BY NATURE EQUAL

NEW FORUM BOOKS

Robert P. George, Series Editor

A list of titles
in the series appears
at the back of
the book

BY NATURE EQUAL

THE ANATOMY OF A WESTERN INSIGHT

John E. Coons and Patrick M. Brennan

With a foreword by John Witte, Jr.

PRINCETON UNIVERSITY PRESS

PRINCETON, NEW JERSEY

LIBRARY OF CONGRESS CATALOGING-IN-PUBLICATION DATA

COONS, JOHN E.

BY NATURE EQUAL: THE ANATOMY OF A WESTERN INSIGHT /

JOHN E. COONS, PATRICK M. BRENNAN.

P. CM.—(NEW FORUM BOOKS)

INCLUDES BIBLIOGRAPHICAL REFERENCES AND INDEX.

ISBN 0-691-05922-5 (ALK. PAPER)

1. EQUALITY—PHILOSOPHY. 2. EQUALITY—RELIGIOUS ASPECTS. 3. EQUALITY BEFORE THE

LAW. I. BRENNAN, PATRICK M., 1966– II. TITLE.

HM146 .C66 1999

305'.01—DC21   98–41031 CIP

THIS BOOK HAS BEEN COMPOSED IN BERKELEY BOOK MODIFIED TYPEFACE

CHAPTER 5 OF THE PRESENT WORK APPEARED AS PART OF THE AUTHORS' ESSAY,

"NATURAL LAW AND HUMAN EQUALITY," 40 *AMERICAN JOURNAL OF JURISPRUDENCE*

(1995): 287–334.

THE PAPER USED IN THIS PUBLICATION MEETS THE MINIMUM REQUIREMENTS

OF ANSI/NISO Z39.48-1992 (R1997) *PERMANENCE OF PAPER*

HTTP: //PUP.PRINCETON.EDU

PRINTED IN THE UNITED STATES OF AMERICA

1 3 5 7 9 10 8 6 4 2

To the best—whoever you are

There is a powerful strain of thought that centres on a feeling
of ultimate and outrageous absurdity in the idea that achievement
of the highest kind of moral worth should depend on
natural capacities, unequally and fortuitously distributed.
(Bernard Williams, "The Idea of Equality")[1]

CONTENTS

Distinguish two questions: (1) Are humans equal by nature in some significant way? (2) Should society create artificial equalities? The first question—not the second—is the subject of this book. Human equality is a relation. If it exists, it is a "double" equality, springing from a property that could vary in extent from person to person but which in fact is possessed uniformly by all rational individuals. That property is the capacity to achieve moral self-perfection.

"Human equality" is a linguistic convention. To grasp its meaning requires interpretation. Our method is dialectic, a conversational sorting and shuffling of the range of things that have been said about descriptive human equality. Because we conclude that most people believe the convention about human equality to be true, we also must ask whether and how they might be right.

Many have argued that law should impose artificial equalities. Some also assert that we humans are all "created equal," but few have analyzed *how*, prior to law, this might be so. What does the idea of a descriptive equality entail? Scrutiny of what has been said and left unsaid provides starting points for a statement of what could be meant by a belief in human equality.

The relation called human equality springs from some significant property common to rational persons. The convention about human equality identifies this special "host property" as the capacity of the human self to accept or reject a real order of obligation to other humans. Only if human equality is founded on this capacity can we explain the goodness and importance with which convention invests it.

The belief in a real order of lateral obligation is characteristic of natural law in its many interpretations. Naturalists, however, tend to hold that one is perfected only by grasping and doing correct actions. Moral self-perfection is not distinguished from correct behaviors; thus the honest blunderer falls short of natural moral perfection. Following Bernard Lonergan, however, natural law could be reinterpreted to recognize that obtension works moral self-perfection. This reinterpretation of natural morality would introduce the possibility of uniform capacity, hence of human equality.

To be intelligible to Christians, our question must be understood as one concerning an opportunity for personal salvation extended to all rational humans on the same terms.

The model for a Christian belief in human equality is an invitation from God to all rational humans. God makes the salvation of every rational person (professed believer or not) available on the sole condition of an honest search for the terms of the real good. The personal power to commit to or reject the good could thus be uniform among all rational persons. This version of moral theology will be controversial among the varieties of Christian belief.

Many Christians have had doubts about the human capacity to contribute anything at all to salvation. Predestination, differentiated grace, baptism, and other beliefs would divide mankind into sheep and goats. From the days of Pelagius (early fifth century) to the end of the Middle Ages, Christianity worried that recognition of human efficacy entails a contraction of God's own power. Over the centuries Pelagius's belief in human agency is often down but never out. Gradually most of the Catholic—and perhaps the Protestant—West has quietly accepted the reality of a created human liberty that can say yes or no to the divine invitation. So far, human equality remains a belief open to most Christians.

ACKNOWLEDGMENT AND APOLOGY

FEW OF THOSE whose early example inspired this book are still around to read it. A litany of their names would be a nostalgic self-indulgence. Let the one exception be my toast across the void to Patrick J. Lyons—counselor to the Chippewa, hope of delinquents, emboldener of singers, and incurable believer in the improbable good. We were more equal just for knowing you.

The scribbling for this essay began in the late 1970s, continuing in brief spurts such as the 1987 paper given for Kent Greenawalt's seminar at Columbia. In June 1988 John and Anne Bodner set me quietly to work in their retreat in the Jura; that summer culminated in five more weeks of writing in the stimulating environment of the Rockefeller Center at Bellagio. Over the years my Deans Sanford Kadish and Jesse Choper of Boalt Hall encouraged the enterprise in various ways; two generous grants from the Earhart Foundation gave me indispensable free time. For all these expressions of confidence I am grateful. These patrons deserved the book sooner. I can only hope that it is better for the deferment; so far as I can tell, human nature has not changed in the interim, and the question we ask here remains unconsidered.

My most profound thanks are reserved for whatever providence delivered Patrick Brennan to my exploitation. (The immediate cause was a typical good work of Steve Sugarman assisted materially by generous support from the Robbins Collection through Laurent Mayali.) Patrick's genius, wisdom, and energy have, since 1991, assured that the thing would get done—and with a scope far exceeding my solo grasp. Had our subject been justice, his name might have come first.

Brennan and I have been buoyed by specific insight, criticism, and encouragement from Lawrence Chickering, Melissa Clemens, William Clune, Cliff Cobb, Willy Coons, Meir Dan-Cohen, Kate Day, Scott FitzGibbon, Fred Lawrence, Jerry Lubenow, Frank Michelman, Gene Outka, Joanne Riddle, Salvador Rus, Richard Schenk, Philip Selznick, Michael Smith, Jeremy Waldron, John Witte, the law students and theology graduate students from three Boalt Hall seminars on equality—and others whom doubtless we will remember too late. Unforgettable is the crucial scrutiny of citations faithfully executed by Kelly Flood. The only miracle of competing distinction was the editing of Rita Bernhard.

Wendy Hargrave, Sheila John, Kristin Largent-Moyes, Ken Matthews, Susan Peabody, Sharon Robinson, Amatullah Alaji-Sabrie, and Rita Tidwell managed with unflagging tolerance to do whatever was necessary at the word processor to give my antiquarian strokes the sheen of modernity. May your tribes increase.

Though my own descendants have progressed from adolescence to the brink of middle age during this project, I note with satisfaction that their mother has remained young in her unflagging hope for its completion. I could not have asked for more.

The belief that men are equal was an orthodoxy of my cradle. Sometimes it returns as a child's interpretation of the lonely men who wandered the roads of the 1930s. They came asking for odd jobs and were content with food and a chance to thaw. I was told that they were people like us, but few of them looked like us, and some looked in a way to make a child wonder. They managed without the soap and razor that I associated with my father. And some of them spoke and acted strangely. But I was assured that they were the same as we, which meant they were very important. It was a prodigious revelation. Later it turned out that many of my contemporaries held this same creed; so where it truly originated for me is hard to say. But I remember those weary men.

I invested this idea about strangers with considerable importance and was not surprised to learn from Sister Marcelline that it had the interesting name equality. It took some doing to believe that evil-smelling beggars might be as good as my parents. But I accepted the dogma and still do, though, having thought about it, I no longer understand. Perhaps only children can grasp it.

Nursery politics can carry us a long way. Human equality has been a part of my emotional world through two generations and a variety of causes most of which still seem sane. But somewhere between Selma and sixty I tumbled to a basic division among those of us who worry about the idea. Equality talk has increased in volume and complexity, but this division remains a simple one: There are those who worry because men are different, and there are those who rejoice because they are the same. This latter notion—that human beings, here and now, in some interesting way are the same—is one that connects to my childhood and to my intelligence. Paradoxically those who start with this premise easily see that people are diverse in their hopes, needs, deserts, and every capacity (but one) and conclude from all this variety that moral or political claims that are plausible for one person would be absurd for another. They argue for differential treatment of individuals without embarrassment or guilt and do so because the worth of a person is never at issue. Like the law (at its best), they are not respecters of persons but only of the person. For them justice in a free democracy properly entails an accounting of differences, but the duty to count anything at all rests upon a common something that is beyond our power to spoil or improve.

Such people often refer to this unfailing source of human dignity as "human equality." Politicians and priests are full of talk like this, and even the man in the street seems a willing consumer of the notion that we are "created equal." For me this idea that equality is some kind of brute datum—an unchangeable fact of life—remains interesting, but it is puzzling to the point of exasperation. Whether and how it might be understood is the primary question of this book. In the end Patrick Brennan and I conclude that descriptive "human equality" has a conventional meaning that can be clarified and grasped. Whether that convention can be believed is another question, and the answer may be consequential. Jefferson himself believed and thought it important; yet not even in the Declaration of Independence did he hint what it is to be "created equal." Today this great problem of the nature of human equality remains virtually unconsidered in serious literature. Recalling the pleasure its contemplation has given me, my deepest gratitude might be reserved for the philosophers and theologians who have left it so.

John E. Coons
Berkeley, 1998

FOREWORD

The Context

OLIVER WENDELL HOLMES once said that the great questions of theology and philosophy must ultimately come to law for their resolution—lest they remain shrouded in speculative mists. This splendid volume shows that the great questions of law must also turn to theology and philosophy for their edification—lest they become mired in mechanical formulas. Theological narratives might well need legal norms to ground them. But legal norms also need theological narratives to guide them. Philosophical propositions might not decide concrete cases. But concrete cases cannot be decided without reference to philosophical propositions.

Questions of the nature of human equality illustrate the virtues of such interdisciplinary inquiry. We jurists tend to view human equality at once as a mantra and a myth of the law. The American Declaration of Independence proclaimed it a "self-evident . . . truth" "that all men are created equal [and] . . . are endowed with certain unalienable rights." But the reality of revolutionary America in 1776 was that women, blacks, natives, the poor, non-Protestants, and the vast majority of others seemed to enjoy rather little equality and even fewer rights. The Universal Declaration of Human Rights proclaimed without pause "that all men are born free and equal in rights and dignity." But the reality of the war-torn world of 1948 was that freedom and rights were hard to find anywhere, and that equality and dignity had blatantly betrayed themselves in the gulags, battlefields, and death camps of the previous decades.

In part, these disparities simply reflect the inevitable tensions between legal ideals and legal reality, between the law on the books and the law in action. And happily, in our day, these disparities have abated somewhat, owing partly to the aggressive extension of legal protections. In America, strong new laws—from the reconstruction amendments to the modern civil rights acts—have begun to close the historical gaps between blacks and whites, men and women, conformists and dissenters. At the international level, new legal instruments—from the 1966 covenants to recent declarations on the rights of women, children, religious minorities, and indigenous peoples—have brought new hope to many desperate persons around the globe.

In part, however, these disparities also reflect the limitations of our rights-based legal discourse on human equality. Inspired by Jefferson's Declaration, we jurists tend to view human equality as a function of human rights. All persons were "created equal," it is argued, *because* they were "endowed with certain unalienable rights." To enhance the reality of human equality, therefore, we must expand the regime of human rights. The more rights for all, the more equality of all. Inspired by the equal protection clause, we jurists also tend to equate human equality with legal egalitarianism. We must expand the guarantees of equal protection, treatment, and entitlement under the law. For the more the law treats all like persons alike, the more equality all persons will enjoy. Inspired by the due process clauses, we jurists also tend to connect human equality with human autonomy. We must free individuals from the traditional structures and strictures of patriarchy and hierarchy that encroach on their autonomy. For the more each person can claim the same zone of privacy, the more all persons will become equal.

The limitations of these legal constructions of equality are now becoming too plain to ignore. As we have expanded the ambit of human rights in the past five decades, the goal of human equality seems to have become increasingly opaque. As we have widened the zones of individual autonomy and privacy, the disparities between the haves and the have-nots seem only to have increased. Although the legal inequalities of Jefferson's day may be closing, new inequalities are opening between city and country, ghetto and suburb, straight and gay, old and young, the indigenous and the immigrant, the moneyed and the maligned, the armed and their victims.

Legal critics and deconstructionists have seized on all this as a veritable field of dreams. The law review literature is teeming with gleeful exposures of the fallacies and distortions of the traditional lore and law of human rights and equality. Even the iconic Thomas Jefferson no longer escapes repeated attack. Some critics urge us to dismiss the human rights paradigm altogether—as a tried and tired experiment that is no longer effective, even a fictional faith whose folly has now been fully exposed. Others urge us to dismiss all talk of human equality—as an atavistic ideal that inspires false hope, even a stubborn fallacy that will not face up to the natural inequalities of aptitude and achievement among genders, races, and cultures.

This is a bit of the professional context in which these two distinguished law professors have crafted their book. Deconstructionists of equality and rights are more than amply represented in the law schools and the broader academy today. Reconstructionists of equality are precious and few. Professors Coons and Brennan are of the latter rare sort.

Coons and Brennan regard rights talk as the wrong talk about real equality. They do regard the modern rights movement as a laudable legal achievement—and indeed have elsewhere contributed ably and amply to the rights of families and religious groups. They do regard the Declarations of 1776 and 1948, among others, as sublime statements of Western ideas and ideals of human equality. And they do regard as rather persuasive many criticisms of current legal formulations of rights and equality. But their accent and agenda are altogether different from those of conventional law professors. Their interest is in the first phrase of Jefferson's "self-evident truth" (that persons are "*created* equal"), not the second phrase (that they are "endowed with certain unalienable rights"). Their concern is with the ontological nature, not with the jurisprudential nurture, of equality. Their thesis is that human equality is a created condition for the law to confirm, not a constitutional ideal for human rights to pursue.

This thesis compels the authors to stand Holmes's method on its head. Holmes urged theologians and philosophers to turn to law to resolve their hard questions. Coons and Brennan urge the opposite method. We must step back from our legal rights constructions, they argue, and reflect more deeply on the essence of human equality, on the origin, nature, and purpose of this "self-evident" concept and command. To be sure, law has some other tools, besides human rights, to engage this task—criminal law and tort law doctrines of action, intention, and causation, for example, which the authors employ with great skill in this volume. But the Western tradition of theology and philosophy has other, more refined tools at its disposal, they argue, and these must now be put to the task of probing the "self-evident truth" of human equality. This exercise is not designed to abandon the law but to bolster it. It does not aim to deprecate our rights talk about equality but to deepen it. Coons and Brennan are pursuing interdisciplinary legal study in its best sense—enlightening the law with the methods and insights of other disciplines while enlivening other disciplines with the conundrums and constructions of law.

The Content

Professors Coons and Brennan offer a "realist" theory of human equality. They first distill a "conventional" definition of human equality—combining the conversational method of "common sense" philosophy with the law professor's method of constructing a "reasonable person standard." They then move with acuity and alacrity down the long honor roll of Western philosophers, theologians, and natural law theorists in search of antecedents and allies for their theory. Plato, Aristotle, Cicero, Seneca, Augustine, Aquinas, Calvin, Luther, Hobbes, Locke, Jefferson, Kant, and a host of others are all put in the dock for close examination of their theories of equality. Coons and Brennan let these historical luminaries speak on their terms, sometimes at length. They do not coach their historical witnesses to use language or to reach conclusions that suits the thesis of their book. Virtually all these luminaries give credible testimony to support portions of the authors' thesis. But none expounds it outright. The authors then stitch together the testimony they have gathered from the tradition and restate their thesis about human equality. The last section of the volume sketches the pertinence of the thesis for contemporary discussions of liberty, equality, and fraternity, justice, rights, and the common good.

I intend no insult to the authors by reducing their long and elegant argument for human equality to three propositions—each delightfully controversial; together an almost irresistible cri de couer.

First, the authors argue, there is a set of transcendent goods and goals that objectively define our moral choices. In the Western tradition, such goods and goals are captured in classic notions of natural law, the law of nations, the orders of creation, the dictates of conscience, the categorical imperative, the Golden Rule, and other such moral coda. These moral coda invariably differ in their definition, content, and fecundity over time and across cultures—though certain precepts seem to be universal. The authors want to leave an ample margin of appreciation to each person's and each community's definition, and redefinition, of these moral codes. They rehearse, with rather gentle equanimity, sundry Hebrew, Greek, Roman, Christian, and Enlightenment formulations of these moral codes. But they insist that such "authentic" moral codes exist, and that these antedate and transcend any particular understanding of human nature, human equality, or human law.

Second, what creates "real equality" is each person's *rational* capacity to apprehend this objective moral order and *voluntarist* capacity to seek moral self-perfection with reference to it. This natural quality of the person the authors call the "host property." It is this ability to combine reason and will in the pursuit of moral ends that distinguishes persons from beasts. To be sure, rational persons have various degrees of rational apprehension of this moral order. (A few persons, such as the infant, the irrational, or the comatose, might not have sufficient reason to apprehend it at all.) And, to be sure, rational persons will voluntarily pursue self-perfection with varying degrees of intensity. But what is critical to the definition of human equality is that each person has the same natural *capacity* (in reason and will) and the natural *telos* (in the transcendent moral order) to strive toward moral self-perfection.

When the person exercises this capacity to seek the correct way, the choice to do so is labeled an "obtension"—an in*tention* for an *ob*jective good. Human equality, the authors write, "does not rest on the claim that well-intending individuals can, in every instance, discover the content of the real good nor that they are equal in their power to perceive its details. The discovery and performance of good acts are, to be sure, the behavioral ideal, but it is in honestly searching for this good—not in grasping it—that one achieves one's own moral fulfillment."

This is the "singular" and "uniform" quality that renders all persons equal, the authors argue. Each person will ultimately be held accountable for how he or she engages this capacity and responds to this telos. Each person's accountability will turn not on whether he achieves the correct outcomes of this transcendent order; few, if any at all, will. Rather, it will turn on whether and what he *intended* to achieve in light of his own grasp of this objective moral order. A person, by this calculus, can become good, without necessarily doing good. The authors are rather optimistic that most people are inclined to strive for moral self-perfection, that most such efforts yield morally acceptable results, and that the collection of such efforts produces a sturdy formulation of the common good and a sturdy foundation for a legal and social order.

Third, "real" human equality is inherently communal and "lateral." The biblical story of creation is the primordial metaphor and message of this "lateral" human quality. When Adam encountered God, he apprehended the transcendent moral order by which to guide himself. When Adam encountered Eve, he acquired the means to achieve both his humanity and his equality. Before the creation of Eve, human equality was impossible: there was no rational, moral creature by which Adam could understand or compare himself. God was above reason and morality; the beasts of paradise were below it. With the creation of Eve, Adam's inherent rational and moral capacities were awakened. Eve became the mirror in which Adam could see himself. Only by watching another person's reason and will respond to God's moral commandments could Adam appreciate the nature of his own rational and voluntary responses. Only by watching another person strive for moral self-perfection could he discover the same capacity and imperative for himself. To be human and fully equal, Adam and Eve needed each other. Solicitude for the other's survival thus became part of their own moral goods and goals. The path to their own moral self-perfection included the duty to seek the good of the other—a duty that could be freely embraced or rejected, as their children Cain and Abel demonstrated.

This haunting rendition of the creation story gives one expression to a universal truth about our human nature. We are, by nature, social creatures, who need one another to survive and to flourish. Our reason and will are naturally drawn to concern for the other. Our moral codes command us to do good unto others. The principle of reciprocity is a deep human instinct. Some understanding of the Golden Rule—"do unto others as you would have done unto you"—suffuses the moral sentiments of virtually all cultures. To be human, we must be communally engaged; to be moral, we must be vertically attuned; to be equal, we must be laterally related.

For Coons and Brennan, therefore, "real equality" is not political, biological, or sociological in nature, as numerous authors argue today. Nor is it an unattainable Platonic ideal, as Hobbes, Nietzche, and their modern disciples believe. Human equality is an ontological property—something created, something natural—which ultimately must be defined by some point of reference outside human nature, human society, and human law. This reality of equality is inadequately captured in modern concepts of human dignity, hero worship, racial and ethnic identity, or in emerging constructions of a global man universally threatened by a nuclear or environmental holocaust. All these loci are incomplete descriptions of equality, which the authors devote a good deal of their text to deconstructing. The only universal, and enduring, "property" of personhood is the capacity of each person to strive for moral self-perfection.

This is a profound and highly original offering. The authors have mined some of the deepest concepts of the Western tradition—reason and will, conscience and synderesis, individuality and community—in search of the core meaning of equality. They have not been content simply to recite traditional answers or to speak only to technical philosophers. Their approach is decidedly interdisciplinary, with illustrations drawn from and for a variety of fields—not least their own professional field of law.

Coons and Brennan are firmly rooted in the best of the Catholic tradition. In one sense, their book is a modern confession and commentary on St. Augustine's famous adage: "Our hearts are restless till they find their rest in thee, O Lord." In another sense, it is an attempt to cast in more universal terms the Second Vatican Council's astute pastoral insight for Christians. "Conscience is the most secret core and sanctuary of a man," reads *Gaudium et Spes*.

> There he is alone with God, whose voice echoes in its depths. In a wonderful manner conscience reveals that law which is fulfilled by love of God and neighbor. In fidelity to conscience, Christians are joined with the rest of men in the search for truth, and for the genuine solution to the numerous problems which arise in the life of individuals and from social relationships. Hence the more that a correct conscience holds sway, the more persons and groups turn aside from blind choice and strive to be guided by objective norms of morality. Conscience frequently errs from invincible ignorance [but] without losing its dignity.

These cardinal Catholic insights lie at the heart of this book. But the authors do not revert to theology or to homiletics to expound them. They aim, instead, to describe and defend universal propositions about human nature and human equality that happen, in their own tradition, to have distinctive Christian theological forms and norms. Such propositions about human nature and human equality can find ample anchorage in other faiths, besides Christianity, and in other disciplines, besides theology. No one faith and no one discipline can claim a monopoly on so deep an ontological truth.

The Challenge

To praise this book comes easily. To predict its reception is more difficult. By avoiding traditional lines, and ruts, of analysis, the authors will invariably draw criticisms from those whose favorite arguments have been traversed or avoided. By rummaging through the desks of many Western lights in search of supporters, the authors will invariably draw fire from specialists who have organized these desks in a particular way. By adducing and combining afresh ancient arguments and concepts, the authors will invariably draw charges of both historicism and iconoclasm. This is the bane of any serious work of interdisciplinary scholarship that challenges convention. And a big, bold book like this one—for all its elegance and gentility—will certainly draw a methodological indictment of some length.

Such methodological criticisms, however, are generally as transient as they are inevitable. The more serious criticisms will come from those who take this argument on its own terms, and then take the authors on. Some parts of the argument will doubtless inspire at least some grumbles of discontent. Many Catholics—prone to more specific formulations of natural law and the common good—might find the authors' generous and generic definition of the moral order too ecumenically phrased. Many Protestants—prone to find the source of human equality in total depravity and common grace—might well still see too much of Pelagius and Arminius at work in this thesis, despite the authors lengthy ratiocinations to the contrary. Many libertarians—prone to minimal nominalist constructions of the individual—will likely flinch at the thought of a person's inherent vertical duties and lateral relationships. Many jurists—prone to following Holmes's dismissal of the "brooding omnipresence in the sky"—might well see this book as a Trojan horse designed to smuggle dangerous natural law theories back into legal scholarship.

After these inevitable grumbles of discontent have been raised, the question that will remain is the one the authors themselves pose throughout the book: can theologians, philosophers, and jurists accept a definition of human equality along these lines and use it with profit in their own disciplines? Have the authors done enough to cajole specialists to look up from their favorite formulas and to see in this volume a glimpse of the essence of human nature and human equality? Have they convinced theologians to look behind platitudes about human dignity for something deeper? Have they persuaded "post-modern" philosophers to take seriously again the prospect of right reason and real will? Have they coaxed jurists into translating their easy rights talk into a richer, but more demanding, language about equality? This is the challenge of this book. The authors have pressed their case forcefully. They have adduced ample evidence for their propositions from many quarters. They have rested with a stirring conclusion. No one who reads the book can help being moved. Have the authors met their burden of proof?

John Witte, Jr.
Jonas Robitscher Professor of Law and Ethics
Director of the Law and Religion Program
Emory University

BY NATURE EQUAL

INTRODUCTION

IN SEARCH OF A DESCRIPTIVE HUMAN EQUALITY

> What was present to his imagination was character—
> a thing which is not only more important than intellect,
> but is also much more entertaining.
> (G. K. Chesterton, *Charles Dickens*)

THIS BOOK EXAMINES the belief in *human equality*—the common conviction that equality is a fixed characteristic of human persons. It scarcely touches the political and moral ideal—also called "equality"—that would make our lives more nearly the same. Just why a uniformity of economic and social circumstance would represent a hope for the world is to us a mystery. Insofar as we understand what egalitarians seek, it is hardly worth the hoping. People who are hungry do not need equality; they need bread and respect. To offer them sameness of whatever sort is to mistake both the human condition and the ordinary person's sense of justice.

This may be one reason that in drafting the Declaration of Independence Jefferson and his colleagues very deliberately declined to draw any political conclusions from the "self-evident" truth of our having been created equal. The egalitarian political option, so soon to be exercised by the French,[1] was carefully considered and rejected in favor of the straightforward claim of fact that men simply are born equal. What we know of this fateful decision in the summer of 1776 provides a proper first encounter with the history of descriptive equality. At an early point in the drafting process Jefferson had selected human equality as the unique property that could serve as the *source* of the rights to be claimed by the colonists. He made this connection between the asserted fact and political rights explicit in the original complete draft delivered for review by the Committee of Five.

> We hold these truths to be self-evident; that all men are created equal & independent; that from that equal creation they derive rights . . . among which are . . . life, & liberty, & the pursuit of happiness;[2]

In its style and content most of the draft shows direct descent from a variety of European and American sources. "Created equal," however, is a Jefferson original.[3]

"Equal" is for Jefferson a description—a statement of fact about men. It is not a social aspiration but a natural attribute. If this were not sufficiently clear from the words, "men are created equal," it would become so on the far side of the next semicolon. Jefferson there announces that it is *from* this created equality that "rights" emerge; these rights are a phenomenon distinct from, but causally dependent upon, the human attribute. No suggestion yet appears that equality itself is to be understood as a right; it is, rather, the material precondition of rights. Persons have rights, because as humans they are equal beings; the rights derive from the fact of their equality.

Before the final draft was submitted to Congress these words of Jefferson were to be altered more than once. Whoever proposed the changes, their intent is clear enough. Carl Becker's representation of the "Lee" copy allows us to display them together:

self-evident

We hold these truths to be ^ ~~sacred & undeniable~~; that

they are endowed by their

all men are created equal ~~& independent~~; that ^ ~~from that~~

creator with ~~equal rights, some of which are~~   rights; that

~~equal creation they derive in rights~~ inherent & inalienable ^

these

among ~~which~~ ^ are ~~the preservation of~~ life, & liberty, &

the pursuit of happiness;[4]

We focus upon the changes that are here printed in *italics*—those changes that were retained as well as those eventually lined out. (The one substitution in roman type—"self-evident"—was made by Jefferson as part of the original draft.) These alterations suggest that at one point the evolving language was to read as follows:[5]

> . . . that all men are created equal . . .; that they are endowed by their creator with equal rights, some of which are . . .[6]

What had changed in this intermediate draft? First, the creator of equality is now egalitarian in his politics. For this one moment in the drafting process, he who made men equal has decreed that their rights shall be equal as well. In the final draft these "equal rights" were to disappear; having been carefully considered, they were snuffed and discarded. The drafters excluded normative equality from the Declaration *ex industria*.[7]

But this intermediate draft shows something even more important: the various declared rights (including even this short-lived right to equality) are no longer drawn as an inference "from that equal creation." Created equality, though still announced as a fact, withdraws as a source of rights. In short, the descriptive has been disconnected from the normative. "Created equal" has ceased to be a factual premise for rights which now, indeed, require a separate decree of the creator for their authority. This disconnection of fact from norm was retained in the final version:

> We hold these truths to be self-evident; that all men are created equal; that they are endowed by their creator with certain unalienable rights.

Whether by Jefferson's initiative or acquiescence, the rights that survive the drafting process remain surgically separated from the fact of our human equality.[8] In the end, all rights spring not from our equality but directly from the will of the creator. This leaves both the structure and function of equality obscure. Men are (in some sense) created equal, but so what? With great care the drafters had driven a literary wedge between the fact of equality and the aspiration.

Though popular, the most naive appraisal of the committee's work is that of Becker himself:

> None of the alterations of Jefferson's draft is of importance for understanding the philosophy of the Declaration, since none of them touches either the premises or the logical structure of Jefferson's argument.[9]

The committee has stripped from the draft the crucial claim that the rights of man spring from the fact of equality. It is hard to imagine a more fundamental shift in the "logical structure" of the single most important paragraph in the Declaration of Independence. Legion commentators, nevertheless, have chosen to ignore this studied severance of the hope from the fact.[10] The Declaration has been consistently misdescribed as a proto-egalitarian lever awaiting the hand of Lincoln at Gettysburg. Almost everything supporting that view has recently been said by Garry Wills.[11] We concede that the Declaration has often been used just as Wills reports. Nevertheless, this has been an invention for which even Lincoln artfully avoided responsibility. If he would have us "dedicated to the proposition," his expression of its terms at Gettysburg remained resolutely descriptive. We think these scraps of history contain a lesson: Those who would draw egalitarian conclusions should first ask what "created equal" was supposed to mean as a fact. Of this Jefferson said nothing at the time. Later we shall see what can be made of his other expressions.

Everything that follows here depends upon our emulating the drafters of the Declaration. We must keep bright this distinction between equality as a natural human feature and equality as somebody's political ideal—what is properly called "egalitarianism." For us that word is a pejorative. Its spawning and inconsistent use as a premise of morals and policy deserves an early burial; in modern social discourse it has become an intellectual drug, an expensive and befuddling habit that corrupts social argument. It is also easily mistaken for the whole of the question about human equality; the social agenda of the egalitarian merges with the claim that equality is a human truth, and we risk sending these discrete ideas to a common grave. This is the deadly drift of modern political writing, and neither Left nor Right seems prepared to draw the saving distinction.

In this book we will think about equality not as a social goal or as somebody's legal claim but, rather, as some characteristic believed to link the individual self to others. As in our title, taken from Samuel Johnson, humans *are* by nature equal.[12] This is not the familiar course of contemporary academic minds. To think of equality specifically as a distinctive and constant reality of related human persons goes against the grain. Conversations on this subject, like a car out of alignment, tend to drift from the center line; instinctively we slip back into the comfortable grooves of egalitarian argot and begin to replay old issues of social entitlements, equal protection, minimums, redistribution and John Rawls. And this easy relapse into egalitarianism is only the first threat to communication. The path to understanding any pure descriptive human equality is mined with difficulties of definition and analysis.

With this in mind, at the risk of getting ahead of our story, we will introduce the most mischievous of these threatening confusions. It lurks within the peculiar form of being that we call "relation." To see this problem at so early a stage will alert us to various difficulties ahead. A silly fable will get us started: A zoologist discovers a new species of mammal that he dubs the "Omoh." This beast is awarded a special scientific niche because it has three horns. The announcement of this discovery kicks off an exchange between two earnest intellectuals over lunch at the faculty club. Mary is a moral philosopher whose obsession for animal rights makes her the occasional mark of her more cynical friends. Peter is a linguist. Between soup and quiche Peter provokes the skirmish:

> Peter: Mary, I see that the Omoh has three horns; in your view is that a basis for calling him "equal"?
>
> Mary: Well, I confess that having three horns seems an odd sort of equality, but why not? After all, if having reason makes a man equal, maybe having three horns makes Omohs equal.
>
> Peter: As I understand it, only one Omoh was found. For all we know, he is an evolutionary sport, a singleton who will never reproduce. I'm surprised to hear you attribute equality to an individual thing considered by itself. If the word gives us any information at all, it says something about two (or more) things. To speak of the equality of one thing is nonsense.
>
> Mary: Of course, that is obvious, and I was assuming—
>
> Peter: Furthermore, even if there were two Omohs, to speak as if the sheer possession of horns or reason—or of any other property—amounted to equality, would get it all wrong. Equality then becomes simply a synonym for the fact that two beings have some specific property—it would not refer

us to anything new at all. It's merely an echo of some other real property of these individuals.

Mary: Hold on. Synonyms sometimes identify a special sense or context. For example, "Sodium chloride" captures something not conveyed in the word "salt"; it adds an analytical statement about chemical composition. It is a synonym for the same reality, but it is worth using because it is clarifying.

Peter: Maybe, but equality lacks even that virtue. When we use it as a synonym for horns or human reason or some other property of individuals in a set, we only obscure the reality we already see; equality adds nothing and is simply a distraction. We call these beasts with horns "equal," but this identifies no new trait. We merely rename a property that is already identified. I mean, if somebody says that equality consists in "having reason," this would tell us zero about what it is to have reason—which is all that counts. It would be nothing but the application of the word-sound "equality" to some property that already has a more suitable name.

Mary: When people say that human equality consists in our sharing reason or free will or the like, they intend to identify something different from reason and will. Even if reason and will have some necessary role in constituting human equality, people mean that equality is more than the sum of these two properties.

Peter: No doubt people imagine that equality does some special work of its own; they suppose that it identifies the uniformity of some real property. To capture this sameness they add a word such as "equality." This is still nothing new but the sound.

Mary: Peter, look! What the word "equality" identifies may literally be no property of any of these individuals; nevertheless, it is indeed something. The term specifies a certain relation that exists among them. Each of the individual Omohs has three horns; but, in addition, there is a relation of each to the other exactly because they share this strange property. By definition, plurality is a condition of relation. When you have only one creature with a certain quality that you already have described, that description exhausts the subject. But when two share that quality, something additional is generated. Of course, this new thing added is not always an equality. Where there are minor differences between the two in respect to the particular feature—horns or whatever—that added reality is properly called a similarity; only when the two are the same is it an equality. And it is something distinct. For example, if the particular sameness of these creatures were their common possession of reason, the equality would consist not in reason itself, but rather in the relation that arises *between* these two beings by virtue of their sharing reason.

Peter: In effect you've made my point, Mary. I agree that without actually abusing the language you can assert that something is added to each of these entities—or exists between them—by the existence of the other. Go ahead and use the word "relation" but remember Hume's point that relation is a "fiction or imaginary principle of union." There is in fact nothing to which the label equality can actually be pinned.

Mary: Forget Mr. Hume! It was you yourself who pinned it a few moments ago by suggesting that it takes two beings with a common property in order to generate an equality. The label equality signifies the relation; a relation is indeed something, and that something deserves to have its own name. If it happens to be an equality, that's the name by which that particular relation goes. I do concede, however, that the ways in which things are related to one another by equality can seem pretty trivial. If two Omohs are equal in their having three horns, it matters not a whit. But that's not to say that every variety of equality is so unimportant.

Peter: Mary, equality is not just trivial; it's nothing at all except perhaps a round-about way of talking about the property of each individual that you say gives rise to this relation.

Mary: Peter, at this very table I have heard you speak rather strongly in support of what you called "the fact of human equality." Indeed, it occurs to me that just last week both of us signed the proclamation of the Skeptomist Society asserting that all persons are equal. Indeed, it may have been you who pointed out that an assertion of that sort might bolster our argument for world government. Were you just kidding?

Peter: I don't remember the details all too clearly. In any case I wasn't kidding, and I can tell you just what I thought then and now. It is one thing to discover these so-called equalities—relations that are based upon horns, good looks, SAT scores, speed, or gender. If that sort of stuff is equality, my reaction is, who cares? But the human equality that we wrote into our proclamation is totally different. As a linguist I can tell you that when people pontificate on human equality, they intend something more substantial than the shallow observation that we all have two eyes or three horns. Now, if I'm put under oath I'll stand agnostic on the question whether human equality is something "real"; what I do believe is that if it *were* real, it would be something not only unique to humans but crucial to who they are and to how they understand themselves. Otherwise it would not satisfy the sense of the words "human equality" as that expression is commonly understood.

Mary: Peter, I'm beginning to think we can work this out.

We identify and empathize with Peter and Mary. Equality is, indeed, some kind of relation, and relations do tend to resist analysis. They resist analysis even by—or, perhaps, especially by—lawyers such as ourselves for whom relations are supposed to be bread and butter. A prominent law teacher once described the legal mind as one "that can think of something that is inextricably connected to something else without thinking of what it is connected to." This was at best a left-handed compliment to lawyers; indeed, we would accept it as a criticism and push it a step further. To think properly about a connection, one needs to understand both things that are connected. But that is only the beginning. When one has grasped both ends, one must go on to reckon with that other thing that is the connection itself. There are not merely two realities to be grasped. And, if relation is a third and distinct reality, it sometimes will take the form of an equality.

Mary and Peter's conversation is but the latest round in an ancient debate among philosophers and linguists about whether this third thing really exists. Since Aristotle, the experts have been divided on the issue; by contrast, the general community seems to have reached agreement.[13] Whenever a relation of any sort "happens," people see this as a creative event, the new third thing consisting precisely of the particular relation; this thing is not understood merely as a word sound or a thought in someone's head. When my daughter is born, people perceive her, they perceive me, and they affirm the relationship—the connection—that would not exist without both of us but which is neither contained in nor exhausted by the sum of our individual properties.

The common belief in human equality exemplifies this grassroots attitude toward relation. People implicitly regard human equality as a claim about a distinctive existent. But if indeed it were real, that reality could be nothing other than a relation; to say that equality is real but not relational would reduce the belief to nonsense.

So far as we can discover, the peculiar role of relation itself never has been considered in the literature of human equality.[14] The arcane and ongoing controversies of Aristotle, Boethius, Aquinas, Ockham, and Whitehead concerning relation are simply ignored, even though this neglect furnishes the critic an invitation to declare equality a work of merest fancy. The authors must reject this strategy of avoidance out of respect for common belief and usage. The bricklayer may be amused to learn that he is an Aristotelian, but his confidence in the reality of equality does indeed entail some such metaphysics. Our project is not to argue for Aristotle (and against those, such as William of Ockham, who deny that relation can be real); it is merely to observe that if human equality is real, that reality is a relation.

We can now turn to a second and similar problem that confounds communication between Peter and Mary. Not surprisingly the term *equality* is used in various senses. Perhaps it would enhance the coherence of their next conversation if they could start with some rough taxonomy of the types of relations that people call equality. If Peter and Mary think as we do, they will find it useful to carve the universe of common usage into four parts consisting, respectively, of what we call *false*, *trivial*, *double*, and *human* equalities.

False Equality

This is the attribution of equality to an individual isolated self, as in this sentence:

Equality is the capacity of an individual for reasoned choice.

The error is plain. Equality, if it means anything, is a relation between two or more beings, not a property of an isolated singleton.

Trivial Equality

Every individual being—including the human sort—has hordes of specific properties, and two or more beings that share the same property automatically are related as equals in a certain way. In other words, they are equal in their common *possession* (or lack) of something. This something that both have (or lack) could be an intangible, such as location. Or it could be tangible, as when two of us possess toes or bicycles.[15] So the following statements are true:

Stones are equal in their common possession of mass.
Most humans are equal in their common possession of reason.

These statements honor the connective or relational nature of equality. Among stones there are many relations of equality, one of which is grounded upon the possession of mass. As physical beings, humans also have that relation to one another; as rational beings, they have an additional relation of equality. The latter is an equality that is not shared by stones or irrational humans (who, however, are themselves related as equals in their shared *lack* of rationality).

Equalities that are based upon the mere possession (or lack) of a property, however, are generally of little importance, and most, indeed, are trivial. Common possession in itself is an unimportant connection between two beings, as we see from the case of our two stones. One may be very heavy, the other very light. They are still equal in their possessing mass, but it is hard to invest such an equality with much significance. This becomes even more obvious when equality involves humans. Each of two men may possess what we call wealth. One has fifty million dollars, the other fifty cents. There is a real relation of equality between them, but, as Peter just said, who cares?

To focus upon mere possession misses the way in which the relation of equality might become important. Our examples so far were *having* reason; *having* mass; and *having* wealth. But possession is an *invariant* trait; it cannot come in degrees. It is defined that way. Either you possess the thing or you don't. Now, this bare fact of possessing a particular property might be useful for assigning certain kinds of legal rights;[16] for the purpose of explaining the phenomenon of human equality it is trivial and misleading. Equality becomes interesting only when there is the possibility that, in respect to some common and significant human capacity, we might—or might not—*differ by degrees*. Were it important that both Ella and I *possess* some property— say, rhythm—it would be enough to say so. Equality becomes significant once we come to compare degrees; it is when we have agreed that I've got rhythm and she's got rhythm that we can ask for anything more.

The significant inquiry, then, is the *degree (if any) by which individuals differ* in their possession of a property that could, but might not, vary. To assert that a genius and an imbecile relate as equals because both possess the property of reason is true but trifling. The important relation is not their equality but their inequality.

So, we switch to examples involving *possession in the same degree*. When the characteristic chosen is a variable property, we can recognize a third kind of equality that is not so obviously trivial.

Double Equality and Disequality

In those cases where variable characteristics such as weight, reason, and money are shared by two beings in the same degree, the resulting equality deserves a separate name. We call this relation "double equality."[17] Here is an example of a double equality—an equality both of possession and degree:

Jones and Black have an equality of swiftness.

   1. Jones and Black have a certain common property (call it the capacity for locomotion) and therefore are equal in respect to its possession. They have a relation of *single equality*.

   2. This shared property—the capacity for locomotion—is variable among humans, but Jones and Black happen to have it in the same degree. They have a relation of *double equality*.

Double equality comes in countless forms. You and I share the characteristic of having an IQ score, and we have the second property of having the same IQ score. You and I also have height—the same height. And so on. It appears we are getting somewhere. Having made this new distinction, however, we encounter an initial difficulty in finding an example of a double equality that could deserve the label human equality.

The impediment is twofold. First, like single equalities, all the double equalities that we can *measure* appear to be trivial; second, for the race considered as a whole, there seem to be no measurable double equalities. Consider these two problems in order.

At first glance, having equality with another person in both possession and degree in respect to some significant property may seem as important as having the property itself. But consider the ordinary example of intelligence tests. The IQ score is a significant fact—one of a sort that varies among us; indeed, we might say that the very point of IQ scores is to vary. However, because you and I both score a 75, a relation of double equality exists between us. We have, first, the equality of possessing an IQ; second, we have the equality of having the same IQ.

Nevertheless, though the score by itself is significant to each individual, the relation of equality is not. Put it this way: few of us would seek such a sameness simply for its own sake. It is seldom of importance to me to be equal; by contrast, it is often important (i.e., good or bad for me) that I have a 75. What matters most is not my equality or inequality with Jones in this matter but my own score. And this holds even if the score I share with him is 200. Again, it is the actual IQ that I prize or regret—not the equality.

Note carefully that we have not said that people are indifferent to their relative standing. To the contrary, they often care very much where they stand in a lineup. In respect to every property that is both variable and benign many of us probably wish to have a score higher than anybody else. In very special cases some few of us might wish a score lower than some other individual (maybe we want to boost the sagging confidence of a friend—or qualify for a tutor). And, doubtless, one *could* want exactly the same score—whether high or low—that somebody else gets. (Please, God, make me the modal American girl.) But surely, this aspiration to sameness for its own sake is not the norm. It is seldom important to us to be the same as someone else in respect to our variable qualities. People in general do not greatly prize sameness in height, intelligence, wealth, age, or looks (though for some reason—as we shall see—they really do prize what we call their "human equality").

If such double equalities fail for insignificance, they also fail for the second and even more basic reason that they become *disequalities* when we consider the race as a whole. Any empirical property that grounds an equality for one human subgroup by definition creates a disequality between those who are inside and those who are outside that subgroup. All 75s are equal to one another but unequal to everyone else. On empirical grounds, therefore, the instances of double equality noted above are irrelevant to the quest for human equality; that is, each includes but a fragment of humankind. The terms of conventional human equality are elusive, but one is plain enough: it embraces the vast majority of humans. And it is not the case that the vast majority have uniform capacities for locomotion, reasoning, or anything else that can be measured. This, of course, is an empirical claim and may be challenged by the critic who can identify some universal double equality that we have overlooked. We would add only that the trait supporting this relation of double equality would also have to be a characteristic of a sort worthy of the veneration that attaches to human equality. All this is discussed thoroughly in part 1.

Human Equality

This relation—the focus of the entire book—consists of a special form of double equality. It involves the sharing of a unique and potentially variable property by all rational humans in the same degree. Eventually we shall identify that property as the capacity of every rational person to advance in moral self-perfection through diligent intention of correct behaviors toward other persons. This capacity for good intention has no empirical measure, but (1) it *could* vary in strength, and (2) it *might* be uniform in strength among rational humans.

Exactly why is this one form of equality uniquely important? This book will answer that question, but at this point we will be content with a few preliminary observations about its nature. First, whatever else it may be, "human equality" is a widely shared belief—what we later consistently refer to as a "convention." It is a linguistic sign that, by implied agreement, ordinary people have attached to a particular relation that they invest with importance. Human equality is a significant relation because those who recognize the term think it so—even those who, like Nietzsche, think it importantly false.

That judgment will be both explained and fortified when later we observe that the term signifies not only the pure relation but various other components of the moral self. It is our task here to determine how these elements become integrated in the idea of human equality. In the end, the terms of the belief become reasonably clear. It implicates a composite feature of the person that is distinctively human: the power freely to seek or avoid the good of our fellows and thereby to forge our own moral identity. To believe in "human equality" is to believe that every rational person has this power and has it to the same degree. Such an interpretation assures the special place for equality that is required by the spirit of this common understanding. If real, equality is important. It confirms some primordial rumor of good news.

Repeatedly we will emphasize that equality does not rest upon the claim that well-intending individuals can, in every case, discover the content of the real good, nor that they are equal in their powers to grasp its details. The discovery and performance of good acts are, to be sure, the behavioral ideal, but it is in honestly searching for this good—not in grasping it—that the person achieves his own moral fulfillment. Though I mistake a specific duty owed to another, my good conscience still does its positive work in me. It morally perfects me even as I proceed to injure my neighbor. For example, I praise the inferior work of some emotionally fragile friend, because I honestly—though incorrectly—think it my duty in charity to do so. It is a lie that injures him by distorting his judgment; nevertheless, following my conscience is for me morally nourishing.

This idea (correct or not) that a good intention can produce disparate effects in the subjective and objective moral orders will occupy much of our attention. We will conclude that, in practical terms, belief in the moral perfection of the self through intention is consistent with the common good; it is an efficient instrument of justice. In chapter 3 we give this act of moral self-perfection a name. After describing human equality in more familiar language, we introduce "obtend" (a legitimate term but with no technical history) as the root verb for the operation of a diligent conscience that is seeking the good of others. We describe the connection between the internal and objective good as "obtensional"; the individual achieves his own moral good by adopting the *objective* good of others (the "lateral" good) as his own in*tention*. It is in this act of "obtension" that each of us chooses and creates his or her own character.

The work ahead falls into four parts. Continuing the analysis begun in this introduction, part 1, step by step, produces an interpretation of "human equality." It confirms that this shared belief is about a relation; it is a belief that equality is real—that is, instantiated in the world. Part 1 also invokes our conception of a "double equality" to help account for the importance people attach to human equality. More specifically, chapter 1 explores what little has already been written on the subject. Chapters 2 and 3 project into a clear idea what we take to be the common and half-conscious convention. We sculpt a meaning judged to represent the shared belief in human equality. Here, then, in a set piece is our conclusion about that meaning:

> *Human equality is the relation arising from the uniform capacity of rational persons to perfect themselves morally by committing to the search for the real lateral good.*

Of course it is open to anybody to challenge and to correct our picture of the convention. Moreover, even if we have gotten the convention (roughly) right, whether such an equality exists in the real world remains a matter for belief or disbelief.

Parts 2 and 3 then address the question that this definition makes intelligible, that is, *who could believe in this human equality?* We put this question to three views of the human self that are typical in Western cultures. Part 2 imagines the reception our definition will receive among philosophers of Individualism and natural law. Part 3 does the same with respect to Christianity. Finally, in part 4 we scan certain practical implications of such a belief.

We claim no special qualifications for this venture beyond a native (and possibly naive) enthusiasm; what the right credentials would be is, in any case, unclear. Furthermore, no one who is more—or even less—qualified seems poised to identify the terms and significance of human equality. Contemplating this vacuum, our diplomatic friends occasionally have suggested that on this subject there just might be nothing to say. They display a kind of polite distraction that we concede to be unsettling. We are heartened, however, by others who view the enterprise as vaguely ominous. Their unfocused anxiety oddly reassures us that we might be on to something. And happily a remaining few see human equality as virgin intellectual territory waiting for a crude map that can be tested and perfected in the market. For better or worse, their enthusiasm also has encouraged us. This uncommonly disparate reaction among wise counselors suggests there is something specially risky about the subject. We hope so.

PART I

HUMAN EQUALITY:

WHAT DOES IT MEAN?

8 *May*—I began to fear as I wrote this book that I was getting too diffuse; but now I am glad I went into detail from the first, for there is something so strange about this place and all in it that I cannot but feel uneasy.
(Stoker, *Dracula*)

INTRODUCTION TO PART I

He said true things but called them by wrong names.
(Robert Browning, *Bishop Blougram's Apology*)

JEFFERSON'S "created equal" may have captured the spirit of the Western insight, but it mistook the difficulty of the issue. Whatever else it may be, human equality is not self-evident. (Jefferson had come closer to the mark in the early draft where he had man's "equal creation" merely "sacred and undeniable.") Any analysis of descriptive human equality is in fact problematic and faces serious methodological hurdles. We have already said a bit concerning method but now must expand, assisted by Snarks and unicorns.

Discourse about unicorns can be intelligible only because linguistic convention has established what a unicorn would be, if there were one. In this one respect equality is like the unicorn. Those who would debate the question need a definition clear enough to allow intelligent conflict. With a common meaning for the term, each could assent to or reject equality in accord with his or her private views of the real world. Each could ask: Do I or do I not believe that the human self includes those defining properties that, if true, would entail equality? If, for example, the definition should require the population of equals to have an identical capacity for moral responsibility, could I believe in such a capacity? If not, I would not be a believer in human equality.

The lack of such a shared understanding was one of the many problems facing Lewis Carroll's intrepid hunters of the Snark: an expedition launched in a vacuum of information—no known color, no size, no shape, no characteristic call. The Snark was an existent without an image. The sole clue to its identity was a humanly fabricated word-sound, a name as yet unattached to any particular thing. Presumably the Snark had mass, hence literally could be imagined; but one mental picture of it would be as likely as any other. Given two unidentified candidates, which should the explorer choose? The real thing might go unrecognized; the pretender might get certified. With a word-sound as his sole guide, the hunter is tempted to fire at any strange object. Yet, as Carroll well understood, people can make prodigal investments in the pursuit or avoidance of Snarks. And sometimes they simply attach the label to whatever new beast they happen to encounter or even to imagine.

Carroll presents the Snark as a real beast lacking a conventional image. But one could imagine the exact opposite: a convention rich in images of a nonexistent thing. One thinks here of the unicorn, Santa Claus, and the Easter Bunny. No one supposes them to exist, and the convention confirms this disbelief. Were a one-horned equine beast to be spotted, we might call it a unicorn—but the discovery itself would change the meaning of the word. For the "unicorn" we knew had no such existence in the real world. (Of what such words signify, the medievals said they are merely "beings of reason" for they have no extramental existence. The chimera was their favorite example.)

Still a third kind of conventional linguistic signal uses images to identify things that either may or may not be real. The term "spotted owl" could become an example; the term passenger pigeon is so already (there might be one left). The conventions describing them will persist whether or not the thing signified is instantiated in our world. Convention here answers the question of what a spotted owl would be if there were one, leaving open the other question about existence.

Distinguishing these forms of convention helps clarify our hope for this book. The enterprise is not a Snark hunt; for much can and will be said about the properties that inform the conventional conception of human equality. Neither, however, is it a hunt for the unicorn; the properties of conventional equality are not so well defined as that famous horn. Nor, finally, is equality conceived by convention as merely mythical; it is a claim about reality.

Is equality, then, a spotted owl? On the one hand it is; it may or may not exist. On the other, however, the owl convention is as plain as the unicorn, while human equality surely is not. At the very least there is grave difficulty conceiving the thing in anything like physical terms. These animal metaphors, indeed, are more useful in capturing the content of conventions that consist of images which can be tested "empirically" than in describing a convention about an equality that might or might not be real. For even a real equality may have no property that could be the subject of an image.

In any case we need to deal with both questions: the conventional meaning and the reality. And the two must match. We have no commission to attach this term to just anything we can identify. The signal "human equality" does not belong to us. Others have already given it such shape and meaning as it possesses. That is the very point of its being a word, and as a convention it remains the property of the community. Its sound may well signify something that is real, but the assertion that the particular uniform reality we have identified as this thing they call human equality requires validation by the society that spawned the expression. The explorer may encounter something real, but until convention has been consulted, he cannot be certain of its name or whether it has one. We apply our best judgment, experience, and amateur metaphysics to this task of describing an equality that is simultaneously convention and a plausible state of the world. It must be both, if only because ordinary people plainly understand equality as a claim of truth to be believed or disbelieved.

As for method, we approach the first question—the meaning of the convention—as something that is accessible through readily available linguistic phenomena. As we shall see in chapter 1, these are seldom the words of scholars. Rather, the primary data are the words and attitudes of ordinary people, contemporary and historical. This is not esoteric stuff. Anyone of common sense (with a taste for word games) is in a position to frame a hypothesis about the meaning of the convention and argue on the evidence for his or her interpretation.

As for the second question—whether the convention, as interpreted, could be a correct understanding of the real world—the method consists principally of adaptations of well-known theories regarding the human capacity for moral self-perfection. If all this seems a case of common sense making the best of available materials, we are content. To converge in this manner on an insight or belief that has surfaced in countless ways over several millennia requires a process of sorting and shuffling. Following Aristotle, it might be given the fancy label of dialectic. Edgar Bodenheimer captures its essence and tells us its uses:

> The term "dialectic" is derived from the Greek word *dialegesthai*, which means to discuss a matter with someone, to argue out a problem with him. Ordinarily, where this method of communication is used, two or more parties to a conversation endeavor to arrive at the truth by means of a dialogue or debate, by posing and defending contradictory arguments. It is, however, also possible that a person will carry on a dialectical conversation with himself, by weighing the merits of opposing viewpoints, by considering the practical consequences of their respective adoption, and by arriving at a conclusion after a thorough appraisal of all facets and angles relevant to the problem. In contrast to a rigid, apodictic demonstration of a proposition, a dialectic discussion of a problem by two or more persons will under optimum conditions move in an atmosphere of open-mindedness and fluidity which leaves room for a full elaboration of differences of opinion, for a free and mutually advantageous give and take, for concessions of points of debate and adjustments of positions.[1]

As we proceed to give, take, concede, and adjust, we ask of our readers to keep bright the distinction between the convention and reality. There are two inquiries that must proceed together while remaining distinct. To ask the conventional meaning of human equality is not to ask whether equality is a fact. But the plausibility of a real equality will have a good deal to do with interpreting the convention. The West has invested too much in human equality to suppose that it has the status of Santa Claus.

1

WHAT HAS BEEN SAID?

*Of making many books there is no end, and much study
is a weariness of the flesh.*
(*Ecclesiastes* 12:11)

IN A 1987 ESSAY the philosopher Harry Frankfurt noted that the card catalogue in Yale's main library contained 326 book entries under the subject heading "Equality";[1] a decade later the catalogue had been supplanted by a computer that registered many more than 400 books under this label. This spectacular overdose can be credited to the current generation; from 1977 to 1987, books in English were catalogued under this heading at a rate of 40 per year.[2] And no one has tallied the articles and chapters on equality that could outnumber the books 25 to 1.

What, then, could justify yet another essay on equality? The sufficient answer is that this formidable mass of existing literature is devoted almost exclusively to the problem of whether and when society should *treat* people alike. On the very different question of whether, in some crucial respect, people here and now *are* the same, surprisingly little has been written beyond the familiar political slogans. Although the possible fact of human equality has been asserted since antiquity, there still is no set of shared analytical terms by which this claim can be attacked, defended, or even defined. "It is precisely because everyone thinks he knows what equality is, that it appears to be difficult to explain exactly what it is."[3]

Another brief fable illustrates the problem that such conceptual poverty creates even in ordinary conversation: You are at a Fourth of July party listening to your enthusiastic neighbor exclaim how right Jefferson was about the equality of man. Your friend seems to be reporting some scientific fact. Standing there swaying and quoting the Declaration, he speaks in the indicative—no "shoulds" or "oughts." Something drives you to ask the question: "What do you mean by 'created equal?' " He's glad you asked. But soon you wish you hadn't. You had supposed he would explain step by step that human equality consists in a relation grounded upon this or that characteristic. Instead he delivers a familiar speech; our political system is unfair, and somebody ought to do something about it. In short, he is not responsive. Your request for the description of a particular claim about reality has evoked only another homily on justice. Your neighbor seems unaware that you expected otherwise. For you, the experience is not a hopeful one, especially if you have an interest in how people perceive descriptive equality. Maybe they don't perceive it at all.

But things get even worse. You and your Jeffersonian friend have been overheard by a gentleman who insists upon giving your question a responsive answer. The fellow is a belligerent skeptic who ticks off a dozen crucial respects in which humans plainly are not equal. Struggling for declarative sentences, poor Jefferson is tongue-tied. He can't assert that we are all equal in talent or speed or age or virtue. Nevertheless, before he knows it, he hears himself saying that the most competent scientists find no inborn difference in the intelligence of large groups. The skeptic nails him:

> That only tells me that there are stupid whites and stupid blacks. That is exactly your problem. If intelligence is what counts, we can forget about individual human equality.
>
> *Jefferson:* That's not the point. Any experienced person knows that people are essentially the same.
>
> *Skeptic:* Ho, ho! Tell us about this common essence!
>
> *Jefferson:* Are you prepared to argue that you're essentially superior to this fellow who's mixing your martini?
>
> *Skeptic:* I'd be happy to make such an argument.

At that moment the skeptic's wife discovers an urgent need for their departure. The rest of the conversation proceeds only in Jefferson's mind: "There must be a crushing answer to such arrogance. What if I'd said that God loves us all? Or that equality is simply the dignity of being human? Or . . . something else?"

The Confused Jeffersonian is oblivious to the distinction between a normative and descriptive equality. Your question to him merited a descriptive answer; what it got was the patented egalitarian sermon. This, however, was not because this speaker avoids description on principle. To the contrary, he is not only willing but compulsively eager to answer the nasty stranger on his own terms; his very anxiety to do so makes him overlook the easy, if meaningless, escape, namely, "I believe I said only that people should be *treated* as equals." Instead he recklessly asserts the fact of human equality; to speak this way is so natural for him as to be quite irresistible, even if he finds the description itself—well, indescribable.

The story is not apocryphal; it is typical. Conceived as a human reality, equality is at the same time popular and neglected. It is often invoked but seldom explained. The consequence is miscommunication both at cocktail parties and in the academy. This failure even of the professional verbalists cannot be explained as a conviction that belief in a descriptive human equality entails metaphysical nonsense (though it might) or that it has little consequence for political theory (also possible) or both. They invoke the slogan too frequently and with too great a reverence, and they could not all be hypocrites.

To be fair, moral philosophers occasionally flirt with the notion of a real human equality, even if they shun definition. Like the Confused Jeffersonian, by intuition they invoke the genie of natural sameness. The moral enterprise, they think, wants a descriptive ground; equality as a goal seeks equality as some preexisting fact. With John Rawls they worry that "we still need a natural basis for equality."[4] Among egalitarians, however, not even Rawls has taken seriously the task of discovering just what a real human equality might be. Human equality as a description has been both a low-tech and low-priority enterprise for political philosophy.[5]

We will become more specific now as we comment on distinguishable divisions of the literature that can be said to deal with descriptive equality. Four of these sets are populated exclusively by modern empiricists, one by moral objectivists, and another by religious commentators.

Westen's Descriptive Equalities

The first set is a singleton. Here in remarkable isolation we find Peter Westen, an American lawyer. With singular clarity Westen apprehends the distinction between descriptive and prescriptive equalities. His 1990 book, *Speaking of Equality*, correctly explains that descriptive equality is a particular kind of comparative relationship. It is not the one that obtains between two or more things that are similar; that relation is one of similarity. Nor is it the one that obtains between things that are identical in *all* respects; that is mathematical equality, absolute equality, or identity—not ordinary descriptive equality. Ordinary descriptive equality is distinct from these; it is the relationship that obtains between two or more distinct things that are identical or indistinguishable in some respect but distinguishable in others.[6] Westen summarizes descriptive equality as follows: " 'Equality' . . . signifies the comparative relationship that obtains between two or more distinct persons or things by virtue of their having been jointly measured by a relevant standard of comparison and found to be undistinguishable by that standard."[7]

From his examples we could understand Westen to mean "undistinguishable" both in *possession* and *degree*. If that were so, his formulation would not only be an excellent general definition of descriptive equality but a useful elaboration of what we termed, in the introduction, a "double equality." Westen rightly identifies descriptive equality as relational and comparative—the measurement of two or more things by the same measure. An equality exists whenever a measurable quality turns out to be the same (in degree?) in the things or persons measured.

Nonetheless, Westen's analysis of descriptive equality has only limited usefulness for us. He very properly crafted his definition (and chose his examples) as the sufficient instruments of a lawyer's criticism of various popular theories of *pre*scriptive equality. These tools served his worthy but narrower purpose by confining the examples of equality to those human traits that can be measured as *material* characteristics of *material* substances. Looking only at Westen's examples of descriptive equalities and his discussions of what it means to measure,[8] readers might suppose that immaterial beings could never stand to one another in a relation of equality. If that were so, Westen would have excluded as a possible occasion of equality the one really unique feature of human existence—namely, the capacity for moral choice. We doubt he intended this. There must be more to the historic and enduring claim of human equality than our common possession of certain material traits.

Westen himself virtually says as much at the point where he concludes that the contemporary passion for egalitarian forms of justice rests ultimately upon a descriptive premise. Quoting Bernard Williams he emphasizes the point as follows: "Prescriptive equalities 'have force because they are regarded as affirming an equality which is believed in some sense already to exist' . . . [T]he normative conclusion that people 'ought to be treated equally' rests on the factual premise that they 'are equal.' "[9]

Westen here seems poised to identify the descriptive human equality that for centuries has given such furious energy to the claim that humans ought to be treated equally. Is he about to introduce some moral or even spiritual human feature to stand as the ground of the relation? Or has he discovered some unique material characteristic that humans share in uniform degree and that justifies the egalitarian passion? His answer is, for our purposes, disappointing:

> Thus, the assertion "all men are equal" is capable of stating both an "is" and an "ought": an "is" if it means "all men are descriptively equal in their possession of certain empirical traits"; an "ought" if it means "all men are prescriptively equal in certain ways in which they ought to be treated." As a statement of fact it is uncontroversial because all men are factually equal in numerous ways, including their common possession of X chromosomes. As a statement of value, it is essentially contestable. However, since prescriptive statements take the same form as descriptive statements, and since the latter are generally uncontroversial, a speaker can make prescriptive assertions that *appear* to be incontrovertible. . . . The upshot is a form of argument in which people are inferred to be prescriptive equals *simply because they are descriptive equals.*[10]

X chromosomes? The historic moral conviction that people in similar circumstances should be treated the same rests upon human properties that can be exemplified by the fact that they all have X chromosomes? Westen is certainly correct that the egalitarians have hoped for some fundamental descriptive equality as a ground for their moral programs, but could chromosomes (or any other material feature) exemplify the common property they might select as the necessary foundation of the relation? We think this was a slip in an otherwise remarkably clean analysis.[11] It gives too little credit to the good minds that have labored like Sisyphus (and with equal effect) to make egalitarianism plausible.

Viewed in the round, Westen's contribution is impressive. He clarified descriptive equality and glimpsed its possible importance; maintaining his limited purpose as a critic, he confined his inquiry to traits of the empirical sort typically used for legal classification. This focused lawyer's inquiry never denies that traits of a nonempirical order could support a more fundamental concept of human equality. Nothing in Westen's work shakes our conviction that if there is a relation that deserves to be called human equality, it will rest upon some very significant moral trait shared in the same degree. Others have given more emphasis to this proposition—what we shall later call the "criterion of importance"—and we turn now to examine their work.

The next three categories represent egalitarians—most of them empiricists—who have either asserted the reality of a descriptive human equality or implied the importance of identifying the convention or both. These writers have focused more than Westen upon the belief that equality is based on some uniquely human reality. However, though the object of their inquiry is occasionally more than normative, the outcome is seldom satisfactory as description. We earmark these three clusters, respectively, as the *insightful*, the *wrong-but-helpful*, and the *marginally relevant*.[12] Each is briefly exemplified. We have not nearly exhausted the enormous corpus of promising titles. We think, nonetheless, that our sample in each set is sufficient to conclude that the great preponderance of the work devoted to "equality" falls short of the analytical clarity the subject deserves. We shall speak of what we know to be relevant, with apologies for oversights. Readers are asked to attend patiently to a few examples of work that is only tangential; it is important to see what has been offered in the intellectual market as answers to the two questions as to whether human equality is a fact and what sort of fact people suppose it to be.

Intimations of a Significant Human Equality

More than thirty years ago the English philosopher Bernard Williams produced an often-cited essay entitled "The Idea of Equality." Most of its scant twenty pages were devoted to Williams's conceptions of egalitarian social reform. Our interest is in the few passages focused upon "what purport to be statements of fact—that men *are* equal." Williams here presents his own version of our Confused Jeffersonian. He says that when confronted with the crucial respects in which humans are unequal, the Jefferson in each of us tends to take an intellectual dive: "Faced with the obvious objection, the defender of the claim that all men are equal is likely to offer a weaker interpretation. . . . [W]e should not seek for some special characteristics . . . but merely remind ourselves that they are all men."[13]

To accept "men are men" as the substance of human equality is to reduce our subject to vapor. Williams concedes this; nevertheless, for his particular enterprise the slogan "men are men" remains highly relevant:

> The point of the supposedly factual assertion is to back up social ideals and programmes of political action. . . . [These] have their force . . . as affirming an equality which is believed in some sense already to exist. . . . [O]f what it is to be human, the apparently trivial statement of men's equality as men can serve as a reminder.[14]

Descriptive human equality serves Williams principally as a watchword of liberal politics. Nonetheless, for one important moment Williams addresses the substance of the question of whether a real and significant factual equality might be discovered among human capacities and, specifically, among moral capacities:

> These capacities . . . would naturally be thought to differ . . . like other capacities. . . . But . . . there is a powerful strain of thought that centres on a feeling of ultimate and outrageous absurdity in the idea that achievement of the highest kind of moral worth should depend on natural capacities, unequally and fortuitously distributed.[15]

What sort of human capacity could be identified or imagined that is free from this deadly variation by degree? Momentarily Williams is reminded of Immanuel Kant who he thinks might be read to support equality of moral capacity both in possession and degree. Kant, he says, detached the moral powers from all contingencies and made them a transcendental characteristic. This move would make a real human equality possible.

Having said this, Williams immediately backs away, specifically rejecting the insight that equality might somehow be located in moral agency. Like Peter Westen—though perhaps for different reasons—Williams focuses exclusively on measurable traits. He does so in part out of a candid contempt for nonempirical philosophy in general and for metaphysics in particular. Further, Kant's notion of the free and rational gives off an unsettling aroma of religion. "Though secular, it is equally metaphysical: in neither case is it anything empirical."[16] And there was that other sufficient reason for avoiding the transcendental: it appears to be politically ineffectual: "This transcendental, Kantian conception cannot provide any solid foundation for the notions of [political] equality among men, or of equality of respect owed to them."[17] For Williams, Kant's sin is that he implies neither the correct design of the civil order nor the proper programs of economic redistribution; what is the only promising theory of descriptive equality could not translate into equal treatment. Williams therefore turns from Kant and descriptive equality to assertions about "respect" and other notions, statements he supposes to support his political program.[18]

Nonetheless, we are grateful to Williams for the very insight he rejected. Any descriptive human equality would have to spring from a universal and uniform capacity to achieve moral self-perfection. If this noble concept was useless to the particular enterprise of one philosopher, it is central to our own, for, as Williams apprehends, the popular belief about equality entails the hope that *somehow*—transcendentally, even—personal goodness is a wide human possibility. So long as self-perfection is possible despite conditions of social iniquity (and inequity), life remains interesting. To believers in "human equality" nothing is more intriguing than the possibility that every rational person, whatever his or her circumstances, enjoys the same opportunity to achieve "the highest kind of moral worth." In chapter 4 we shall try to understand how Kant might be read to support that possibility. In the end, what Williams discards as conceptual slag may well constitute the most promising ground of human equality; whether it will pass muster as somebody's political tool is not our immediate concern—we merely wonder that it might be true.

The American philosopher Thomas Nagel shares Williams's impulse to locate a descriptive equality that could precede and justify egalitarian proposals. And though his systematic attention to such an equality is scant, he seems—at least for a moment—to transcend Williams's fear of the metaphysical. Nagel's factual equality consists in our being equal to one another in "importance."[19] This equality of importance can be discerned only by taking the "view from nowhere"—the super-perch Nagel urges us to occupy in order to gain objective knowledge of reality. Among the wonders Nagel would have us see from that perspectiveless perspective is that everyone both possesses the property of "importance" and does so in the same degree. Here is the apparent ground for a significant, very human—and double—equality.

Readers begin straightaway to look for an analytical explanation of "importance," including identification of some specific property to which it is ascribed. At least we hoped Nagel would tell us that it means something like *moral* importance. Sadly, in the rest of his work there is no suggestion of this. Indeed, the opposite may be implied in his assertion that we must "continue our unsteady progress toward moral equality."[20] This possibility was confirmed in an academic colloquium in which Nagel was asked the analytical content of "importance." Nagel's only answer was that the equality of importance one sees from the objective point of view is that "everybody counts the same."[21]

This, again, does not address the descriptive content of an equality based upon importance. Nagel moves directly from the slogan to a particular social program. We are told so little about "importance" that it could be a quality shared by rodents and redwoods. Nor is Nagel interested in the possibility that ordinary people might want more detail before they assent to his usage of the word as the descriptive anchor for the relation of equality. Conventional understanding seems to carry no weight for him. This private sculpting of meanings for equality is hard to justify. How can we speak of equality without connecting to the content of this term as understood by the mass of those who use it? If every speaker is free to apply the term to whatever phenomenon he or she pleases, the hope for conversation vanishes.

Nevertheless, Nagel's assertion of an equality of importance constitutes a significant intimation of a descriptive form. Here is another mainline philosopher who has verged upon the issue and seen that, in principle, it is resolvable. Indeed, he resolves it. His solution is scant, but it is a probe in the right direction. The abstraction "importance" seems to implicate the very kinds of transcendental human properties from which Bernard Williams turned away. At least at that point in his thinking Nagel shared the insight that, if we are equal, it is because we all have the same opportunity for moral fulfillment.[22] What else could he mean?[23]

John Wilson's Excellent Error

In 1966, in a book called simply *Equality*, the English philosopher John Wilson produced what may be the most sustained discussion of "Equality as a Fact." It is coherent and professional in the best sense that even its vulnerabilities are left undisguised. Wilson, like nearly every other writer we describe, is pursuing a social program, and predictably this distorts his vision; nevertheless, for most of a chapter he pauses to describe what he labels "intrinsic equality." Like our own term, "human equality," this is clearly intended to identify a unique descriptive phenomenon—a crucial relation of sameness that characterizes all (and only) rational decision makers: "The claim of intrinsic equality is essentially the claim that every man has an equal ability to frame his own world view. . . . This claim is a factual one."[24]

Wilson appears to accept the task that other liberals refused—that of fashioning a "metaphysical" doctrine by which "all men are equal—now and forever in intrinsic value, inherent worth, essential nature."[25] Wilson proceeds toward this end from the liberal premise that individuals have the capacity to make up their own morality and that they must do so, because there is none other to be found. "If two people differ in their . . . rules for behaviour . . . they have no higher . . . rules by which to settle their difference."[26] Wilson applies this extreme moral relativism to the question of equality in the following way:

> Because each man can shape his own ends and can choose his own values . . . it is impossible to say that one man is superior. . . . This is a natural and not an artificial equality: the whole point, indeed, is that it does not depend on any status which we give to particular people as creators of value, but upon the natural abilities of rational beings.[27]

The locus of Wilson's equality, then, is the familiar autonomous hero of modern subjectivism whose glory—whose fate—it is to invent the good as he goes along. This is a plausible strategy. It begins with Bernard Williams's insight that human equality must be a relation grounded upon our individual moral powers. It adds the standard assertion of the liberal moralist, that anyone who has a will is entitled—at least until he consents to the social contract, and possibly after as well—to will what he chooses. The common possession by all individuals of this originally unfettered will is what equality means. Wilson's claim is that all rational persons are in a relation of "intrinsic equality" grounded upon this uniform capacity to will their own ends.[28]

If rational humans were free to invent the terms of morality, there would, indeed, be a form of equality existing among them. Unfortunately it would be a wholly trivial equality, a problem Wilson ignores. His equality among autonomous selves is one of possession only; it is a single, not a double, equality. Indeed, if humans all have this crucial property—this capacity to justify a choice simply by making it—they will have it in wildly varying degrees. As he himself insists, intrinsic equality depends "upon the natural abilities of rational beings," and these abilities are dramatically variant. If value is self-determined, those who by nature or circumstance are relatively more creative in devising alternatives will have a wider set of life options. Humans will be not equal, but unequal. Wilson has by misadventure returned us to the absurd world rejected by Bernard Williams where we find the most important "natural capacities unequally and fortuitously distributed." Wilson's form of human equality is self-defeating.

Wilson—like Nagel—also undervalues convention. There are limits to the kinds of relation that terms such as "human" or "intrinsic" equality can signify. These limits are ambiguous but they exist, and of these conventions Wilson tells us nothing. For him the question to be answered is purely metaphysical. He asserts the reality of a particular human property he believes to exist; then, blithely, he applies the label "human equality" to the relation he thinks to be grounded upon that property. Even if he were correct about radical human autonomy and the unfettered moral powers of individuals, we still would challenge his authority to christen the resulting relation "equality" without consulting convention. Where did he get the right to attach this name to the Individualist Self? So far as we can see, Wilson has pitched his own tent in the desert and called it New York City. This is perfectly legal, but convention need not respect his peculiar usage.[29] Of course it might do so, but that is a point for him to establish. Until he does, Wilson's usage could be arbitrary and parochial. Ordinary people may not agree that we simply make up morality. They could find it a bit high-handed of Wilson to take what is their own term for a relation in which they do believe and attach it to the Individualist Self in which they do not believe.

Wilson's attempt at a descriptive equality also suffers from the standard liberal preoccupation with questions of social policy. Even in the course of description he slips into the language of aspiration: "It is our failure so far to see *why* a belief in intrinsic equality is a necessary moral belief—our failure to defend intrinsic equality as an ideal of practical living—that makes nonsense of many of our liberal assumptions."[30] By some undisclosed process Wilson conflates the supposed fact of equality with some "moral belief" and with an "ideal." The difficulties of his identifying a clear descriptive human equality continue to multiply. Still, for all our objections, we applaud Wilson's serious engagement with the problem of description. He has helped to set the terms of the debate and, if only by contrast, to suggest the way the structure of the moral self ought to be viewed, if it is both to provide the base for a real equality and to satisfy the criteria set by convention. Ultimately, however, we shall show that consistent moral individualists cannot believe in conventional human equality.[31]

The Marginally Relevant

A sampling of other modernists who speak of equality discloses a literature focused on the question of what makes a society good in political and economic terms; in these works the occasional claim that there is a descriptive equality of persons is rarely more than an unexplained assertion or a passing reference to some canonical source. We will illustrate this with a specific case or two and suggest their marginality for our task. The process helps to clarify the real quarry. There is no better example than John Rawls, the doyen of liberal egalitarianism. If a coherent descriptive equality were part of the liberal package, it is here one would expect to find it. As noted, Rawls himself insists that "we still need a natural basis for equality."[32]

Unfortunately Rawls leaves this seemingly important point in confusion. The only sustained discussion of anything like human equality comes in his allegory of the "original position." This is an imaginary primordial setting in which individuals ignorant of their own circumstances bargain to a set of social rules. This fictional legislature is designed "to represent equality between human beings as moral persons, as creatures having a conception of their good and capable of a sense of justice."[33] However, this state of affairs is not proposed by Rawls as a discovery but as a philosophical artifact; it represents no reality and could be ascribed to no actual person. Indeed, it is designed precisely to avoid facing the inconvenient reality that people are quite unequal in exceedingly important respects. The "original position" could satisfy neither convention nor metaphysics as a description of human equality, nor does Rawls ever claim that it would.

Toward the end of his now classic book, however, Rawls does provide a section entitled "The Basis of Equality," which restates and attempts to explain the remark about a "natural basis."[34] On close inspection it turns out that the equality referred to in this expression is nothing more than the congeries of legal and political *rights* that Rawls would insist upon for his version of the just society. And the "natural basis" from which he would infer this array of egalitarian social claims is not the relation of equality. The descriptive term, rather, is the human capacity for moral personality. As he says: "The capacity for moral personality is a sufficient condition for being entitled to equal justice."[35] It appears that equality itself has no descriptive sense at all; it is only a political goal.

The unwary reader, nonetheless, could suppose that Rawls really does claim equality as the factual basis for his social program. For he adds the curious suggestion that the capacity for moral personality should be thought of as a "range property." By this he seems to mean that the varying *degrees* in which people *possess* this capacity are morally irrelevant:

> Now whether there is a suitable range property for singling out the respect in which human beings are to be counted equal is settled by the conception of justice. But the description of the parties in the original position identifies such a property, and the principles of justice assure us that any variations in ability within the range are to be regarded as any other natural asset. There is no obstacle to thinking that a natural capacity constitutes the basis of equality.[36]

When read closely, this merely repeats the claim that, by itself, the mere *possession* of this *variant* capacity for moral personality suffices to qualify the individual for a particular set of political and economic rights.[37] The important assertions about equality remain normative. Of course the sharing of the capacity for moral personality (like any other trait) does in fact generate a descriptive equality among those who have it; but, once again, this relation is only the trivial form of equality that exists between any two people who possess *any* property in common no matter how much they vary in the degree of its enjoyment. It is one of the many ways in which Leonardo da Vinci and I are equal. There is something missing here.[38]

Why does Rawls leave this all so vague when he seems so keen to find a descriptive base for political equality? We suspect that the answer is this: He recognizes the emptiness (or worse) of any equality that is founded upon mere possession of a property that varies in degree from person to person. If he were plainly to acknowledge that humans differ in the degree of their capacity for moral personality or for a sense of justice, this would be a dramatic admission of descriptive *disequality.*[39] Rawls's allegory of persons ignorant of their own talents and circumstances struggles to obscure and defang this embarrassment; these are real and important human differences that he is anxious never to encounter.[40] Thus Rawls finesses the problem and grounds his egalitarian social program upon a human capacity that entails a descriptive inequality.[41]

Ironically this was an unnecessary concession. Eventually we will show that, properly understood, the capacity for moral personality may not be a "range property" at all but rather one that is uniform in degree. And if it is uniform, it might be the host property for the relation of human equality. Of course it is not our purpose to supply the premise for Rawls's politics. We are nevertheless grateful for his confirmation of Williams's ever-widening insight that any believable descriptive equality will take its stand upon the human moral capacity.

Rawls's fleeting engagement with description is the signature of the modern egalitarian. Ronald Dworkin's work displays the same bent. In three long articles entitled "What Is Equality?" as elsewhere in his massive published corpus, Dworkin manages to avoid his own question.[42] His title would be better understood as "What Would Equality Be if We Could Get It?"; for his interest is, once again, those social and economic arrangements that he thinks deserve the sympathetic political label of equality because of their fairness and justness in distributing benefits and burdens. Dworkin's work is rich in theories about our collective obligation to assure "equal concern and respect" to all, but he lacks altogether a theory of how the people he insists are to be treated "as equals" *are*, in fact, equal. Dworkin's vast jurisprudential project is an effort to give moral and legal effect to a descriptive human equality he never specifies.[43]

Religious Commentators

It is not merely the secular philosophers whose descriptive claims are unsatisfactory. Commentators on Western religion regularly assume without argument that Judaism or Christianity contains some theory of descriptive equality.[44] From this they deduce moral and social consequences with little concern for the difficulties at either end of this supposed logical connection. They observe, for example, that Christians see all humans as "children of

God" and that we are "neither Jew nor Greek"; from these obscurities they conclude that Christians believe in equality as a fact.[45] Historical movements for political equality also get reinterpreted as an implicit religious recognition of "the natural equality of men"[46] without the faintest concern to define terms.[47]

An example of several of these related tendencies appears in this assessment of the attitude of Judaism toward equality:

> It is more than equality before the law that God had willed. Indeed, even at creation did He will human equality as a *fact*.

> That all men have only one progenitor, whereas animals were created by God in the plural number, was held to mean that all human beings are born equal. They enjoy this equality by virtue of the very fact that they were born, even if they never attain to the faculty of reason.[48]

In these passages the word "equality" is seemingly crucial. In fact, however, it does almost no work. It is merely the name for the relation among those humans who happen to be born. And this suggests nothing significant about what we *are* beyond human tissue. The relationship arising from the fact of birth is, by definition, merely a single—not a double—equality. It does not vary in degree; it could not vary in degree. It is therefore trivial.

Consider an older example. Though it relies on antiquarian and secular sources as well as religion, a curious essay of Samuel Pufendorf (1632–1694) still deserves brief notice. Wedged into his bulky treatise on the law of nations it is titled "All Men Are Accounted as Naturally Equal."[49] Its author collects a menagerie of classical sources to assure us that "human nature belongs equally to all men." This assertion—and others like it—are provocative, but their descriptive potential is swamped by Pufendorf's conflation of fact and value. The thing is saturated with admonitions to Everyman to "treat every other man as his equal by nature." Nor is there one solid clue to the meaning of such quasi-descriptive passages, unless it lurks in the pregnant aside that God will judge men "according to the sincerity of their piety."[50] That tidbit, unexploited by Pufendorf, will be worth remembering. Because it would forge a link between equality and sincerity, Pufendorf's baroque theory of natural equality is a significant, early modern intimation of the conventional belief in human equality.

Pufendorf's insight into human equality does service in no contemporary analysis of descriptive equality that we know. In its stead one often finds the early-twentieth-century work of A. J. Carlyle, the eminent English historian. Even today Carlyle's strange amalgam of Stoic and Pauline ideas is taken to represent a coherent statement of a descriptive human equality.[51] Carlyle's work is a rich trove of learning about Western probes in the direction of a belief in natural human equality; but in his zeal to identify antecedents for the "Liberty, Equality, Fraternity" of the French Revolution,[52] he locates equality where there is only similarity.

Carlyle discerns the beginnings of a belief in "natural equality" in the movement of thought from Aristotle to Cicero and Seneca. Aristotle had taught that some men naturally are slaves because they lack the mental capacity to deliberate and to choose how to act. The broad experience of empire, however, had revealed no "natural" slaves; nature had given *all* men the reason required for self-determination. Cicero, Seneca, and the Stoics discovered that reason was a common possession, evincing a natural unity notwithstanding the differences in human customs and mores. While they seem rarely to have understood this common possession of reason specifically as a human "equality," Carlyle cheerfully supplies the missing term. In his hands the Stoic discovery of the common possession of reason becomes an early passion for descriptive human equality:

> Over against Aristotle's view of the natural inequality of human nature we find set out the theory of the natural equality of human nature. There is no resemblance in nature so great as that between man and man, there is no equality so complete. There is only one possible definition for all mankind, reason is common to all.[53]

Carlyle is correct that the Stoic discovery of universal reason was the ground for new ruminations about human unity, sometimes even expressed as a natural equality. If equality is rooted in reason, however, it can be only a trivial, single equality of possession; more important are the dramatic differences in capacity.[54]

Carlyle, like Pufendorf, has scripture teaching an early version of a natural equality. He finds it in Pauline passages such as the assertions that among Christians "there is no respect of persons" and that masters should "render that which is just and equal, knowing that ye also have a master in heaven":

> St. Paul's attitude to the question of slavery is obviously founded upon his conviction that all men are at least morally and spiritually equal in character. To him all men are in God's sight equal, distinctions of condition belong only to the outer man, men are to each other brothers.[55]

Consider but a few of the problems this passage raises. First, men are equal "in character." Does this really mean that they are equally good (something too hard for us to imagine) or only that they have equal capacity to be so? If the latter, what is the nature of this personal power by which, at the start of the race, both St. Paul and the ignorant (and unbaptized) slave are equally equipped to reach the finish line together? Second, regarding "God's sight," how is it that the value God attaches to particular humans can be inferred from the two Delphic assertions of Paul—the one about God's being no respecter of persons and the other about the proper treatment of slaves? There is nothing in words of this sort to justify the conclusion that God invests all of us with the same value; before we conclude that he does, we might remember that many Christians have believed (supposedly on Paul's authority) that God made us wholly different in our opportunity for salvation. Third, that we are brothers does not foreclose the possibility of little brothers with feebler powers. And so on.[56]

Again, the point is not that any of these descriptions of fact is right or wrong. That is not the question we ask (nor could answer). Our question is what meaning writers have attached to their assertions of an existent human equality. What we find over and over, whenever the assertion gets any content, is an unanalyzed alliance of equality with human moral potential. Frequently the connection is made in terms that allow only a single, and therefore trivial, equality. But the enthusiasm of the assertions raises a suspicion that much more than a single equality is at stake.

Consider an essay of the French philosopher Jacques Maritain (1882–1973). While he was moderately egalitarian in his social thought, Maritain's overall approach is almost opposite that of the egalitarians which we have sketched above. Their instinct is first to imagine forms of political and social equality and only then—if at all—to go looking for some descriptive notion of human equality to support them. Maritain starts with an inquiry into the nature of man, finds a certain form of descriptive equality, and (rightly or not) draws conclusions about the society that would be just for such beings.[57] He proceeds from what is to what should be. Writing in the tradition of Thomas Aquinas, Maritain shares none of the modern empiricists' allergy to metaphysics and the transcendental.

Human equality, according to Maritain, is an equality in human "nature," "essence," or "substance."[58] It is a "real relation" that is "ontological and concrete,"[59] "primordial," and "fundamental."[60] Where the empiricist sees only difference, Maritain discovers an equality of human nature[61]—an equality that "lies at the root" and coexists with inequalities "in the branches."[62] "This equality . . . in nature is revealed . . . as a very precious thing, . . . more important than all the differences and inequalities superimposed upon it."[63]

This all sounds promising but sketchy. The single most difficult problem is Maritain's silence on the question of degree.[64] Is this a single equality, or a double? It appears to be merely an equality of possession—possession, indeed, of what cannot vary in degree: human nature. (To possess only part of a human nature is to have some other nature.) Such an equality would allow rational humans diverse capacities for moral self-perfection.[65]

There are, nonetheless, clues in Maritain's equality about the convention that Maritain himself ignored. That equality is said to be "very precious," more important than any and all difference. But what else could this be than the capacity for goodness (or, in Maritain's own Catholic terms, salvation)?

This in fact is the form of human equality Yale professor Gene Outka associates with the Danish theologian Søren Kierkegaard (1813–1855);

however, the concept is now recast in a strange linguistic medley of Protestantism and Kantianism. Outka's article presents the most subtle and sophisticated analysis of descriptive human equality we know; it does so as an exegesis in which Kierkegaard understands every human to be uniformly obligated and able to achieve his highest good, union with God.

> "The eternal in speaking about the highest assumes calmly that every man can do it, and merely asks, therefore, whether or not he has done it." *Every man*: the commitment to equality appears wholly unqualified, with "man" referring to male and female alike. *Can do it*: our relation to the highest good is characterized chiefly on our side by what each of us is equally capable of willing to do. *Whether or not he or she has done it*: every person is judged by the sole criterion of actual performance, a performance undetermined by natural advantage.[66]

This is, in our terms, a double equality, approaching in nearly every detail that unique double equality that—we shall argue—is conventional human equality. "[The person] who is victimized by an unhappy parent, who proves unable all his days to secure from others what he needs though he gives lavishly of himself, and whose death goes unrecorded [—t]hat person can nonetheless do 'the highest thing of all,' he can will the Good."[67]

Kierkegaard well knew that none of this can be proved; it remains a matter for religious *belief*. But for him the alternative, which is to condition the highest human good on unequal external advantage called "fate," is to "make nonsense of" and to "betray" our "ethical reality," the way we become fully human.[68] "The process of attaining individuality is never foreordained for anyone; it awaits the free action of each of us."[69]

Tucked away in the remote corners of Kierkegaard's extensive corpus are the makings and intimations of a robust theory of human equality, which Professor Outka has knitted together and set in contrast to Bernard Williams's assertion—an assertion Outka judges typical of modern moral philosophy[70]—that undeserved natural advantages affect individuals' chances for moral goodness. We are grateful to Outka for his forceful demonstration of Kierkegaard's Christian commitment to human equality and, even more, for his confirmation that human equality is a question about the extent and range of the human capacity for goodness.

Conclusion and One Final Clue

The popular expressions of a real human equality are thus—with rare but critically clarifying exceptions—left unrefined in the scholarly literature. This much, however, seems agreed on: equality implicates what is best and most important among human powers. We have good reason to seek its meaning among conceptions of moral self-perfection. Discovery of that meaning would not prove equality to be either fact or fiction, but it might allow us to see how that question might be framed as one about morality. Human equality cannot be approached except as a plausible proposition. Moral powers are nonempirical. They and the equality they may generate are properly matters for intelligent belief or disbelief, not for proof or demonstration.

Arnold Brecht understands both the modesty and the hubris in this enterprise. His dialectical interpretation of the convention is worth quoting at length, for it forecasts much of what follows in the next two chapters:

> Sometimes the eighteenth-century argument that all men . . . are "born equal" is still heard today in the somewhat more precise form that . . . all men are by birth "in the same plight." . . . This [argument] needs proof in order to be scientifically acceptable. It is not self-evident. On the contrary, it obviously needs correction or modification, for it would prove much more than merely the equality of human beings: all animals are in the same plight from birth.

Brecht does not leave things there, however:

> In order to limit the postulate to man, one must add a rational ground on which men, and all of them, deserve such a distinction. If then reference is offered to the eminence of man because he alone is "endowed with reason," we are again up against the old objection that there are considerable differences in the breadth and depth of reason in individuals.

Trying to make the convention intelligible, Brecht proceeds to the necessary last step:

> One significant feature in which all humans are alike may be their ability to choose to be good or evil in any moment of their lives. It makes sense to consider this feature so essential that all other differences, even those between high and low degrees of intelligence, are held negligible in comparison. This way of arguing (which is in line with my own convictions) would then lead logically to the proposition that all men are "essentially" equal. But in allotting such a high rank, and even top rank, to this one feature we render a value judgment which cannot be sanctioned by science.[71]

If there is confusion in these passages, there are also uncommon insight and clarity. The convention is about something *worth believing*, or so Brecht concludes. Proceeding in this spirit we address three questions: the meaning of the convention about equality, its plausibility as a feature of the real world, and the connection between the two.

2

THE HOST PROPERTY

Man remains a person only in the magnetic field of a
fundamental relationship. If he leaves this field of energy, he
will crumble into bits, like iron filings when an electro-
magnet is switched off.
(B. Schellenberger, *Nomad of the Spirit*)

THIS CHAPTER and the next contain the heart of the idea. Here we ask what conventional "human equality" means. Concluding that the convention expresses a belief in an existent human relation, we go on to ask what this would require. Throughout we make judgments as to what evidence is relevant to these issues and roughly how each piece should be weighed. We identify a set of five criteria for a plausible meaning of "human equality." These criteria emerge from our own experience and re-flection, both on what we hear on the street and on the little help to be found in the literature. In any case they seem rather obvious; they must, for we are interpreting a linguistic convention—a shared possession. We have sculpted the figure of conventional human equality from common clues about the meanings people attach to the expression. These fitted together well enough and in due course formed the clear outline of something per-haps already inchoate in our thinking. The process remained throughout a matter of trial and error, but gradually the errors began to betray themselves even before we could specify the precise flaw. There was something more natural about this development than we are able to articulate. The result is as ungainly as the selves that experience their own human equality.

Clarifying the Quarry

Every equality, as we have seen, is a relation. Human equality, if it exists, is a relation connecting those who share some uniquely important characteris-tic in the same degree. Perhaps every rational person has this characteristic, perhaps not. We have called it the "host property." To identify the host prop-erty is to describe at least part of the human self that anchors both ends of the relation. This task of description is entirely different from the work of those social philosophers who keep reinventing the good society. They con-fect notions of social or economic equality that could obtain even among selves that were, by nature, unequal; their hope is that by some splendid rescue society will homogenize the estate of persons who are presently in very diverse circumstances. Much of recent moral philosophy has been a search for such a measure of justice; as we have seen, few of these scholars who pursue equality as a social good have paid more than passing attention to the possibility that we already are equal in a manner recognizable to any Jeffersonian.

This essay is, then, the converse of modern social philosophy. While egalitarians specify social justice and ignore the equality of the self, we describe the equal self and skirt the details of justice. Our point is not that justice ceases to be important among persons whom nature has related as equals; indeed, it could be that only in discovering their equality do we make justice worth specifying. But we leave that question to those with more social vision.

What could it mean to say that persons who are diverse in their readiness for life's various races are in fact equal? In what respect are we to measure and compare them? The answer may be that human equality will concern some achievement that involves no contests among us, resting upon a specific capacity that is always able to reach its end in a plenary way, on its own and without competition. Given the importance commonly ascribed to equality—indeed, its perception as something good—it may be, as Bernard Williams suspected, that the host property is to be found in our peculiar faculty for morality. How the power of this faculty might be uniform among rational persons will be considered in chapter 3. Our project in chapter 2 is to give it a plausible description.

A Working Premise: Equality Is Perceived as Important

Our quest begins with the observation that most people think the relation of human equality is a significant attribute of the person; it is—simply—important. This allows us conveniently to discard various versions of the self that otherwise might compete for the role of host property. We will soon show that convention gives human equality not only weight but approval. No theory of conventional human equality could remove this "halo" and remain recognizable; human equality is something both significant and good, or it is nothing at all. For the moment, however, we are concerned only with its significance (for good or ill).

This premise of importance allows us to disqualify as the host property all those characteristics of the self that could generate only trivial forms of equality. How do we distinguish the trivial from the significant? Happily there is no need to canvass the whole list of human properties, comparing them for their functional and aesthetic weights. The great multitude of human samenesses can be eliminated straightaway because they generate nothing more than "single" equalities. In other words, they are merely cases of common possession of some property that *varies in degree* from person to person. Recall from the introduction and chapter 1 that common possession of a trait can by itself generate only a trivial form of equality regardless of the significance of the shared property. To be relevant for our purpose, the equality needed is one that springs from possession of some property in the same degree. The search for the host, therefore, can ignore those many properties of the self that all of us enjoy "more or less" or as "range properties."[1]

The trait of rationality is an example. A true relation of equality does exist among all those who possess reason. However, this particular equality that holds among rational selves obviously will not do as "human equality." Reason might at first seem a plausible candidate because of its capital importance. But upon reflection we see that this very importance works against reason as the ground of equality. Our individual endowments of this crucial good differ radically in degree. Some minds are powerful and thus valued; others are dim and less valued. As a candidate for host property, reason fails precisely because everyone agrees that (1) the relative amplitude of one's intellect is a terribly important fact; and (2) some minds have only a little whereas others have a lot. As the host property, reason would allow us to be equal only in its possession; but human equality would thus be reduced to a relation that to ordinary persons seems empty and formalistic. The observation that Einstein and I have a relation of equality by our common possession of reason is valid, but, if reason is the standard of ultimate excellence, I am not flattered. There must also be equality in degree.

This rule often is acknowledged in an obscure manner by egalitarian moralists. When John Rawls speaks of "human beings as moral persons, as creatures having a conception of their good and capable of a sense of justice," he is careful to say that humans thereby have a "similarity."[2] Implicitly he has identified two types of relations among persons: (1) humans have a relation of *equality* based upon their common *possession* of a certain "capability"; and (2) humans differ in the degree that each enjoys this capability and, in this respect, have at most a relation of *similarity*. Restated in our own terms, Rawls has identified only a single and not a double equality.

If human equality holds, then, it will be as a relation emerging from the possession of some host property that, by definition, *could* vary in degree but in fact does not. This point may be partly aesthetic. Equality first becomes interesting when conceived as a possible but not necessary state of human affairs. The term identifies a factual condition that might or might not obtain; those who believe it does obtain will claim this state of affairs as an exciting and unexpected truth. It will be a bit like the news that all of us are equally gifted at golf—a clear if implausible form of descriptive equality. The host property of human equality will have to be something more majestic than the talent for golf, but we will experience this same agreeable surprise that so variable a trait could in fact be uniform from person to person. It will be a provocative claim about the human condition.

Though the term itself is new, the possibility that "double equalities" may hold among subgroups (not individuals) has long been the concern of systematic professional inquiry. Social science has looked for evidence of sameness between and among racial, social, ethnic, and gender groups, seeking some variable human faculty (often some aspect of intelligence) that in fact does not vary significantly *on average* from one group to the next.[3] The candidates for the host of such an equality often have proved elusive even with respect to large clusters of humans—for example, races and genders.

With respect to individuals—our subject—the difficulties of finding such a property increase exponentially. Scientists are unlikely ever to discover any such universal trait. In whatever manner they may redefine the object of their search, any double equality that could hold among the mass of human individuals seems an unrealistic expectation. Our gifts and intelligence may get measured according to every imaginable calculus; each metric will involve an important quality, and each of these qualities will be potentially variable; and we could possess these significant characteristics either uniformly or in different degrees. In theory, then, such properties would be candidates for the role of host property. The difficulty, that is, the empirical difficulty, nevertheless will remain— that manifestly we *do* possess them all in widely varying degrees. Our gifts differ in extent if not in kind.

Many double equalities do exist but only among relatively small clusters of individuals. On any imaginable metric, groups of individuals score the same; indeed, if the sample is large, almost everyone will find another person who scores at the same level. Among such persons there will be a true double equality. Larsen and Johnson are equally clever at chess, a variable skill; the two of them thus have the necessary double relation. This, however, does not alleviate the difficulty. Such petty clusters of uniformity are not instances of "human equality." The convention is about a company more inclusive than the puny collection of individuals who happen to get the same score on a test (and which test?). To put it more generally, any variable human feature that—in respect to individuals—turns out in fact to be so empirically diverse in degree as do looks, brains, skill, or experience never could serve as the host. What the convention requires is a double equality that holds for the mass of mankind. The great run of us must possess some crucial human property, and possess it in the same degree—or there is no human equality.

This may seem all smoke and mirrors. We have made human equality depend on individuals' sharing some supposedly variable host property that never in fact varies, but it begins to look as if no such property exists. This is not yet certain, however; all we really have said is that we can think of no such property that is measurable in the manner of the laboratory. If a double equality is what we need, we still could hope for a host property equal in degree among all individuals but identifiable by rational processes that do not depend upon scientific measurements.

This would be an unsurprising part of the convention; few suppose that the idea of human equality has much to do with anything that can be weighed, measured, or counted. Their attitude is constantly confirmed in ordinary conversation. Defenders of descriptive equality may at first rely on brains or skill as the host property, but when that foundation crumbles, their favorite refuge is some untestable property of the individual such as "moral worth" or "soul." Even empiricists such as Thomas Nagel recognize "importance" as a more plausible sort of candidate for the host. It was improbable from the beginning that the host of the relation would be some element detectable by scientific observation. Human equality is bigger game than this, and the promising hunting ground is less the statistical than the moral wilderness. Maybe the host will be, as Arnold Brecht supposed, something like the power of the self to fix its own ideal. A power that could vary so among us might, after all, be the same.

Equality as Relation Plus

Our initial premise that equality is something important is helpful in eliminating all empirical properties as candidates for the role of host of the relation. At the same time, however, this premise of importance could constitute an unintended threat to the whole enterprise, for there is a common tendency to treat relation itself as an inferior order of being. Even Thomas Aquinas, a champion of its reality, conceded relation to be the least of all real being.[4] Relations, even of the real (i.e., nonmental) sort, are derivative. The host is the foundation, which, in combination with another host, generates relation. The equality is one *of* will or *of* reason—or *of* moral capacity. Attention commonly fixes upon the substantive feature by which individuals are related, and it should; what we have termed the "host" property also should be thought of as the *generative* property of the relation.

This devaluation of relation qua relation creates a problem for us; the psychological effect is that equality, analyzed as pure relation, becomes demoted almost to a word-sound—a metaphysically marginal tail wagging a substantive dog. And if the relation is perceived to be so vapid, what judgment is rendered upon it by our first premise—that of *importance*? So long as this premise maintains its authority, the pure relation may have insufficient dignity to satisfy the equality convention. Obviously something has to give.

One path is closed—we cannot simply ignore the relation. If human equality were to be identified as *nothing but* the host property, it would cease to have independent reality and would become redundant for that property; it would be a property attributable only to each solitary individual, losing all intelligibility as a connector. How can we simultaneously maintain both the independent status of the relation and its importance? The answer seems plain enough. Any intelligible interpretation of "human equality" will need to implicate *both* the relation *and* the property that generates it. The term must be understood as the name for the package.

This trifling insight leads us to a new and broader set of relevant terms. Once we grasp that understanding human equality requires understanding its host, our interpretation will include *whatever* has contributed to the constitution of that host—including other forms of relation. Relations come in endless varieties, all of them separate and distinct from the special relation—human equality—that is our subject. Some of these other relations may be relevant to human equality even to the extent that they are necessary sources of its host property. In other words, there may be some relation X that generates some property Y which, when shared by the mass of individuals, becomes host to the relation we call human equality.

Simply stated, relations themselves can in turn become causes. Some relations (which we tend to call "relationships") produce new host properties of individuals, thereby generating the potential for still other kinds of relations (including various forms of equality). Insofar as a particular relation has this generative effect, we here call it a "source relation." The specific source relations that could interest us are those that might help to generate the host property of human equality. The critical host property could be more than some raw potential we are born with; it might, for example, be that raw potential after it has been awakened, activated, and transformed by human encounter. It could be an artifact of social experience and thus dependent upon some antecedent relationship.

An example suggests the relevance of this obvious, but so far abstract, point. Consider the deaf child who is cured by some medical process, one that enables him to experience sound. Because he lives in society, he learns that certain sounds are messages conveyed in a conventional code. He becomes an active consumer of such sounds; the greatest gift from his cure turns out to be his newly activated potential to transform these sounds into the meaning those who utter them intended. But this capacity can emerge and function only because of the existence of that peculiar set of semiotic relations we call language. Because of language the spoken word is a transforming experience for the child. He literally becomes more than he was, a dynamic locus of auditory perception and understanding. His self has a significant new *property*.

This is relevant to our inquiry as we understand that such a new aspect of a person can in its turn become the host for new relations, including those of similarity, dissimilarity, and equality. In fact our formerly deaf child has clearly acquired one specific relation of equality—the form that holds among all individuals who possess the capacity to receive and interpret spoken language. Of course, as appears to be the case with every equality except human equality, this is a relatively trivial relation. It is but a single equality—an equality of *possession*. The capacity to interpret spoken language varies in degree among those who have it. Its possession does not generate a double equality.

There is nonetheless an instructive analogy between the equality that links humans who can hear and the other (double) equality we call "human equality." In both cases the host property may spring from sources that are deeply relational, and in each case the consequent relation of equality cannot be understood without reference to those sources. The equality that holds among those who can hear requires the preexistence of the complex of relations we call language. Those relations are inseparable from a child's capacity to interpret spoken messages.

Similarly, the meaning of "human equality" must include more than the pure relation, reaching back to incorporate all the stuff—relational and substantial—that goes into forming its own host property. Equality would thus be relational in a richer and more comprehensive sense than at first we supposed. The convention could constitute an allusion to those generative relations that have preceded and contributed to *the* relation by shaping its host property. These source relations would suffuse the concept of human equality with their own independent significance, contributing to the dignity of what thus has become a constellation of relational and substantive properties. Such a synthesis of individual traits and relations would more easily satisfy our initial criterion—that of importance. In our search for the host property, we will therefore be dealing with two interacting but distinctive forms of relation: (1) those relations that help to generate the host property for human equality; and (2) the specific relation that is human equality.

Five Criteria for the Host Property (and the Relation)

The five criteria for which we argue are plainly interrelated and overlapping in content. Their connections to one another are not primarily logical but experiential. They are not wooden assertions about what human equality *must* be, but our observations about what people in fact believe it to be. "The criteria," that is, are not analytical propositions that entail one another; rather, they are mutually consistent propositions comfortable together as elements of custom and usage tend to be. They are our insights into a particular usage—an interpretation of the boundaries of the conventional term "human equality." They will seem tendentious, a kind of setup. And so they are. Every convention is self-referential and self-affirming. The real question here is whether we have read this convention correctly. Obviously, individuals may disagree.

Our arguments for these five criteria (or conditions) of any theory of human equality share this tendentious quality. They aim to show that each criterion is a component of a plausible interpretation of the convention, but they do so in part by construing ambiguities in the convention in a manner congruent with our personal and vicarious experience. All the same, we are borne along by that experience and hope not to manipulate it. As we have stressed, convention generally is a probe in the direction of reality; we can cooperate in this collective impulse by not substituting our private views of the world. The authors believe there is a reality that the term "human equality" would fit. Our task, however, is to ask honestly whether convention agrees. If it does, this term and our belief may be linked.

Here, then, stated tentatively and cast in declarative sentences that will serve roughly as the conditions of any plausible definition of equality, are what we conclude to be the basic requirements of the host property and the relation:

1. *Importance.* Human equality is a significant relation generated by the sharing of some important property.

2. *Goodness.* Human equality is a positive relation arising from the capacity of each rational self to work its own moral perfection through free submission to the real good.

3. *Laterality.* This order of the good embraced or rejected by the self consists of correct behaviors regarding other rational persons (and reflexively the self).

4. *Singularity.* The relation that is human equality is distinct from any relation of equality among humans that might be based upon a capacity to accept moral obligation toward other beings such as God or animals.

5. *Uniformity.* The capacity of rational humans to accept or reject lateral obligation is uniform both in possession and degree.

In the remainder of this chapter we attempt to show that the first four of these propositions represent the convention. If that is so, and if the convention postulates a real equality, we can then ask in chapter 3 whether and how this property of the self can be conceived to be uniform in degree among rational humans.

The Criteria of Importance and Goodness

Equality as Halo

The *importance* and *goodness* of human equality are closely related and can best be considered together. Whatever this elusive relation may be, convention regards it as a significant good. It is never a defect but a merit of those related.[5] This justifies our confidence that the host property which generates it is also esteemed, giving us a clue to its nature as convention understands that nature. Note that this initial question about goodness and importance is directly concerned only with the content of the convention, not with the host property's plausibility as a reality of our world. However, the convention thereby directs our subsequent efforts to locate such a real property. For if human equality is widely valued, this is because it is perceived as a claim of something real, not a fairy tale of politicians. It is for a similar reason that our criteria include what we have called singularity; its very importance requires that human equality be distinct from other human qualities.

Note that although it contains a moral element, the assertion that equality is conventionally valued is itself a description of fact in two senses. It is, first, an empirical account of the common mind. Any collective understanding—even of moral phenomena—constitutes a certain state of affairs; that people hold such and such a view is literally a fact. Convention itself is something. But the claim is descriptive in another, more cogent sense. When it is understood only as social philosophy, the idea of equality is cast as an optative; it is a hope that some nonexistent sameness (say, of economic wealth) will one day become widely valued and will come to pass. By contrast, a descriptive human equality is admired in the present. A unicorn can be valued only as something to wish for; but Everest is valued because it is there. Descriptive equality is so regarded, not as a perfection to be pursued because of its absence but rather as a reality to be cherished (or, by some, despised) because of its presence. It is valued precisely for being a fact. And that is the initial sense in which we use words such as "value" and "good." People approve of the human equality they believe to be a fact. Its host property, therefore, is likely to be one associated with human goodness.

This says nothing in particular about the implications that a descriptive equality may hold for the design of the good society. Only after the constituent parts of the host property (and thus of the relation) had been identified would there be opportunity to consider whether a descriptive equality points to some Utopia—egalitarian or otherwise. Until that description is accomplished, the unanalyzed word-sound "equality" cannot by itself yield a single moral clue. We are said to be "equal"; therefore . . . what? The daily tide of egalitarian non sequiturs is nonetheless helpful to our argument for its mere persistence; it confirms our observation that human equality is believed to be a significant and positive fact. As an article of faith it is valued whatever its capacity to generate a theory of the good society.

So we believe, but at this initial stage we must also recognize an apparently inconsistent strand in the data whose interpretation yields the convention. Some regard the notion of descriptive equality as profoundly negative, a product of moral depravity. Such a view of equality in the descriptive order parallels certain plausible complaints against egalitarianism in the normative order. Since Nietzsche (indeed, since Plato), the distinctive objection has been that proposals for redistributing wealth and power are animated by simple envy.[6] The have-nots are eager to pull down the haves, even when there is nothing to be gained. Historically there is something to this; envy seems the driving spirit for some portion of democratic social theory. But could this partial explanation for egalitarianism also explain the common enthusiasm for a descriptive human equality?

It might. Emphasis upon equality as a shared human characteristic does not necessarily represent a generous impulse. One could take a wholly un-worthy comfort in being by nature equal. The notion is easily transmogrified into the sneering absurdity, "I'm as good as you are,"[7] and the belief in equal-ity then reduces to a simple projection of *ressentiment*. Nor is this an asser-tion from a particular social class. Even the well-fed man can be tormented to discover that in some particular he is "unequal" to someone else. For him a descriptive equality—human equality—offers a bit of verbal therapy. Maybe we are unequal in this or that, but as humans we are equal; I'm as good as you. His pain is tranquilized by the news from his metaphysician that everyone's need for equality already has been descriptively satisfied. If such a neurosis explains the common reverence for human equality, our proposed interpretation would be false. To the extent that spite and envy insinuate the general view, the relation of equality is not easily interpreted as a positive phenomenon. And insofar as we hope to understand the defining convention, we would be wise to seek some host property that is irrational, devilish, or Manichaean.

If indeed there is a link between envy and descriptive equality, it is not one of a logical or analytical sort. If people generally accept the fact of equal-ity, this in itself cuts neither for nor against envy as their motivation; such a consensus would be ambivalent in a way egalitarianism is not. The egalitar-ian begins by reporting to us (correctly) that there is someone available to be dragged down (relatively or absolutely), and envy thus becomes his natural confederate. By contrast, insofar as human equality is thought to hold as a fact of nature, there is neither anyone to drag nor anywhere to be dragged; we are all already there (wherever "there" may be). Among naturally equal creatures—be they essentially malevolent or benign—the act of envy loses its object. At least this is so with respect to the specific qualities in which they are equal. Within the domain of human equality, envy is functionless. Only where equality is absent can one aspire to it; so far as it holds, the aspiration ceases. You can envy a man for having what you lack; you cannot envy him for being what you are.

The critic might of course reply that precisely because human equality excludes envy can we be confident that the convention confirming it is the product of envy. Individuals suffering from envy invented the notion of equality as self-therapy. Logically this is possible but unconvincing. Fiction is a tool to any hand. Perhaps it is envy and not equality that was invented.

Envy is a convenient story for those (like Callicles[8] or Nietzsche[9]) who would justify dominion by the lucky few with fables about the spitefulness of the degraded crowd. Which one, then, is the chimera—the vicious mob or superman?

Were descriptive human equality the work of envious minds, its content would reflect its source. But envy is an ego-debt that must be discharged in ultimate human value. Its coin is goodness—not mere capacity to become good but present actual goodness. Again, it can be expressed only in the contemptible chant: "I'm as good as you." Envy requires us to be equal, not in mere potential but in *achieved* moral state, now and always; it disallows distinctions created by free acts of heroism or cowardice. Envy insists upon an equality of outcome. This world must be one in which no one *could* be morally superior to anyone else. Hence goodness (or worth) must consist precisely in whatever it is the individual has actually chosen as his or her own—independent of any external measure of the good.

Envy could not, therefore, abide an equality that is defined as individuals' uniform *capacity* to achieve *degrees* of real perfection. It must reject contingent propositions of the following sort:

> Possibly I am as good as you, but you may have become better (or worse) than I by the exercise of your equal capacity for self-perfection. The reality of our chosen states is indeterminate; I cannot read your heart. Our equality of capacity allows for every degree of diversity in actual perfection.

To the contrary, envy insists that I *am* as good as you regardless of the choices I have made, and to most humans this is nihilistic nonsense.[10]

Finally, if the convention were somehow the product of envy, two questions would remain: (1) whether this condition called equality is nonetheless true; and (2) whether it is benign. If both were the case, the possibility that equality is therapy for the morally defective might be interesting but would cease to be a criticism. If equality itself were the good and the true, why should we worry that the envious find it consoling?

In any case, whatever the envious feel, the general assessment of human equality must be read as positive. There is an unmistakable popular allegiance to those canonical sources that historically have exalted the idea. The West, indeed, is obsessed with its goodness. Jefferson did not start all this—nor explain it—but he caught the spirit nicely in the Declaration.[11] That testament contains no egalitarian claims to uniformity of treatment; it draws no inferences whatsoever from the fact of equality. The whole of the reference is a simple declaration of the self-evident truth that we *are* "created equal." Equality is not our goal but our natural condition, and it is a glorious condition—or so it would appear.

It was glorious enough that Lincoln in his turn saw the nation "dedicated" to it as a proposition. Just what sort of proposition he did not say; the context of Gettysburg and the idea of "dedication" may make his usage implicitly prescriptive. But it is also explicitly descriptive and, as such, is wholly positive. Equality is so true and so good that we surrender our lives in its appreciation. These eloquent scraps of political mythology still make Americans cry for joy.

But are we entitled to ignore the historic testimony of human slavery, the treatment of the American Indian and twentieth-century genocide? Barbarities of this sort have been defended on theories of the descriptive inferiority of the target groups. Ironically, these venomous perceptions of human difference unintentionally support our claim that convention values equality. For even the racist recognizes human equality to be a positive state; he merely supposes particular people to lack it. Who does lack it, we shall soon see; but the immediate question is not who is equal but, rather, *is equality believed to be a good thing to have?* And that much is clear. If the members of an enslaved or despised group lacked this particular property, this was for them a tragedy. And it was thought to be so by their tormentors.[12]

The perception of human equality as benign is no American monopoly. Its generating spirit has been broadly Western, and equality is widely accepted as a good throughout the Atlantic world. Seldom is it pictured as a condition of insignificance or shame. Even Nietzsche's antipathy only confirms the attitude of the crowd whom he despised. Far from imagining itself degraded by equality, mankind—at least the West—plainly deems itself honored. Equality is a leveling up in which even the rich and powerful see themselves enhanced in dignity along with the rest. This may be the deeper meaning of sarcasms about the rights of all to sleep under bridges—and it is the consensus view. Unlike the many neutral samenesses we share, the equality that is human equality elevates everyone's self-perception.

To understand equality in this way, as a kind of dignity, introduces a happy element of paradox. In its application to the rest of experience, equality is purely comparative.[13] Only in its application to the mystery of the ultimate self does this note of the absolute appear; here alone is it transmuted into a kind of moral bedrock, becoming a condition valued for its own sake. It is not another word for some set of noble properties. It is itself a noble property. Further, this value is independent of circumstance, even of ruin; men do not lose it in spite of the most atrocious conditions of servitude, starvation, or ignorance. The dignity that is equality cannot be forfeited, and tragedy (of which we shall have more to say) only confirms it.

Why does the idea of a descriptive human equality enjoy this halo? To a degree the answer is a mystery lodged in the recesses of the Western mind. Most of us commit to the belief without conscious choosing. Many suppose equality to have religious meaning and value; perhaps they find this in those scriptural clues that drive bigwigs to wash the feet of beggars, hoping paradoxically to inherit the Earth.

Equality's affinity with religion is indirectly, if unconsciously, acknowledged by liberal moral philosophers whenever they associate it—as they do—with the concept of "human dignity." When the 1990 *Platform*[14] of the "Communitarians" asserted the "equal moral dignity" of humans, its signatories joined a trail of ideology that originates in *Genesis*. It is a staple of Western culture and tradition that we acquired our dignity in the Garden as the "image and likeness of God" and could not shed it if we would. Note, however, that there is no logical connection whatsoever between dignity and equality; compared to your dignity, mine may be distinctly wanting. One could indeed view dignity as a "range property" or even as the ideal metric of inequality.[15] Nevertheless, this frequent conflation of the two ideas is a ringing confirmation of the positive weight conceded to the fact of human equality, a compliment some believe to be expressed unconsciously in the ancient symbols of Western theology.

In part 3 we argue that this identification of human equality with Western religion is possible but chancy, requiring a particular interpretation of God's relation to man; equality may be consistent with, but is scarcely required by, the Hebrew and Christian traditions and the metaphors of Scripture. And it may be more the "sense of the faithful" than the teaching of the churches. The common association with religion is important, nonetheless, because it confirms that we are dealing with the sacred. Descriptive equality is not a claim of human right but a premise of human nobility. That premise preceded democracy in the order of historic time and continues to do so in the order of value. Equality is more than democracy; it is universal aristocracy. This naive and transcendental joy in sameness is the ground for all possible understandings of the elusive claim that the relation of equality is a fact. It is a clear signpost as we continue our quest for its host property.

Reason and Will as Part of the Halo

The halo that crowns human equality betrays the popular association of the idea with the capacity for moral choice. Equality is vaguely associated with the personal struggle between right and wrong, good and evil; its reality is implicated in the liberty to decide what sort of person to be. Equality is cherished precisely because it is entangled in moral freedom and responsibility. It is part of whatever makes it possible for us to attempt the good.

The search for the host property, then, must proceed in light of the popular perception of our moral powers. There is little mystery about this. The ordinary person has an implicit theory of moral choice that is rough-hewn, traditional, and serviceable for the run of cases. To begin with, he is no determinist.[16] The most up-to-date criminal codes attest that individuals are widely regarded as responsible for their behavior with rare exceptions that require rather dramatic proof. The burden is on the wrongdoer to show his or her incapacity to perform as a moral agent.

The ordinary person thus assumes free will and choice. Indeed, one is constantly making decisions that matter both for self and others. Where shall I live? Whom shall I marry? Shall I give up alcohol? Without much self-reflection the individual—parent, lover, worker, beggar—gathers and understands what relevant information he or she can and then chooses a path. Reason and will are the stuff of everyday life. They are what make us different from our pets and from the madman who runs amok on the subway. This association with reason and will is what makes equality a positive word. Nothing else in the infinity of possible human samenesses could approach the importance of moral autonomy; whether we are as smart or as quick as the Turks or the Tasmanians is at best a passing concern. If we are indeed "created equal"—equal to complete strangers—this special form of equality springs not from our muscles nor even our knowledge but from the unique power to commit, and thus to constitute our own moral selves. This power to direct our lives is lodged in our reason and will, and any theory of human equality must account for both these faculties in its defining structure.

This sense of equality as an aspect of the moral self is a strong but obscure theme in Western history. The Enlightenment was driven by the premise that humans are rational choosers who, in the fullness of historic time, have come to apprehend the possibility of fixing their individual agendas. Man at last had begun to make himself through reason and will. Eventually portions of the Enlightenment came vaguely to suppose that this moral liberty entailed descriptive equality. Strictly speaking, this was a non sequitur. As we have seen, a general assent to reason and will as constituents of liberty does not usher in human equality as a matter of simple inference.

It was revolutionary politics that in 1789 united liberty and equality in the familiar French slogan. It was, however, typical of the age of revolution (as of ours) that it left the descriptive content of equality unspecified. The philosophy of the eighteenth century made equality the constant companion of liberty, but it traveled as liberty's shadow. Its nature remained largely unconsidered and thus ambiguous. No effort was made to separate the elements of liberty and equality (and fraternity) either as distinctive aspects of the individual or as forms of human relation. Understood as a description, equality may well have been perceived as nothing more than the real but trivial relation that holds among those who simply *possess* natural liberty however much they may differ by degrees in their individual abilities to exercise it.[17] The Enlightenment never considered such questions, nor does modern philosophy show promise of ending this neglect. We must proceed with a few philosophical clues and our perception of the common mind.

But first consider two interesting consequences of our accepting will and reason as elements of the self that are necessary (though insufficient) for the host property. The first is that certain "lower orders" of creation might be included as equals. There is an overlapping between humans and other mammals in regard to reason—and possibly in regard to will. Some chimps are smarter than some people, and some dolphins make arguably rational choices. The resemblance to human agency evokes claims of what the ancients called *oikeiosis* (a moral sameness with human agents)[18] and what moderns invoke as a basis of "animal rights."[19] The real question here, as with humankind, is which among the beasts can choose their own ends. If certain animals could exercise a truly moral choice, they might be difficult to push outside the select circle of equals. Most people seem content to put them out and leave them out. This is a reasonable opinion, or at least it is our own while we await demonstration to the contrary. Let the animals carry the burden of proof. When porpoises persuade us that they ponder their own ends, their inclusion should be reconsidered; there might be still other hurdles for such brainy beasts to clear on the way to equality. In any case, our task is to interpret the convention, and the convention is strictly limited to *homo sapiens*. It is a convention of *human* equality.

If we continue to assume that no animal but man makes free choices, we have finessed one problem but another emerges. Our focus upon the capacity for reasoned choice may be less objectionable for the beasts it might include than for the humans it definitely excludes. To require it as an element of the host property denies the equality of those humans who can neither think nor choose. These may include people of three sorts: those who from illness, accident, or age have permanently ceased to think and choose; those who for whatever reason never have, and never will, think and choose; and those who will have the opportunity to do so only if they are allowed to be born.

At first glance, many would want to include some or all of these. Apart from disputes about the status of the unborn, they would resist John Wilson's description of a senile elder or a mentally challenged child as an equal "only by courtesy."[20] Despite the Enlightenment's prejudice against the nonrational, a broader version of community endures and sometimes claims the mantle of "equality" for everything identifiably human. Earlier we saw a spirited theological objection to the monopolistic claims of reason in the definition of equality: "All human beings enjoy this equality by virtue of the very fact that they were born, even if they never attain the faculty of reason."[21]

This view would be highly expedient in one respect. If the class of equals included all (and only) Adam's progeny, we would have put nonsapient humans safely on board while conveniently excluding bats, baboons, and other clever pretenders.[22] More important for the fate of this essay, if human genetic origin sufficed for equality, it would follow that rationality and choice were utterly superfluous. This view, however, would render the popular recognition of equality's importance quite unintelligible, shrinking the concept to a single equality based upon common possession of a property that could not vary—the property of birth to human parents. Equality would be real but trivial.

Of course our inquiry concerns convention, and in theory this vacuous meaning could be correct. Membership in the species could constitute the host property. That, however, would eliminate the moral dimension commonly ascribed to the idea of human equality—and this will not pass. The convention certainly links equality to man's moral potential. The rationality and free will of the self are necessary to the theory, even though they exclude certain beings who are obviously human.

Their exclusion should not be seen as a threat. Regarding the rights of a specific individual, nothing in particular may turn upon his or her being among the "equal." In any case, those persons who lose their equality do not slip into the status of animals and would deserve protection on religious or other grounds. They certainly would deserve more than that conferred by a trivial equality grounded upon common genetic descent.[23]

Granted, there is an obsession in some quarters to attach the label "equality" to everything good. These enthusiasts would include their nonreasoning human brothers and sisters even though this would empty descriptive equality of substance. If this were the consensus, the direction we have taken would be a mistake. However, we rest on our apprehension of a popular belief that the relation called "human equality" carries moral weight. Most would insist that equality be a significant reality that embraces the overwhelming majority of humanity rather than an all-inclusive but vapid abstraction. Of course, whether the faculties of will and reason actually do lead us to some distinct, robust, and plausible reality that can be the host for the relation of human equality is something yet to be shown; however, if will and reason are not sufficient, they are rather clearly necessary and provide a promising structure within which to search for this elusive element. That is the task next in order.

The Criterion of Laterality

Here is a restatement of the criterion we called laterality: Human equality presupposes a moral order that the self can freely embrace or reject as an ideal and thereby determine the degree of its own moral perfection; this order precedes positive law and consists of correct treatments of other rational persons (and reflexively of the self).

This or a similar conception is necessary to the intelligibility of conventional human equality. In addition to their duties to themselves, individual humans have the capacities potentially to participate in various separate orders of moral behavior involving either humans or other beings. In theory, the number of such moral orders is unlimited. So far the race has experienced three: self/God; self/beast; and self/other. The entry of the self into each of these orders is triggered by a specific form of encounter. For example, one discovers one's responsibility in respect to animals by meeting them (in the flesh or vicariously). Understanding their natures as best we can, we recognize (somehow) that our authority over their fate is finite. We may call this relation between animals and ourselves the "descendent" moral order. It is very different from what we will now describe as the "lateral" order of obligation—the order that binds two rational wills that have taken the measure of each other. We will conclude that the relation of human equality can be grounded only upon such an awakened capacity to accept or reject duties toward other rational agents (and oneself) that correct reason would identify. Human equality entails a plurality of rational human selves among whom reciprocal moral obligation arises out of mutual recognition.

The claim of such a lateral equality to be the relation conventionally known as "human equality" can be clarified by contrasting it to real equalities that might be supposed in the ascendant or descendent moral orders. A conscious and active capacity to discharge (or to neglect) duties to either God or the beasts would constitute a true moral self. If all rational humans had such a capacity in respect to either God or animals, this would be the basis for a real relation of equality among those human persons. It might even be an equality of some interest here; for if, perchance, all humans had this ability in uniform degree, the relation among them would constitute a double equality. It would rest upon no mere range property. This capacity could also be of paramount importance; it would indeed be so if it were the unique medium of self-perfection for the individual—the key to moral achievement. It would in that event be a true and significant equality of humans. It would not, however, be "human equality." For duties of divine worship or care for animals are distinct from the form of obligation that arises from consciousness of other rational actors within a shared moral environment. The relation of human equality can be ascribed only to human choosers who live in conscious interdependence with other human choosers.

We will try to put this distinction less abstractly. The crisp example of human equality comes in the awakening of the solitary Adam of *Genesis*, chapter 1. Here is history's only authentic loner, lacking even memories of a lost society, hence without consciousness of the possibility of social duty; before woman, Adam was isolated in a sense stronger than any of us could know. Still, that isolation was far from absolute. Adam already had a moral life or, more accurately, moral lives; he was obligated toward beings of two separate and significant classes—one superior, one inferior.

On the nether side he was obligated to treat the other creatures reasonably according to their simpler natures. This noblesse oblige receives no specific mention in *Genesis*; perhaps it was too obvious—an unnecessary distraction from that more interesting business about the tree. It has found revelation enough in our own time; the scriptures of environmentalism would have us protect every tree as if it were the tree of knowledge. Wherever one draws this line of duty, today all agree that the moral issue about these creatures is real. But it was real before Eve; the goodness God saw in his initial works suggests that the indiscriminate burning of forests and the torture and extermination of animals were not among the legitimate pleasures of the peculiar fellow he created to oversee them. Likewise, on the ascendant side, Adam confronted the divine will; here was a unique moral object toward whom Adam had that one narrow responsibility. His free nature faced the distinctive moral issue of obedience.

Thus Adam already had two moral lives, but neither the brutes nor God himself had exhausted the potential variety of his obligation. Each imposed on Adam a morality of a truncated and unilateral sort; his reason and powers of choice encountered a narrowly bounded set of issues. Animals and trees cannot will to support or resist man; they cannot choose to join or frustrate his enterprises; they are incapable of true hatred or true love. Nor does their own self-perfection lie in the moral order.

And as for God, Adam's reason and will faced the opposite problem. God is impervious to man's will; there is no medium through which Adam could either oppose or embrace him except by his leave. God can be neither assisted nor hindered—only loved or rejected by man's exercise of the very freedom God created. Thus, so long as this one man stood "alone," his moral relationships, both ascendant and descendent, remained purely unilateral. Adam's moral capacity was dressed up for some other affair to which as yet he had received no invitation.[24]

A world of persons could be imagined in which, like Adam, we each stood hermetically apart and incapable by our choices of affecting the options open to other moral creatures. We could be conceived in test tubes and lodged in isolated spheres or be sent alone on one-way trips into deep space. But in such a world our capacities for lateral obligation would remain unactivated, hence unexplained. Once we lift man from his familiar social cocoon and view him apart and alone, certain of his constituent properties do not make sense. He is like a boat in the desert.[25] He might stand in some relation of moral equality to the unexperienced others of his race, but this would hardly be what the West has meant by "human equality."

It is precisely the presence of the "other who is the same" that introduces the specific kinds of moral choices we all face every morning. Eve is a being who must, by nature, reason and decide. She is physical, but she is capable of choosing ends, and she is potentially both competitive and cooperative

with Adam. Upon her appearance Adam and she, through their own concrete choices, begin for the first time to alter the set of choices open to
another being. Each awakens the other's latent potential for a lateral and
reciprocal morality. Both have suddenly become inescapably vulnerable.
Whatever the one does, proposes, or even neglects by itself changes the
moral universe of the other. The ascendant and descendent duties to God
and the lower orders remain, but, ever after, the more immediate issue is
what to do about her—and about him. And eventually about them. Suddenly
we have a world in which chosen action implicates other beings who must
also, by their nature, make free choices.

The meeting of Adam and Eve is important as a type for much of what
follows here. We need names for three aspects of this story. One is the event
itself, to which we shall often refer as the "encounter." It is a metaphor for
the universal experience of the other. All who reach rationality bear the
mark of engagement with other moral beings. The encounter becomes what
we have called a "source relation" for "recognition," which is the second
important aspect of the tale; it is the specific effect of the encounter as it
generates the self's consciousness of a new form of moral relation.[26] That
consciousness emerges (we assume) exactly as Adam and Eve realize that
the other is also a being both reasoning and free. Each by this discovery
becomes bound in a way that is distinct both from the obedience explicitly
owed to God and the respect implicitly due the beasts. Recognition is the
grasp of the reality of lateral obligation. Third, this discrete order of substantive obligation needs a name. It can be a very general name, because, as we
explain in chapter 3, equality involves only the recognition of the fact of
obligation and not its specific content. To help distinguish this order of
obligation, we have so far called it lateral morality. We should stress the
ordinariness of this particular moral connection between interacting human
agents by giving it a second and more common name—"reciprocity." So, we
say exactly this: The encounter triggers the recognition of reciprocity.

Now this use of reciprocity involves one small risk. It is a term often
associated with the idea of exchange or contract in which freely bargaining
parties either offer each other a quid pro quo or—on a grander scale—make
an implicit social contract, determining through mutual consent how the
society shall be run.[27] For us, reciprocity will mean almost the opposite of
this bargaining model of moral relation. The lateral obligation to which we
here refer arises whether we discover and consent to it or not. The act of
recognition entails the judgment that we are obligated to the Other simply
because of what we both are and quite apart from any agreement we might
reach.

Reciprocity is nevertheless an appropriate term, because the obligation is
mutual. The reader might even expect us to slip into the language of
"rights"; if I owe you a duty, it may be said that you have a right against me.

It is hard for lawyers to think otherwise. But—again—we are not interested in rights as such. It is not in rights but in our awakened capacity for moral self-perfection that we hope and expect to find the host property of the relation of human equality. Hence we speak of the capacity for reciprocity only as the power to accept or reject an order of duties we owe to one another.

The shouldering of this obligation is a primary means of our own moral self-perfection. Put another way, by convention our moral fulfillment is significantly a function of how we pursue our responsibility to others. However, this capacity of ours to self-perfect through commitment to reciprocity might be either variant or uniform in degree from person to person. Unless it is uniform, it could not satisfy the fifth criterion for the host property. We devote chapter 3 to that difficult question.

Finally, observe that this criterion of laterality or reciprocity provides another reason for excluding animals from the scope of human equality. Even if their rationality were sufficient, they still would be outside the circle by reason of their incapacity to acquire obligation toward humans.[28] None of them owes us anything.

The Criterion of Singularity

Human equality could be "singular" in either of two ways: First, its *host property* could be some moral power that is importantly different from that by which the self discovers and responds to obligations owed to God or animals. Second, *the relation* that emerges in human equality could be distinct from those relations that arise among humans as bearers of duties to God and animals.

Singularity is cousin to the criterion of importance. By convention, the idea of human equality requires the dignity that is thought to attach to discrete metaphysical status. This relation must be one that is distinguishable from all others. This need for singularity could be served by the host property itself, if it were a property unique to this relation. We have tentatively identified the host of human equality as the capacity of the self to accept or reject lateral obligation. Is this capacity distinct in any way from the general human power for moral commitment? In one important respect it is different. To show this, we again invoke Adam, Eve, God, and the animals, and we rely upon the analysis already made of the obligation of reciprocity that emerges from the relation between the two human persons. We are not, however, asking what distinctive moral duties each order imposes on the individual. The precise question, rather, is what changes the emergence of these ascendant, descendent, and lateral moral orders works on the human actors themselves. We are looking for a distinctive effect on Adam and Eve as each first experiences human society. Is there something new that emerges in their own persons?

Adam's reason and will already had experienced two sets of duties—ascendant and descendent. Necessarily Adam had made reasoned choices in relation to God and the animals. These were made on the basis of his understanding of who God was and what the animals were. He was, then, already functioning nicely in two distinct moralities, and he had yet to lose his rib. Even in this dualistic moral economy, however, Adam was importantly incomplete. This point is straightforward and not merely allegorical. No solitary individual is fully human. We have it on good authority that "it is not good for man to be alone," and this assertion is as much about man's identity as about his morals. What it would mean to be utterly alone, none of us can experience, but the nature of true isolation can be clarified analytically. So long as the self remains unaware of other moral selves, it lacks a crucial element of humanity. Full personhood requires consciousness of some other who inhabits the same medium and who also exercises the preexisting capacity for choice. This is definitional to the reciprocal self. It takes two for any one of us to be completely human. And that other must be human. Neither the brutes nor even God himself could satisfy this condition of Adam's humanity.

In the encounter with Eve, then, we not only witness the introduction of the third or lateral morality, but we see that the change is plainly descriptive in the sense important to equality—Adam himself is altered.[29] In experiencing this source relation he acquires a new characteristic that is itself simultaneously individual and relational. What to that point had been an unrecognized possibility was now rendered conscious and concrete in him (and in Eve) by this new world of interdependent persons. It is in the advent of this mutual consciousness that the two become indissolubly linked. She is mother to the complete Adam—and he her father. With Eve humanity is born.

Strictly speaking, all that is new in Adam and Eve, considered separately, is their *consciousness* of the other and of their distinct lateral relation. Even before the encounter, the capacity for reciprocity already existed in each as potentiality lacking a known object. The encounter activates and discloses to each this third order of morality. What is specifically new to the self is the experience of participation. Whatever we call this added aspect, however, it is "there" in Adam in any responsible sense of the word. It is there as the inevitability that his preexisting capacity for morality will hereafter serve as the host of unprecedented relations of similarity, dissimilarity, and equality—possibly even of human equality.

This capacity thus becomes active—it accrues as a practical power—by virtue of the individual's consciousness of membership in a human social order. An economist might describe this effect of society upon the individual as "value added." To be sure, this new possibility for interrelation has a potential for chosen activity that is hostile as well as cooperative, but this merely underscores the fact that the self's discovery of the other has existential moral consequence. For Adam and Eve the encounter is creative. Here is something new in the self—something plausibly sufficient to satisfy the requirement of singularity imposed upon conventional equality by the metaphysicians of the street.

Nevertheless, it is the weaker of the two arguments for singularity. The stronger claim rests not upon this emergent consciousness and exercise of a preexistent power but, rather, upon the wholly new relation that is formed by the encounter. The host property is not itself new but merely awakened. By contrast, the *relation* of mutually conscious persons is a metaphysical *novum*. It literally springs into existence with the encounter.

Nor are the human relations that arise from the other two orders of morality even of the same form. In each of the three orders the human self confronts an entirely different object—God, the spotted owl, my sister. Each order is a unique moral medium. To be sure, any one of these orders might provide a milieu sufficient to the need of the human person to work out his or her own moral self-perfection. Had we never experienced a human neighbor, our freely chosen responses to God or beast might have been adequate to the plenary fulfillment or frustration of our moral potential. But that is not how it happened; we have, instead, encountered the *homo sapiens* next door and in her discovered a different kettle of moral fish.

This means that human equality would be singular and require separate description even if it should be the case that humans are also equal to one another in their capacities for ascendant and descendent morality. Assume for the moment that all rational humans have a real obligation freely to worship God (or to protect the spotted owl) and that, by giving assent to this responsibility, humans can achieve moral self-perfection. Add to this that the ability to give or withhold assent is uniformly distributed. In that event a certain relation of double equality would hold among us based upon this uniform host property—this ability to commit to (or to reject) a particular order of responsibility. Were this so, the singularity of *human* equality would nevertheless hold. Any equality of humans that involves obligations to God or the creatures would itself be a relation distinct from all others. Each would be a true equality of humans, but neither would be human equality.

In seeing this we grasp the meaning of singularity. There is, in theory, an unlimited number of true equalities that humans might have with one another by possessing in the same degree the capacity to self-perfect by making free acts of submission to various distinctive orders of obligation. But the existence of such relations of equality between humans would not depend upon whether the *content* of the obligation had anything to do with humankind. In the case of a human responsibility to God or the animals, the relation of equality (if any) is between humans; but the content of the duty concerns only a nonhuman third party. It would be a relation of equality that holds *between* humans, but it would not be one that is *about* humans.[30]

This point is cognate to the one made earlier about laterality. We said there that the obligation had to be horizontal; in order to be strictly human, it had to involve a mutuality of persons. Only an order of interpersonal obligations can be the proper object of the host capacity as it generates the relation of human equality. Otherwise, that relation would in one very important dimension not be human at all. *It could exist among humans who had never encountered another human.*

Thus the unique relation that is generated in mutual human encounter is the only serious candidate for "human equality." In the environment of reciprocity we might be equal in our powers of moral self-perfection precisely because self-perfection is achieved by freely seeking the good for other humans. Facing God or nature we humans might be moral equals; it is only in facing one another that we could initiate human equality. The various equalities *of* humans stand distinct from the one equality that *is* human.

The Reality of Obligation

A major problem remains. This awakened capacity for lateral obligation rests upon a problematic premise. It assumes that lateral obligation itself is real and that it binds us quite apart from the rules and institutions created by social contract or other human authority. The lateral obligation necessary to equality comes with the human territory; its existence is recognized by the self. "A genuine subjectivity . . . knows . . . that it has to allow itself to be at the disposal of something objective which it has not established."[31]

If this premise of an authoritative, preinstitutional moral order seems unnecessary to distinguish the host property, try assuming the contrary. Suppose the obligation of reciprocity to be nonsense—that nothing of the sort binds us without our individual consent. In that case our recognition of moral linkage is simply false—a piece of self-deception. Rules might come to govern our daily lives, but they could only be rules made up by us or received adventitiously. In such a world, where duties are never more than self-legislation or chance reception—where Adam's own will or some human legislator is the sole source of rules—no real change takes place in the encounter and no distinctive relation to other humans is created. The epiphany of Eve would alter such an Adam as little as the appearance in the Garden of any other new creature he might treat as he chooses. It is true that Eve's free intelligent nature would introduce the possibility of contract and entail certain new dangers and opportunities about which Adam and she could negotiate. This is a difference, but a difference only in the environment in which Adam continues to pursue his purely self-defined ends. Any serious alteration in the moral relations of Adam must rest upon an order of lateral obligation that is real. It must be one that he and Eve have the potential, indeed the exigence, not as gods to create but as humans to recognize.[32] The existence of such an order is not conclusively demonstrable; modern philosophy has been at pains to convince us that none exists.

Social science is uncertain that modern culture believes in a morality that is binding apart from our own wills. Commentators such as Robert Bellah report the decay of personal "commitment" in both private and public life and conclude that many people have reconceptualized the sources of obligation.[33] Freud, it seems, has reduced the question of duty to the level of mental health, and rampant individualism interprets human community as an instrumental convenience.[34] No theme is more popular than the high incidence of aggressive and corrupt behavior in modern society. Critics see Americans withdrawing from civic and community connections on a large scale and infer from this a general disbelief in an objective moral order.

We are skeptical of such broad indictments. There may well be a decline in correct behavior both in public and private life. But by no means need this imply that natural and revealed orders of obligation are disbelieved.[35] They may be widely flouted, but that is a separate question. Violence can be fun precisely because it is perceived to be evil. Regretting his adolescent plunder of a neighbor's pears, Augustine recalled that "our only pleasure in doing it was that it was forbidden."[36]

Still, we suspect that there is some real decline in the recognition of a binding order. It would be hard to live in the academy and remain blind to education's general drift into skepticism, and, to some extent, this is effectually transmitted to the social scene. No one should be particularly surprised. Once it becomes de rigueur to "question authority," it will be questioned; indeed, this is a classic American cultural theme now intensified by the wealth and technique of modern culture. In any case, what is surprising to us is how few of the general population actually do reject the concept of a preinstitutional morality. What is our evidence for this optimistic reading of the public mind? The first exhibit might well be the widespread approval given to Bellah's own warning. His assertion that we need to refasten our moral seatbelts proved to be immensely popular, making Bellah a bit of a culture hero and discrediting his own thesis.

The consensus on this question is more likely to be found in the constant tribute paid to authoritative morality by political hypocrisy. Even the guiltiest parties in our public scandals invoke these same truths. So far, not one political aspirant has offered his extramarital larks or financial overreaching as evidence of his enlightened liberation from musty morality. Without exception, such public figures are serious consumers of opinion surveys that measure religious belief, church attendance, and allegiance to traditional communitarian values. Plainly, those whose careers depend upon their grasp of public attitudes continue to suppose that ordinary people perceive obligations that bind independent of political institutions and legal rights.[37]

If, however, the literature of moral disintegration does not prove that ordinary Americans have rejected preinstitutional sources, it clearly shows that they have no *theory* of them. Over and over Bellah's own subjects display confusion about the ground of their responsibility; when they try to explain it, they are philosophical bunglers.[38] This is to be expected, even—or especially—among the educated, who (unfortunately) seem to be the chosen targets of such surveys. Given their political structure, the schools that form them must shun the issue of moral sources,[39] and can even stigmatize the child who is committed to traditional morality. This cultural censorship is strongly reinforced at the university where notions of tradition, natural obligation, or revealed morality may be reported as history but dismissed as authority in any serious argument about the good. Academics who resort to them run professional risks. Few suggest to their students any sources beyond the social and political institutions that mankind creates for itself. This general academic scorn for preinstitutional morality has hobbled ethical discourse; paradoxically the school and the university have become instruments of moral ignorance. This inarticulateness has not, we think, converted America to a philosophy of radical individualism.[40]

Samuel Scheffler, a Berkeley moral philosopher, gets it more nearly right. Scheffler interprets "morality by consent" as wholly out of touch with the crowd in respect to beliefs about the real sources of reciprocal obligation. Indeed, he warns aspirant statesmen of the political risks of grounding liberal social programs on the moral quicksand of liberal philosophy:

> This would not seem to be a promising climate in which to argue the virtues of a reduced conception of responsibility . . . [A]lthough the perceived boundaries of individual responsibility are to some extent in flux, and although . . . there is a widespread sense that traditional notions of responsibility are under attack . . ., there is no evidence that the impulse to employ the concepts and categories of responsibility is disappearing or even diminishing significantly in strength.[41]

By "concepts and categories of responsibility" Scheffler means specifically a "preinstitutional" order of obligation in which the terms of duty and desert are conferred by religion or nature and not by our individual or collective wills. This ethic of responsibility remains regnant in American life. Those few who reject it tend to be established in vocations whose practitioners can flourish in spite of—or even in proportion to—their ideological eccentricity. We would add only the obvious point that in the course of *practical* affairs traditional morality carries the day even within the academy and the media. Intellectuals committed in theory to moral individualism often are the last to practice it in their own lives or to approve its practice by those who share their environment.[42]

Nonetheless, we concede that nobody has a firm grip on the question of just how many of us still believe in a moral standard that we do not invent for ourselves. On this issue nothing can be proved, and each must interpret the scene for himself. If one concludes that belief in a natural and/or revealed order of morality is no longer typical, then for that individual our conclusion that Americans believe the convention defining human equality to be a statement of truth is simply wrong. Indeed, even the shared definition of equality could have evaporated along with the belief in an unchosen morality—another victim of modernity.

In that event our thesis would remain as one private view of the *real* nature of reciprocal morality. That reality would be something well worth describing, even if it could be the foundation only of an unrecognized and as yet nameless human relation—and this book would be a claim about the reality of a connection in which people have merely ceased to believe. We of course accept the claim of a binding reciprocal morality; so far as we can see, belief in it is universal and, indeed, ineradicable among rational humans. The "recognition" of lateral morality is more than a piece of intersubjective reality; it is the common experience of the race reconfirmed in the daily decencies of those who in practice accept the authority of that morality. We admit that this stubborn prejudice of ours is a posture ill-suited to a neutral interpreter of convention, but we deny that any such neutral person could be found.

In any case, in our estimation, though its particular duties may be disputed, misunderstood, and violated, the fact of lateral obligation commands consensus. It is one of our common understandings—and one of the criteria that fix the possible meanings of human equality. It will be our task in chapter 3 to show that the capacity of the self to achieve moral perfection by participation in such a real order can be conceived of as uniform among rational humans both in possession and degree.

The Host Property

Obviously we have attempted more than a bare elaboration of the first four criteria set by convention for the idea of human equality. Much of this chapter turned out to be an account of shared Western beliefs about moral personality. This accords with the method we earlier adopted. We seek the content of the convention in the discourse of ordinary persons and their philosophers, but our interpretation is governed by the broad consensus—perhaps the prejudice—that "human equality" is a claim of something real. This popular impulse sets limits upon the theories of moral personality that could nourish the convention; they must be theories that could acknowledge equality to exist, not just as convention but as reality. So we move back and forth among common experience, the world of intellect, and the requirements of our own common sense. This does not mean that we have gotten either convention or reality right; this book is an invitation to a dialogue. But it does mean that our candidates for the first four necessary constituents of the host property and of the relation are clear enough that we can proceed.

If it exists, human equality will be a relation springing from the capacity to commit to the lateral good. In exercising this choice individuals assign meaning to themselves, forging a principal portion of their identity. Thus the specific capacity to accept or reject the search for the content of our obligation to others confronts us as both opportunity and fate. It is opportunity insofar as the freedom to seek correct behavior makes moral self-perfection an option; it is fate insofar as that choice either to honor or to flout this obligation is inescapable. Each of us determines whether the dignity of others shall be honored; in so doing we settle our own identity. This capacity is the obvious host for the relation of equality, but only if it satisfies the final criterion of uniformity. If, instead, humans enjoy this capacity in varying degrees, it becomes the source of disequality in human worth.

3

MAKING THE HOST PROPERTY UNIFORM

We may be as good as we please, if we please to be good.
(*Mother Goose*)

A ROBBER BACKS his way out of a bank juggling shopping bags stuffed with cash. Bundles of bills spill onto the floor. One is retrieved by a lawyer who promptly returns it to the bank. Another is snatched by a socialist who pockets it and passes it on to a hungry family. Still another is recovered by an imbecile who returns it to the robber. The episode ends when a fourth citizen seizes a gun from a fallen policeman and blazes away—aiming at the robber's foot but killing both the robber and the imbecile.

What has this tale to do with human equality? Here is a set of people of varying sophistication who—at least apart from the robber—seem to choose as best they can among courses of action that vary in their practical effect from "correct" to catastrophic. Each actor would probably tell us that he tried to do the right thing. And that may be so. But it is also possible that Citizen Four relished the opportunity to shoot regardless of the risk; maybe the socialist acted out of envy; the lawyer may have been moved only by concern for his reputation; and perhaps the imbecile simply wanted to do something bad and supposed this to be an opportunity. In any story of moral decision there are (1) good or bad *intention*; (2) a correct or mistaken *understanding* of either the facts or the governing rule of conduct; and (3) *choice* among possible courses of action. Moral actors can differ by their intention to seek or ignore the lateral good, by their ability to grasp that good in particular cases, and by their choice (and opportunity) to perform or reject what they understand to be the correct behavior.

But which among these three make(s) a person good? In chapter 2 we concluded that the relation of human equality is plausible only if it rests upon a certain capacity of rational persons to achieve moral self-perfection; the fifth and final criterion requires that this capacity be uniform in degree among all the actors in our little story. It must be a double equality; the imbecile cannot exceed the lawyer in potential for personal goodness, or equality becomes a myth. But if either correct knowledge of the lateral good or correct behavior is required for moral self-perfection, belief in the necessary double equality will be problematic. For some people seem to be able to find and execute the right answers more efficiently than others. If the talent for finding or executing right behaviors is unevenly dispersed, it may be for the human race as Satan perceived the condition of the fallen angels; we will stand equal in *possession* of moral freedom, but arrayed in disparate *degrees* of moral power:

> Ye know yourselves
> Natives and sons of Heaven
> . . . and if not equal all, yet free
> Equally free; for orders and degrees
> Jar not with liberty, but well consist[1]

If rational humans vary in their power to perfect themselves through the practice of lateral morality, equality fails.[2]

The Good Person: An Inside Story

The credibility of the necessary uniformity turns on which of three human achievements—intending, understanding, or behaving—is (or are) required to accomplish individual moral fulfillment. If the imbecile in the bank is to be included among the equal, his access to moral self-perfection needs to be grounded upon something other than his relative power to discover and execute correct answers.[3] It may have to rest upon something like "good intent." If an individual *becomes* good by *intending* the good as his reason presents it, equality might be possible. The capacity to intend the apparent good *could* be uniform among us. We emphasize could, because such a uniformity of degree will rest upon premises that are unprovable. Not every fair-minded reader will accept them, and the question is not an empirical one. We cannot weigh the strength of this variable capacity within each individual. We can show only that its uniformity is believable; but this credibility is sufficient.

As we consider the subjective springs of morality, we need a vocabulary adequate to our purpose. Speakers of English often use the same words to designate the relevant subjective act *and* its manifestation in correct deeds. The word "good" is a primary example. We speak of a good woman without our audience's knowing whether we mean that she does deeds that are correct or only that she is striving, successfully or not, to discover and do such deeds.[4] Obviously the difference can matter, and any hope to explain equality depends on our not conflating the two meanings.

Bearing this in mind we have settled upon two sets of terms by which to distinguish this purely subjective act from its external manifestations. The latter—the *behavioral* elements that lie at one pole—will be called the order of obligation; real good; practical good; order of the good; lateral order of obligation; responsibility to others; real obligation; lateral good; common good; object; objective morality; specific commands; mutual obligation; revealed obligation; correct moral answers; correct treatment; right behaviors; and—most frequently—correct behaviors.

In describing the *subjective* states and decisions of the moral actor we prefer phrases from the following set: personal moral state; moral self-perfection; subjective moral goodness; personal goodness; moral self-fulfillment; commitment; good intention (and obtension—soon to be introduced); the inner forum; conscience; and the like.

But if we distinguish correct deeds from good intentions, it is not simply to separate them but also to clarify their connection and overall unity in the moral economy. Behind both is the subject, the person who advances (or regresses) morally by committing to seek (or flout) the order of correct actions in the world. Regarding the metaphysical makeup of this human actor, it is sufficient for our present purpose that *someone* is at home making moral choices; the self is continuous and stable, at least insofar as it consists of the free rational capacity to seek the real good. This is a necessary presupposition of *human* equality; most readers will find it uncontroversial (the few exceptions tend to inhabit the academy). What may raise eyebrows is our clarification of the silent premise of conventional human equality, namely, that this enduring subject or self works his own moral perfection by committing to treat his neighbor in the manner that appears correct, even if he is innocently mistaken about which treatment is truly the right one.[5] The self's capacity to make this commitment is what we have nominated as the host property of the relation of human equality.

The actor may "intend" correct behavior in two senses. First, before any understanding of the practical good in a given case, he may commit to seek it; his intention, then, is an affirmation of the authority of the lateral good and the obligation to search for its content in the particular instance. Second, at some point in the course of the search he may conclude that he has discovered that content; that conclusion may be right or wrong, but his intention will now be directed to the specific deed that is *apparently* correct. So we could say that the actor has a general intention toward the real good and a specific intention toward the apparent good. The first sort of intention can exist without the second; that is, one can be searching for the correct deed without yet having reached a specific answer. But in *either* case the actor would have a *good* intention, so long as he was seriously committed to the task.

How "serious" a search is required for self-perfection? We describe the necessary degree of commitment with terms such as "diligence." We use quotation marks, because the minimum standard of good intention is ambiguous. No science can quantify what is required either in intellectual search or in compliant behavior. We suspect that the settled obscurity of this question is a useful part of human experience; often it may operate as a subtle incentive to exceed what would be the content of merely correct behavior. In any case, it is sufficient here to say that if we are to advance in moral perfection, we must intend—that is, commit diligently to—the real good.[6]

We do not declare the capacity for this act to be uniform in degree. We see that among individuals it *could* vary in its power—as must be the case if human equality is to be a double and not a single equality. But if in fact it should be the same, what we behold is the most democratic of all moralities; the means of moral self-perfection would be fully available to anyone who can make a choice, however feeble one's grasp of the specific good in the particular case. The test of a person's moral excellence is not his or her grasp of correct solutions but the diligent pursuit of them. One must want to know the right way and must act upon the understanding of it that one's intellect can manage. The capacity of human actors to commit to this search might be uniform in degree, and we will say what we can on that issue.

As we proceed we must take account of those competing theories that hold, in one way or another, that the moral fulfillment of the person depends upon his or her discovery and performance of correct behaviors. Who believes this, and how deeply, is a critical clue to the meaning and extent of the convention. For equality to be believable, so too must the necessary features of its host property; one good (though not the only) indication of whether something is credible is who, and how many, actually believe it.

The moral theories at cross purposes with the convention can be usefully divided into two types: one claims that *knowledge* of the correct behavior is *itself* moral perfection, the other that such knowledge increases the *power* of the individual to achieve self-perfection (or its opposite). A summary statement of the position required by equality may be set in contrast to each of them:

1. *Knowledge of specific correct behaviors as irrelevant to moral self-perfection (the position presupposed by conventional human equality).* The only knowledge necessary for *moral* self-perfection is the understanding that there exists a real order of obligation that holds us responsible honestly to seek the correct treatment of others. It is the commitment to this search, not the degree of success in getting or executing the right answers, that fulfills the moral self. The capacity to will the necessary commitment obtains in all rational persons and is plausibly uniform in degree among them.

2. *Knowledge as empowering.* Moral sophistication is empowering; insofar as one grasps the terms of correct behavior one has a greater capacity for moral self-perfection or its opposite. Human equality thus fails as a description of reality, for we differ in our intellectual capacity to grasp the correct moral answers.

3. *Knowledge as determining.* The understanding of correct answers and moral self-perfection are identical terms. No distinction is to be made between act and actor.[7] He who knows the good does the good and is thus perfected to the extent of his knowledge. Since the capacity for acquiring correct answers varies, the capacity for moral self-perfection varies, and equality fails.

Convention and Intention

That moral perfection is advanced by a certain kind of intention is not a particularly exotic idea; indeed, it is basic, but its importance is obscured by various practical barriers. Intention is not only invisible at the surface of daily life but is generally irrelevant to the conduct of quotidian affairs. We cannot stop to discover or applaud what may be the admirable mental state of the driver who runs the red light. It cannot be our first concern that she could have been distracted by some noble mission to prevent a neighbor's suicide or to deliver food to a hungry family. Whatever it was she was thinking, we will judge her guilty of a misdemeanor that risked the common good. Judgment in the public square is often, as lawyers say, a "strict liability" affair.

Most of our social life has to be like this; we judge the surface and move on.[8] But that practical necessity obscures the answer to the crucial question about the moral state of the actor;[9] our judgments about external events involve only the most superficial assessment of the self. We all understand this. Ask me whether this bad driver is a good person, and I concede that I have virtually no information. And if I do get credible evidence of her benign intentions, my complaint of her misdeed will nonetheless survive alongside my independent admiration for what I hear about her "true self." In my mind her self has, to this extent, become distinct from her overt behavior, and I will judge the two separately. In short, daily social practice can be a poor indicator of the weight that ordinary people put on intention.

Suppose that somehow we could be spectators of one another's intentions—witnesses of our neighbor's subjective acts of moral choice. Would we care about his intention, or would we still judge him by the correctness of his behavior? Our own view is that we would care so greatly about motive and intention as to make ordinary social life exceedingly difficult. Our daily equanimity may depend, more than we realize, upon the invisibility of our neighbor's benevolence and hypocrisy. That we never will have direct evidence of his intention is a very great convenience. Paradoxically this only emphasizes the importance we attach to the state of a person's heart. We tend to fuss very little about this matter only because it is a riddle. We grasp the humor when someone worries about what is *really* meant by his neighbor's cheery "Good morning."

Nor do intentions have significance only when they concern our self-interest. Perhaps the most common form of subjective moral accounting is both disinterested and relatively cool; it occurs as we monitor moral commitment on the screen and in literature where art removes the mask from heroes and villains. The spectator infuses the fictional role with his or her own values. Such self-referential viewing and reading may offend professional critics, but this very difficulty of the ordinary spectator to maintain neutrality only confirms the universal concern for intention. Whether or not the protagonist in the story eventually does the right thing, the spectator has a separate and central concern about whether he or she *intends* the right thing. It is this intention that qualifies any character, in real life or fiction, for the moral role that, in popular eyes, is the highest human achievement.

A critic might observe that in the vicarious adventures of fiction, it is the villains that most of us really enjoy. We would agree. Our point is only that the moral detectors of the spectator scrutinize the outside of any character less than the inside. Of course we object to what Lady Macbeth actually does, but we are appalled—and utterly fascinated—by the awful state of her heart. It is bad enough that she commit murder; that she should be murderous is worse yet.

This focus on intention is independent of the objective elements of the plot. In some of the most exciting romances the least important thing is what "happens," and, indeed, very little need happen. We think of Conrad, James, Cather, or Mauriac, for whom every morality play, however ordinary, is a crisis of the heart. It could be the tale of a dull, paralyzed, and speechless old woman on her deathbed. She faces with full intensity the moral choices familiar to us all; she must decide to forgive or curse her enemy, even if she cannot communicate or pursue her choice in the external order. No matter that her enemy is insulated from every material effect of her decision. Her ill will is itself the morally crucial fact, though she may scarcely recall the occasion of this particular enmity and though she barely grasps the idea of moral obligation.

In the contemplation of the audience, this woman is no less responsible for the state of her will than is the robust and intelligent young man who also has an enemy but who grasps precisely the ground of his own hostility and the options available to deal with it. It does not count that this second moral chooser is an ethics student of great promise nor that he has open to him a multitude of practical alternatives, both objective and subjective. In short, though they differ in their intellectual grasp of the situation and in the practical consequences of their actual choices, the young man remains the moral equivalent of the "helpless" woman. Indeed, the point is precisely that she is not helpless. Circumstances do not alter our capacity to make the choices that determine our individual moral state.[10] They don't even count. In everyday affairs we do not get many occasions to think in explicit terms about intention. But this, the authors believe, is a faithful representation of the substantial weight most of us give it.[11]

This subtle and widespread fascination with intention can serve here as a secular analogy to what Christians invoke as the "*sensus fidelium*" or the insight of faithful believers on a specific issue of theology. On a question such as the means to moral self-perfection—so resistant to ordinary analysis—it would be profligate to disregard the weight of popular perception. And if the belief in human equality is so common, we would expect a corresponding enthusiasm for its premises (at least once they are clarified); the alternative would be an incoherence in the common mind.

Intention among the Philosophers: Two Historical Forms of Autonomy

For two millennia philosophy has increasingly shared and nourished this emergent popular emphasis upon the subjective. Moderns often associate the celebration of intention with Immanuel Kant, whose moral philosophy seems to demote the behavioral aspects of choice while focusing upon the "good will." Whether Kant can embrace the premises of human equality is considered in detail in chapter 4. Whatever the case, his emphasis upon the will was hardly revolutionary; early and systematically optimistic Western religion had elevated the importance of intention in the moral calculus.[12] This creeping subjectivity has had its limits among scholars, but few today would entirely neglect the internal state of the actor.[13]

Classical Greece had taken almost the opposite view; because of the powerful objectivity of the culture of antiquity, even Oedipus was not absolved by his well-intentioned ignorance. The calculus of moral accomplishment has altered so decisively, however, that, for many, tragedy has become an incomprehensible concept. Unlike the Greeks, we and our literature suppose that a man can have every sort of rotten luck without the slightest danger to his soul.[14] This shift in perception has rendered even our secular versions of the worthwhile life notoriously subjective. "Success" lies in the good wish and the honest effort. The poet who is lost in the fire along with his unpublished work has not failed as a human person (even if his poetry was bad). His fate may be pathos but not tragedy. If there are losers in his story, they are we the living.

If the Enlightenment did not invent intentionalism, it radically redefined and expanded the moral autonomy of the individual, thereby giving intention a wholly new significance. The work of Thomas Hobbes and his intellectual descendants was to be decisive; their extreme individualism was to affect the ability of modern moral philosophy even to make sense of descriptive equality. We consider this at length in chapter 4. It is sufficient here to observe that since the beginning of the eighteenth century, the idea of exercising moral autonomy through subjective action of the self has borne two contradictory interpretations. The pre-Enlightenment outlook which survives and flourishes holds that every individual is free to embrace (or reject) a preinstitutional moral regime that is objective and authoritative. This version we call "traditional"; it understands autonomy as the capacity of the person to flout the authority of this authentic canon of good behaviors and to accept the consequences of that choice for his or her own moral identity. Belief in a real moral order of this sort did not keep Marcus Aurelius from insisting that the soul "makes itself such as it chooses."[15]

In contrast with tradition stands a certain version of the Enlightenment (typified by Hobbes and rejected by Kant) that flourishes among our secular elites. Broadly speaking, it too makes each person autonomous, but now in the very different and radical sense of appointing him creator of his own moral order. The individual is born unburdened by obligation; any duties he might choose either to honor or to flout could never arise at all except by his own consent. His subjective choices create the only law to which he is answerable.

Either the traditional or the Enlightenment view of moral autonomy could, then, justify the familiar and ambiguous adage that "man makes himself." From either historical standpoint, the individual becomes the particular moral being that she chooses. Each picks his or her own ideal and, in making that choice, produces his or her own character. Plausibly this moral self-construction can proceed independent of the circumstances of the actor and thus may be favorable to human equality. If you are minimally rational, you choose your own moral identity. This act of self-definition is pure will; intention is the core of the matter. Moral choice "is the work of the free and responsible subject producing the first and only edition of himself."[16] Here is a game all of us might play on the level playing field of the human heart.[17]

But there remains a profound difference between the "autonomy" associated with traditional morality and that of Enlightenment individualism. Granted, each is a subjective affair; intention is for both a crucial feature of our moral identity. Nevertheless, the two conceptions are at ground utterly different. In traditional thought, the subjective commitment of the individual is for or against a lateral morality that is real and binding in its endorsement of particular behaviors. The traditionalist is puzzled and commonly appalled by arguments for a pure subjectivism in which decisions have no moral meaning other than what the actor chooses to give them. The philosophers who (broadly) represent the traditional point of view insist upon the authority not only of the will of the individual but also of a precast moral structure of the world in which he lives, including his own nature. There are deeds good and bad.

Tradition has tried to keep the behavioral and subjective aspects of moral choice in a kind of rough balance. Its defenders recognize among moral phenomena an analogy to Aristotle's analysis of material substances.[18] Aristotle insisted that material things require both form and matter in order to become reality. Matter never exists in a formless state; conversely, forms are nothing except as they are materialized. In the moral analogy favored by tradition, our exterior acts (behavior) substitute for matter, while intention supplies the form. When a jury member votes, this act in itself is morally meaningless without the form consisting of his intention. And what might otherwise be a good act (vote) of a particular juror—because it is consistent with the evidence—would be rendered evil *in him* by an intent to serve a purely private end such as revenge or racial discrimination. One who is indifferent to the evidence is himself corrupted, even though his vote is juridically "correct."

Traditional moralists, however, often employ this analogy in a curiously narrow manner. They invoke it to impeach those who do good works with evil intentions, but seldom to justify those who do bad works with good intentions. For them the right intention is *necessary* to justify the moral actor (and move him toward what we call "moral self-perfection"), but it is never *sufficient*.[19] This view would contradict our claim that tradition makes room for moral autonomy. For whenever any actor makes an honest mistake about his duty, he would be corrupted by following his own conscience. And anyone invincibly ignorant on some important matter would be incapable of autonomy; though diligent in search of the real good, he would be morally imprisoned by the limits of his intellect. The perplexed actor could achieve autonomy only if the decisive autonomous act were the *seeking* of the good and not the *finding*; for his one invulnerable freedom is the choice to intend the lateral good.

We note this feature of traditional morality to suggest the crucial distinction that would be sufficient to vindicate the honestly mistaken actor and—in the process—allow descriptive equality. If intention cannot transform an evil *act* into a good one, it might, nevertheless, convert the *actor* into a good person. Tradition did take a half step toward an intentionalism of this sort by exonerating the actor who is innocently ignorant of some fact—one, for example, who appropriates another's bicycle which he had sufficient reason to suppose his own. Such an error of fact would not cancel the good in a man's intention.

What remained fuzzy in tradition was the possibility and the effect of ignorance, not about the facts but about the rule of correct behavior. Could a rational person who knows the facts ever mistake the governing principle? If one person can grasp the right answer, can others in good faith believe the opposite? And if so, what effect does their well-intended misbehavior have upon their moral state? Can the status of actors ever be considered apart from the good or evil of their behavior? Might we even applaud them as moral victors for doing what they wrongly think is right? Maybe. At any rate, later we shall see that on this question, if traditional Western moral philosophy is often opposed to our solution, Western religion has tended to become more open-minded. The reality of a bounded moral autonomy based upon a freely chosen intention to seek the lateral good is not a belief confined to the margins of Western thought. In our society intentionalism could not survive as a theory denying that behavior by itself can be good or bad; but it might do so as one that identified moral self-perfection with diligently intending the lateral good.

It is, then, plainly plausible that while humans have a primary obligation to seek correct treatment of others (and self), their honest pursuit of that ideal effects whatever moral perfection is possible to the individual. This is a balanced and even banal perception—a loose union of the subjective and objective. Recognition of both the outside and inside is congenial to the common sense moralists of the street. "Schultz was wrong, but he was only trying to do the right thing; Lucy meant well—though what she did was wrong." Such judgments do not disclose whether Schultz and Lucy are morally perfected by honestly willing their mistaken choices, but rarely is there anything to be gained by putting it in those terms. We have relatively few occasions publicly to judge actors' "real" character. Our objections to their destructive behaviors can coexist with a belief that whatever harms they *do*, they may still *be* good people. One would not live cheek by jowl with such bunglers but might be willing to exchange moral states with them. Though Steinbeck's half-witted Lenny was objectively a murderer, one could prefer being Lenny to being, say, Bertrand Russell or Carl Sagan. Where the issue is personal goodness, IQ may not be the criterion.

But if we judge a person's moral state by his or her commitment to seek and honor the lateral good and not by success in finding or achieving it, we have found a host property that satisfies the final criterion of the relation of human equality. The host emerges as the individual's capacity to give internal assent (or dissent) to whatever picture of the correctness of behavior he or she is able in good faith to recognize. This means that every rational person could be fully capable of the only act that produces moral self-perfection; all could, in theory, enjoy in the same degree the capacity diligently to seek this real good. With Pascal, all of us can "endeavour . . . to think well; this is the principle of morality."[20] Here is the essence of the convention.

Again, assent to this proposition does not dispense with the need for correct answers. If the order of right behaviors were fantasy, perfection of the self would in turn be nonsense. One might, of course, pursue or flout a purely imaginary canon of good deeds, but there could be no coherence to this choice as a moral activity. A good intention requires a truth for which the actor can aspire, even when its terms elude him. The reality of a lateral order of correct behaviors is the very condition of free morality, providing the will its crucial opportunity to reject or embrace the good.[21]

This need for correct answers is enhanced by their function in the perfection of the social order; right behavior constitutes the practical good that the individual is obligated to seek and, with luck, to realize for others (and himself). Society embodies for every actor the opportunity to concretize his or her choice for or against the imperative of reciprocity; to the extent that we are able (by intention and effort) actually to discover and pursue what would be best, we are empowered to contribute to the common good. Conversely, to the extent that we fail (despite our diligent intention) to discern the proper way or—discerning—to achieve it, harm is done; the potential common good is unrealized. It is this practical truth that underlies our constant duty to *educate* ourselves and one another in its specific terms. These themes are given close attention in chapters 5 and 9.

To some, this division of the good into objective and subjective orders may suggest a lawgiver as well as a law. Would (could) blind nature bestow its highest perfection upon honest bunglers? Could natural selection secure the moral survival of the fatuous? An assumption of conscious design no doubt would ease this tension between the subjective and practical orders of the good. Belief in a cosmic rewarder of good intention may be necessary to make belief in human equality coherent. That, of course, does not entail the existence of such a being, but only that without him human equality may be hard to swallow.

Dealing with Objectivist Criticism

A moral self-perfection that is achieved by diligent intention of correct behaviors would not, then, be radical doctrine; its very moderation further reinforces its credibility as part of the convention. Nevertheless, this resort to subjectivity as the hermetic arena of moral self-fulfillment inevitably will cause some to reject human equality or to look for it elsewhere. It is entirely healthy to doubt that one who mistakes the practical content of justice is morally perfected simply by his warm heart.[22] And the more consistently the blunderer misreads reality, the more uneasy the objectivist becomes. The pages immediately ahead deal with such criticism. Exploring and—eventually—rejecting possible compromises with stringently objectivist theories clarifies the inescapable dependence of any theory of human equality (true or false) upon a good intention/diligence model of moral self-perfection. We will neither satisfy nor criticize the hard-nosed objectivist; we will only suggest that he cannot (coherently) believe in human equality.

By an objectivist theory we will mean—for the present[23]—one that sees (progress toward) moral self-perfection to depend upon (1) the individual's *correct* understanding of the behavior that would be right under the circumstance; (2) his or her assent to the duty to perform (or at least attempt) that particular act; and (3) performing (or at least attempting) the act. If one holds this view of moral self-perfection and believes, in addition, that the ability to distinguish correct answers to ethical questions varies among persons, then objectivism also entails disequality; differences in individual acumen entail a hierarchy of moral capacities. Now we concede, as we must, that any morality—objectivist or otherwise—must give some place to cognition; earlier we excluded persons with extreme mental disability from the very possibility of equality. Reason is an elemental condition of moral life; praise and blame presuppose choice, and choice itself requires at least some understanding of alternative courses. What, then, happens to the idea of a uniform human capacity as we move along the cognitive spectrum from an individual with the barest grasp of alternative possibilities toward another who is the epitome of practical sophistication? In an objectivist moral order we face the problem of relative capacity in an aggravated form. The person with the talent and opportunity to become a philosopher appears impossibly distinct in his potential for virtue (or vice) because of his sophistication; is he not superior to the dull-witted and beleaguered busboy in his capacity for moral self-perfection (or degradation)?

Many heroes of the Enlightenment were prepared to answer yes. Galileo meant every word of his obsequious dedication to an aristocratic patron:

> Most Serene Grand Duke:
> Though the difference between man and the animals is enormous, yet one might say reasonably that it is little less than the difference among men themselves. . . . Such differences depend upon diverse mental abilities, and I reduce them to the difference between being or not being a philosopher; for philosophy, as the proper nutriment of those who can feed upon it, does in fact distinguish that single man from the common herd in a greater or less degree of merit.[24]

Before suggesting escapes from Galileo's conclusion that might interest objectivists, we should repeat that if a person's sophistication has an effect upon his or her capacity for moral self-perfection, this effect can be conceived in either of two ways: in one view (associated with Aristotle) knowledge is an *empowerment* (and a responsibility); with each insight of correct behavior the self achieves broader possibilities for its own good and evil.[25] In the other view (associated with Plato) such moral knowledge and self-perfection merge; they are *identical*, because when we know the good, we always do it.[26] For the moment this latter, stronger role for objective knowledge will be our primary focus.

The identification of knowledge with virtue is at least as old as Socrates. "The source of sin is ignorance or error, the mistaking of evil for good."[27] Today this view is represented by neo-Socratics who under various forms

hold that "he who knows the good does the good" (and vice versa, for ignorance is from this perspective equivalent to vice).[28] This idea of "good" as
the object of knowledge is ambiguous; good that compels us when we know
it may consist either of a very particular correct behavior, some broad aspect
of human flourishing such as friendship or—at the religious ultimate—the
beatific vision. However, for purposes of explaining the difficulty this poses
for equality, we can lump these diverse forms together.

In rough harmony with its intellectual history, we use the label "gnostic"
for this belief that self-perfection is a function of increasing moral knowledge. Gnosticism is usually depicted either as a variety of religious experience or as a deliverance from that experience into some more exalted and
independent spiritual state. Contemporary American churches have been
interpreted as gnostic in their tendency to exaggerate the true believer's
autonomy in his special relation to God.[29] The elect consist of an elite with
superior knowledge. In our own judgment, this religious element, though
historically important, neither exhausts the phenomenon nor is even necessary to it. Gnosticism exists wherever a human self perceives the possibility
of achieving moral superiority by possession of knowledge—of whatever
sort. A gnosticism consisting of purely secular knowledge is a coherent form
that might flourish under specific historical conditions (or in specific sectors
of society as, for example, the modern academy or media).

In our own time the gnostic slant on human excellence was given extravagant support by the American president who repeatedly associated the
"brightest" with the "best"; this formula first surfaced as a flattering soph-
istry uttered at a university commencement and, not surprisingly, became a
watchword of the politically enlightened. Taken literally, this marriage of
brains and virtue would foreclose the idea of a uniform human capacity to
achieve moral self-perfection. The "bright" can know the best, hence potentially *are* the "best." The effect of good intention is subordinated, and self-
perfection becomes a function of the relativized capacity for having clever
ideas about good things to do. We "blush before the frown or smirk of superior knowledge."[30]

So far as he makes a factual claim about the relative abilities of individuals
to find correct behavior, the gnostic is convincing. There are indeed variations in sophistication. If to this we add the claim that this sort of acumen
is what counts in the struggle for moral self-perfection, how can the ungifted
busboy and the bishop occupy the same moral pew? Obviously they cannot,
and our enterprise thus can proceed only by dissociating "bright" from
"best."

There are two possible strategies. The first may be facile but is certainly
to the point. As a moral theory, gnosticism has a peculiar vulnerability.
Wherever the intellect grasps the objective good plainly and without error,

a serious question arises whether morality is even possible.[31] This, we think, was a vexing issue for the late Lawrence Kohlberg who told the world in specifically gnostic terms that "he who knows the good chooses the good."[32] Kohlberg also believed that it is possible for some of us, on occasion, truly to know the good. In those instances it followed for him that the good is done—inevitably. But this entails great cost for the very idea of personal morality. Those who seek moral knowledge apparently do so at the risk of their own freedom, hence of morality itself. For our knowledge deprives us of that power of choice that underlies the possibility of moral action. The consistent gnostic implicitly views moral success as self-canceling.[33] Too firm a grasp is "an insuperable difficulty."[34]

This suggests an interpretation of equality recognizable even to the gnostic. If the acquisition of specific moral knowledge does in fact annihilate segments of our freedom to choose, a real morality might yet survive in the world of intention; it could consist not in the grasp of specifics but in the free response of the self to its general knowledge that lateral obligation exists. We could concede that a person who knows he should pay income tax is thereby driven helplessly to do so. To acquire one or more captivating insights of this sort might still leave this person subjectively free to commit for or against any *general* search for specific behavioral goods. The two acts are different in kind. The more fundamental commitment to seek out and submit to the imperative of the lateral moral order still could for that individual remain voluntary. In freedom he or she would choose whether to start down the path that could lead to the enslaving grasp of additional specific moral insights.

But would the gnostic question not then arise in respect to the freedom of this more fundamental and subjective submission to the behavioral good? Would the very recognition of the *existence* of a lateral moral order not annihilate our freedom to reject it? He who knows the good does it; but—what may be the same thing—he who knows that the lateral good exists also necessarily forms the general intention to seek and submit to it. If that were so, the intentional order would also be a pseudo-morality, collapsing into a second and more complex form of determinism.

The question becomes this: How could we at the same time be determined by the enthralling knowledge of a particular correct behavior but still be free regarding the general obligation to seek such insights? The possibility that our freedom to form a good intention could survive might be stated this way: Knowledge *that* the good exists is different in its nature and effects from knowledge *of the good itself*. Whatever be the forms of knowledge that could compel us, they are different in kind from that primary and general knowledge that there is an order of obligation whose commands would compel us if we actually found them. Knowledge *that* (instead of knowledge *of*) is only an invitation and never coercive. Perhaps it should not be called knowledge at all, though we would oppose such a verbal shift. We would prefer to leave it that knowledge *of* the content of behavioral good might indeed compel us, while knowledge *that* we are obligated to seek it does not. This is not an argument; it is the lesson of our own moral experience and what we perceive others to believe. It receives fortification in our discussion of Bernard Lonergan's moral psychology in chapter 5. For the moment, we have said enough to allow the summary of a plausible compromise with the gnostics.

It would entail a split-level version of what had started out as a purely objectivist moral economy. On its behavioral side, it would continue to be potentially gnostic in regard to particular correct treatments; that is, it would be involuntary in respect to any particular right act correctly grasped. To that same extent, the objectivist order would become morally irrelevant to the individual; for he or she would be in this respect unfree. In the internal forum, however, it would remain a real morality, for the individual could commit to or reject the search. The overall effect would be only trivially undemocratic in its distribution of moral capacity; paradoxically this slight inequity would favor the unsophisticated. For as the educated, gifted, or leisured individual grasped a greater repertoire of specific obligations, she would to that extent be removed from the population of moral choosers. In gnostic terms, she would become the prisoner of her own benign wisdom. The practical significance of this loss of moral capacity would be small, however, for even the wisest among us can master only scraps of the universe of specific (and ever new and surprising) questions about correct behavior.

A More Aggressive Response to
the Gnostic Problem

An alternative response to gnosticism would deny its basic premise that one can know any specific good in a manner that compels moral submission; it would assert the counter proposition that one's grasp of specific correct behaviors is unfailingly incomplete. Even where the actor's inquiry is honest and earnest, his or her grasp of the right way lacks cognitive finality and is therefore nondetermining. This explanation for the possibility of moral choice holds quite apart from those cases of culpable pseudo-ignorance that are generated by voluntary self-delusion—a phenomenon that will also require our consideration.

Giving a place of honor to the incompleteness of moral knowledge in particular cases confronts Aristotle's question: "If [a man] acts by reason of ignorance, what is the manner of his ignorance?"[35] Is it possible to give the very absence (or limitation) of knowledge a place in moral theory without falling into a skepticism that would be unacceptable to ourselves and to the very convention we seek to interpret? One starts down this path with the promising observation (from their own reports) that theologians and ethics professors experience the same anguish as the rest of us in making moral decisions.[36] Not only their theories but their personal lives seem as filled with indeterminacy as Archie Bunker's. Their temptations to cruelty and injustice may come in different forms; the pain of their indecision may be more exquisite[37] (we doubt it). But so far as can be seen, it is not always sophistication that determines their actual responses to personal moral challenge.[38] Whatever it is, these experts differ as greatly among themselves on specific ethical issues as do dropouts, bus drivers, little sisters, and movie stars. Nor are these lively professional conflicts—and all this personal ambivalence—confined to cosmic issues of life and death; the masters divide on premarital sex, the rights of children, smoking cigarettes, owning a mink coat, and driving carefully over the speed limit.[39]

The democracy suggested by this cognitive incompleteness was vaguely recognized by Kant himself; though he lived in a culture that was a great deal less pluralistic than our own, he could still say the following:

> The most remarkable thing about ordinary reason in its practical concern is that it may have as much hope as any philosopher of hitting the mark. In fact, it is almost more certain to do so than the philosopher, because he has no principle which the common understanding lacks, while his judgment is easily confused by a mass of irrelevant considerations.[40]

Kant, however, did not mean that "ordinary reason" actually hits the mark where philosophy fails. His point is that both fail. It is our fate to decide without certainty, "a reproach which we must make to human reason generally." Kant is followed in this lament by all professional moralists.[41] This consensus intensifies the rashness of the alternative view we now suggest: this frailty of human judgment may constitute not a defect but a positive aspect of our moral life. This very cognitive infirmity can be understood and embraced as a moral empowerment—and coincidentally a premise of human equality. If the thought is paradoxical, it is nonetheless benign.

The point is essentially that morality requires freedom, and freedom entails a peculiar relation of the mind to its real object. On the one hand, were intellect to be flooded with knowledge of the good, morality itself would suffer the gnostic fate—for choice would be eliminated.[42] On the other hand, ignorance also eliminates choice; a man blind to alternatives is no more free than the beasts. Now if ignorance and knowledge alike are a threat to self-perfection, the exact relation of reason to morality becomes puzzling.[43] Nev-

ertheless, the practical conclusion seems clear enough and involves no contradiction: moral choice, hence human equality, is possible only in a state
of knowledge—but of imperfect knowledge. *Pace* Aristotle, one prong of
the gnostic slogan seems plausible; a clear knowledge of the particular good
might determine the will. But such knowledge could well be forbidden
us. The race could be so encoded that man is spared a will-crushing grasp
of moral truth.[44] Maybe the world satisfies Robert Nozick's injunction
that there be no "coercive arguments."[45] In such a nondetermining intellectual order, moral decision could have a significance that is identical for
both Socrates and the imbecile in the bank who enjoys only the faintest
flicker of choice. Each, within the arena of his own awareness, would be
spared the captivity of clarity. The imbecile experiences a range of moral
struggle narrower than that of an ethics professor or a senator, but for each
the act of choice could be the same in its interior difficulty, and thus in its
consequence for personal goodness. The knowledge available to each agent
is sufficient to make him responsible for a good-faith (not necessarily correct) answer to whatever range of moral issues presents itself. The possibility
of morality is sustained by the very obscurity that afflicts our images of
good behavior; the shadows of Plato's cave are the substance of our moral
freedom.[46]

The Role of Self-Delusion

To this point in our response to the gnostics, we have spoken as if the happy
shortfall in moral knowledge were to be accounted for solely in terms of our
cognitive limits; that is, humans simply cannot grasp the whole of moral
truth in particular cases. But, in reality, two distinct mental elements cooperate to produce this liberating imperfection. The flickering insecurity of reason is ably assisted by the cunning resourcefulness of the human will when
it decides to mask the act of moral mutiny even from itself.[47] The deliberate
choice to flout our responsibility to the lateral good is facilitated by the free
act of self-distraction. Semiconsciously we are able to kid ourselves about
the propriety of our aims; we talk ourselves into choices of objective evil by
viewing moral issues uni-dimensionally under some narrow aspect of the
good.[48] This perhaps is obvious; but we would emphasize the democratic
quality of the trait. Deceiving ourselves about our motives is no specialty of
the unlearned and the stupid; perhaps the most effective self-deluders in our
literature are the elegant villains of *Faust* and *Paradise Lost*. And even Judas
had his reasons.[49]

When we try to distinguish cases of honest error from those of a corrupt
self-delusion, we find that art is plainer than life. As the literary creator of

Faust, Goethe could authoritatively ascribe to him an evil intent; Dorothy Sayers could establish in subjective detail the anguish of the actor (possibly conscientious) who recognizes the danger of self-delusion but who must choose one of two paths, both bearing the name "duty":

> For a full half-hour Miss Climpson sat alone, struggling with her conscience. Her natural inquisitiveness said "Read"; her religious training said, "You must not read"; her sense of duty to Wimsey, who employed her, said, "Find out"; her own sense of decency said, "Do no such thing"; a dreadful harsh voice muttered gratingly, "Murder is the question. Are you going to be the accomplice of Murder?" She felt like Lancelot Gobbo between conscience and the fiend—but which was the fiend and which was conscience?[50]

It is in the real-life cases that the state of the heart remains opaque to the observer. Sometimes it seems the most dedicated, and even professional, do-gooders (Judas himself is an example) who commit the most atrocious wrongs with a wholly ambiguous attitude toward duty. It is, for example, not unknown for apparently conscientious policemen and prosecutors to conceal or even fabricate evidence in the good cause of removing dangerous people from society. A vivid recent example is that of the British police and prosecutors—even judges—in their injudicious treatment of cases involving suspected killers from the IRA.[51] It is certainly possible that some or all these objectively injurious decisions were made by individuals in a sincere effort to meet their moral responsibility. They supposed they were doing their duty as required by a real external imperative of justice. If so, they were not self-deluding. They were simply wrong; they were destructive of the common good; and they were morally self-perfecting.

The same could hold for Robin Hood, John Wilkes Booth, people who murder abortionists, the abortionists they murder, and the court that burned Joan of Arc. Our judgment of their motivation must be that we have no judgment.[52] And these cases are merely spectacular examples of the perplexity faced by actors and observers in everyday life. Many a wife, like Anna Karenina, has plausible justifications for cheating on her husband. Is she merely adjusting her blinders to obscure the sin, or is she only innocently wrong and—paradoxically—perfecting herself morally by her good intention? In all probability even she would not recognize the degree of her own complicity in the objectively wrong result, nor is anyone else in a position to provide the answer.

Combined with the universal moral fallibility already discussed, this knack for self-delusion presents the practical possibility that the capacities of each of us to commit to the behavioral ideal are uniform in spite of the vast differences in our general practical sophistication and life circumstances. If knowing more about the rules prevents neither doubts nor self-delusion, these accidental distinctions in brain power might be irrelevant to our capacity to perfect ourselves through moral choice.

This description of fallibility and self-delusion might seem to flirt with moral nescience. This too would frustrate our purpose, for in interpreting the convention we would have put ourselves crosswise with its affirmation of a real lateral good.[53] This popular objectivism, however, does not necessarily conflict with the morally self-perfecting efficacy of good intention. Indeed, as already noted, the common view seems to be that the right answers often are hard to discern, and that we are supposed to keep looking for them while—in the meantime—following our consciences. The imperative presented subjectively to the actor is plain but only as an invitation to seek and do correct acts. If we wish to perfect ourselves morally we may do so by pursuit of the elusive terms of the lateral good and by submission to whatever judgment of these terms our diligent conscience reaches; the knowledge of this option to seek or not to seek does not determine our wills. Finally, every rational person receives this same moral invitation from nature and experience; thus the gnostic hierarchy fails, and equality is at least possible.

Simplifying the Basic Propositions

Moral fallibility might be a natural condition that holds in uniform degree among all rational actors; or it might not. If the former—if, in effect, every person has the same access to the right answers to the specific questions he or she faces—an argument for human equality might be made in a form that could satisfy either Socrates or Aristotle. For all would have equal opportunity to grasp the content of those correct deeds that the ancient Greeks insisted must be seen and done if one is to advance in moral self-perfection. Everyone would have the same chance to get things right (or wrong).

That, however, is not the use we make of the premise of universal moral fallibility. Ours is a simpler proposition that would support equality whether or not there is uniform cognitive access to the right answers. Fallibility— the incompleteness of all particular moral knowledge—serves equality sufficiently by ensuring human freedom; it is enough that there are no Socratic occasions on which anyone is enslaved by knowledge. If, despite this liberating fallibility, some humans have a richer repertoire of right answers, this is unthreatening to equality so long as we accept one final condition: one must reject the other Greek proposition that perfection comes by getting right answers to questions about behavior. The issue of personal goodness cannot turn upon right behaviors but only upon the free active aspiration to find and execute them. The capacity for moral self-perfection is plausibly uniform to those who can believe that one advances by freely doing the best one can in realizing this practical hope for the common good. This belief is solely about the correctness of intention, not of behaviors; we believe it to be very widespread among ordinary people and implicit in their belief in human equality. Who among the philosophers and theologians could agree with it we consider in greater detail in parts 2 and 3.

A Fragment on Habit

A threat to the plausibility of equality appears from yet another quarter. Conceding the original uniformity of our individual capacities for moral self-perfection, how could this state of affairs endure *over time*? Some humans develop habits of virtue, others of vice, and most a bit of both. The behavioral choices that produce these habits may have differential effects upon the individual's capacity to commit to the quest in the future. Over time some may become inclined to the moral search, others disinclined. If so, no matter how one comes down about bishops and bartenders, it could seem naive to equate the capacity of the hardened hypocrite with that of the persistent pilgrim. Perhaps good habits not only make it easier to find the good but even to choose to look for it—and vice versa for bad habits. One speculates about the difficulty for a dying Lord Marchmain to submit to a real good that he has long flouted.

An obvious solution to this problem would be a shift in definition. Jefferson's "created equal" could be reduced to its literal minimum; that is, the capacity for moral self-perfection might merely *originate* (be created) with a uniform intensity that over time becomes differentiated in the course of making specific choices in our treatment of others. Equality thus would cease to be a constant state of affairs; indeed, at no historic moment would it exist except as a relation among those—mostly children—who happen at any given time to be acquiring the use of reason. At every moment those individuals who stand at the threshold of rationality would have the same capacity to acquire moral perfection during whatever time they are given in this life to seek the good. But it would be *only* at this ephemeral beginning point that equality would hold, and it would hold only for those who reach that point of moral development simultaneously.[54] Such a descriptive equality could provide the same moral *opportunity* for all rational persons;[55] but as choices are made they would continuously differentiate the strength of this power of individuals to commit to the search. Such a moral economy would be the terrestrial counterpart and prelude to Dante's hierarchy in paradise. Dante suggests that the blessed, while still on earth, made diverse moral choices that influenced the capacity they were to enjoy in paradise to behold the beatific vision;[56] our concern here is that these same choices might alter their capacities *while on earth* to achieve moral self-perfection.[57]

Such an ephemeral equality in its peculiar way would be a democratic interpretation of human experience. Irrespective of fortune, every rational person would have the same access to the one ultimately important good of life. Even Bernard Williams could concede that the achievement of "the highest kind of moral worth" would have no dependence upon natural capacities, unequally and fortuitously distributed. But we doubt that Williams or anyone else could accept this picture either as true or as morally satisfying. The ordinary person disdains the sort of uniformity that would diminish human equality to an evanescent moment. By ceasing to be a claim about *all* rational humans (at whatever moment in history), equality ceases to be an existential and psychologically compelling concept.

Indeed, the idea that humans differentiate their originally equal capacities for moral self-perfection could appear as the sinister invitation to society once again to identify in positive and negative ways those individuals who already have begun the moral shuffling of the deck. Nor would the winners in this contest be the old Calvinist elect who arrived there by luck. The new elect would get there on their own, constantly augmenting their own capacity to transcend the rest of us. This will not work. The uniformity that is a criterion of human equality must hold for all rational humans simultaneously and across time. But, again, how could this be when we consider the force of habit?

Before we panic, let us be certain that we are confronting the specific aspect of moral habit that actually threatens equality. What we have conceded so far is that for a person to reject the quest for the lateral good in one case can affect the power of his or her rational moral faculty to find correct answers in future cases.[58] Simply put, the moral acumen of the actor is diminished (or enhanced); even add the less plausible assumption that this degradation (or increase) of cognitive power occurs whether the incorrect behaviors proceeded from a good will or a bad will. If a diligent conscience tells a man to fight in a war that is in fact unjust, let us suppose that his participation injures his capacity thereafter to distinguish the just from the unjust.

All this, though plausibly true, would be irrelevant. The threat to equality lies not in the damage that moral renegades and blunderers do to their own perspicacity. Their progress in moral self-perfection does not rest upon regaining their former acuity but only upon their willingness to do so. The resolute degenerate may descend to a state of moral insight as feeble as that of our imbecile in the bank; recidivism may erode his sensitivity, reducing it to the preconversion level of a Magdalene, the Samaritan woman, or the Good Thief. The only question for us is whether this sinner nevertheless retains full capacity to embrace the lateral good as his or her ideal. And that is a question wholly separate from the relative power of the moral intellect. Equality does not rest upon our ability to discover correct behavioral answers. Uniformity is required only in respect of our capacity to commit to those answers, and moral self-perfection comes precisely in their diligent intention, not in their accurate perception. The only (and difficult) question about intention, then, is this: Does a bad intention in one case diminish the capacity to form a good intention in the next case?[59]

The answer is clear enough, so long as we resist the impulse to accept sheer *consistency* of behavior as evidence of alteration (either erosion or increase) in the person's original capacity to commit to the real good. A forty-year-old woman may from an early age have been indifferent to the call of obligation; let us further suppose that even when her behavior has been objectively good, it has been chosen exclusively out of selfish motives. She has been, throughout, an evil-intending person. We deny that anything follows from this fact concerning the strength of her capacity for moral self-perfection.[60] If her stubborn consistency were to tell us anything, it might suggest stability rather than variation in her capacity to make the relevant decision; the truth is, of course, that it suggests nothing either way on this subject. Her consistency begs the very question we need to answer. We still know only that she has not changed her mind on the fundamental question. She has stuck to her bad answer. Nor is our judgment about the stability of her capacity to commit to the good altered if, instead, we suppose that she has been a consistent seeker (even a finder) of good behaviors. No inference would be justified that her capacity to revolt has been affected.

It may help once more to identify the specific activity of which our forty-year-old woman must be capable (in constant degree) if human equality is to obtain. It is not the decision either to continue or to break her particular habit (good or bad). To secure human equality, constancy is required only in the strength of her capacity to reverse her old commitment for or against the order of correct behaviors. The question is whether, in spite of her objective failures and successes—and even her subjective rejection of all obligation—she can still opt for correctness as vigorously as ever. We see no reason to suppose otherwise. Indeed, if she has failed freely and often, that very failure could contribute to her appetite for the tantalizing good that so far she has fled.[61]

This last remark is not meant to suggest that the person who ignores what she knows (or could know) perfects herself by her very act of rejection; that would be a contradiction. By turning from her own conscience she commits the fundamental act of moral self-destruction. What we do mean is that for many (not all) who reject the quest for right acts, the consequence is not the experience of satisfaction but of misery; for them the flight from the lateral good seems often to generate the very moral energy by which they can reembrace it. Oscillation between moral poles is a wrenching personal experience, but a poor index of diminishing moral capacity. Nor is the number of these fluctuations necessarily the mark of anything but the enduring invitation of every person to a fresh beginning. The Christians seem to mean something like this when they speak of the impulse to *metanoia* or change of heart. Even as the sinner freely abandons the search for correct answers, he may rediscover the power to recommence. The moral coward who flees responsibility remains "hounded" by an invitation to reconnect his will to the good.[62]

Our conclusion: Whether habit alters the degree of individual capacity to commit to the lateral good cannot be settled finally either by empirical or metaphysical inquiry. It remains plausible that every sane person retains the option in all its strength. Human equality continues to be a real possibility.

A Word on Intention and Obtension

We have favored the verb "intend" to label the subjective act that works moral self-perfection. To commit diligently to the independent lateral order of correct behaviors is our definition of a good intention; to commit to anything that subordinates the authority of this preinstitutional order is a *bad* intention. With the meaning of intention thus cabined, it does a serviceable job of designating the point on which personal moral progress pivots. But equality's morality of "good intentions" is ambiguous and risks being mistaken for a pure subjectivity in which the goodness of an intention does not turn on the subject's diligent commitment to the real good. Some single and singular word is needed to clarify the idea that the moral decision that occurs "inside" relates to the good behavior to be realized "outside." There should, in short, be an English verb "to obtend," which would encompass both the subjective (tend) and the objective (ob). It would identify a specific subjective act—namely, the choice to seek practical outcomes[63] that are good according to a standard not controlled by human consent. To obtend would mean to commit to the search for the content of the real order of the behavioral good and to its realization. This mental act of the individual would be labeled an "obtension," which would make the adjective "obtensional" or "obtensive." "Obtensionalism" would be the formal term for this conception of the moral life.

To our considerable surprise, a casual pass at the unabridged *Oxford English Dictionary* (*OED*) turned up something very like this pattern of words. To "obtend," it seems, is obsolete; it is also vague (and possibly contradictory) in its meanings. The *OED* gives it this meaning: "to put forward as a reason." The noun "obtension" is then defined simply as "the action of obtending." The *OED* cites Samuel Johnson's dictionary of 1755 as its source and notes that no quotation has been found for this noun. The word "obtent" also appears and is defined as "purpose, intent," a rendering supported by the following quotation—obscure but memorable: "Origenes . . . did gelde hymselfe . . . for the obente and wille of chastite."[64]

If we accept "to put forward" as the meaning for the verb "obtend," this may at first seem to render the term a bit *too* objective, suggesting an external audience to whom an argument is being made in justification. "George, here is why I plan to move to Sacramento." This dialogic aspect is irrelevant to the moral act we have in mind, for that act is wholly internal to the deciding individual. Still, this usage is roughly consistent with what we are trying to express, for presumably one "puts forward" to another exactly what one has adopted subjectively as one's own "reason." It would be a scant extension to apply the word "obtend" to the act of presentation in which one puts forward *to oneself* the choice of a justifying external purpose. "I obtend that outcome" can be an internal comment. We think that the word signifies well the fundamental act of commitment to the lateral good as a general ideal and to its specification in individual cases.[65]

Thus, when I decide to honor my real obligation by providing food to my children, I obtend in two senses. I do so as my general commitment to seek and perform the correct behaviors discoverable (or at least to be sought) in the order of lateral obligation; I also obtend in choosing specific means to consummate that commitment. In sum, by my subjective acts, I intend the fulfillment of a real lateral imperative.

A Conclusion

These, then, are the plausible parts, the criteria and basic vocabulary of a real relation of human equality as Western convention would have it. Descriptive equality must be limited to humans with reason and will. It rests upon the premise of an innate and slumbering capacity of the isolated self to recognize the obligation to seek and honor the details of a distinctive order of obligation. This is the lateral or reciprocal morality that contains the terms of correct behavior toward other humans. Its binding force is brought to consciousness only by human encounter. Individuals puzzle and divide over its specific content. Every rational person, however, recognizes this preexisting and obligating order as a fact. Each has the capacity to will that it be realized in its details through his own choices; necessarily the individual exercises this capacity in the free choice he makes either to seek and embrace or to ignore and flout whatever of its truth he could find through the diligent exercise of whatever power of reason is his. In addition to the capacities to seek what is correct toward self, God, and creation, this awakened capacity to will correct behavior toward other humans constitutes the instrument by which each individual can achieve whatever moral self-perfection is possible for any human being. The relation of human equality must rest upon this common capacity to will whatever of the lateral good we can know when we make the honest effort to discover it. That capacity must be uniform in degree; it is plausibly so, hence worthy of belief—and equality with it.

PART II

COULD THE PHILOSOPHERS BELIEVE

IN HUMAN EQUALITY?

The will of philosophical men of power and artist-tyrants will
be stamped upon thousands of years: a higher species of men
who, thanks to their preponderance of will, knowledge, riches,
and influence, will avail themselves of democratic Europe as
the most suitable and supple instrument they can have for
taking the fate of the earth into their own hands, and working
as artists upon man himself.
(Nietzsche, *Beyond Good and Evil*)

INTRODUCTION TO PART II

What is there to respect in what alone is common to all men—
membership of this particular biological species?
(Benn, *Egalitarianism and Equal Consideration of Interests*)

UNLIKE NIETZSCHE, most Western writers pay at least a superficial respect to descriptive equality. This is riskless, so long as the concept remains undefined. But now we have a meaning and must put this question: Who could believe in such an equality? Whose ideological commitments harmonize with, and thus support, the convention? Some of us obviously could not assent. If I am a Nietzschean or a determinist (or Professor Benn), my premises disable me. I might acknowledge the existence of the linguistic convention; but, as with the passenger pigeon, I must deny its representation in the real world.

The case of the determinist is an easy one, and, as for Nietzsche, he will be glad to be excluded. Which other systematic philosophies fit or do not fit may be less clear. Some who account themselves true believers in equality may in fact hold premises about the nature of man that are incompatible with the definition. If that proves to be so, this essay will stand as an invitation to them. Any one of three responses is requested: revise your premises about humankind; correct our interpretation of the convention; or stop insisting that you believe in equality.

For clarity's sake we will assume our interpretation to be correct. Through the next two parts—in five chapters—we shall suppose also that Hobbes, Aquinas, and the other philosophers and theologians we encounter share this definition of "human equality." This will not commit them to belief in the actual existence of the relation; whether their premises allow belief in such an equality is the very question we mean to answer. But even to put that question we must hold the meaning constant. If we are to ask Hobbes whether he believes in human equality, there must be a clear idea for him to accept or reject.[1] Of course, an incidental consequence of this inquiry may be a confirmation of or a challenge to our interpretation.

What specific commitments are required to believe in the reality? We can compress the now familiar litany: The philosopher must agree that rational humans have the capacity freely to choose either to seek or avoid the details of correct behavior; that there is a preinstitutional order of such correct behaviors that each human owes to every other; that moral self-perfection is achieved precisely by diligently seeking the content of that order; that all rational persons uniformly possess the capacity to make that effort.

Human equality is the specific relation that springs from the uniformity of this moral capacity; that is what the term means. Any claim to believe in it must accept these structural criteria. For example, it would be a contradiction to profess human equality as a fact while simultaneously supposing that the capacity for moral self-perfection varies in degree among rational individuals. Such disuniformity might be true, but, in that event, it would entail the further belief that equality is not the case in the real world. Our definition will be compared for fit with various theories of the structure of the moral self. The question in each case will be whether persons with a distinctive view of human nature—say Calvinists—could recognize as part of the world about them this uniform human trait we call the host property. Calvinists? A worthy group, but why them instead of Zoroastrians or neo-conservatives? Just how does one select the "who" in the question, "Who could believe in equality?"

Three considerations determine our choices. *First*, we can put the question only to those philosophies and faiths of which the authors know something, and these are mercifully few. *Second*, the examples we choose should be broadly familiar to the Atlantic audience that is our natural target; they should be drawn from some recognized Western tradition. Readers then can replicate the process with respect to other worldviews as they like and are able; having put the question to themselves, they may extend it in every other ideological direction familiar to them. For example, some sophisticated critic may conclude that the criteria of the convention will fit certain arcane philosophers or Eastern religions; we will be agreeably surprised and ask for details. In the process we all may learn something. *Third*, and perhaps most important, certain ideologies have obvious relevance to equality. Thus in part 3 we do in fact single out the Calvinist; it is natural to ask him whether human equality can cohabit peacefully with what he calls "double predestination." Indeed, as we shall suggest, many moral theories (religious and secular) seem to have been shaped with a view toward settling whether human equality is true.

A Brief Example of the Inquiry: Jefferson and the "Moral Sense" Philosophers

Before we tackle the ideologies represented in the worlds of the "Enlightenment," "natural law," and "Christianity," we will illustrate the sort of inquiry we intend. For purposes of this brief exercise we have chosen a specific historical school of moral psychology; it is one that, in any case, we should mention because of its surface resemblance to our own picture of human equality. These thinkers are known collectively as the "Scottish realists" or the school of "Moral Sense."[2] We can afford to be brief with this interesting set, because Garry Wills has already described how the moral sense, as they understood it, allows a certain concept of equality among humans. In his *Inventing America* Wills showed Jefferson's debt to this school in reaching his "self-evident" proposition.[3] We have considered the extent of Jefferson's accord with us and conclude that moral sense philosophy (and Jefferson) are ambiguous in their endorsement.

The exercise will be truncated for simplicity's sake. We will simply assume that the Scottish school accepts certain of the premises that are necessary to belief in conventional human equality. The criterion of "laterality" is one: It is not absolutely clear that the moral sense, as the Scots use it, entails a *real* (as opposed to conventional) responsibility to others. And there are other ambiguities that could justify an entire book probing their implicit view of equality. For this sample encounter, however, we confine ourselves largely to the issue of uniformity or "double equality." Could the Scots believe that all humans possess the moral sense in the same degree? It is one of the specific questions we will put to various ideologies in a more plenary analysis in the succeeding chapters, and here we provide a rough idea of how we intend to go about these inquiries.

In glancing at the set of moral sense thinkers, we (like Garry Wills) intend to focus upon the work of the eighteenth-century Scottish divine Francis Hutcheson (1694–1746), a theologian-philosopher and professor of philosophy at Glasgow. He had been a student of Locke and became a friend of Hume and a teacher of Adam Smith. Hutcheson held that ensuring moral behavior is the specific function of a distinctive moral sense that is analogous to the five physical senses. Roughly speaking, it is by this sixth sense that each individual distinguishes good from evil within a moral order that Hutcheson, in at least an ambiguous way, considers to be real and authoritative.[4] That order consists in benevolent acts or "public good." And, to put it in our terms, we must ask whether personal commitment to this benevolence is, in Hutcheson's eyes, the engine of one's own moral self-perfection; is that perfection advanced wherever the individual attempts to realize the apparent version of the real good that is discoverable under all the circumstances including his own level of moral sophistication? Here is one of Hutcheson's summaries that sounds especially promising for an alliance with our interpretation of human equality:

> Since then in judging of the goodness of temper in any agent, the abilities must come into computation . . . and none can act beyond their natural abilities; that must be the perfection of virtue where the moment of good produced equals the ability, or when a being acts to the utmost of his power for the public good; . . . no external circumstances of fortune, no involuntary disadvantages, can exclude any mortal from the most heroic virtue. For how small soever the moment of public good be which any one can accomplish, yet if his abilities are proportionably small, the virtue may be as great as any whatsoever. Thus . . . we must judge this character really as amiable as those whose external

splendor dazzles an injudicious world into an opinion that they are the only heroes in virtue.[5]

Hutcheson would be an important trophy for equality because of his influence upon American revolutionary politics. Before we could declare him an implicit believer, however, we would need to know more. Specifically, is the self morally perfected even by the errant choices of the well-intending individual who mistakes the acts that would fulfill the obligation of benevolence and who thus accomplishes objective evil through ignorance? If so (if intention alone suffices for Hutcheson), it would seem that any rational person of whatever intellect or circumstances would indeed have the same capacity to self-perfect. Human equality would be consistent with such a belief.

If, on the other hand—in order to self-perfect—the actor must be both well-intending *and* find the correct answer, Hutcheson would represent a view different from our own. Or, alternatively, if Hutcheson should hold that the actor who is well-intending *always gets it right*, the issue of honest error could never even arise;[6] that position would also be hard to reconcile with the common sense moral premises of conventional human equality.

Does Hutcheson tell us whether honest mistakes are possible and, if so, their effects? He is difficult to interpret regarding the relation between correct moral reasoning and the moral sense,[7] but he does say this much: "Partial views of the tendency of actions make us do what is really morally evil, apprehending it to be good."[8] But can the person who takes a "partial view" be well-intending? Hutcheson adds this note: "No mortal can secure to himself a perpetual serenity, satisfaction, and self-approbation, but by a serious inquiry into the tendency of his actions and a perpetual study of universal good according to the justest notions of it."[9]

But, again, is this "serious inquiry" in itself sufficient for moral self-perfection, or must the individual actually find and attempt the correct action? This never becomes entirely clear. We read Hutcheson implicitly to assume that the actor must get it right.[10] Granted, he does ask who is "rewardable" in what degree for the appropriate internal disposition toward behavior intended to affect others.[11] This is promising, but his examples of such persons are limited to a set of moral agents who specifically (according to Hutcheson) have gotten the *correct* answer; their various motivations or "affections" only differentiate the degree of virtue resulting from their uniform choice of *proper* behavior. There is no suggestion that an unapproved behavior executed in good faith could generate moral self-perfection. And in a related comment Hutcheson appears finally to close the door on human equality:

It is no way inconsistent with perfect goodness [for God] to make different orders of beings and, provided all the virtuous be at last fully content, and as happy as they desire, there is nothing absurd in supposing different capacities and different degrees. And during the time of probation there is no necessity, not the least show of it, that all be equal.[12]

Carefully read this could leave our question open; that is, it would also be *consistent* with "perfect goodness" if God had provided the same capacity in the same degree—and Hutcheson does not specifically deny this possibility. But it would be a considerable stretch to locate Hutcheson in equality's corner.[13] And we will find the central question left unclear in other authorities from the school of moral sense, even though they too seem superficially to stress the importance of good intention. Thus Hutcheson's Scottish contemporary, Thomas Reid (1710–1796), obscures both the accuracy with which good intention produces correct judgments and the efficacy of honest but incorrect judgments in producing moral self-perfection:

> Every man of common understanding, who wishes to know his duty, may know it. The path of duty is a plain path, which the upright in heart can rarely mistake. Such it must be, since every man is bound to walk in it. There are some intricate cases in morals which admit of disputation; but these seldom occur in practice; and, when they do, the learned disputant has no great advantage: for the unlearned man, who uses the best means in his power to know his duty, and acts according to his knowledge, is inculpable in the sight of God and man. He may err, but he is not guilty of immorality.[14]

How "rare" are those moral conundrums in which we are likely to err? We suspect that our natural limitations and our special circumstances may cause any of us innocently to take the wrong side on many a disputed moral issue. And even if we are *excused* ("inculpable") for such honest mistakes, we still do not know whether our good intention positively perfects us. Where exactly does our hope for self-fulfillment lie?[15]

The school of moral sense is by no means extinct. In the early twentieth century it enjoyed a revival in the works of W. D. Ross and C. D. Broad. It remains inscrutable on the question of human equality, and its ambiguity has been reinforced and extended in the recent work of James Q. Wilson.[16] It was Wilson's hope to give scientific respectability to the reality and nature of the moral sense. Unfortunately for equality, Wilson's "evidence" for the moral sense turns out to be the familiar Darwinian arguments for a biological/psychological evolution of moral capacity.[17] The persuasiveness of those claims as science is beside the point. Were they all true, this could only establish different degrees of human moral capacity—a sort of evolutionary moral queue. Moral evolution is a theory of elites.[18] This was not Wilson's point, but it is impossible to blink the gnostic implication.

Our reservations about the Scottish moral school would not, however, settle the specific question about Jefferson's belief, in spite of his apparent assent to their general understanding of the moral sense. Jefferson could have improved upon Hutcheson et al. and brought the Scots' self-conflicted version of human equality into full intelligibility. Given the quality of his mind and the political exigencies of his times, this would not be surprising. It was he, not the Scots, who stood in practical want of such a theory. It needed, of course, to be a concept of considerable subtlety were it to accommodate his participation in human slavery.

Garry Wills thinks that Jefferson actually came to believe in a universal, descriptive, human equality in spite of his personal practice and beliefs in respect to blacks.[19] Unfortunately, nothing in this legacy speaks clearly on the point; very little even speaks ambiguously. Wills's argument is nonetheless credible. Here we confine ourselves to fragments of the Jeffersonian record that cut in both directions and that illustrate how we propose to test ideological systems for their compatibility with our interpretation of human equality.

Unfortunately, what the Scots left obscure Jefferson allowed to stand; Wills reports little beyond Jefferson's enthusiastic agreement with their equivocation. He (Wills) puts great weight upon the distinction Jefferson favored between the heart and the head.[20] Jefferson is said to have believed that "the moral sense is not only man's *highest* faculty, but the one that is *equal* in all men."[21] It was this that allowed Jefferson to include slaves in the circle of equality in spite of his conviction of their intellectual inferiority.[22] That sort of difference did not matter for moral purposes. All this is indeed promising. And the case is further advanced by an aphorism Jefferson borrowed from Reid: "State a moral case to a ploughman and a professor. The former will decide it as well, and often better than the latter, because he has not been led astray by artificial rules."[23] This is positive in two respects: It not only makes the necessary heart/head distinction but recognizes that the heart's specific responsibility is to command the search for correct answers (whose reality otherwise is left in a state of confusion by the Scottish school). The ploughman dictum does not, however, suggest either the uniformity of the capacity to find correct answers or the irrelevance of those answers to moral self-perfection. In fact Jefferson proceeds to deliver the poison pill to equality. In the very same paragraph he eliminates the possibility that a double equality—one both of possession and degree—could be based upon the moral sense:

> This sense . . . is the true foundation of morality. . . . The moral sense, or conscience, is as much a part of man as his leg or arm. It is given to all human beings in a stronger or weaker degree, as force of members is given them in a greater or less degree.[24]

All of us, then, have this "highest faculty"; we merely have it in different degrees. Everyone possesses it, but some get more than others. Note that this does not eliminate the possibility that slaves as a group are equal to all other groups; that would depend on how the capacity is distributed among groups. It only means that *humans as individual members of the race* are unequal to one another in their most significant attribute.

Is that all that Jefferson and his colleagues meant by "created equal"? We doubt it. Indeed, we suspect that they would find the idea of a "double equality" to express more precisely what they felt but failed to bring to full intelligibility. The convention that today supports equality probably owes a great deal to the conspiratorial understanding in Philadelphia that never quite made it to the consciousness of the eighteenth century.

We are finished with this introductory exercise, except to emphasize that none of the foregoing is intended as criticism of the *truth* of the claims made by these protagonists of the moral sense. Our inquiry is whether the premises of thinkers such as Hutcheson and Jefferson allow them to embrace the obtensional structure of human equality. And that will remain our central aim as we move through various philosophies and theologies in the chapters ahead. Whether Hobbes, Aquinas, Luther—or none of them—got their moral theory right is not our concern; we want to know only whether their views of what makes a person good are consistent with, and thus supportive of, conventional human equality.

The Plan for Parts 2 and 3

Parts 2 and 3 thus examine separate clusters of thinkers who—within each cluster—are related by the structure of their moral psychology. Some of these would not appreciate the company into which they are thrust; Kant, for example, was not an admirer of Hobbes. And the use of such broad labels as "Enlightenment," "natural law," and "Christianity" will seem too elastic even after we have pruned them, as we are about to do. Still, such terms identify a rough historical and substantive kinship. Although we will elaborate separate pictures of all three groups, it will be useful to have in mind what we consider to be the principal relevant features of the moral psychology of each.

- The term "enlightenment" here will comprise two historically related, but sharply contrasting, subspecies which we shall call "individualism" and "Kantianism."
- By "individualism" we mean a strong moral relativism grounded upon an individual self that wills its own rules—what we have already called a "radical autonomy." It is exemplified with clarity in the work of Thomas Hobbes; it loses that clarity in most works of his successors (and may lose its nature in Kant). Its core in Hobbes is the idea that the individual is born lacking duty to others and can acquire obligation only by his or her own consent. Self-perfection—if it has meaning—is self-defined.

- "Kantianism" is simply the transcendental moral psychology of Immanuel Kant with its peculiar marriage of autonomy and duty.
- "Natural law" will refer to those moral theories in which the individual self discovers obligation in the "natures" that are disclosed by experience and reason. Unable to avoid confronting this natural obligation, the individual, nevertheless, is free either to obey or to rebel. With the important modern exception of Bernard Lonergan, natural law theories hold that self-perfection consists only in finding and performing the good deeds that are inferable from nature.
- "Christianity" assumes a moral capacity similar in some ways to that of natural law, but it identifies God as the source of the order of correct behaviors to which that capacity is directed. The precise implications of a descriptive human equality for the believer would depend upon the sort of God he or she believes in and the character of the divine commands. Because of their considerably greater complexity, these issues of moral theology will be separated from the philosophers and discussed in part 3.

Again, the point throughout will be not to criticize either individualism, natural law, or Christianity for its stance on equality (or anything else). Our picture is not detailed enough; our definition of each is too narrow; and, in any case, it simply is not our purpose. We stress only those concepts of the self within each worldview that are relevant to the convention.

The sole question is whether human equality could be squeezed into—or out of—each of these systems of thought without serious discomfort to either equality or the particular ideology. How many persons today actually hold the premises that we ascribe to these systems is a separate question. The radical autonomy Hobbes preached, for example, may be an aberration confined largely to the academy. Understanding Hobbes's premises could, nevertheless, tell us a good deal about who *could* believe in a real equality of the sort signified by the convention. And that is the inquiry.

4

COULD THE ENLIGHTENMENT BELIEVE?

INDIVIDUALISM, KANT, AND EQUALITY

I did it my way.
(Paul Anka)

A T THE THRESHOLD of modernity looms the great Hobbes, the architect of liberal man. Of the Enlightenment moral philosophers, he was
both the earliest and the plainest. Counselor to kings and prudent
survivor of revolutions, Thomas Hobbes (1588–1679) initiated his own in-
surrection in the Western conception of the moral self. His candid—even
crude—style is an advantage to us. He set great store upon simplicity of
method. Supposing himself to stand in the tradition of Euclid, he proceeded
from axioms and theorems that he declared self-evident; he is seldom subtle,
and the butcher can hear him plainly. We invite Hobbes here as the primordial (but also classic) representative of moral individualism. Our interest in
him is limited to the single question of whether the structure of individualist
thought admits of human equality.

Hobbes made sparing use of the term "equality" in his great treatise, *The
Leviathan*. It was he who taught our contemporaries to be short on the description of equality and long on its supposed political inferences. Indeed,
the factual equality Hobbes asserted is not merely scant but most peculiar
in content. Early in *Leviathan* he makes the arresting keystone assertion that
all men are essentially equal in their mental and physical abilities:

> The difference between man, and man, is not so considerable . . . as to the
> strength of the body. . . .
>   And as to the faculties of the mind . . . I find yet a greater equality amongst
> men, than that of strength.

To show precisely how far Hobbes proceeds along this descriptive limb, we
have reprinted his words in their entirety in the endnote.[1]

Hobbes refers to this state of affairs as the "equality of ability."[2] He apparently felt that he needed some such notion, however improbable, as justification for a political regime that he hoped to base upon contract, a society
in which all persons would necessarily participate as rational, self-interested
actors. Prudently he separated his fabulous assertions of equality by a full
chapter from the political use he intended to make of them. For it is these

same feeble claims—reasserted now abstractly, as if they were self-evident—
that serve him ambiguously, on the one hand as a supposed natural truth,
and on the other as a "law" or "precept":

> The question who is the better man, has no place in the condition of mere
> nature; where, as has been shewn before, all men are equal. The inequality that
> now is, has been introduced by the laws civil.
>
> If nature therefore have made men equal, that equality is to be acknowledged:
> or if nature have made men unequal; yet because men that think themselves
> equal, will not enter into conditions of peace, but upon equal terms, such equal-
> ity must be admitted. And therefore for the ninth law of nature, I put this, *that
> every man acknowledge another for his equal by nature.*[3]

Here we see Hobbes laying the foundation for the current confusion between descriptive and normative equality. We humans are equal, or, if not,
let us pretend so, because the political program requires it. Hobbes has invented the first "range property" whereby men are simultaneously different
and the same depending upon how one wants it.[4]

Happily we can ignore this subtlety, for the particular descriptive elements
chosen by Hobbes would not by themselves even implicate the idea of
human equality. Whatever that equality may be, it entails a moral dimension.
Physical strength and "faculties of the mind" belong to animals as well as
humans and bear no necessary moral significance (as Hobbes presently confirms with his focus upon the will). Hobbes to this point withholds precisely
what we would need to know in order to speak either for or against human
equality.

The decisive questions are whether humans are connected by natural ties
of moral obligation; whether these ties are distinct in kind from those that
link us vertically to God and the animals; whether it is by shouldering this
lateral obligation that we perfect our own selves; and whether our capacity
for doing so is one of Hobbes's equal "mental faculties" or, if not, whether
that essential capacity might nonetheless be equal in degree. In short, the
two factual equalities Hobbes asserted are not only improbable; even if true
they would be inadequate to support human equality. Conversely, even if
they were untrue, this would not foreclose a human equality based upon a
uniform capacity for moral self-perfection.

This does not mean that Hobbes's version of the human moral self tells
us nothing of his potential allegiance or hostility to human equality, but we
must look elsewhere than the factual equalities he invented for his own
political use. Scanning the *Leviathan*, one can in fact get a rather clear picture
of the human building blocks with which Hobbes is working and which
would determine his position on our question. What is important for our
immediate purpose is the moral structure of the natural self—the self before

government is instituted. Hobbes tells us that there is "no obligation on any man, which ariseth not from some act of his own; for all men . . . are by nature free." In this state of nature, having consented to no rules but his own, each man enjoys a right of choice that is limitless:

> *Naturally every man has right to every thing.* . . . [T]he condition of man . . . is a condition of war of every one against every one . . . [I]n such a condition, every man has a right . . . even to one another's body.[5]
>
> [E]very man has right to every thing; and consequently no action can be unjust. . . . [W]here there is no commonwealth, there is no propriety; all men having right to all things: therefore where there is no commonwealth, there nothing is unjust.[6]

Though he was not consistent, Hobbes gave the propositions just quoted a central place in his thinking. His view of man's moral nature was strongly untraditional. The revolution he wrought did not lie in his association of morality with a free will; the reality of choice had been an assumption common to Western culture and religion—to natural law and the mainstream of Christian doctrine. Hobbes, however, gave choice a special twist. The will is not merely free to choose evil; it is morally unbounded. For the natural self there is simply no idea of duty at all. Here is a twist from which the modern mind is still spinning.[7]

Let us call this notion "radical autonomy." Its core is this: The human individual has no innate moral obligation; until he submits freely to the sovereign state, each person chooses his own law (if the word "law" can be used here). He wills it into existence by a faculty of choice that is utterly free. If Cain is to be subject to a rule that forbids him to strike Abel, Cain himself must will that rule into being. He chooses his own ends, and he wills any constraints upon his behavior in pursuit of those ends. He wills the limits of his own will. In this he is assisted by a faculty of reason whose sole function is to display to the will its practical options.[8] The individual is influenced by circumstance and by his own preferences and passions, but morality imposes no natural fetters upon his choice.

In Hobbes's picture of society, however, this radical autonomy of the individual quickly becomes dissipated. Though created with boundless liberty, every person is irrebuttably presumed to make the same choice; that is, he consents to the rules ordained by the common sovereign. By social contract each of us promptly surrenders his freedom in exchange for security. However stridently he may declare otherwise, his consent is nonetheless imputed. This freedomless freedom leaves radical autonomy thoroughly vacuous within the Hobbesian system, but, again, that is not our concern. What specifically interests us is the notion of an unbounded moral freedom of the original self. It would be too much to say that this view was to become the signature of the entire Enlightenment; what is true is that once and for all Hobbes had legitimated the expression of extreme individualism as an intellectual option. From his time, whatever the literati really believed or practiced, they were entitled to talk as if morality were entirely theirs to invent. For them, aside from sheer survival, nature tells us nothing in particular concerning the good life. This stripped-down model of the moral self was a plain invitation to the political imagination of Europe; it became the pole star for legions of moral adventurers. The dreary relativist so familiar to our time traces his pedigree to Hobbes.

How do the natural humans portrayed by Hobbes stack up as candidates for the relation of human equality? Can their moral apparatus satisfy the criteria we have labeled "importance," "goodness," "laterality," "singularity," and "uniformity"? To state this fivefold division may suggest distinctions sharper than we can in fact sustain, but the loose framework they constitute allows an intelligible evaluation of Hobbes and his intellectual descendants. Our principal focus for the time being will be upon his encounter with the criterion of laterality; equality assumes the existence of an order of real obligation to other persons—an order that serves as the ideal for the self to embrace or refuse. Hobbes is in obvious conflict with that concept, and this dissonance implicates the other four criteria. Indeed, we have focused upon Hobbes precisely because he epitomizes a common form of moral wisdom whose premises exclude the possibility of human equality.

Flunking the Test of Human Equality

At the outset, however, to the extent possible, let us encourage détente. First, assume that the relation among Hobbes's moral selves in their pregovernmental state is what we have called a "double equality." In other words, we will concede that his most plausible host property—the unencumbered will—*could* vary in the degree of its force, but that in fact it does not. This assumption is important. If Hobbes's candidate for the host property were merely the *possession* of will, those who had it would indeed be equal but only trivially so. In order to serve as host for the relation of human equality, the will would need to be potentially variable but actually uniform in potency.

With this assumption, Hobbes at first may appear encouraging to human equality. The radical freedom of the individual to choose his or her own course seems cousin to the kind of moral autonomy that in chapters 2 and 3 we found necessary to the structure of a descriptive equality. Each of the two forms of autonomy includes reason and will as constitutive elements, and each is a capacity through which man "makes himself" to the ideal he chooses. To this extent Hobbes flirts with the convention of human equality. That, however, is the end of the affair.

In truth, Hobbes's radical autonomy is so different as to be virtually the opposite of that required by the convention; for the latter asserts not that the will of man legislates what is good, but that the good has already been legislated for man whether he chooses or rejects it. Equality could concede that the will is "absolute," but only in its freedom to accept or reject real obligation; the self is at liberty to rebel, but it is limited to a rebellion against this preexisting order, for there is nothing else against which to revolt. The more precise term for this human condition is "bounded autonomy," and we will use that label to distinguish our own view from that of Hobbes and company.

The gulf that separates "radical" from "bounded" autonomy is wide. Bounded autonomy, which represents the stronger tradition in the West, claims to be the exclusive form of moral liberty. It rejects the Hobbesian idea of an autonomy that is empty of duty and declares it a contradiction; for law itself is a condition of freedom. The capacity—the freedom—for *moral* choice would not even exist were it not for the order of real, preinstitutional obligation. When the individual chooses, he chooses for or against that order. That is how moral choice is defined. Cain is absolutely free to reject the law and to kill Abel; he is not free to convert that act into a fulfillment of law. Cain does not create law. His autonomy is limited to the option to obey the law or to rebel. That is what freedom is.[9]

Hobbes defines freedom negatively, as the absence of constraint. One can give this a positive form by saying that the individual will is the sole author of whatever rules it chooses to recognize; in any case, Hobbes represents a strong form of "moral subjectivism," but we must pause to clarify this usage. The subjective/objective distinction does not capture the crucial difference between radical and bounded autonomy; the bounded version, too, is subjective insofar as the recognition of and submission to the lateral moral imperative also occur within the self. In bounded autonomy reason interprets its own experience, striving to present to the self the specific behavior that would fulfill the lateral imperative regarding fellow humans. But the self's consciousness of its own subordination, its search for correct answers, and the act of choice itself produce no empirical trace. To this extent, bounded autonomy indeed is subjective.

It definitely is not subjective, however, in the Hobbesian sense that choices are made in isolation from all authority but the choosing self. In Hobbes's version of natural man, moral choice is nothing but the action of will exploiting its subordinate faculty of reason and discriminating among the various passions that compete for satisfaction in every particular decision.[10] There is no external moral order to be sought. Indeed, order exists neither inside nor outside until the self decrees it. It is this picture of naked will—a morally empty self, disconnected from other selves—that made it possible for various of Hobbes's successors to view moral judgments as reports of mere sentiments peculiar to the person judging. In an act of moral lobotomy Hobbes reintroduced the ancient possibility of nihilism. Much of Western moral philosophy since 1700 has consisted of the struggle to preserve this exaggerated individualism while distinguishing it from anarchy.

By reducing value to individual preference, Hobbes is already at odds with the convention. Ordinary people see the moral faculties as important precisely for their aid in separating real good from real evil—not for their Promethean power to create the one or the other. Few of us picture ourselves as the originators of the good; fewer yet concede that power to our neighbor.[11] This is not to deny our tolerance for variety. The butcher may cheerfully overlook eccentric preferences. What he rarely does is admire their substantive content simply on the ground that the choice to pursue them was made without moral constraint. Mrs. McDevitt's calculated decision to get drunk or to despise her neighbor is no occasion for his admiration, even though she made her choice with ever so much gusto and contempt for rules. Pluralism of such an extreme sort is an acquired taste, and few butchers acquire it. Or so it appears to us. Doubtless this could be wrong. Possibly this generation has come to accept "doing your own thing" as the ultimate meaning of the good. Our experience of people at every point in the age spectrum runs to the contrary. It is difficult to see how human equality can peacefully coexist with radical moral autonomy, for the one is commonly cherished and the other is rejected.

Note that the exaggeration of autonomy is a problem for Hobbes quite apart from his reliance upon social contract to set the rules. Contract is merely a device and could serve as the instrument of a real, lateral good that is congenial to equality. The Hobbesian difficulty is that *all* obligation is made to rest upon contract alone. And to make the human will the author of all value is to cripple moral discourse. If there can be no morally intelligible evaluation of the choices of individuals, the concept of the good appears empty. People simply choose what they choose. All decisions are, by definition, right; but it would be as meaningful to say that they are all left. In either case Hobbes has eliminated every hope to distinguish the one from the other except by force or ballot (neither solution having the moral advantage). Our relations to other humans and, for that matter, to the beasts, are brought under the same master—the ego. What Hobbes would offer as the host property for human equality is the individual capacity for caprice.

Now we observe that this absence of a morality that precedes human institutions also leaves a second criterion of equality unsatisfied by Hobbes; this is the requirement that the relation be distinctive or "singular." Recall from chapter 2 that convention requires human equality to have its own metaphysical status. We showed how this singularity is possible: equality is a *third* relation arising as humans encounter one another, discovering a form of lateral obligation that is distinct from the two already owed—the one to God above, the other to the animals below. Singularity has two subconditions. One is the reality of the unique order of potential lateral obligation between persons; the other is their becoming conscious of that order, an event that creates the relation and brings the individuals under its thrall.

Hobbes implicitly denies this singularity; for him the mutual recognition of persons raises no distinct kind of moral connection; indeed, it raises none at all. We may use one another as we would use the trees and animals. In the human encounter we become related to one another in the manner that each of us was already related to the pig.[12]

Hobbes Replies

Assuming that Hobbes nevertheless cares to register as a true believer in a descriptive equality, how might he respond? An argument along the following lines might be made: There is an innate and stable property even in the radically autonomous self; humans do not will just anything at all. It is only by this lawlike aspect of our nature that individuals finally all consent to— indeed create—the sovereign whom they agree to obey. The self's consciousness of this regulating impulse is initially triggered by its perception of other persons; they are the occasion of its animation. This event—this "encounter"—generates a transformation no less dramatic than the one we chose to call the "recognition" of lateral obligation. Hobbes would say that the same occurs for radically autonomous man when he, like Adam, encounters his own kind. In this moment of recognition each human self experiences a mutation significant enough to be the foundation of a new relation; we might even declare this new consciousness a "capacity" and, if it were uniform in degree, it would be fit to serve as the metaphysical ground for the relation of human equality.

None of this, however, is correct. To be sure, in Hobbes the experience of recognition alters something. Specifically, the human encounter discloses particular risks and opportunities that the wholly isolated self had not yet faced. But awareness of these new possibilities is the only alteration in the self, and such a change is insufficient. There is nothing about these risks and opportunities embodied in other human persons that could distinguish them from those already presented in dumb nature. There is death; there is pleasure. These existed before the human encounter, and they endure thereafter. The advent of other humans may alter the probabilities of imminent death or pleasure and may multiply their potential forms. But only if the recognition of others initiates the consciousness of obligation is there anything distinctive in the relation among humans. Perceiving the other person, Hobbes's self experiences fear and hope, but this is hardly new. It is, rather, the same radical egoism, and it exhausts the content of the natural moral self. Even if Hobbes could conceive of fear and hope as "law," that particular law had already been activated before the arrival of the Other by every prior experience that befell the lonely individual; for Hobbes there is no other law of which one could become conscious merely by experiencing the human encounter. Fear and hope were familiars of the isolated individual. These remain. Nothing is added.

This is a basic but tricky point, and an eccentric perspective may help to clarify it. Hobbes's problem here can be thought of as the mirror image of the difficulty that would be raised were we to write a chapter asking the equality question about purely spiritual beings. Specifically, could angels have among themselves a relation of equality analogous to human equality? We have in mind the medieval angel of Aquinas who was pure spirit and not his incarnations by Milton or Scripture.[13] Aquinas and his age stripped the heavenly hosts of their flaming swords and bulging muscles. In doing so they denied the angels the kinds of moral commerce that are possible among men. Having no bodies, angels cannot, qua angel, affect one another's lives (or even ours) except, perhaps, by permission or by special divine deputation. In any case, let us suppose this to be so. There could, then, be no issue of an angelic morality except in the ascendant order. As Lucifer discovered, that particular order is real, but it is unidimensional. Angels answer only to God. When sin is their aim, their sole choice among the seven deadly varieties is pride; for there is no medium in which they can affect another created being. Angelic selves are so thoroughly isolated, even from one another, that Aquinas regarded each as a separate species.[14]

Like Hobbes's men, such creatures could not generate a real and positive relation of equality grounded upon their moral powers, for they lack the necessary properties. Assuming they could become mutually aware, that awareness would add no morally relevant information to their original selves. No new responsibilities would emerge. They would experience no inclination to declare a code of "angelic rights and duties." Though angels might (or might not) appear "the same" to one another in the structure of their individual rationality and free will, they would lack a medium in which either to threaten or nurture one another; they would lack moral reciprocity. Beings who can neither suffer nor make suffer cannot be brothers. And herein lies the curious counterpoint to Hobbes. For him, men are merely flesh without order; by contrast, angels are order without flesh. Mutual recognition among beings of either sort could generate no distinctive moral relation of equality—human or angelic.

Changing the Assumption

So far we have assumed that if Hobbes's candidate for host property satisfied the first four criteria of equality, it would satisfy the fifth; that is, we supposed the radically autonomous will to be uniform in both possession and degree. Now let us test this by reversing our assumption. Let us suppose now that the relation which would be generated by such a will meets the four tests of importance, goodness, laterality, and singularity. Let the question now become whether this unbounded Hobbesian capacity to choose could in any case claim uniformity.

The answer is determined by the role Hobbes assigns to reason in the process of moral choice. In the conventional view of choice the autonomy of the self is bounded; the will's function is either to seek or reject the real good of others. In such a view, reason's part is to identify that good as best it can. It has the specific task of being diligent in this quest, and that mission of diligence can be fully accomplished even by the person with the weakest power of reason. By contrast, in a radical autonomy of the Hobbesian sort where the will *creates* the good by its own choices, reason's function is quite different. Its task is not to seek the good but to display the array of options available to be chosen; it is a scout that reports the alternative possibilities to the sovereign will. The will then chooses among the specific outcomes presented. First, it decides what it likes best; then it decides which strategy will yield the most of what it likes.

In such an enterprise, any variation in the degree of intellect affects the individual capacity to choose and to get the most of what it chooses. It determines what one *can* choose, because to choose requires that one be able in some degree to conceive of the object. For Hobbes's choosers this is a serious problem, for they must select specific outcomes; that is, there is no possibility of their simply aspiring to the good itself as an ideal, for there is no such thing. Indeed, there is nothing good—whether ideal or objective—until it is already chosen. By contrast, for the obtending person there is always a good; the problem is to find it, but it is the very effort to do so that works moral self-perfection. For Hobbes there is nothing like this— there is no good to be sought but only an endless kaleidoscope of neutral possibilities. Hence the smarter person has the advantage in power; he can conceive the greater range of possibilities from which to confect his own good.[15] Uniformity of capacity is thus unimaginable.

Uniformity of a sort could be achieved, perhaps, by reconceiving the will as the end in itself; that is, the good would somehow consist in the very act of willing. With the will recast as a purely formal power, perhaps all rational persons could be said by Hobbes to have uniform capacity; since everyone can will, there is some relation of equality among them. They are descriptively equal in having a will. So far so good. This is indeed a uniformity—a relation of equality. This, however, does not get us very far toward anything justifying the label "human equality." First, the purely formal capacity to will *could not* vary in degree. Being uniform simply by definition, it creates an equality of no interest to us. It is a "single" equality—one of possession only. To attach the adjective "equal" would be almost a redundancy; for once we have said that rational persons have wills, we have said everything important.

Furthermore, a self that wills only for the sake of willing has no capacity to self-perfect or even to regress. It simply wills, and that's the end of it (even if its will were to refuse to will). Any concept of self-perfection obviously requires the possibility of change of the self through particular choices; the self must have something at stake, the will becoming not the end but the instrument for attaining the chosen ideal. Thus in what we call bounded autonomy there are real human chips on the table; by its choices the will effects the transition toward a good or bad intention, hence toward a particular altered moral state.

In radical autonomy of the purely formal sort (will for will's sake), there is really *nothing* at stake, for no altered state is even relevant but only the will as it was and is—and whatever it wills. The individualist could of course shift ground yet once again by reintroducing the relevance of particular choices. He could tell us once more that the self auto-determines the particular objects that will constitute its own self-perfection. But such a move (apart from its offense to convention) only takes us back to that state of disuniformity that is fatal to human equality; even if what one designs on one's own terms could be called self-perfection, our individual cognitive power would affect the degree of our capacity (1) to conceive possible objects and states; and (2) to attain them.

There is one other possible reconception of the Hobbesian will. It would not be a sheer contradiction to assert that the human will as such *could* vary in power. Indeed, it is often said loosely of individuals that they have special "strength of will." Let us assume that wills can vary in strength wholly apart from any particular object. The wills of Alice and Marylyn could then, in like proportion, be devoted to the object of being elected president, but Alice could will that specific objective with greater absolute strength. She could do so because, from the start, she had more capacity to will anything at all—whether it be apples, shoes, or a ride in the park.

If wills could vary thus in their strength, it would still be theoretically possible that they do not vary in fact. In that event there would exist a double equality, and to that extent it would constitute what is required for human equality; the relation would rest upon a host property uniform both in possession and degree. Again, however, the problem is that the ordinary person would attach no importance to this possibility. There is nothing interesting in the uniformity of a capacity unless it is a capacity *for something* (other than the capacity itself). There must be some matter at stake before anyone could care about the uniformity of our capacity to seek or avoid it. And that is just what will for will's sake denies.

Contract and Equality

We will give Hobbes still another chance for harmony with human equality. Let us consider his radical demolition of the moral self to be merely the windup for his real pitch, which is social contract. Hobbes had strategic reasons for slaughtering preinstitutional obligation. Principally he wanted to clear the way for an order of public sovereignty that would be insulated both from ecclesiastical claims and from the constraints of the law of nature, as those claims and constraints had been understood by prior generations. In doing so, he initiated Western philosophy's obsession for grounding law and morality upon contract.[16] For Hobbes, the incentive to the social bargain lies in the individual's fear of lethal competition. Terror inspires the universal submission to a sovereign whose unchallengeable will promises security. Hobbes's idea of the social contract was so general as to be applicable to virtually any form of society he knew, including absolute monarchy. It was a conservative notion and accepted as such by contemporaries; with few exceptions, whatever the appointed sovereign ordains represents the good for his subjects. Furthermore, they have consented to it; their obligation is to obey any recognizable and minimally stable government whether it be a person or an institution.

Is it here that the individualist might locate some substantial relation of equality? If Hobbes's view of the natural self was unable to support it, perhaps it could be grounded instead in what becomes of the self within this apparatus of social contract. As the self moves from its original isolation and amorality into participation in the sovereign state, does it acquire something separate from the will and reason that it already had? If so, could this new self support a relation that would satisfy the convention and be worthy of belief?

Perhaps. Contractarians might argue that the necessary supplementation of the naked moral self occurs in the individual act of consent; here is the place to seek the emergence of a distinctive relation of human equality. Before that consent the individual was free; by it he becomes forever bound. There could be no more substantial alteration of the self. Here is an assent by the individual to whatever forms of lateral duty the sovereign may decree. The self is suddenly linked to a moral objectivity considerably more definite in content than the wispy ordinances of natural or religious law. Adam has embraced the internal revenue code; what could be a more dramatic instance of a new relation between him and other persons and of a new moral consciousness of a real obligation?

This claim can even be restated in something like our own terms. Consent is equivalent to Adam's "encounter" with the Other; in this decisive act of consent there is "recognition" of real "obligation" in the lateral order. This experience is new to the self and inaugurates a discrete relation between persons. In some sense it is even more distinctive than the authors' claim about the effect of awakening to an extant preinstitutional morality. In Hobbes's tale, consent does not arouse some slumbering capacity that recognizes a preexisting order of obligation. The event is not an awakening at all but a creation. When consent is given, obligation springs ex nihilo from the will of unobligated man.

Maybe, but there are difficulties. We concede straightaway that the legal order decreed by Hobbes's sovereign, unless it be exceptionally wicked, is deserving of obedience; that is, under proper circumstances social contract creates genuine duties. But real duties require real moral actors for their formation. Social contract can be the work only of moral beings who are already aware of their preinstitutional obligation to seek a just social order. Where such a social order comes to exist they indeed are bound to honor it, but only because they were already bound to recognize the common good whichever political form it might assume.[17]

Hobbes's problem is to create a real order out of fake people. When the moral starting point of his actors is zero, how are they to bind themselves by promise? Social contract for Hobbes is a case of something from nothing. Further, even if this unpromising creature could—godlike—create duty by his own consent, why can he not uncreate it? Finally, there is no sanction for violations that go undetected; the self is uninjured by its own secret crimes, and the "duty" that is created by contract thus can only be understood as the duty not to get caught by the civil authorities or the neighbors; it has nothing to do with the moral perfection of the self. And of course for Hobbes it cannot. Once he got himself committed to radical individualism as human nature, the idea of virtue—of character, of moral self-perfection—became very hard to sustain. Indeed, his successors have been reduced to talking about legal rights; in the process, the possibility of a human moral vocation has largely evaporated.

When Hobbes's individual makes law through social contract, he may achieve practical order, but he does not achieve auto-alteration. Nature is unchanged. Consent to the command of Leviathan is merely the device chosen by the same unobligated ego as its strategy of survival and self-maximizing. The social contract as conceived by radical individualism is a deal that is negotiated at arms' length by hostile parties. Grounded specifically in fear, the contract is a legalistic relationship among wary self-seekers. Within this negotiated regime the self, though domesticated, remains precisely as it was—both inward-turning and morally vacuous. There is nothing new here that could serve as the host property of the relation of human equality. Each of us is as he was—a lone gun and every man's enemy.

Social contract appears to fail as well on uniformity grounds. Here it is not easy even to identify the subject of the question; Hobbes's candidate for host property of the relation of human equality is elusive, because the only concern of social contract is enforceable rights and duties, not moral perfection of the self. If an analogy to self-perfection is even possible—we are unsure—it would have to be located in the capacity of the rational self to observe the terms of positive law. From Hobbes's perspective, the nearest an individual can come to perfection is in honoring the letter and spirit of the community compact. Certainly all rational people have some capacity for this. But is that capacity conceivably uniform? Plainly not, for the rules of social order are an object of intellect, and the ability to grasp them is affected by talent and circumstance.

A last possibility: One could have a sort of "good will" toward the content—known and unknown—of the civil and criminal codes and the whole apparatus of man-made law. Using our own terms, law itself could be the object of an obtension; one commits oneself to search and to submit. The subjective product of this personal commitment would consist of the most law-abiding citizen this individual could be. It would be a self-perfection in which the objective ideal of the obtension is supplied by Caesar. Examples? One thinks first of Socrates and the respect he paid, even unto death, to the social form of law. The trouble with the example is that Socrates was willing to die for human law precisely because he was already committed to a higher law. By comparison, the man who loves law simply because Leviathan has uttered it seems a rather puny moral type. Still, the subjective law-hero is a possibility. We all know examples of the person whose chief moral advice is "obey the law, whatever it is." In principle, all rational persons could possess, in uniform degree, this capacity to will the objective realization of the purposes and particulars of law qua law. The real stopper to this idea is not the disuniformity of this capacity, but its triviality. There is simply no *moral* point to willing the realization of the law unless, like Socrates, you have some independent moral reason that makes this a thing worth doing.

These various conflicts with equality probably hold for all forms of moral relativism of which individualism and Hobbesian social contract are examples. By relativism we mean the notion that lateral morality and law can be nothing other than artifacts of culture and thus may differ fundamentally from society to society. In this view whatever rules come into being and pass away do so either by consent or by imposition of superior power. Society may always change the terms. Some individuals will internalize the newly proffered rules, and some will not. At any given moment, different individuals assent to conflicting versions of the rules en route to a new consensus.

The patterns of their allegiance determine which among competing assertions can credibly claim the status of rules at any instant in the social flux. Either the relation of human equality rests upon sterner stuff or it is nonsense. What is surprising is that many in the academy continue to suppose that Hobbes has provided the clue to equality. Something in his view of man tantalizes Western philosophers, and they return to it perennially seeking to reconcile radical autonomy with moral stability. With his universal solvent Hobbes has stripped away every moral distinction; nevertheless, egoistic philosophy continues to hope that this very emptiness may prove the doorway to some equality of the infinite. Like the dead Ahab, Hobbes vaguely beckons. And they follow—into the void.

It should by now be plain where this chapter is headed. If Hobbes faithfully prefigures his "liberal" successors, any claim that they have supported a descriptive human equality could be a historic misunderstanding. It may be that the idea of equality became popular in Western history just as intellectuals began to abandon the only commitments that could have sustained it.

The Career of Radical Autonomy

Did Enlightenment politicians announce human equality at the very moment that Enlightenment philosophy made equality impossible? The answer is not so clear; or at least Hobbes is not the whole story. If Hobbes was the first liberal, in an important sense he was also the last—at least until our own day. Certainly this is so with respect to the question of man's metaphysical makeup. None of the succeeding giants of the Enlightenment was ready to reduce man to quite the moral vacuum Hobbes perceived; that final embrace of nihilism had to await the despair of elites in the consciously unenlightened twentieth century. Even in Hobbes's own time John Locke (1632–1704), to a considerable degree, revived the traditional interpretation of natural man as a being subject to a moral imperative that is innate, authoritative, and recognizable in broad outline by the individual.[18] Such a natural order did not of course preclude—indeed it invited—authentic social contract. The good society was to come as a perfection wrought by all of us through reason and choice; but its negotiated terms were to be monitored by preinstitutional constraints imposed by God and nature.[19] Locke proclaimed, of course, with historic effect the terms of a new political order of self-governing men. In this we see him as the quintessential liberal, and so he was; that is, he was a political liberal.[20] Metaphysically he remained relatively conservative, recognizing a structure of preinstitutional obligation that is evident to men even in a state of nature, one that holds simply by virtue of their being human.

Radical autonomy, nevertheless, was out of the bottle. Among Hobbes's immediate successors perhaps David Hume's (1711–1776) picture of man comes the closest to the amoral egoist—at least at the surface. Hume took considerable pain to assure us that morality was sheer sentiment and wholly relative to the culture into which one is born. He tells us, indeed, that mankind invented the laws of nature. At the same time Hume concedes that at some deep level all known human societies are in agreement about morality.[21] This in itself may not convict Hume of contradiction. Maybe this deep universal agreement came about by coincidence—some amazing moral accident. The real tension arises from the concessions by Hume that mankind could hardly have invented any moral law other than the one it had chosen.[22] Did he or did he not accept Hobbes's radical autonomy? Hume was destined to become a common intellectual type in the West. His shuffling between the subjectivism of Hobbes and a kind of quasi-objective morality prefigures modern versions of relativism that scorn all dogma yet can march on moral crusades that discredit their own skeptical premise. It is not apparent how such minds in his age or ours could coherently address the question about a descriptive equality.

Jean Jacques Rousseau (1712–1778) is an even more exaggerated example of trying to have it both ways regarding man's nature. In the *Social Contract* he first tells us:

> Man loses by the social contract his *natural* liberty, and an unlimited right to all which tempts him, and which he can obtain; in return he acquires *civil* liberty, and proprietorship of all he possesses. [W]e must distinguish natural liberty, which knows no bounds but the power of the individual, from civil liberty, which is limited by the general will; and between possession, which is only the effect of force or of the right of the first occupant, from property, which must be founded on a positive title.[23]

Rousseau's autonomous individual thus seems as Hobbesian as one could wish. And this is confirmed by his identification of the transformation that civilization works upon the natural man:

> The passing from the state of nature to the civil state produces in man a very remarkable change, by substituting justice for instinct in his conduct, and giving to his actions a moral character which they lacked before. It is then only that the voice of duty succeeds to physical impulse, and a sense of what is right, to the incitements of appetite. Man, who had till then regarded none but himself, perceives that he must act on other principles, and learns to consult his reason before he listens to his inclinations.[24]

This change in the self takes place with the formation of social contract. It is not the inevitable effect of man's encounter with man but of his submission to the "general will." As with Hobbes, this would seem to leave Rousseau in conflict with our interpretation of conventional equality. There may be a "remarkable change" in the individual, but it is a change only in the external order that the egoistic self has ordained by its own consent. It remains the same old self, though now adorned with the particular legal duties and rights for which it has bargained.[25] Rousseau's *Discourse Upon the Origin and Meaning of Inequality Among Mankind*, however, suggests a different outlook. Not only is man a good deal more amiable in his original nature than Hobbes would have him; he has a concern for others that is innate. Furthermore, this latent empathy rises to consciousness at the moment of the human encounter:

> Pity is a natural sentiment, which, by moderating in every individual the activity of self-love, contributes to the mutual preservation of the whole species. It is this pity which hurries us without reflection to the assistance of those we see in distress; it is this pity which, in a state of nature, stands for laws, for manners, for virtue, with this advantage, that no one is tempted to disobey her sweet and gentle voice.[26]

Pity, however, is merely a fact for Rousseau. It is an impulse that comes "without reflection"—a kind of autonomic, hence amoral, response in which reason could play no part except possibly to corrupt pity with self-interest. We find here no order or rule challenging man to respond with intellect and will. Essentially an animal reaction, this capacity for pity could not constitute the host property. It is an involuntary response irrelevant to morality. Further, it adds nothing singular to the self; reason receives no constitutive glimpse of authentic lateral duty. The self remains feral and morally uncompleted. Conventional human equality is out of the question.

Equality, Luck, and "Homo Noumenon"

Immanuel Kant (1724–1804) provides a rather different example for our purposes. Kant, though arguably the epitome of the Enlightenment, is the philosophical apostle of human equality. His moral philosophy is studded with literal affirmations of an "equality" that arguably is grounded upon the five premises of conventional human equality. The modern literature on human equality—such as it is—is saturated with Kantian concepts.

Kant philosophized long after the invention of modern science, even as it portended the eclipse of its own inventors. Science with a capital "s" had promised wonderful new knowledge. But among its deliverances was the report that man is merely a determined cog in a mechanistic universe. This worried Kant. For as one of Kant's modern interpreters puts it, "if Nature were responsible for the realization of 'moral character,' that would counterproductively result in determined, that is, amoral character."[27] If human conduct is causally determined, goodness and evil, virtue and vice, are non-sense. Morality—the moral evaluation of humans—requires that humans be free, rather than determined; but human freedom was exactly what the emergent science seemed to render illusory.

Kant set about rescuing freedom. As Kant conceived his task, it was no minor labor but rather a revolution he modestly styled Copernican. Kant essentially conceded the determinists' claim that what we can see of man, his "phenomenal" nature, is causally determined; but he deprived that concession of its sting by asserting that man is no mere this-worldly phenomenon. Man's "true self," according to Kant, is a "noumenon." This strange word is Kant's way of designating a pure intelligence, which together with other "noumena," makes up a "noumenal world." Though beyond empirical examination, that world of pure intelligence is not at all remote. As a rational being, man is already a part of it. There alone he truly is himself—an autonomous and self-determining actor, not just a determined confluence of external causes.

If this noumenal realm seems unfamiliar, it should. It lies, according to Kant, utterly outside human experience and knowledge. But—and this is the linchpin of Kant's ethics—man must, if he is to understand himself as free and thus subject to moral evaluation, *regard* himself as a material and determined phenomenal being, and *simultaneously*—in his true self—a purely intellectual and undetermined noumenal being. This is Kant's much maligned theory of the "two viewpoints," in defense of which Kant wrote:

> There is not the slightest contradiction in holding that a *thing as an appearance* (as belonging to the sensible world) is subject to certain laws of which it is independent *as a thing* or being *in itself*. That he must represent and conceive himself in this double way rests, as regards the first side, on consciousness of himself as an object affected through the senses; as concerns the second side, on consciousness of himself as intelligence—that is, as independent of sensuous impressions in his use of reason (and so as belonging to the intelligible world).[28]

Though man cannot be certain that he (or anyone else) is part of this purely intelligible world, its existence is, for Kant, a necessary postulate of morality. Making sense of Kant's moral metaphysics, then, requires keeping clear this strange idea that man must *regard* himself as a pure other-worldly intelligence and, exactly thus, capable of autonomy.

But if freedom from compulsion fits man for moral evaluation, autonomy alone does not make a person morally good or virtuous. If he were free but subject to no law, there would be no standard by which to judge his use of his freedom. Man is capable of morality exactly because his "true self" is not only free but also *under a law*.[29] That law is pure reason—reason functioning on its own terms, without the influence of man's phenomenal side.[30] Reason can be a law without vitiating man's autonomy, because it does not coerce man's choices but leaves him free to follow or flout its directives.[31] Choosing according to the law of pure reason, and thus refusing to be determined according to his sensible interests and personal preference, the rational person lives "autonomously."[32] Hence, in a carefully considered juxtaposition, Kant calls pure reason the "law of autonomy."[33] Freedom and law are, according to Kant, "so inextricably bound together that practical freedom could be defined through the will's independence of everything except the moral law."[34] The Law of Autonomy is a "universal law"—*universal* because it provides the reasons for choice and action for all rational beings, without exception; *law* because it is mandatory for all rational beings, without exception.[35] "For Kant . . .," as a recent interpreter explains, "the road to autonomy," and thus to morality, "is through that self-imposed discipline or self-mastery necessary to adopt rules by which we transcend individuality in favor of universality."[36]

A rational person thus imposes the law of pure reason on himself, and what pure reason commands a rational person, according to Kant, is this: Act upon a maxim that can also hold as a universal law.[37] This is Kant's first and most famous formulation of the "categorical imperative," the form that the Law of Autonomy takes as it guides man's choices.[38] The categorical imperative commands that man adopt "maxims." These are internal principles of action, expressions of how a man means to act. The categorical imperative commands that he should will to act solely on the basis of reason and thus on grounds that would be valid for any rational agent. The categorical imperative

> is concerned, not with the matter of the action and its presumed results, but with its form and with the principle from which it follows; and what is essentially good in the action consists in the mental disposition, let the consequences be what they may. This imperative may be called the imperative of *morality*.[39]

The will is made good, and the person virtuous, by acting from respect of the moral law as the only determining ground of the will.[40] Kant's famous way of putting the point is that what makes a person moral is acting *from* duty. "We stand," in Kant's words, "under a *discipline* of reason, and . . . we must not forget our subjection to it, or withdraw anything from it, or by an egotistical illusion detract from the authority of the law (even though it is one given by our own reason)."[41]

Sometimes Kant is interpreted as making virtue depend on one's actually being reasonable in all one's choices; Kant's stress on *reason* does vaguely suggest a cognitive morality more within the reach of some than of others.[42] There is ambiguity, sometimes even contradiction, in his moral philosophy, but at curtain time Kant seems to settle on conditions of morality that make virtue possible for every rational person. The most basic premise of Kant's moral theory is that only if people are *capable* of morality can they be under a moral *obligation*; for him, "ought" always implies "can." But since, according to Kant, we can never know the depths of our heart and the purity of our motives, to require that we act solely from the motive of duty might be to obligate us to do what we cannot know that we can do. What alone every rational person can do is to *adopt the maxim* always to act from duty alone and strive "as well as lies in our power" to do so.[43] "It is a human being's duty to *strive* for [moral] perfection, but not to *reach* it (in this life), and his compliance with this duty can, accordingly, consist only in continual progress."[44]

Such a morality of "good intentions"—as Kant's is sometimes described—will harmonize with conventional equality so long as it is not a pure subjectivity. We need to ask whether Kant's ethics satisfy equality's demand for "objectivity." Kant's infamous assertion that man must be "self-legislating" has to some ears the haunting ring of Hobbes. But there can be no question that Kant postulates preinstitutional obligation; indeed, it consists in the categorical imperative. True, man has a *choice* about whether to follow this universal law; but such freedom is (as we argued in chapter 3) a necessary condition of human equality, regardless of whether the source of preinstitutional obligation is called nature, God, or the imperative. Moreover, Kant certainly believes that the correct application of the categorical imperative specifies an order of lateral correct behaviors.[45] He even believes that what a person is doing in the world raises an inference about whether he has a "good will."[46]

But where Kant broke decidedly with the tradition was in his insistence that what alone has *moral* worth is what everyone can achieve, the will that is made good by adopting the maxim always to act from duty:

> The good will is not good because of what it effects or accomplishes or because of its adequacy to achieve some proposed end; it is good only because of its willing, i.e., it is good of itself. . . . Even if it should happen that, by a particularly unfortunate fate or by the niggardly provision of a stepmotherly nature, this will should be wholly lacking in power to accomplish its purpose, and if even the greatest effort should not avail it to achieve anything of its end, and if there remained only the good will . . ., it would sparkle like a jewel in its own right, as something that had its full worth in itself.[47]

Kant satisfies the criterion of uniformity by making morality pivot on an act of which everyone is equally capable: committing to duty and then pursuing its terms as best one can.[48]

Human equality is no accident in Kant's moral metaphysics. Facing a deterministic world in which people might excuse themselves from morality by their inability to satisfy morality's commands, Kant cut to the quick. He eliminated excuse by making morality accessible to all. It is exactly because man is under a moral law which he can fulfill that he possesses "*dignity* (an absolute inner worth)." And it is exactly because all rational beings are under this law which each is equally capable of fulfilling that a rational person "can measure himself with every other being of this kind and value himself on a footing of equality with them."[49] Kant's second formulation of the categorical imperative in fact enjoins every rational actor to make his maxims regard his own humanity as possessing the same dignity as every other rational person.[50]

Kant's ethics is a thoroughgoing morality of equals, supported by a tailor-made metaphysics. For Kant, as Bernard Williams aptly puts it, "the success-ful moral life, removed from considerations of birth, lucky upbringing, or indeed of the incomprehensible Grace of a non-Pelagian God, is presented as a career open not merely to the talents, but to a talent which all rational beings necessarily possess in the same degree."[51] The hard question that remains is whether the equality Kant's moral philosophy yields is an essen-tially *human* equality.[52] Kant's work, according to Williams,

> contains the working out to the very end of that thought, a thought which in less thoroughgoing forms marks the greatest difference between moral ideas influenced by Christianity, and those of the ancient world. It is this thought, that moral worth must be separated from any natural advantage whatsoever, which, consistently pursued by Kant, leads to the conclusion that the source of moral thought and action must be located outside of the empirically condi-tioned self.[53]

The Kantian capacity for a "good will" is believable as a host property for a relation of equality exactly for the reasons Kant has accumulated so many modern enemies; that is, he has reduced the "self" to the pure noumenon under the law of reason. A "shattering failure"[54] is how Williams describes the result, because "no human characteristic which is relevant to degrees of moral esteem can escape being an empirical characteristic, subject to empiri-cal conditions, psychological history and individual variation."[55] There just *isn't*, from where Williams sits, a noumenal self—a "true self" exempt from empirical determination. Nor in any event, according to Williams, would locating a noumenal self solve the perceived problem, for it would be too thin, too other-worldly to count as *human*. Kant's Herculean efforts to shelter some "true self" from ineluctable empirical degradation result—to Wil-liams's mind—in a "*reductio ad absurdum*."[56] The human whom Kant would shelter from fickle fortune has been shaved down to a metaphysical noth-ing—a noumenon.

Williams is not alone in these trenchant objections. But even if the nou-menal aspect of Kant's world was interred with its architect, the broader themes and ideas of his ethics have flowered (as in Kierkegaard). As one of his leading current interpreters observes, "the Kantian view or something closely akin to it seems clearly to be the way many people think about morality even today, particularly those reared in the Judeo-Christian tradition. Kant often says what they themselves would say about their own moral life, were they to articulate it."[57] Kant does what no earlier philosopher had managed: he separates the highest form of human achievement, *moral* goodness or the "good will," from every other form of human good. That separation is absolutely critical to human equality; without it people's access to the highest form of human worth varies with their empirical opportunities. The belief in factual human equality requires a belief in some nonempirical human capacity for a nonempirical form of human goodness. The pressing question is whether such a capacity can be identified this side of an imagined noumenal realm.

Our own answer began with the refrain that human equality and its host property are matters for belief, not proof. If human equality is true, it is not in respect to any host property we can see or touch; it is, as we have urged, because all rational persons share uniformly the capacity to be morally good. But that is believable if, first, all rational humans have a uniform capacity freely to strive to discover and realize the correct way and, second, if this striving works a person's moral self-perfection. This belief is not at all exotic; indeed, this is the element of Kantianism that, we think, has passed into the common mind (or vice versa).[58] Nor, so far as we can tell, does it *require* belief in Kantian noumena. So long as human freedom is real, and goodness crowns the faithful commitment to lateral duty, equality is possible.

What Williams and the other "moral 'luckists' " (such as Thomas Nagel and Martha Nussbaum) eschew is the idea that goodness is equally available to all. Advocating the idea that a person's moral makeup is (partly) determined by fortune, Williams et al. deny—primarily on the authority of Greek philosophy, secondarily on the authority of their interpretation of common moral intuitions—that there is any kind of human worth which is even partially independent of external advantage (that is, of luck). Kant's moral philosophy is a protest of exactly this idea, as Williams realizes:

> The idea that one's whole life can in some . . . way be rendered immune to luck has perhaps rarely prevailed (since it did not prevail, for instance, in mainstream Christianity), but its place has been taken by the still powerfully influential idea that there is one basic form of value, moral value, which is immune to luck and—in the crucial term of the idea's most rigorous exponent—"unconditioned."[59]

That exponent of course is Kant, who marshalls—against the Greek philosophical position—the common judgment that morality is universally obligatory because it is universally possible.

The ostensible subject of this continuing debate is the seemingly abstract question, what is morality? But the driving subtext—of which both Kant and the "moral luckists" never lose sight—is this: Who has the aptitude for this precious achievement? It cannot be surprising that elites—whether ancient or modern, Greek or English—discover morality to be a function of (their own) good luck. By contrast, the conventional belief in human equality is the butcher's nontechnical way of saying that "moral luck" is nonsense. It may also be, as we intimated in chapter 3, that the idea of a totally nonempirical form of goodness would make sense only if there were someone (God?) to recognize it.[60] In any case, such a goodness is part of the common mind, given voice in the convention about human equality. We turn now to a more extended discussion of the Greek philosophical tradition; it is one that Kant protested but which in our own time is discovering Kantian connections.

5

NATURE, NATURAL LAW, AND EQUALITY

If morals and ethics are not based on nature or on reality, then
what else are or can they be based on?
(Henry Veatch, *Human Rights: Fact or Fancy?*)

Nature loves to hide.
(Heraclitus, fragment 22 B 123 Diels)

I N COONS'S FAVORITE movie Humphrey Bogart defends his taste for
gin, explaining to Katharine Hepburn that it is "human nature" for man
(or at least men) to drink. She demurs: "Nature, Mr. Allnut, is what we
are put in this world to rise above."[1] In a novel dear to Brennan, Lord Henry
rejects the precious moralizing of Basil: "If you want to mar a nature, you
have merely to reform it."[2]

Whether nature is a clue to the good (or indeed *is* the good) has engaged
the mind of the West since antiquity. The Greeks conceived the question
and elaborated its answers; the Romans took it up, invested it with legal
significance, and bequeathed it to the medieval theologians, philosophers,
and canonists; they in turn made it a cornerstone of ambitious and influential moral systems. Eventually it became the preoccupation of the Protestants
Grotius and Pufendorf and the Anglican Hooker, passing through them to
moderns such as Locke and Rousseau who, as chapter 4 implied, gave it
their own twist. Nor is it merely of literary or historical interest. In the 1990s
"natural law" became the stuff of American politics. In successive years during hearings on Supreme Court nominations, the same senator first com-
plained that Judge Bork rejected natural law and then that Judge Thomas
embraced it. An alert press noted the apparent tergiversation, but the senator
explained it all in *The Washington Post*: There are, he said, a good natural law
and a bad natural law.[3] Grateful for this insight, the authors are committed to
a search for the latter, all in the hope of understanding whether good natural
law will harmonize with human equality.

There are countless conceptions of this natural morality and no one dominating example that we can test for compatibility with human equality.[4] Nevertheless, in the midst of its "many mansions"[5] there is a common element
that disposes all natural law theory toward what we have called obtensionalism. Every version of natural law claims to rest upon an order of good and
evil that holds apart from human preference and obligates the individual.

Rejecting the fickle commands of individualism, subjectivism, and pure convention, natural law declares nature to be an immutable guide for human conduct.[6] Unlike human devices, it will not bend on command to ratify our personal or collective preferences. For "whatever else it may or may not be, the natural law philosophy is not relativist."[7] It challenges our prejudices and warns us from even the most exigent or alluring.[8]

Natural law thus seems to satisfy several of the criteria of descriptive equality. It asserts that the individual must seek diligently the specific terms of a distinctive order of lateral obligation that is antecedent to any human law. But the hard question remains whether, by demanding that we grasp these terms correctly and successfully adjust our conduct to "correspond" to them, natural law forbids equality. For equality's sake, natural law would have to allow the achievement of moral self-perfection simply by obtension—the diligent search for the terms of a lateral obligation generated by nature. It also must concede to every rational human an ability to obtend that is *uniform* in degree.

Can natural law satisfy these final two conditions? For that inquiry we will examine separately four distinctive understandings of natural law.[9] The first we call "Common Sense." It is the stuff of cocktail parties and Senate hearings with an ancient and enduring appeal. Second, we examine the "renaissance"—or what we shall call the "Classic"—view of Francisco Suarez; although Suarez invokes the Common Sense notions of nature, we will find his theory more divine than natural in its origins. Third, we look at the most prominent contemporary account of "natural law," one that seemingly replaces nature with "reason"; adapting an expression of its creators, we call this version "Integration." Fourth, we develop the natural law implications of the work of twentieth-century philosopher Bernard Lonergan; for the moment let us call this "Authenticity."[10]

Our general conclusions will be that neither Common Sense nor Classic views of natural law accord with conventional human equality; both make self-perfection depend upon accurate moral judgments followed by corresponding action. The fallible self's conscientious quest for the good is not sufficient. In short, these two traditional versions of natural law are forms of moral gnosticism; they require correct grasp of specific duties. If, between them, they exhausted the resources of natural law, human equality would be left as unsupported by nature as it is by individualism. This would leave us a bit uneasy. Natural law is often portrayed as the sole morality shared by all humans. So viewed, it has broad importance to the possibility of a human equality. Could the convention survive without the support of the morality that is allegedly the most democratic?

The answer may depend upon whether natural law can get by without the insistence on getting things right. The third and fourth versions have been selected for scrutiny here specifically because of their self-conscious departures from at least some parts of the gnostic standard. We pursue a fleeting hope that the third version, which we call Integration, will accept moral self-perfection by obtension. Finally, in Bernard Lonergan, we discover a staunch ally for human equality, the only question being whether his conception of morality can properly be designated "natural law."

Natural Law as the Matching of Natures: The Common Sense Position

The Common Sense version of natural law received its shape from the biology, physics, and metaphysics of Aristotle, though he himself probably would find it an extravagant extension of his own premises.[11, 12] In any case, this habit of moralizing from the appearances of nature is too ubiquitous to ignore; nor is it confined to the uneducated.[13] It is also a valuable entrée to the other three versions, and we shall try to see it in the round.

The Common Sense analysis of morality begins, as did Hobbes, with a picture of what is unique and essential to being human. But where the Individualist focuses on the human will, Common Sense identifies *reason* as the key element. Rather than *willing* morality into existence in a series of choices, reason grasps an already extant morality through its characteristic activity: knowing. Knowing, in turn, occurs in complete dependence on the senses. According to Common Sense, as touch, sight, taste, and the rest go to work, they bring man into sensate contact with material reality, and from sensation there immediately follows understanding. Sense experience fructifies into knowledge. Finally, as reason delivers this knowledge of things, it also delivers the content of responsibility.

How does reason accomplish this final feat? At the center of Common Sense morality stand sensible things; but at the center of each and every one of these things stands, in turn, what Common Sense calls a nature. This nature is its core or stable essence. It is what a thing *really* is. It is by knowing this that one knows the thing (as distinguished from its variable or "accidental" characteristics). By knowing what things are, we know—so the story goes—how we ought to act.[14] Obligation is said to be "intrinsic" to things. Common Sense teaches, in short, that the human mind knows the natures of things and that this knowledge is (1) necessary, and (2) sufficient to put us under specific moral obligation.

The sense in which knowledge of things is *necessary* to morality is plain enough. Even if morality were but a collection of divine (supernatural) commands, one would still have to be able, by use of the senses, to distinguish particular things and persons (for example, spouses) from other things and persons. But the sense in which such knowledge is *sufficient* to morality is not so clear. How does knowing what a thing *is* show what anyone *ought* to do? How, in other words, does knowing the nature of a thing put one under an obligation to treat it—or anything else—in a particular way?

The systematizers of Common Sense offer something like the following explanation:[15] We come to know a thing's nature not all at once, but by experiencing it as it goes through change. Most of the change things undergo is not random but orderly and the result of principles internal to them. By discovering a thing's principles of change and growth we discover not only what that thing essentially is but what it is trying to become. And these dynamic principles are the basis of obligation. In the dynamic connection between potentiality and actuality, "the ontological and moral orders are ultimately one. . . . A basis for value exists only in the tendency of something incomplete to complete itself."[16] Man's responsibility with respect to the things of his experience is not to inhibit (and perhaps even to assist) their achievement of their given potential.

What its nature tells a thing to seek to become is called its "finality" or "final causality." This concept was not new with Aristotle, but he put it on the Western map, and with him it is forever associated.[17] According to Aristotle, a thing's finality is its end or goal, and what it already is potentially; it is this inner, constitutive principle of a thing that specifies what the rational agent must do. This is the core of Common Sense morality: "The very essence of any natural-law ethics is that there should be a veritable natural end, or natural perfection, or natural *telos* [end], of human life, discernible empirically and directly in the facts of nature."[18]

Common Sense itself grasps that this picture is too simple. For one thing, there are conflicts among the yearnings (finalities) of the natures that persons encounter and experience. The food chain consists of such conflicts; the yearnings of the hungry human conflict with those of the growing carrot and the grazing cow. And among the contending natures one experiences is one's own; we notice contradiction among our own dynamic yearnings to move from potentiality into ever greater actuality.

This array of conflicts poses a deep problem for any theory in which *things* determine the content of morality. If it is to remain rooted in reality, Common Sense cannot leave man's undirected preferences to resolve the conflicts. That would be a form of subjectivism. If Common Sense is not to sacrifice its objectivity, nature must identify the correct alternative. According to Common Sense, it does. While the fundamental location of obligation is in the dynamic principles within all things, nature itself has worked out the pecking order. Nature tells reason which sorts of finalities trump others. It does this through the real relations or "matches" that exist among things.

Prior to ethical rules expressive of types of right actions are those objective and real relations between persons, between things, and between various interpersonal dealings. These relations are understandable "ratios" (in a wider sense than the arithmetic) which provide an objective basis for reasoning to moral judgments. Some of these practical judgments are general in form, for example, that children should respect their parents, or that parents should take care of their children. In other words, there is a right ratio between parent and child, not simply because I think so but because of a universal relationship.[19]

"The order of nature," it turns out, "is a vast complexus of such intelligible relations."[20]

Can a Common Sense natural lawyer accept obtensionalism? Plainly he believes in the raw availability of the information that is necessary to moral choice, and that at first seems promising for equality. No revelation, rarified intuition, or heady calculus must be had in order to know what things are, hence what to do. Still, even if Common Sense rarely notices the point, people differ in their capacity to know the natures of things and to discern the serpentine twists of the "*complexus.*" It is a point we have already considered. But this discrepancy in relative acumen is not the limit of the problem. Knowledge is perspectival. With every cognitive nature goes the baggage of its personal history. Things cannot be known in splendid purity. Things and their relations do not speak for themselves as the Common Sense moralizer would have it. There is grave reason to worry that people will have uneven success in finding the way.[21] None of this would be fatal to equality if Common Sense also taught that self-perfection is not impeded by "unnatural" acts as such. But that is not its message.

On this crucial point, even today Common Sense draws its spirit from Greek antiquity. Its intellectual forebears—such as Aristotle—put the moral question in this form: "What am I to do if I am to fare well?"[22] The Greeks merged—or did not distinguish—morality and earthly happiness, and they thus set the tone for legion successors bearing the banner of "eudaemonism."[23] This is unsurprising and requires no apologies from Aristotle, but identifying morality with happiness does compromise equality by commissioning luck as an instrument of self-perfection. Aristotle's own elaborations of happiness make this clear. He explains in detail that happiness is the attainment of a "complex totality: the best and most beautiful life, the accomplished fullness of human nature, happiness—consisting in the true order of the parts which compose it."[24] It is the achievement of a whole range of earthly goods. Man must live in a polis; he must possess goods and leisure enough to contemplate things divine; he must possess and exercise the virtues with pleasure; he must enjoy art and be completed with friendship.[25]

Antiquity was by no means unanimous in locating human happiness in this constellation of human excellences and contentment.[26] Plato had earlier identified human happiness with the philosopher in the state of contemplation. That answer appealed to him because it minimized happiness's vulnerability to the fates. His is still no easy path, because few can climb to the philosopher's heights; but the happiness to which Aristotle aspires is even more elusive, as Maritain laments:

> Happiness . . . involves . . . so many conditions which are hardly attainable—even for a small number of individuals, for a limited aristocracy of philosophers. . . . Our whole moral life, all our effort and striving toward rightness and virtue, are suspended from an End which, in fact, eludes us, vanishes within our grasp.[27]

Conventional human equality, too, is an implicit protest of this old Greek version of self-perfection and its merger in the Common Sense tradition. Identifying goodness with human happiness makes room for so few among the blessed. To begin, there are no children to be found among the moral heroes of Common Sense and Aristotle. In an ethics formed around finality, perfection is apt to be understood as what is attained "at the end of a long term, after long exercise, at a ripe age when the hair is beginning to turn silver."[28] Kings, savants—and perhaps soldiers and farmers—can all be pictured as reaching their natural finality.[29] But such ripeness is impossible to the child. This picture of moral gradualism, of a perfection realizable only by survivors, is just what equality forbids. Self-perfection cannot be the special achievement of those who fortuitously survive to apply the final touches in maturity (and who, paradoxically, must perceive death as irrelevant).

Equality requires plenary moral power for every rational being, including those who are new at the game. It somehow must swallow even the hard case of the child who dies (or who loses rationality) having experienced only the "faint flicker of choice" and only the promising beginnings of natural excellence. By posing the question as they did, the Greeks may have ensured human aspiration toward all that is good and fulfilling within a human culture, but simultaneously they guaranteed that achievement of what matters most to the person would be confined to a few. Those who fall short, despite their best effort, could be left with little of worth.

Consider but one example—the fate of Oedipus. Subjectively he was innocent of the atrocities that crushed him: Oedipus himself understood them as his destiny; it was the will of Apollo that he kill his father and sleep with his mother. Yet his lack of "responsibility" for such unnatural acts—our anachronistic appraisal of the case—was no moral redemption. Oedipus' "status" was determined precisely by this behavior. His "innocence" was beside the point, and the question of whether he was morally self-perfecting is subsumed in his "tragedy."

Now Oedipus surely is to be pitied; the harms he caused were for him a humiliation. He was not to be happy, and his life was an objective failure. Sophocles has ensured him the permanent label "tragic." But though this usage survives, it is an antiquitarian view of tragedy—one that largely reduces the significance of a life to its objective deeds. As we have noted, and will again, Western religion and its humanism initiated the historic drift away from such extreme objectivity and toward a competing understanding—one that limits tragedy to cases of voluntary withdrawal from responsibility. Immanuel Kant ensured that shift its place as a secular orthodoxy. Strictly speaking, tragedy is no longer necessary; it must be chosen.

If we still perceive Oedipus as tragic, this could only be in some third sense; namely, it was a tragedy for him to have lived in a society that had not yet distinguished happiness from goodness.[30] We would only add that to the extent Common Sense natural law still lacks this distinction, it turns the hope for equality into this third sort of tragedy; conventional human equality requires for its existence that goodness be accessible to the innocent regardless of their "fate."

The Natural Law of Conformity and Divine Command: The Classic Position

Between the fourteenth and seventeenth centuries, Common Sense and its purely natural sophistications lost their monopoly over natural law. While "final causality" was to remain an important concept in natural morality, increasingly it was regarded as insufficient by itself to ground obligation. Modern critics explain what was missing: "The trouble with natural law was precisely that it had no author. . . . The point of the matter has always been that natural law itself needed divine sanction to become binding for men."[31] Some moralists responded by junking the natural law for God's commands discoverable directly in revelation. Others were not so ready to give up on natural law, and in their hands the old edifice was reconstructed by infusing nature itself with God's command. Divine will was invoked to reinforce nature's own causality, providing the necessary authorship.

Unlikely as this combination of nature-plus-God may seem, it is the quintessential presentation of the natural law that emerged from the medieval period. It descended to this century by way of the Latin "manuals" that dominated much of moral debate in the West until recent days, and so we denominate it the Classic position.[32] The manuals tended to treat the natural law as a rigid edifice of highly specific rules (mostly prohibitions), and for this these works are today regarded as an embarrassing excess of moral theory. But notwithstanding the scorn that has been heaped upon the manuals, the detail and specificity of much contemporary natural lawyering illustrate that their spirit continues. To assess the compatibility of this brand of moral theory with equality, we focus upon Francisco Suarez (1548–1617), who conferred its modern charter.[33] Standing Janus-like at the beginning of the seventeenth century, Suarez was enough of a traditionalist to suppose that nature founds an objective morality; at the same time he was enough of a modernist—and a legist[34]—to conclude that moral obligation requires a surer source than nature. What it wanted was sovereign will—a command. Finally, Suarez was enough of a theist to believe that God issued that command.

If we squint just a little, Suarez's notion of natural law reduces to an academicized form of Common Sense.[35] The traditional references to natures and the "intrinsic" quality of obligation are there (2.15.18; 2.5.2). Still prominent is the "match" between natures that remains, as it were, the basis of specific moral solutions. Suarez refers to it as the "conformity" or harmony between human rational nature and some other nature (2.5.9; 2.5.3).[36] Finally, such "conformity" is just as real as "things" themselves; it arises automatically once human rational nature and the relevant other nature are posited (2.15.18).[37]

Opening wide our eyes, however, we see that Common Sense has receded some. Its champions had held that our knowledge of the "match" or conformity emerged from the simple experience of natures, their growth and possible interaction. A match was a discovery about how *things* ought to interact; knowledge of matches was a grasp of the fixtures of the real world. By contrast, the Classic understanding severs[38] moral knowledge from its root in the being of things. Where once there were real things, now there is language. Gone is the empiricality of Common Sense, and in its stead looms a labyrinth of propositions. With serene confidence, Suarez declares that from the most general principles to the most specific conclusions (2.7.5), "every judgment derived from the natural law is of such a character that it rests either upon self-evident principles or upon deductions necessarily drawn therefrom" (2.13.3).[39]

The component premises of this deductive edifice are of three classes. Those in the first class are primary, general, and "self-evident," for example, "one must do good, and shun evil" and "do not to another that which you would not wish done to yourself." Those in the second class, though "more definite and specific," are also self-evident. "Examples . . . are these principles: 'justice must be observed'; 'God must be worshipped'; 'one must live temperately'; and so forth." Finally, there are those in the third class—conclusions that are "deduced" from the more general principles. "Of these conclusions, some are recognized more easily than others, and by a greater number of persons"; thus adultery, theft, and "similar acts" are plainly wrong. For other acts, the conclusions come with greater difficulty, requiring "reflection . . . of a sort not easily within the capacity of all"; we must struggle to see "that fornication is intrinsically evil, that usury is unjust, that lying can never be justified" (2.7.5). Indeed, some of these conclusions require "a great deal of elaborate reasoning" (2.7.6).

But Suarez understands that even if one manages all the deductions with the rigor of Euclid, one still might deny that the natural law actually governs us. The only thing that correct deduction can reveal is that certain acts are *suitable* to be done—not that anyone is actually obligated to do them. In discovering a "match," the Common Sense natural lawyer knew at once *what* to do, and *that* he must do it. By contrast, the Classic natural lawyer learns only what would be suitable; these conformities among natures are not, for him, law.[40] Indeed, properly speaking, there is no natural law without a divine command, coming from within rational nature, telling us to realize what reason discovers to be a potential conformity and to avoid disconformity.[41] Absent the divine command, acts can be unsuitable but not prohibited.[42]

Obviously humans do not have formal knowledge of this divine command. Else the law would not be natural. Instead, according to Suarez, God's command that we obey nature is promulgated to us obliquely—and not without more effort on our part. Proper *reflection* shows us that it is *necessary* that a fitting Providence should issue such a command (2.6.23).[43] This oblique awareness, Suarez concludes, is sufficient, "no other notification [of the divine command] being necessary." The natural light of reason can make clear to man that God wills us to do the good and avoid evil (2.6.24).[44]

Would this hybrid natural law square with the structure of human equality? Within the Classic version can moral self-perfection be achieved by obtending the real good? Suarez's answer appears as he considers, with conspicuous candor, the likelihood of ignorance of the content of the natural law. Ignorance of the primary principles is impossible; of the more particular principles, ignorance is possible, "yet such ignorance cannot exist without guilt; not, at least, for any great length of time." But with respect to the other precepts that require "greater reflection, invincible ignorance is possible, especially on the part of the multitude" (2.8.7). One indication of the possible scope of this ignorance is Suarez's judgment that many know the Decalogue (part of the natural law, according to Suarez) only through scripture.[45] For him knowledge of the natural law is both incomplete and diverse among individual humans (2.8.3, 5).[46]

Nonetheless, Suarez blithely asserts that this spotty obscurity is of "slight importance" (2.14.6), even though it results in moral culpability. The existence of a precept obligates a man to know it (2.10.10), and "the moral question"—man's culpability—is not "particularly affected by how much reflection is involved" (2.7.10).[47] That common people are most typically ignorant of the particular precepts also is irrelevant. These precepts are the means of perfection, and the person who is not in fact guided by them will remain—as Aristotle supposed—morally incomplete; he or she will not be self-perfecting. The content of the natural law, correctly perceived, is necessary for the perfection or felicity of human nature (2.7.7; 2.8.4). Ungoverned by the precepts of the natural law, human conduct lacks "rectitude." The subject who fails to *do* the natural law stands imperfect, his potential unfulfilled.[48]

More complex than Common Sense natural law, the Classic version is at one with it in rejecting fulfillment by good intention—even by the specific good intention to seek the content of the Suarezian rules of conduct. The wrong choice never produces moral goodness in the actor. Hence the savant with his or her superior grasp of details will have the easier access to self-perfection. This is descriptive inequality.

The Natural Law of "Integral Human Fulfillment"

Much of post-Enlightenment theory would take seriously Kant's off-handed declaration that morality "has nothing to support it in heaven or earth."[49] In such a climate the gradual petrifaction of the Suarezian propositions in the seminary manuals made the stewards of the Latin moral theology increasingly uneasy. By the late nineteenth century a crisis of confidence drove them to reconceive the basic idea.[50] The new work has appeared since then in two basic types. The first consists of revivals and restatements of Common Sense with its ancient notions of nature and finality—all to support traditional morality. Today, with Henry Veatch, these thinkers continue to ask where morals could ever be based if not in nature or reality.

The second new type is the subject of this part of our discussion of natural law. This contemporary school also is unimpressed with Common Sense; it agrees that morals are to be grounded in reality, and even in natures, but it denies that nature itself is the source of the moral "ought." And resisting the temptation to invoke divine command, it locates the moral "ought" somewhere between heaven and earth—in a reality at once familiar and obscure, the self-evident principles of practical reason. When we learn what these are, we can ask whether they harmonize with the moral self required for human equality. Because its proponents are at great pains to limit nature's function in founding morality, some have suggested that this is not a natural law theory at all.[51] It is nevertheless regarded as such by its primary proponents, John Finnis and Germain Grisez, as well as by a host of collaborators and critics. We accept their judgment. "Integral human fulfillment" is the name they prefer for the achievement of moral self-perfection; our shorthand for this is Integration.

Integration tends to define itself by its enemies. It takes its shape from the Charybdis of Common Sense, on the one side, and from the Scylla of the Classic position, on the other. The Classic view is to be avoided because a quasi-natural divine command solves no problems and creates new ones. Quite apart from the eventuality that no such command reaches people, the

Finnisians insist that even if it did, it would give us no moral guidance; we would still need to know how to treat quasi-divine commands. An infinite regress looms.[52]

The Integration school notes that the divine command was necessary to the Classic position because nature gives no moral messages. A nature is only what is, and is thus impotent to say what ought to be. To coax an "ought" out of it is to commit what the professionals know as the "naturalistic fallacy." While many defenders of Common Sense deny that it indulges the dreaded fallacy (the ought is given with the is, no inference being necessary), Integration takes the fallacy seriously, thinks Common Sense is the Charybdis that entails it, and so looks elsewhere for the moral ought.

To be fair to Integration, it does not divorce itself altogether from nature. Indeed, it is as we experience human nature that we become familiar with its possibilities and grasp what, for this nature, would be fulfilling and worthwhile. We know, in other words, what is *good* for it. And presently we grasp that the good is to be done—but, crucially, this is not by a process of *inference*. Rather, simply in grasping what is good for human nature, we know *at once* that it is to be done. According to Finnis and Grisez, the most basic source of human obligation is a group of self-evident, intrinsic goods. These "intrinsic goods are basic reasons for action precisely because they are (intrinsic) aspects of human well-being and fulfilment."[53]

> The most basic reasons for action are those reasons whose intelligibility does not depend on deeper or still more fundamental reasons. As *basic* reasons, they cannot be derived; for there is nothing more fundamental that could serve as a premiss for a logical derivation. Therefore, they must be self-evident.[54]

Finnis and Grisez have equivocated somewhat regarding which goods are basic, but they seem to have settled on a list of seven: life, knowledge, play, aesthetic experience, sociability (friendship), practical reasonableness, and religion (understood as peace with some more-than-human source of meaning and value).[55]

In this little package of self-evident goods we have, according to Finnis and Grisez, the nucleus of morality. Now it may seem that everything in their basic formula happened much too fast; the rabbit sprang undetected from the hat even under our watchful gaze. But this is to be expected in a theory that rests upon self-evidences. Finnis and Grisez have, "in effect, excuse[d] themselves from providing metaphysical or ontological grounds" for morality.[56] There is, of course, nothing that can be said to *prove* (or *disprove*) what is self-evident; the basic goods are bedrock. Yet knowledge of the basic goods is neither irresistible nor immediate.[57] What is in itself self-evident is not equally accessible to all people; it takes time and experience to grasp the basic goods. But *once they are grasped*, "there will not be mistakes about the goods themselves, as the categories of benefit people have reason to seek."[58]

Because each of the basic goods is a first principle, they cannot be distinguished in dignity, either from one another or from some more basic standard. All seven are—simply—fundamental.[59] It follows, say the Finnisians, that the possibilities for human action cannot be reduced to some uniquely correct solution. No preexistent pattern of behavior is prescriptive; countless valid combinations are possible. It is because "human persons have possibilities which are not yet defined, [that] there is . . . room for them to unfold themselves through intelligent creativity and freedom."[60] "Practical reasonableness" requires only that human choice be directed by the basic goods—that those goods provide the point to what one does.[61]

"Practical reasonableness" is not yet morality, but just one among the several basic goods. It fails (creating evil) when one chooses some *partial* good, thereby effecting the (unreasonable) neglect of that whole good that ought to dominate the moral quest. Choice of a partial good is indeed reasonable so far as it goes. "Even morally bad actions have their point."[62] Thus, to the basic goods that demand that one be *reasonable* in one's action, Finnis et al. add what they call the *first principle of morality*—namely, that one not simply avoid pointlessness but that one be *entirely* reasonable in one's practical deliberation. This means, at least, that in all choices reason must pursue exclusively the basic goods.

> The fundamental principle of *moral* thought is simply the demand to be fully rational: In so far as it is in your power, allow nothing but the basic reasons for action to shape your practical thinking as you find, develop, and use your opportunities to pursue human flourishing through your chosen actions—be entirely reasonable.[63]

This formulation of the "first principle of morality" seems ripe for equality. It identifies "reasonableness" as the criterion of morality, but it explicitly limits this requirement to *what is in one's power*. Moral achievement no longer is hostage to correct knowledge and the realization of a completely predetermined natural finality. Rather, it is the consequence solely of choices made in personal commitment to the self-evident goods. Although Finnis and Grisez do not specifically say that best effort by itself is perfecting, equality would be at home in the moral universe so far described. The alliance between natural law and human equality becomes plausible.

For better or worse, however, this flirtation with equality vaporizes when Finnis and Grisez add their final criterion of moral achievement, which they label "integral human fulfillment." Up to this point they seemed to agree that conduct motivated exclusively by the basic goods (i.e., fully reasonable conduct) is morally perfecting. This could mean, however, that even if one's conduct were to be directed exclusively by only a few of the basic goods, the benign effect would follow. This possibility properly worries Finnis and Grisez. Moral self-perfection could be achieved while neglecting any number of the basic goods; the perfected person could be lopsided—zealously pursuing knowledge, for example, to the exclusion of friendship. It is particularly worrisome to them that religion might be among the basic goods that get slighted.[64]

The final requirement for morality is integral human fulfillment. Each person must seek and achieve a *balanced* menu of the basic goods:

> Integral human fulfillment is not a basic good alongside the others, nor some sort of supergood transcending all other categories of goodness. For integral human fulfillment is not a reason for acting, but an ideal whose attractiveness depends on all the reasons for acting which can appeal to morally good people.[65]

Finnis and Grisez are careful to emphasize the ideality and nonbasic status of integral human fulfillment, and thus to try to remain true to their starting point in the foundational authority of the seven basic goods. Nevertheless, we suspect that they have here introduced what is a theoretically unmotivated and unallowable ghost of moral theories past. The person of integral human fulfillment looks surprisingly like the human nature of the traditional natural law theories.[66] He also looks a lot like the "ideal Christian." Significantly, Finnis and Grisez attribute a large, though disputed, role to religion in *clarifying* the ideal of integral human fulfillment.[67] If, as it appears, the "revealed data of faith" enter into the very foundations of the theory, we have here a fideism that blocks equality by giving weight to correct perceptions impossible to many.[68] Integral human fulfillment may not lay down a detailed template of the perfecting human life, but its prescription of a pattern of choices that is necessary to moral fulfillment raises doubts of the possibility of equality.[69]

So far as we have been able to detect, Integration's implications for human equality have never received Finnis's or Grisez's explicit attention. But their ally, Robert George, has written enough to confirm that Integration is no friend of conventional human equality. George claims—contra Aristotle and his "elitist" doctrine of natural slaves—that persons are *"equal in dignity, however unequal they are in ability, intelligence, and other gifts."*[70] Standing alone, this would be a promising probe in the direction of conventional human equality, even if it falls short by preferring "dignity" over the capacity to obtend as the host property of the relation. But the hope for a genuine human equality is disappointed, as George explicates the point.

Persons are equal in dignity, George tells us, "as loci of human goods and of rational capacity for self-determination by free choices."[71] Anyone with rationality enough to be self-determining and to realize the basic goods in his or her own moral person is a locus of dignity. But as we have emphasized, rationality, and with it the knowledge necessary to appropriate the basic goods, varies among persons. All rational persons, then, are equal in *possession* of rationality, in their *possession* of the capacity to achieve human goods, and in their *possession* of human dignity; this, though, is merely a single equality, and George could not plausibly claim that this meets the conditions of a double relation founded on a uniform rational capacity to instantiate basic goods. If dignity hinges on the rational capacity to achieve basic goods, conventional human equality again fails.[72]

Jesuitical Echoes of Kant: A Natural Equality?

This result can be avoided—as we have avoided it—if moral achievement comes not to those whose free choices actually correspond to the external order of correct behaviors, but to those who *try* to achieve such correspondence. This is obtensionalism, and it allows human equality, because everyone plausibly has the same capacity to try. But so far this view has not gained the allegiance (or even the attention) of natural lawyers. Indeed, to most natural lawyers perfection by obtension may appear to finesse the need to require "objectivity" of all. Too blithely obtensionalism concedes that the capacity for correspondence to the external order will vary, while lavishing moral credit upon the mere effort to achieve it. This apparent antagonism to human equality might be eliminable, however, given a reinterpretation of the "objectivity" necessary to a natural morality. It is the singular achievement of Bernard Lonergan, S.J. (1904–1984) to have re-conceived "objectivity" as no longer a "correspondence" to the external world, but instead as the product of fidelity to an *internally* given moral order.[73]

The revolution begins with Lonergan's attack on the ideal of correspondence. The fallacy in the tradition is easy enough to spot. Because we are always on the inside of being, there is no way to get outside to "check" whether our mental content—our supposed knowledge—*really* corresponds to what is "out there."[74] Correspondence in that sense is an otiose doctrine; it presupposes the utterly unachievable act of "checking" the identity between thought and thing.[75] Lonergan anticipated the dictum of Richard Rorty that "we should not regret our inability to perform a feat no one has any idea how to perform."[76]

If correspondence to the "external" world cannot be ratified, nonetheless, "there is . . . a rock on which one can build."[77] To discover it, however, one ends one's fixation with the external world, and attends, instead, to the realm of being inside. The supporting rock is the subject in his own *acts* of experiencing, understanding, judging, and deciding.[78] To explore this "rock" of Lonergan's, we proceed in steps.

First. "The rock . . . is the subject." The rock is not external to me but an aspect of my self. It is discoverable not by the senses, but simply by being attentive to my own internality.[79] The subject—the self (my self) that has been the traditional *threat* to objectivity—is now the foundation on which reliable knowledge may take its stand. If the true conditions of objectivity are to emerge, one must notice, perhaps for the first time, the "neglected subject."[80]

Second. It is not the subject—simply—that is rock, but the subject in his conscious experiencing, understanding, judging, and deciding. We begin with the first three of these activities. Attend to your own cognitive constitution, and in it you will discover, according to Lonergan, three invariant *operations* that together bear your consciousness. None of them is at all exotic. They occur every time you know anything at all. First, the subject *experiences*—senses, perceives, imagines, feels. This is the empirical level, at which the subject's operation is to receive data. Next, the subject *understands*. He grasps the intelligibility in the data given by his attending. By insight into the data, the subject produces ideas, concepts, and formulations and works out the implications of those formulations. Third, the subject *judges*—affirming or denying what he has received, experienced, and then has understood. Here the subject reflects on the formulations produced by intelligence, marshals the evidence given in the data, and ultimately passes judgment: Adverting to the data, the subject says yes or no (or probably or probably not) to the understanding of the data proposed by intelligence.[81]

There remains a fourth and final internal operation to be discovered. It, too, is cognitive in nature; but this fourth operation is not merely to know but to *decide*:

> So far, our reflections on the subject have been concerned with him as a knower, as one that experiences, understands, and judges. We have now to think of him as a doer, as one that deliberates, evaluates, chooses, acts. Such doing, at first sight, affects, modifies, changes the world of objects. But even more it affects the subject himself. For human doing is free and responsible.[82]

On this level, Lonergan tells us, we are no longer just conscious; we become self-conscious. We affirm the real not just as what is but as what is good and valuable and something to be chosen. This is the level of freedom; here we decide what we are to do and to become.[83]

These four operations, then, are the invariant structures of consciousness and self-consciousness. Their existence never can be "proved" by catching a good look at them but only by the subject's redirecting this whole series of operations to the task of understanding the internal process of knowing itself—that is, by attending to, understanding, and judging the very activities of knowing. And here looms paradox or even contradiction. Any meaningful attempt to disprove the structure would itself prove that it exists and operates, for the would-be critic must himself attend to the evidence of its nonexistence, and then proceed to understand and formulate this evidence, pass judgment upon it, and choose to make the denial.[84] "Anyone that cares to deny [the operations'] existence is merely disqualifying himself as a non-responsible, non-reasonable, non-intelligent somnambulist."[85] These operations are rock.

Third, and however: If all you discover in yourself are these four operations, you have missed what is even more basic—the very condition of the possibility of their efficacy. These operations do not function at random. We distinguish them analytically, but in every cognitive act they are *already* assembled and dynamically related to one another; they have a structure and direction.

> The operations . . . stand within a process that is formally dynamic, that calls forth and assembles its own components. . . . It is a unity and relatedness that exists and functions before we manage to advert to it explicitly, understand it, objectify it.[86]

By attending to this already accomplished unity, the subject will discover that "the many levels of consciousness are just successive stages in the unfolding of a single thrust, the eros of the human spirit."[87] The ineradicable desire expresses itself in the curiosity, in the relentless questions that frame our meanings and set limits to our muddle—in questions for intelligence (What is it?), questions for understanding (Is it so?), questions for decision (Ought I to do it?). It is "a self-assertive spontaneity that demands sufficient reason for all else but offers no justification for its demanding."[88] It is rock.

Fourth. Satisfaction of this desire is the criterion of human knowledge and decision. This elemental cognitive satisfaction is achieved only by free adherence to what Lonergan calls the "transcendental precepts." These precepts rule us whether we affirm them or not. "Before they are ever formulated in concepts and expressed in words, those precepts have a prior existence and reality in the spontaneous, structured dynamism of human consciousness."[89] They are four, each prefiguring and governing one of the respective cognitive operations: "Be attentive, Be intelligent, Be reasonable, Be responsible."[90] With these precepts the dynamic desire of the human spirit "teaches" the subject that the point is not just autonomic experiencing, understanding, judging, and deciding. If the dynamic desire to know is to be satisfied, the subject must (1) experience *attentively*, (2) understand *intelligently*, (3) judge *reasonably*, and (4) decide *responsibly*. From within himself, but without his choosing this vocation, the subject is called in freedom to *be* attentive, intelligent, reasonable, responsible.

Fifth. Normativity thus emerges from within the subject.

> [It resides] at root in the native spontaneities and inevitabilities of our consciousness which assembles its own constituent parts and unites them in a rounded whole in a manner we cannot set aside without, as it were, amputating

our own [4] moral personality, [3] our own reasonableness, [2] our own intelligence, [1] our own sensitivity.[91]

This normativity extends to all four operations, not merely the strictly "ethical" imperative of responsibility. It is the nature of responsibility both to presuppose and then to reaffirm the knowledge that emerges from the process of being attentive, intelligent, and reasonable.[92] "We experience and understand and judge to become moral."[93] If the subject is to be moral, that is, responsible, then he must first have been attentive, intelligent, reasonable.[94] Morality requires nothing less than fidelity to all four transcendental precepts.

Sixth. We begin to see the application to equality. It is by adhering to the transcendental precepts that we achieve *objectivity*; that is, "genuine objectivity is the fruit of authentic subjectivity."[95] Though it takes some getting used to, the reason is simple: the dynamic desire for understanding could be finally and fully satisfied by nothing less than what is real. It is the desire not for fantasy or fiction but for what *is*—for what is *real*. It is, in a word, a *transcendent* desire, because its satisfaction moves the subject beyond his interiority.[96] "There is," therefore, "no problem of a bridge [from the subject to the external world]. If you can reach the judgment [or decision], you are there."[97] The *fact* of authentic judgment and decision completes the journey to reality; there is no bridge to be crossed. Immanentism is avoided and objectivity is achieved, not by decamping from our subjective locus (with Thomas Nagel to get a "view from nowhere") but instead by *authenticity* in knowing and deciding.

Authenticity is the key concept in Lonergan's ethics, a linguistic link to a moral vocabulary evolved during the last four centuries as an alternative to the traditional labels.[98] But with Lonergan, authenticity has become the instrument not of self-affirmation but of self-transcendence; it becomes the process by which the subject reaches the real. Lonergan's dual message is that authenticity gets you to reality and that there is no shortcut. If you follow the four transcendental precepts, you'll get there—you *are* there.

But authenticity must be won again in every conscious moment. The dynamic desire to know frequently demands that one judgment be supplanted by another. What we know are "emergent probabilities."[99] A judgment that was authentic when made must yield to fresh attentiveness, intelligence, reasonableness, responsibility. The subject who would be authentic must constantly engage in a self-correcting process.[100] "Authenticity does not prevent mistakes in the short run, but it does tend to overcome mistakes in the long run, when our relevant questions find their quarry," even though "this 'short run' may be the entire life of an individual or a culture."[101]

What our own being obliges, however, is authenticity in the present. The subject cannot "postpone his living, until he has learnt, until he has become willing, until his sensitivity has been adapted"[102]—until he has answered all the questions. We are, "in [Gerard Manley] Hopkins' phrase, . . . 'time's eunuch.' "[103] One must resist the urge to transmute probabilities into pseudo-certainties, repose in those achievements, and give up the search. The necessity of continued search rests upon the constancy of the dynamic and inescapable desire to know. No one is in a privileged position (with Nagel), no one exempt or sent on vacation.[104] You have finally concluded that this war is unjust; OK, keep thinking. Everyone must be—equally and constantly—a seeker. "Emergent probability is the great equalizer of humankind."[105]

The question of whether people have the equal capacity to achieve objectivity in their moral judgments has been transmuted into the question of whether they have the same capacity to be authentic, and the answer seems to be yes. Moving the basis of ethics in from the external to the internal world dissolves the problem of "equal access." Once objectivity's norms are internal, everyone can know and satisfy them. The principle is not correspondence to the external but fidelity to the internally given transcendental precepts. That principle, according to Lonergan, "gives rise to instances of the good, but those instances are good choices and actions. However, do not ask me to determine them, for their determination in each case is the work of the free and responsible subject producing the first and only edition of himself."[106]

This must not be mistaken for moral laxism. Whether the subject is authentic is radically contingent upon whether he has exercised the "relentless devotion"[107] required to meet the demands of a command of which he cannot plead ignorance.[108] This does not threaten but instead assures equality, because it never requires of the subject that he do more than heed the inner commands to be attentive, intelligent, reasonable, responsible. But the work of meeting these commands must not be underestimated; it is the constant business of a lifetime.[109]

So we conclude with Lonergan: Yes, there is a genuine order of obligation; yes, we must heed its commands; no, we never get outside to check whether we have got its terms right. The most we can do is to make the search in the enthusiasm of the dynamic desire for the good that promotes us from one step to the next. Whatever self-perfection is possible lies in making this search; thus, though we cannot be certain, it is plausible that all persons are uniformly prepared to do what is necessary.

To identify these transcendental precepts as the natural law may prove controversial, but it should not. There is some justification for it even in Aquinas, and Lonergan himself, though he did not use the expression (he would not have wanted his solution confused with the hopeless mess of other meanings for natural law), seems to have approved it, as have his intellectual heirs.[110] Terminology aside, Lonergan's influence upon the course of natural law theorizing seems likely to grow. There appears no creditable way for its champions to ignore his invitation to bring the possibility of moral self-perfection in from the cold of external correctness. They may in the end reject it, but first they must deal with it. The experience may prove rejuvenating, and human equality comes as a bonus.[111]

Lonergan's reconciliation with the more traditional interpretations of natural morality could be facilitated by taking one verbal step back (or perhaps forward) in the direction of Aristotle. Recall that both the Common Sense and Classic schools have continued to express individual self-perfection in terms of Aristotle's familiar dyad of the potential and the actual. The natural finality of any being lies in its capacity to achieve a certain perfected state, becoming the realization of that state. In the case of a flower this fulfillment consists in completion of the full cycle of its possibilities—from seed to blossom to seed. That is the flower's perfection, and animal finality is a close if more complex parallel. The real puzzle appears only when we inquire about the perfection of man; what is the natural finality of a rational, voluntary animal?

Aristotle and his intellectual descendants—including Aquinas and Suarez—never broke free of the limiting notion that the natural moral fulfillment of human beings requires a form of realization that is experienced in the external order—one that has cognitive, material, and social achievements as necessary ingredients. For them, no one is completed unless he or she is in some degree a "success"; or, as they would prefer to put it, natural fulfillment entails some measure of earthly happiness. Earlier we saw this eudaemonism still flourishing in modern philosophers such as Thomas Nagel and Martha Nussbaum as well as the traditional naturalists.

We would not denigrate temporal happiness (all of us seek it); but we wonder that natural lawyers remain content with a notion of man's natural finality that is so vulnerable and utterly contingent. There is, after all, another plausible view of fulfillment. There is a kind of finality that is unthreatened by bad luck and—more to the point—one of greater nobility than mere external success. Nor is there anything in the least "unnatural" about the sort of human capacity we have in mind. The traditionalists agree that, by their very constitution, humans are invited to seek the good. What, then, would be the potential that is left unactualized in the person who in fact seeks? The shortfall in his fulfillment could amount at the very most to the ephemera of the external—wealth, leisure, beauty, knowledge, friendships, reputation—all of it blowing in the wind of our mortality. How could these contingent blessings compare in nobility to the unconditional good that is open even to the least-gifted seeker whose moral estate remains incorruptible to every enemy save his own will? If it be true that the free pilgrims of the good achieve moral fulfillment, obtension is man's natural finality.[112] Period.

A Second Fragment on Habit; Virtue and Vice

In their theories of the moral life natural lawyers—particularly of the Common Sense and Classic stripe—often seem to accord a cardinal role to virtue and vice. Aquinas, for example, considered virtue to be, like law, one of the necessary means by which a person is led to his perfection;[113] in chapter 3 we agreed with him that good habits can enhance a person's chances of discovering and realizing specific correct behaviors. We concluded, however, that neither this relative advantage of the well-habituated nor the corresponding disadvantage of the ill-habituated represents a threat to equality. Virtue—like knowledge and intelligence—may be an aid to finding specific correct behaviors, but even the most vicious (or stupid) person is fully capable of obtending. Whether bearing good habits or bad, every one of us plausibly retains in uniform degree the capacity to try for the good.

We do not propose to revisit that discussion. Here we consider briefly the different possibility that virtue is simply a synonym for obtension. To natural lawyers virtue could be just another name for whatever it is that produces self-perfection. At first this seems unlikely. In practice, the naturalists have assigned virtue only a bit part in the morality play. In the Classic tradition, for example, virtue helps (and vice hinders) correct acts, but it is the acts themselves that are necessary and (with proper intention) sufficient to rectitude.

But this oversimplifies the history of natural theories. The moral significance of simply keeping rules is notoriously obscure, and only a crude behaviorist would accept it as the whole story about the moral man. Recently natural moralists have begun to emphasize that virtue is something more than rule-abidingness and even to make it the measure of a man's moral perfection. For them the question clearly becomes less what an actor has done than what is the meaning of the particular act in the context of the person's entire character. This new focus upon virtue has made it to popular media such as *Newsweek*: "What . . . a variety of . . . influential thinkers . . . propose is the renewal of the idea of virtue—or character—as the basis for both personal and social ethics."[114] This turn from rules to *internal states* of the person has taken shapes too numerous for inventory here.[115] Overall it appears congenial to the premises of equality. Indeed, this trend has made it a temptation for us to equate obtension with virtue, and it is important to see why that conflation would be false.

Whatever else it may be, obtension entails *activity*; it is the activity of committing to the good. It is *doing* something; specifically, it is diligently intending the good. It is this dynamic element that the term "virtue" fails to capture. From the time of Aristotle, virtue and vice have been understood to be *passive* states of the person—the one favorable to good behaviors, the other to evil. They are internal environments, the soil in which the plant grows or withers. A person, then, might have every virtue, and these might add up to that medley we call good character; yet he might or might not, at any particular time, be striving for the good. Aristotle insisted upon this very point; virtue is but a passive state, whereas human perfection entails activity.[116] To be sure, with a subtle shift in usage the moral theorist could turn the definition in our direction by limiting the state of virtue to those who are busy seeking the apparent good. But the old conception of virtue is also important, and its distinctive nature might be obscured. Hence some separate term (we prefer "obtension") is necessary to label the act of moral questing and to distinguish it from the state of virtue.

In any case, there is a strong stylistic reason not to equate obtension with virtue. Ordinarily, virtue is said to incline the person toward specific real goods—to correct moral answers. "Virtue . . .," as *Newsweek* puts it, "is a quality of character by which individuals habitually recognize and *do* the right thing."[117] It would be odd to ascribe virtue to the diligent and conscientious bungler who is the picaresque ensign of human equality.

Among the naturalists, in respect to the proper characterization of the elements of moral experience, it is Lonergan who comes closest to a moral theory consistent with—and confirming of—the premises of conventional human equality. Moral life is a series of demands for personal responsibility; moral self-perfection is achieved by the effort to meet each demand as it arises; and the person who is passive in the face of those demands diminishes his own moral personality. The question of whether a person is advancing morally is not whether he is habitually disposed to the real good, but whether he is authentic—whether he is diligently striving to find and to do that good. But on that proposition we must conclude that the multitudes of natural lawyers have gone both ways.

PART III

COULD THE CHRISTIANS BELIEVE

IN HUMAN EQUALITY?

It was the true Light that enlightens every man who
comes into this world.[1]
(*John* 1:9)

INTRODUCTION TO PART III

Whosoever unceasingly strives upward . . . him we can save.
(Goethe, *Faust*)

PERSONAL COMMITMENT to the good seems a plausible strategy for Christian self-perfection. To be sure, in moving from the porch to the altar the perfection is transmuted into eternal salvation; but most Christians perceive that outcome to remain related to our earthly enthusiasm for lateral morality. "Do unto others" is common to Christianity and conventional human equality. Nonetheless, there are serious obstacles to Christian assent. Good intention plus diligence may not so obviously add up to salvation. First, there are believers who, in addition to obtension, would insist upon various objective events such as baptism, good works, and a passing score on the Ten Commandments; second, even if obtension suffices for salvation, the capacity of individuals might differ in degree. One who accepted either of these propositions would—on pain of inconsistency—reject human equality. To conclude that there is no (emergent) Christian consensus in favor of the propositions necessary for human equality would be a signal blow to our interpretation of the convention.

In seeking the Christian version(s) of self-perfection, we focus upon a set of historical-theological problems that have vexed and divided the churches. In chapter 6 we reduce these problems to three specific inquiries crucial to equality. In chapter 7 we answer the first of these: Is it Christian to believe that human actors really have an important role to play in their own salvation? Our general answer being yes, we are entitled in chapter 8 to address the second and third questions: Is it plausible to Christians that God has established obtension as each person's sufficient contribution to his or her salvation? And, if so, may Christians also believe that God has endowed all rational humans with uniform capacity to form the necessary diligent intention?

6

THE FRAMEWORK FOR A CHRISTIAN

OBTENSIONALISM

Sir, the road to hell is paved with good intentions.
(Samuel Johnson)

OBTENSION—striving for the real good—is the mood music of Christian morality whose foremost practitioner stressed the possibility of holiness for the most limited, ignorant, sinful, and misguided; in doing so, he nearly reversed the connection that antiquity had assumed between intellect and self-perfection. Paradoxically, Jesus threatened human equality by hinting the moral advantage of simpler persons; where worldly options are less distracting, pride's hold is loosened.[1] Happily for human equality, Christians seem agreed that the poor and ignorant are sufficiently afflicted by other temptations peculiar to their state. In any event, the unfathomable distribution among social classes of the occasions of sin will be the least of several problems in reconciling Christianity to human equality.

Even to identify these problems, we need a set of premises plausibly Christian but in harmony with the structure of conventional equality—a kind of theological hypothesis. Such a framework may seem to reverse the proper Christian order of things; it makes human equality the stable premise to which the propositions of moral theology are compared. The question will be whether the religious idea can be reconciled to equality. This procedure entails anthropomorphism and analogy; we speculate about the sort of God who could have willed such an order of things, and whether he could be Christian. This method, however, is one invited by both Old and New Testaments and by Christianity's own founder. Even the vegetable world provided him clues to his father's will, and this link between physical and transcendent was confirmed in his own nature. There is no mental activity more familiar to the West than that of groping through images of maculate flesh toward the imageless, perfect Being so oddly concerned for the salvation of bodies. Myth and analogy can easily become reckless and silly, but to disallow them altogether would disqualify the Church fathers and bowdlerize the scriptures.

Nevertheless: The ascriptions to God in this chapter are nothing more than the contingent premises necessary to a conversation about equality. For example, *if* God willed salvation for all, this might be one necessary step toward human equality. Obviously, whatever theologers like us might suppose about him, God will have it his way. Our inventions are brief, and, having constructed the version of God's will necessary to equality, we turn in chapters 7 and 8 to ask the extent to which the core concepts of Christianity might allow such a view. At that point, authentic theologians get their hands on the issue. Withal we make the disclaimer of the amateur, satisfied to have raised an intelligible question.

The Form for a Moral Theology of Obtension

Recall yet again the structure of conventional human equality. Its mainspring is a moral intentionalism of a particular sort. The well-meaning imbecile can be the moral equivalent of Socrates (assuming that Socrates was well intending). Indeed, given certain bizarre psychological assumptions, Hitler might be the moral equivalent (or superior) of Mother Teresa. Men can do bad deeds with good intent and be morally the better for following their erring conscience. Sometimes, in good faith, they misunderstand objective evil as a good; in these cases, individuals know not what they do but are perfected by doing it. What would be the Christian counterpart to this purely human ethic? How would the secular formula be rewritten as a proposition about God's relation to man?[2]

To begin, Christianity personalizes the source of morality. There are not only rules but a ruler. The structures of any possible order come from *someone*, and there is no doubt of the author's identity, even though his nature remains a mystery. This personalism could encourage belief in the efficacy of pure intention; a Christian—a child of God—might suppose that in a Father's eyes, one need only seek in good faith.[3] With this in mind, here is a first cut at such a theological obtensionalism expressed in three propositions:

1. Explicitly and/or by implication God invites all rational humans to loving union with himself.
2. The person accepts this invitation by honestly seeking the author of the good and submitting to his will insofar as it can be discovered.
3. The acceptance is both necessary and sufficient to salvation.

A Christian obtensionalism of this sort would embrace human equality by adding, as usual, a fourth proposition:

4. Every rational human enjoys in uniform degree the capacity to accept or reject the divine invitation.

The divine invitation commingles the ascendant and lateral orders of morality. Except for the special religious obligations of prayer and worship, duties to God and to our fellows become indistinguishable. "If you do it for the least of these, you do it for me." This partial fusing of the two moralities is no problem for equality theory, because in Christianity lateral duty to fellow humans endures, becoming now a distinct element of religious obligation; all that is new is that these lateral duties have their source outside nature. The human encounter with other rational choosers remains the event that triggers personal consciousness of this lateral obligation. The capacity to honor or flout the responsibility for seeking its terms remains a distinctive and real property of the self and continues to serve as the host property of the relation of human equality. Of course, whether Christianity allows all this is the question to be answered.

The Metaphor of the Invitation Elaborated

Invitation is a traditional Christian theme expressed in parables of a host who calls us to celebration. If the invitee accepts, he does so by freely satisfying the conditions of attendance set by the host. These conditions may appear arbitrary. The invitee may have to wear a wedding garment (or glass slippers—the parable is endlessly elaborated in our fairy tales). The point is that we have apparent reasons to decline and are free to do so.

This story of the invitation can also come in a contrasting and competing form, one in which those who are "invited" are expected to attend—or else. In this version the no-shows may even be tortured, their cities leveled, and their crops withered. The message turns out not to be so clearly an invitation, though it may still be a choice. This fork in the tradition may represent some unsettled issue in Christianity about the consequences of sin and the meaning of Hell. Both versions of the invitation (come and be fulfilled; come or else) could be fitted into the convention about human equality; whether the proper metaphor is pure invitation or pure command, our capacity to accept or reject might be both real and uniform. The authors respect the sterner tradition, but our focus will be on the other.[4]

One plausible theology of the divine invitation would be cast in a form something like this: God wills a freely chosen union with each rational soul, and he communicates that message—explicitly or otherwise—to the invitee. Successful union, however, requires the individual's active and particular response. Each must decide; there is no opting out, for stubborn indecision counts as refusal. The specific form of acceptance required is the invitee's commitment to seek and honor duty as God sees fit to reveal it to him.[5] If an individual is unwilling to shoulder that vocation, he has declined the invitation.

For us the question is this: Must one's choice of behavior be a correct interpretation of God's way, or does an honest but erring effort get us to the party? If Christianity is to allow equality, intention would have to be decisive; only thus could the capacity of every rational human for union with

God be identical in degree. We continue to assume that the individual ability to discover correct behavior differs from person to person; but, if one person's superior insight represents an added capacity for self-perfection, equality is lost. While condemning the phony ignorance that is the cultured product of moral evasion, the Christian must deem honest mistakes compatible with moral self-perfection. It must be available to anyone who accepts whatever duties he or she discovers through honest and faithful inquiry.

Here is a basic theodicy for human equality, one to which we will shortly pose important historical doctrinal objections. We see that within this notion of the invitation, man would continue to hold the power to "make himself"—but this, now, in a sense wholly unlike that of extreme individualism or most interpretations of natural law. Christian self-definition would be undertaken in a specifically theological context that is simultaneously confining and liberating. First, it is confining insofar as it constrains us either to submit to or reject the will of another (God) wherever it leads; in the primal act of obedience the self deliberately constricts its own universe of possible choices. In a kind of trusting ignorance one accepts whatever apparent duties the future will present, thereby committing to courses of action that cannot be predicted except in the contingent sense that as we struggle to discover what God wills, we are already pledged to do his apparent commands. We accept in anticipation whatever unknown but specific responsibilities our future understanding will disclose.

Second, however, this primal choice of obedience is less an act of limitation than of liberation. The mere fact that the constraint is self-chosen is enough to remind Christians of the freedom entailed in the act of obedience. Furthermore, Christianity intensifies this libertarian perspective with a paradoxical twist of its own. In the act of submission one discovers oneself empowered, for this is the single positive life option. Its fulfilling abundance is assured by its authorship. Pico della Mirandola puts this all in the mouth of God:

> "Adam, . . . thou mayest have and possess what abode, what form, and what functions thou thyself shalt desire. . . . Thou . . . shalt ordain for thyself the limits of thy nature. . . . [W]ith freedom of choice and with honour, as though the maker and moulder of thyself . . ., thou mayest degenerate into the lower forms of life, which are brutish. Thou shalt have the power, out of thy soul's judgment, to be reborn into the higher forms, which are divine."[6]

Pico's moral outlook is the opposite of radical individualism. The Christian understands that man chooses from a limited menu of possibilities in which the options are, on the one hand, "degenerate" and "brutish" and, on the other, "higher" and "divine." Human decisions are made according to a *standard*. In that sense choice is compassed and confined, but, because the standard defines the real good, our search for it can be holy and self-perfecting, and our rejection of it corrupting. On the one hand, choice is liberated from the prison of moral nihilism; on the other, we are provided the materials with which to "make ourselves."

Pico makes the invitation look hopeful as a home for equality, but it is only a beginning. What Pico does not even consider is that, in assembling his ideal self, the individual may misread the directions that come packaged with the gift of life. Like the parent assembling a toy on Christmas eve, in good faith he may intend one outcome but get another because he mistakenly reverses the switches and connections that would make the thing work. Or some necessary aspect of the required assembly simply exceeds his knowledge or intelligence. Is there a moral analogue to this familiar form of mechanical frustration? Do people honestly mistake the right way? If so, what is the effect of such error? Perhaps it has no moral effect upon the mistaken actor; intention may be the sole determinant of his moral fulfillment. If equality were to be a possibility, we would have to add that particular refinement to Pico's vision. We would keep him a good Christian while reading him to say that, even when we err, it is solely the spirit in which we choose our object that counts for our own salvation. The individual achieves transcendent moral identity simply by striving for it.

Christianity Complicates the Equality Question

As we prepare to inquire whether Christianity conforms to this theological mock-up of human equality, it is important to see that the doctrinal repertoire of religion is more complicated than that of either individualism or natural law. Intuitively one might have expected religion to imply universality. God created us; hence we are in the same moral boat. The fatherhood of God is the brotherhood of man. Perhaps in the end the story will turn out something like this, but getting there is not simplified by the intellectual structure of Western religion. Here is one way to state the problem: When philosophers of the Enlightenment or of natural law ask the meaning of moral fulfillment and self-perfection, they start with the assumption that the subject matter of their inquiry is—simply—rational humanity. It would never occur to either John Rawls or Lon Fuller to begin moral theory by excluding a particular caste of humans for whom morality is irrelevant because of some preordained characteristic. Philosophy long flirted with such principles of exclusion; women, slaves, children, and barbarians were the favorite outsiders. Modern philosophy, however, knows no such disqualifications.

Moral theology is a different kettle of fish—or at least it might be. God could have it whichever way he likes, and perhaps he has drawn lines among us that unaided human rationality cannot apprehend. Some believe that he has. They see the planet's population of rational humans divided by God's will into categories; some never receive the invitation, or (what for our purpose may be the same) some of the apparent invitees are created with diminished capacity to accept, or some with none at all.

To be precise, there are well-known theological propositions that, if they stood at the core of Christianity, could be absolute stoppers for human equality. Predestination is the most obvious. This ancient notion requires that from all eternity and apart from choice, some of us be damned and others saved. Hard-core predestination will not reconcile with the claim that individuals have been given freedom to accept or reject a divine invitation. A second and related threat to the invitation is the puzzle about the relation of God's omnipotence to man's liberty. The invitation assumes such a liberty; that is, man may refuse God's society. Historically this has suggested to many pious minds the possibility that God's own will may be frustrated. This cannot be; Christianity steadfastly maintains divine omnipotence. Is free will, then, an illusion? If so, human equality is also illusory, for it rests upon the capacity for human choice.

Other difficulties arise from the doctrine of original sin and the curative role that baptism plays. If Christian salvation requires a specific form of sacramental deliverance, this obviously poses a problem for equality. Baptism—at least of the formal variety—can be a matter of where one is born. If it is a precondition to salvation, we must say that some individuals do not get the invitation at all. And this suggests yet another set of problems lurking in the doctrine of grace. If God bestows grace unevenly, as many seem to suppose, how could our capacity to submit to his law (or reject it) be uniform? In due course we must deal with all these problems raised by predestination, baptism, and grace.

These "technical" exclusions from salvation require our reconsideration of historical debates over the chances for nonbelievers. Belief in equality would require that every rational person receive the divine proposal—and on the same terms. Thus Christians could not consider the invitation as made exclusively or even preferentially to themselves. Their theology would need some form of universal natural conscience of the sort portrayed in chapters 2 and 3. There we said that all rational humans must grasp a duty of reciprocity among themselves, and the quest for its details must suffice for moral self-perfection. To qualify specifically as Christian, however, such a universal grasp of obligation will have to include at least an implicit recognition of the personal source of mankind's responsibilities. The recognition of lateral obligation by unbelievers somehow has to include the invitation to a union with God; the natural moral equipment of the nonbeliever will include a longing—conscious or otherwise—for its own explanation, moving the unsatisfied seeker and even the honest scoffer within the economy of salvation.

Only if Christianity concedes the possibility that all rational humans can make salvific (or damning) responses to the invitation can we even reach the final question of whether this capacity to respond might also be uniform among us.

The Scope of the Inquiry

A word on the scope and method of the next two chapters is now appropriate. We need not review the range of Christian dogmatics; most of Judeo-Christian doctrinal history has little bearing upon whether obtension suffices for salvation.[7] The same holds for Christian concerns about hierarchy among the just in paradise. Human equality requires only that a uniformity of moral capacity hold during this life; its diverse exercise may populate a seven-level Paradiso, but this would not concern us.

Nor need we canvass all the authorities that confirm the moral vitality of the poor and ignorant. Their potential holiness is so obviously Christian as to be presumable. We raise this point about the ignorant once again only as a reminder that it would not follow from the universality of the invitation that every mind has the potential of the genius or the scholar for salvation. Whether Christianity allows such uniformity of moral capacity will be a different and crucial question reserved for chapter 8. We will, of course, report the biblical clues we recognize, but surely we have overlooked a good many. Whoever wrote the Bible seems not to have had our question in mind.

However much we simplify, the scope of the inquiry remains ambiguous. We have been unable to identify any general test of what is "Christian." In the cases of "individualism" (chapter 4) and of "natural law" (chapter 5), limiting concepts were available. Each of those two bundles of ideologies comprised a manageable core idea that could be tested for its harmony with the convention. We have not found so crisp a standard for Christianity. The difficulty is not the complete absence of shared premises; there is a set of common ideas held by a roughly identifiable community. These things on which there is a "Christian agreement," however, tend to have little to do with our subject, and those concepts that do bear on equality happen to be points on which believers divide along several ambiguous dimensions. Sometimes the split has been along confessional lines (e.g., Calvin and Luther against the rest on predestination). Sometimes the split has occurred within one confession across time (e.g., in chapter 7 we see that the Catholic Church has quietly adjusted to semi-Pelagianism).

Assuming that we identify the right questions, to whom do we put them? Does it matter which view is presently popular in the theological media? Most Christians have never heard of most theologians, past or present; should theology even count? We give the professionals considerable weight but also respect the authority of what faithful Christians in fact believe—the *sensus fidelium*; we only wish it were more accessible. Finally, quite apart from disputes both inside and outside Catholicism concerning the scope of papal supremacy, there is conflict regarding the doctrinal authority of bishops and—especially among Protestants—dispute regarding the dogmatic claims of communities that are organized in a hundred different forms.

Our failure to find a unifying conception of moral theology helps account for the greater number of pages we devote to Christianity than to individualism or natural law. Despite our focus upon mainline confessions, we faced an embarrassment of riches and necessarily have slighted major thinkers. An example is Søren Kierkegaard whose celebration of human equality could have served as the model for our own.[8] Our only defense is that this book is intended to open conversation, not to end it. Perhaps some critic can better answer the question that has vexed us: What is the unitary model of Christianity against which the invitation is to be measured?[9] Lacking such a model, the course of the inquiry is set by a half dozen recurring and distinctive ideas that have been promoted by thinkers who at least thought them to be Christian. Depending upon the interpretation and orthodoxy of these ideas, they may either sunder Christianity from human equality or marry the two.

Insofar as possible we will express equality's encounter with Christianity in the same style and terms employed in the previous parts of the book. Some new labels will be necessary; nevertheless, within the limits of our literary capacities, the discussions should remain linear and plain. Here is the rough and simple sequence within which we pursue the basic questions in the next two chapters. In chapter 7 we ask:

1. Are all baptized persons free to decline or to accept the invitation?
2. If yes, are the unbaptized similarly empowered?

We conclude that affirmative answers to these first two questions are plausible for many Christians; this permits us in chapter 8 to go on to ask:

3. Does obtension (the diligent intention of the good) constitute acceptance of the invitation?
4. If yes, do all rational humans have a uniform capacity to obtend?

Of Freedom, Faith, and Fallibility: Mumbling in Paradise

The idea of a perfection of the self will remain central to the invitation, but, for Christianity, it could no longer be satisfied by any earthly excellence that has a natural termination. Christian perfection may entail moral achievement as a criterion, but the *perfection itself* (in its final form) is eternal salvation—a theological category. It is God who perfects us. The incorporation of this divine aspect of perfection affects our description of the act of obtension. If obtension is "to give a reason," God becomes that reason. Without differentiating the perfecting capacities of individual persons, room must be made for this special theological aspect of the invitation. More specifically, Christian perfection requires what Martha Nussbaum would not—some form of what is called faith. As St. Paul wrote to the Hebrews: "It is impossible to please God without faith, since anyone who comes to him must believe that he exists and rewards those who seek him" (*Romans* 11:6). Few Christians would dispute this point. What may be unsettled among them are those mental and moral conditions that satisfy the definition of faith. Just what faith is and how it is acquired are not so clear. This ambiguity we think to be salutary for equality.

In part 1 we argued that reason apprehends moral truth in a certain way. Equality requires free will; the actor must not be compelled to assent to or reject the real good. Since a clear and distinct grasp of the content of the good would determine the will, a certain ignorance is benign. On the other hand, ignorance pure and simple has a determining effect; one who grasps no alternative course of action is unfree. Moral freedom therefore requires decision in a persistent mix of shadow and light, never achieving a state of compelling clarity nor falling into pure nescience. Such genuine obscurity seems the common experience. The basic decision to seek or avoid the true and the good, as well as every choice among specific goods, is free because of both cognitive inconclusiveness and the human capacity to self-delude. As we continue to hypothesize the terms of the invitation, we need a Christian interpretation of this saving fallibility. It must be orthodox that, though our darkness is related to the Fall, a degree of darkness would in any case be the medium congenial to free human choice.

This curious wisdom regarding the benign obscurity of correct works will attach to belief itself. For, as morality will need to remain in its crepuscular state, faith too will require shadow. This may be as one might expect; faith and sight are distinct ideas. In any case, this half-light is elemental to Christian freedom and cannot be ignored; but how does one describe it?

Both believers and unbelievers have their versions of the divine obscurity, and many find it thoroughly irritating. The late Michael Harrington represents the unbelievers. Mr. Harrington was the quintessential well-intentioned and suffering soul. He had searched the world for God but simply could not find him and wound up a "Catholic atheist." In his autobiography he tells of a late-life conversation with his cousin, a nun:

> My only problem was that I did not believe . . . I told Peggy that if I did die on
> the operating table and discovered, to my astonishment, that there was indeed

a God . . . I was not afraid. . . . I then added that in case I did encounter God
. . . I was going to accuse Him (Her?) of mumbling to humankind.[10]

Earthy types like Harrington are not the only complainers. The thoroughly
academic (believer) Roberto Unger ends one of his long and inconclusive
searches for justice with a feverish "Speak God[!]"[11] Critics have had good
fun with Unger's outburst,[12] but we suspect that some would be as grateful
as he for a revelation. Getting things straight without the aid of an unim-
peachable authority seems so utterly hopeless.

But what would it mean to get things straight? If God really ceased to
mumble, just where would a person be? Let us pursue the question with a
little mumbling of our own in the form of a brief parable presented in two
parts. The discerning reader will note that the first part is about faith, the
second about morals.

Part 1

Four lawyers are playing golf together in Kansas. We choose lawyers because
we intend to make these people boring. They are so ordinary that we will
call them A, B, C, and D; they are not even very good (or bad) golfers. They
are also indifferent husbands and lovers, read the New York Times, jog, and
do not really like one another very well. These are not mystics; none has
ever asked God to speak and each is quite content that God mumble.

Our foursome has finished the twelfth hole and is waiting on the thir-
teenth. The conversation is the usual stuff about the Supreme Court or com-
puters. At this moment God reveals himself to the foursome. We mean they
see him. No—better—they don't see him; they simply know two things: (1)
that he is, and (2) what he is. They know this by a direct and irresistible
infusion of knowledge. They have "it." (Language, you will note, does not
work here, but our point is plain enough.)

Modern psychology will delegitimate this story, saying that one can never
distinguish dream from reality. Hence we allow B (a skeptic who reads Richard Rorty) to say to God, "Don't stop the revelation now, or else by six
o'clock we'll all suppose it was a dream." Presently a hippo materializes and
trots down the fairway out of sight.[13] The episode terminates, and without
a word the foursome heads straight to the clubhouse.

They take their usual table but sit there staring into space, ignoring the
imported beer. Their unaccustomed silence is presently ended by a tumult
in the parking lot, followed by a hysterical announcement that a hippo is
rambling about bashing cars. This is getting harder to explain.

Part 2

At that point God returns to the foursome and reveals that he wants each of them to move to Azerbaijan and help start a law school. C asks, "What happens if we don't go?" God reveals that anyone who refuses to go will be rich, famous, and damned; by contrast, considerable earthly misery awaits the one who accepts the assignment—but he or she will be united with God in heaven. God also gives a perspicuous view of the alternative eternities— the one with him and the other without him. Being without God (damnation) turns out to be a state roughly like earth—not much brimstone, but an endlessly boring concentration on one's own self. On the other hand, being in union with God is just what the Christians always claimed; it is— well—heavenly. In short, nothing is concealed from these four ordinary people. We have no idea what it would mean to conceal nothing, but, in a way, this ignorance of ours is the very point of the parable.

Even—maybe especially—for believers we would suppose that any such invitation to the four lawyers would be nonsense. It is possible in a fantasy to give God's proposal the verbal form of a free option, but in truth there could be nothing of the sort. The encounter would be a terminal intellectual and moral experience leaving no choice at all. No believer claims to have had such an experience—neither Abraham nor the prophets, neither the mystics nor the apostles, least of all Paul. Though he was struck from his horse and never would enjoy another restful night, he still saw through a glass darkly. God apparently continued to mumble to him just as he did to Michael Harrington.

Mumbling about himself and his will for us could be God's choice. For whatever reason or none, God never infuses skeptical lawyers with the beatific vision; nor does he give them perspicuous moral alternatives by which to determine their own state in this life and the next. Instead, all are allowed their liberating obscurities. Even the believer who decides to torture and kill his enemy out of pure hatred, and who expects to burn in hell for it, is able to carry out his purpose only because he cannot grasp whole and entire the transcendental costs and benefits of this choice. More precisely, he never gets to see it all from God's point of view. One possible reason is obvious. Perhaps the actor cannot be *allowed* to see it so, because that would be the end of his freedom, hence an end to the free choice between self-love and self-surrender that God might wish to maintain.[14] It is for freedom's sake that the objective stupidity of doing it "my way" (barely) eludes the Don Giovanni and Frank Sinatra that lurk in us all.

Stand back a bit farther. The sort of God who would have man's friendship would (so far as we can see) encounter an intransigent problem. Men literally could not refuse union and bliss with a loving God whom they had perceived as he truly is. A revelation that revealed so much would make the game of God and man into no game, for the outcome would be fixed, and faith and love would be transmuted into knowledge and involuntary adoration.[15] At various times in history Christian theologians have argued that freedom survives even in heaven. Everyone is said to be "free" to leave, even though nobody in fact does so. Grace is too abounding.[16] To suppose any such "freedom," however, is wordplay, for the beatified would be bound in any practical sense. And beatific bondage would itself be confirmation of the necessity for obscurity in a free, temporal world. The very possibility of choosing God would require that revelation conceal as much as it reveals; faith and love would need a measure of mumbling.[17]

It thus seems to us that at least some mainline versions of Christianity might require both a theology and a morality not merely of mystery but of mist; that is, man would need a cognitive environment supporting the capacity to disbelieve and the capacity to disobey—and the latter could well be a function of the former.[18] And there is more to be said.

More Mumbling: Theology and Doubt

The relation of seeing to believing, then, might not be as the skeptical motto supposes. Seeing is not believing; for faith itself needs the possibility of disbelief, and that possibility in turn rests upon our not quite seeing.[19] Indeed, the mental state of the "saved" who dwell with God is imperfectly expressed in the term "believer." One who shares the beatific vision does not believe—he knows. Belief, by contrast, requires at least the capacity to doubt. In the case of those already saved, doubt is over; and those for whom doubt is over already are saved. Blessed are those who have not seen, for only they can believe.

"Doubt," of course, is an ambiguous word, and in at least one of its forms is condemned by Christians. This is the doubt that consists in the "hesitancy or refusal to assent to the faith" in a spirit of evasion or disregard.[20] Sin makes its appearance in "the indifference, the insincerity, the conceitedness, through which so many men turn away."[21] But excluding this obvious case leaves that other kind of doubt—one that could be wholly Christian—consisting in "every temptation or difficulty against faith."[22] This seems to have its role to play in a full Christian life:

> Doubts against the faith . . . help in their own way to show what faith is. Difficulties are part of faith. They have a positive function. They force the believer to bring the message of Jesus more clearly to mind. They make dedication a more conscious act. They purify faith from accidental motives.[23]

Thus even the certainty of faith is accompanied by difficulties or "doubt."[24] Indeed, this would seem a necessity, at least if Christianity is to maintain mankind's liberty to disbelieve and disobey. Storytellers may see the issue more clearly than the theologians. Isaac Singer compresses the whole into a few lines in his story "Joy":

> On Rosh Hashanah one prays for life, and life means free choice, and freedom is Mystery. If one knew the truth how could there be freedom? . . . Of all the blessings bestowed on man, the greatest lies in the fact that God's face is forever hidden from him. Men are the children of the Highest and the Almighty plays hide and seek with them.[25]

Note the contrast between the attitudes of Singer, on the one hand, and of Michael Harrington and Roberto Unger, on the other. The latter ask for divine revelation that they may grasp truth like a ripe apple;[26] but Singer prays for divine restraint that he may remain simply human. Graham Greene's hero in *Monsignor Quixote* agrees with Singer; he is tormented by the merciless lucidity of a dream about an aborted crucifixion:

> Father Quixote stood there watching on Golgotha as Christ stepped down from the Cross triumphant and acclaimed. The Roman soldiers, even the Centurion, knelt in His honor, and the people of Jerusalem poured up the hill to worship Him. The disciples clustered happily around. His mother smiled through her tears of joy. There was no ambiguity, no room for doubt and no room for faith at all. The whole world knew with certainty that Christ was the Son of God. It was only a dream, of course it was only a dream, but nonetheless Father Quixote had felt on waking the chill of despair felt by a man who realizes suddenly that he has taken up a profession which is of use to no one, who must continue to live in a kind of Saharan desert without doubt or faith, where everyone is certain that the same belief is true. He had found himself whispering, "God save me from such a belief."[27]

Notice, finally, that obscurity works its liberating effect by giving the *appearance* of the good both to the right choices *and* to the evil ones. Man remains free to disbelieve and to sin because both *seem* good. Phyllis McGinley understood such things. Her critique of Graham Greene is a piece of high theology:

> Were all our sins so empty of enjoyment,
> All sinners gloomy as the ones he paints,
> The Devil soon, I think, would lack employment.
> And the earth teem with saints.[28]

McGinley was right about the premise. Sin *is* fun. She was wrong only about the inference. If sin were boring, the world would teem, not with saints, but with moral hostages. Sanctity is won by a choice made among tantalizing alternatives, and boredom is not one of them. In our view Pascal made a similar miscalculation. In his classic wager he conceived the loss of the world to be as nothing; but if a man's submission to God and to the good really entails no serious trade-offs, it ceases to be a free act of fidelity and moral commitment. If choosing God and God's way really means risking nothing, there is no option. Pascal could not choose God at all, for God would already have chosen Pascal simply by allowing him the coercive insight that the world is worthless.[29]

For believers, then, it may come to this: Human freedom—if it is to exist at all—requires a zone of obscurity surrounding the source and content of the good. The truth may make us free, but not if it is the whole truth, or at least not right now.

God! Speak not, that I might believe!

Where Is Love?

We now have our theological framework for human equality ready for inspection by the theologians. If the reader is a Christian, however, he or she may wish to pose a final and basic question about our approach: Whatever happened to love? The framework is a contraption consisting exclusively of faith and morals. Why was it not fashioned, instead, out of faith and love? To substitute talk about correct behaviors for that about love seems excessively rationalistic and not very likely to win Christian approval of human equality.

The "model" could have been so designed. The works of love might be taken as a surrogate for faith, and the host property would become nothing other than the capacity to love; that capacity would, then, be examined for its uniformity among rational humans. Its efficacy for self-perfection would be scrutinized to see whether Christians could perceive this power to love as a faculty independent of circumstance and moral sophistication. If so, human equality plausibly could be a relation of double equality that holds among those with the capacity to love. We suspect that this indeed is a deeper, if unconscious, meaning of the convention of human equality, and it is appropriate to concede the point.

Nevertheless, here we will evaluate the Christian pedigree of equality in more "objective" terms. A sufficient reason for this restraint lies in the perennial focus of theology upon the importance of specific acts in forging our link with God. A fair part of the Old Testament consists of such acts; the Sermon on the Mount, the good Samaritan, the healings all confirm that the behaviors of bodies count also in a Christian economy. Faith too, of course,—but plainly faith without works is dead. And a love that never issues in deeds can scarcely be imagined. Love is a practical project, inviting the application of intelligence. Whatever brainpower one has is to be addressed to seeking the details of our brother's practical good.

We nonetheless face briefly a substantive question arising from the Christian conception of love. It concerns an immense literature that specifically purports to associate Christian love with equality; we must explain our ignoring this resource despite its supportive assertions. The literature of Christian love—or "agape"[30]—treats equality as a feature of the love relation; these claims could be used to the advantage of our argument. However, before showing this possibility and justifying its neglect, we should be as clear as we may be about the meaning of this new term. Agape is not about feeling good or ego satisfaction, and its permanent contrast is eros, or erotic love.[31] Endlessly parsed by spiritual writers, the content of Christian agape has acquired a dominant interpretation that resonates with our own theme. Agape is "equal regard"—the imperative to accord everyone equal consideration (if not identical treatment).[32] It might fairly be deemed the New Testament version of *normative* equality. It is not in itself a descriptive equality, nor does it necessarily imply the possibility of such an equality.

Nevertheless, the agape literature also teems with offhand claims about connections between this normative equality (agape) and some unspecified intrinsic or descriptive equality. Sometimes this crypto-descriptive version is said to be a foundation for the normative version. At other times it is normative equality that is said to be necessary to the descriptive equality.[33] In light of the frequency with which it does service in the agape texts, it is incontestable that most of these writers conceive of themselves as believers in some sort of descriptive human equality. Why, then, do we forego their support?

The justification will be familiar from our early treatment of the secular philosophers who invoke descriptive equality. Like them, no Christian author ever tells us exactly what this equality *is*. The effect of these unsupported assertions (at least the effect upon us) is merely to intensify resistance to the predictable non sequitur that we *ought* therefore to treat everyone the same.[34] Hence, though we find this Christian literary intuition encouraging, it is feeble support for any articulated proposition about a descriptive equality. If Christians in general actually do believe that all rational humans have a uniform capacity for agape, and thus for salvation, this will have to be inferred from the more ponderous (but also more intelligible) structures of Christian philosophy and theology. Superficial affirmations of human equality are a Christian commonplace; the question for us is whether conventional human equality has an enemy or an ally in the deep structure of Christian theology.

Hence we pose the question for a Christian descriptive equality in terms already familiar. We ask simply whether it is orthodox to believe that God has made obtension sufficient to salvation and whether Christianity has supposed that rational people might uniformly possess the capacity to obtend. The reader may anticipate a traditional discourse of faith and works, not the exaltations of agape. The omission of the latter is an investment in intelligibility.[35]

7

REPAVING THE ROAD TO HELL:

THE PELAGIAN ISSUES

Who does his best, God will grace.
(Anonymous medieval saw, known to theologians as the *facienti*)[1]

Trust in the *facienti* has subverted almost the whole Church.
(M. Luther, *Werke*)[2]

WE PROMISED a rational consideration of the theological hurdles Christianity raises for human equality. The story cannot, however, be merely academic and bloodless, if only because all Christian moral theology bears the imprint of Augustine (354–430), that "troubled person"[3] and saint who, as bishop of the remote north African city of Hippo, formed the moral intellect of Europe.[4] The mind and passion of Augustine influenced every Christian doctrine significant to our theme, ever urging against equality. This chapter and the next ask Augustine's reasons and the extent to which the major Christian churches have unlearned them during the last fifteen hundred years.

Augustine's general outlook is familiar from the *Confessions*, his autobiography completed ten years after his conversion to Christianity. Writing now as a Catholic bishop, Augustine recalls his dissolute youth and the tortured path by which he was drawn to God—his resistance to good, his choice of evil for its own sake, his captivity to the sin that was in his very members. "I was at war within myself, and I was laid waste by myself."[5] So completely did mankind's fall in Adam vitiate human nature that moral impotence is now man's "second nature."[6] Augustine's own experience of depravity drove him to identify the saved as those only who are graced "from above." "It is not something that comes from man, but *something above man*, that makes his life blessed."[7]

These very personal themes were transmuted into theological bedrock under the pressure of the Pelagian controversy. Pelagius (ca. 354–418) has been a theological bogeyman since the year 400 when he appeared in Rome with a message he thought Christians needed to hear. Possibly a Celtic monk, Pelagius apparently was living an athletic Christianity, doing his best to cooperate with God's grace in order to be saved.[8] He was convinced that Christians had adopted a deterministic attitude toward salvation, one that made men too ready to let God do all the work.[9] What Christians needed was the recognition that—by the sustaining, but not overwhelming, grace of God—each person held salvation in his or her own hands.

Pelagius seems a well-intentioned activist hoping to clarify moral theory in an orthodox way. He thought he had found the tool to his hand in Augustine's own early theorizing about free will. Shortly after his conversion Augustine had composed his first—and the first[10]—analytical treatment of the link between God's power and man's capacity for moral choice. The immediate purpose of his *Free Will* (*De libero arbitrio*) was to refute certain doctrines of his former coreligionists, the Manicheans. Their theology divided all reality into two coequal sources—one good, the other evil. Working now from the Christian premise that God has no rival, Augustine needed a way to explain evil without implicating God as its author. Late Greek philosophy provided the solution: evil is not itself a form of being but rather a privation or falling away from being. In the case of man, evil consists in the choices he makes to fall away from God, his highest good. By making the choice to reject God, it is man, not God, who creates evil.

But in recognizing human freedom, Augustine unintentionally cut both ways, making the relationship between man's freedom and God's grace into a paradox. He had established that God was not responsible for evil; he did not seem troubled that his solution had the practical effect of building up both God and man—God, because evil had no substance that could rival the divine, but man, too, because he had the power to choose and, by rejecting evil, to realize the good.

It was this teaching of Augustine's that Pelagius invoked with considerable public effect at Rome. Although Pelagius's aim was to reassure the bishops concerning man's freedom, the effect was the opposite, particularly its effect upon Augustine. "Pelagianism was a radical negation of Augustine's personal experience."[11] Augustine looked to something "from above," and would concede no alternative.[12]

Pelagius never denied the necessity of grace. Indeed, for him any disparagement of nature was automatically a disparagement of grace, for grace never implies the gulf between God and man that, for Augustine, made man's salvation exclusively "from above." Pelagian grace comes with, and generally is indistinguishable from, whatever else comes to us in nature. If grace is not nature, it is at least—owing to God's creative and sustaining work—natural. "Free will was grace, because it was the very gift by which God has made man capable of achieving his own salvation."[13]

Augustine, by contrast, held that grace does not abound among men and comes only through the sacraments of the Catholic Church. In the third century the African bishop Cyprian had uttered the fateful thesis that "outside the church there is no salvation"—"*extra ecclesiam nulla salus*"[14]—which Augustine accepted and from which he inferred that the Church's sacraments are the exclusive remedies for man's corruption. Salvation is the result of the direct action of God himself as he reconstructs man by the grace of the sacraments.[15]

Some, of course, have no access to the Church and her sacraments. Augustine made no concessions. The whole of mankind stands condemned in the Fall, and, for reasons beyond our ken, God has willed to confer the free gift of regeneration only on some. The losers have no legitimate gripe. Man's condemnation was deserved, and the condemned have, as it were, no rights; whoever is saved, it is by God's gratuitous mercy, not his justice.[16]

Nor are the lost souls losers by their own choice. To assure that God is ever sovereign and never frustrated, Augustine insists that those who reject God do so not in denigration of his grace but because—according to his will—they lack it. This is double predestination, the embattled doctrine most noxious to equality. Under such a regime, God predestinates some to heaven and others to hell, without regard to his foreknowledge of what merit any might have. When he rewards a man with salvation, he crowns only the gifts he has himself bestowed.[17] Everything is God's work.

Even many of Augustine's contemporaries objected to the notion that "by God's predestination men are compelled to sin and driven to death by a sort of fatal necessity."[18] Twelve centuries later these critics would be labeled semi-Pelagians, even though they joined Augustine in much of his opposition to Pelagian optimism. They insisted only that Augustine had gone too far—glorifying grace by belittling nature and free will. Among the "semi's" of the fifth century were many monks. Looking at their way of life, a life approved by tradition, they could not accept that in the salvation story God is the only actor, nor that his will for human salvation was less than universal.[19] They grasped that the debate concerned the problem of who had a chance to be saved. Against the Augustinians' attempts to make salvation an exclusive affair, the semi-Pelagians pressed for an equal-opportunity God who gives to all that mixture of freedom and grace required to respond to his invitation.[20]

The Second Synod of Orange (529) reached an official resolution of the issue by adopting Augustine's economy of grace wholesale—teaching that man's nature can accomplish nothing toward salvation, that only unmerited grace works any good, and that a person can be restored and saved only if he or she is baptized. All good comes "from above"; the disparagement of nature is profound.[21] Yet the Synod stopped short of fatalism; absent from Orange II (and from every other Catholic declaration) is an approval of Augustine's doctrine of double predestination. The result:

> Shorn of its predestinarian elements . . . Augustine's anti-pelagian doctrine of grace became the *official* teaching of Latin Christianity. . . . "Natural endowment" was to be distinguished from "that good gift which pertains to a holy life," which did not come from nature, but was superadded by God.[22]

Meanwhile, the yet unnamed semi-Pelagianism throve, reminding all that God expected them to reach out to him in an initial act of faith.[23] The necessity for grace had never really been in question. The real dispute concerned the way grace worked. Pelagius supposed that it was communicated in nature itself. Augustine countered that the necessary grace is not natural but "from above"—*super*natural. Drawing a bright line between the natural and the supernatural, Augustine simultaneously carved the universe into the saved and the damned.[24]

Eventually, of course, the theological tides shifted, and the ark of salvation expanded. Exclusivism was supplanted by an ever-widening embrace, the strong medicine of *extra ecclesiam* being diluted a drop at a time. Augustine had taught that the hopeful statement in 1 *Timothy* 2:4 that "God desires all men to be saved" meant "all the elect"—a twist of scripture his personal theological precommitments demanded.[25] In time, as we shall see, the Church would invoke the same text to show that salvation is possible even for the unbaptized.

It took the theologians a millennium and a half to credit this idea and to rejuvenate the possibility of equality. In this chapter and the next we watch them wrench and pull on grace, freedom, predestination, and the sacraments. In the end we will see much of Christianity accommodate a natural human freedom allowing the possibility that all men might be saved by their diligent efforts to accept God's universal invitation.

Grace "From Above" in the High Middle Ages: Thomas Aquinas

Even today St. Thomas Aquinas (1225–1274) frequently is regarded as the leading Catholic theologian. And it is not uncommon to suppose him to stand on the side of a substantial, if limited, human freedom. Were it so, he might be a potential friend of equality. Alas, the freedom with which Thomas credits man is insufficient.

Aquinas shared Augustine's conviction that man can do nothing at all toward salvation. What was necessary to man's perfection was the intervention of the "supernatural." From eternity God has chosen some to receive his grace and to be brought thereby to heavenly glory.[26] These are the elect, whom God has predestinated. He has elected them to glory not because they merit it (they do not) but because of his gracious goodness. Those whom God has not elected and predestinated, by contrast, fall into reprobation not because God positively wills it but because he permits it.[27] God loves all men, says St. Thomas, but only some does he love so as to elect, predestinate, and bring them to glory.[28] As 1 *Timothy* 2:4 teaches, God wills all men to be saved—but only "antecedently." More relevant is God's "consequent" will that "some . . . be damned, as His justice demands."[29]

Predestination, then, is just a technical name for the outcome God ordains.[30] When a man's act is good, "all the credit is God's, and the creature is only His instrument."[31] When man's own feeble influence enters, its name is sin.[32] Thus goodness and evil are asymmetrical. When man does good, it is through God's active agency; when man authors evil, it is in his own name. Thomas's understanding "leaves sin to be . . . due to the sinner alone, and to be a ground for punishment in a way in which merit is not a ground for glory."[33] As with Augustine, salvation is still a "heads I win, tails you lose" proposition.[34]

This is confirmed in Aquinas's treatment of the maxim which introduced this chapter: *Facienti quod in se est Deus non denegat gratiam*. This Latin saw is probably best translated "God will not deny grace to one who does his best" (or, literally, "who does what is in him"). It affirms the need for grace but very significantly divides the work of man's justification between God and man. No theologian who wholeheartedly accepts this axiom could suppose that God is the only actor. Though it concedes (as Orange II required) that salvation requires grace, the maxim gives man a hand in the workings of the supernatural. Its origin is obscure,[35] but Aquinas deemed it sufficiently venerable to require domestication. Attempting its harmonious incorporation into his theology, he paid important tribute to its plausibility, even as he strove to disarm it.

More accurately, he gutted it. For, according to Thomas, God will not deny grace to the man who does his best, "insofar as he is moved by God to do this."[36] Thomas means this literally. "It is impossible that the whole of the effect of predestination in general should have any cause as coming from us; because whatsoever is in man disposing him towards salvation, is all included under the effect of predestination; *even the preparation for grace*."[37] In the order of salvation, God does it all, and so to follow Aquinas is to forsake equality.

Aquinas, however, did not have the last word.[38] Shortly we shall turn to figures more cordial to equality. But first we shift to an alternative vocabulary.

Simplifying the Terminology

The Pelagian story so far has been reported largely in terms that—except for their translation to English—were supplied by the protagonists. This seemed important to capture the historical context. We now can introduce a simplifying terminology. The new terms are "original grace," "special grace," "sufficient condition," and "necessary condition."[39] They will allow us to clarify the distinction between the Augustinian/Thomist and the semi-Pelagian points of view.

The enduring core of Pelagianism comes to this: whatever the crippling effect of the Fall, the human self remains in a state of genuine, if limited, grace. Insofar as it has being, that being comes from God. This transmitted being is good, and it is empowered. The Pelagian question, then, is this: What are the powers that are included in this limited and inaugural bestowal of grace? The Pelagian answer is that every human has been given at minimum the capacity to will union with or separation from God. This supposed universal human capacity to choose God we label "original grace."[40] The rest of material creation does not receive it; in spite of the Fall, we still do.

This capacity to will union with God is, however, not a *sufficient condition* of salvation; it cannot by itself effect its chosen object. Our species cannot merit salvation by willing it. This insufficiency does not mean, however, that our attitude regarding salvation is simply ineffectual. Indeed, the free choice to unite with God is as important to salvation as air is to our physical survival. Air is not sufficient, but it is *necessary*; water is likewise insufficient— and necessary. If either is lacking, life is impossible. The individual will to salvation, like air or water, may be necessary without being sufficient. Our choice of God may be crucial without being enough. The idea that the individual's assent is necessary but insufficient is a simple expression of the benign aspect of semi-Pelagian moral theology.

What, then, is the additional component that is necessary to salvation? Just as water must ally with air to sustain the body, God must join his own will with ours to effect salvation; this is the process (or act) of justification. Note carefully that this separate and *special grace* offered by God is also insufficient in itself to produce salvation; for God has left man free to refuse it. That freedom, indeed, was the essence of God's original grace to us; by nature we are given the capacity to choose God or reject him. But when the two necessary conditions of God's will and our own are satisfied, together they constitute the *sufficient condition* of salvation. The metaphor of the invitation is again irresistible; the feast does not take place unless there are both the special grace of invitation proceeding from the host and an acceptance from the one invited. Each is necessary; jointly they are sufficient.

Adopting this roughly semi-Pelagian view of the economy of salvation would not settle the question about who among us receive the special grace that allows the assent of the individual to make the conditions sufficient. Perhaps not all those who would choose God are themselves chosen; maybe the guest list is not universal. Thus selective predestination would still be a possibility; God could withhold the invitation from some, either for no reason at all or for reasons we cannot grasp. The semi-Pelagians as a group believed that God's offer (his special grace) was open to anyone (at least any Christian) to accept, but this conclusion would not follow necessarily from their belief that natural man has the original grace of choice; for man's own choice is only a necessary condition, and God is free to play favorites.[41]

The Augustinian position ultimately adopted by St. Thomas may be recast in a similar verbal framework but with different content and outcome. For Aquinas, the act by which God sustains us in existence simply does not include "original grace" in the sense just suggested. Whatever powers man is given at birth, he lacks the crucial capacity freely to will acceptance of a divine invitation. It is true that God can and does make such an invitation (and possibly to all) in the form of individual bestowals of grace for which "special" may be the most appropriate adjective. And it is also appropriate to consider this special act of God as *necessary*. Special grace is not, however, sufficient to effect salvation, for in Aquinas's formula, man's movement toward God also is necessary (and only together are they sufficient). On this aspect of the problem Aquinas and the Pelagians agree. The two conditions of God's offer and man's acceptance must be met.

The specific anti-Pelagian element in Thomas's theology is the denial that man has original grace in the form of a free capacity to will salvation. Man does not will acceptance. God alone acts to satisfy both necessary conditions. In effect, he both invites and accepts, thereby satisfying the sufficient condition of salvation. Man does nothing positive to assist this outcome. He can participate only negatively by his one free choice—the choice to sin, thereby effecting his own damnation, if that is not already predestinated.

In these recondite struggles to settle the language of Christian justification, the theologians thrashed out their answers to that question of universal import: Who can be saved? Though only occasionally do they answer by explicitly affirming or denying an equality of opportunity (Calvin will be a conspicuous exception), from at least the time Augustine narrowed the ark, the stakes have been inescapably clear.

The Late Scholastic Shift: Gabriel Biel

One giant of late scholasticism interpreted the *facienti* in a manner congenial to equality. Our simplified vocabulary may be helpful in explaining the development represented in Gabriel Biel (ca. 1420–1495), who appears the first among the proponents of a moderate Pelagian theology to be quietly conceded a place within the mainstream.[42] Biel's own account of the state of fallen man at first seems familiar enough. Man lives in "inner revolt" and is prone to all evil. Sinner that he is, man simply cannot merit salvation—without the healing of grace. To be sure, the individual is never without grace insofar as God sustains his being and empowers him even to abuse his gifts. Man, however, needs more than this minimal divine support; he needs healing grace. Transposing Biel's conclusion into our own terms, man has original grace but cannot be saved unless he receives special grace.

How does the saving event occur in human individuals? Biel converts the issue to a new form with his own understanding of the *facienti*. God has decreed that man, by doing his best, both chooses and merits the special grace necessary to his healing. Man makes this initial necessary move by his own decision, for which God has empowered but not determined him.

> The commitment by which God in eternity obligated himself conveys to man's action a dignity which it would not have in itself: if man goes halfway, God will meet him with the gift of grace. Without this gift of grace man is *helpless*; but it is just as true that, without the full use of man's own natural powers, the offer of grace is *useless*.[43]

With original grace, man can choose to merit the necessary special grace that is always available. His choice fuses with God's own to become the sufficient condition of man's justification.

Just what is this necessary and salvific move that is made by individual men and women? In Biel's view, what every person can do—if he chooses—is to love God above all things for his own sake and to seek his will. Even in his fallen state, God provides man with knowledge of this opportunity along with the capacity to accept or reject it. We would say that this knowledge and this capacity are a part of God's grant of original grace. God creates and starts it all, but what he starts is liberty. By his created nature man can choose to do his best. In bestowing this original grace God tells man to play the part for which he has been empowered: It's your move. Do your part; I'll do mine. Unlike Aquinas, Biel lets the Latin epigram have its plain meaning.

If God puts this option to every rational Christian, predestination is in trouble. And Biel agrees. God does not predestinate but only foresees whether one will choose to merit and reach beatitude. Salvation is achieved not by inescapable divine decree but because the individual freely does his or her best to meet the terms of the invitation.

Whether Biel is a heretical Pelagian is, of course, a matter of definition. Biel, to be sure, emphasized more than Pelagius the necessary action of special grace, but if this grace is assumed to be available to all for the asking—and if all have the capacity to ask—it is a distinction from Pelagius without a very great difference. The theologically offensive thought from the time of Augustine was the proposition that even in his natural and fallen state, man could freely contribute an act necessary—even if not sufficient—to his own salvation. Biel's affirmation of that proposition moves even a friendly modern critic to admit that "it is . . . evident that Biel's doctrine of justification is essentially Pelagian."[44]

Biel does say that by exercising natural powers under the influence of original grace, man comes to *merit* the special grace by which he is saved. But here there is no false supposition or hope that man can climb to heaven by his own achievements whether God likes it or not. God has willed a pact with man; the *facienti* works because God has decided it will.[45] "God had promised, through the covenant, to treat [man's works] as if they were of much greater value, in just the same way as a king could treat a lead coin as if it were gold."[46] God remains God, while inviting man to make his own critical contribution.

Biel saw the threat of psychological isolation that was created by man's relative autonomy. By the power of original grace, the earthly pilgrim knows of the existence of the object of his quest. On the other hand, he can never be certain whether he is in fact doing his part nor, in any case, whether he will persevere. Hence he seeks his salvation—with scriptural warrant—in fear and trembling. Indeed, it is his very oscillation between love and fear that allows the hope that he is on the right path. Greater certainty than this would be a damnable act of presumption.

If this discipline sometimes has seemed to its Christian practitioners more dolorous than hopeful, it is, in any case, a major step toward the premises of conventional human equality. Salvation still may be a long shot for the individual, because doing "what is in us" may turn out to entail moral heroism. The point, in any case, is that it is up to us. Furthermore, Biel seems to have us all playing the same game with the same equipment. Perhaps we have witnessed the epiphany of an equal-opportunity God.

Pelagius Meets Luther and Calvin

Biel's *facienti* is, in one neat package, a theology of freedom and grace that would sustain human equality. The young Martin Luther (1483–1546) learned his theology at the University of Erfurt from disciples of Gabriel Biel, and his reaction was one of appreciation: Luther reportedly considered Biel the only scholastic worth studying. Between 1509 and 1514 he espoused a Gabrielistic theology of salvation: God has promised to reward with grace everyone who does *quod in se est.*[47] "Something happened,"[48] however, to end Luther's affair with the *facienti*. In his 1515–16 lectures on St. Paul's letter to the Romans, Luther broke with the *facienti*, calling it "Pelagian" and denying that salvation depends in any way upon human will.[49] God does not invite man's free contribution. "God himself meets a precondition which man cannot fulfill."[50] This Luther knew from reading St. Paul, but perhaps even more from his own experience:

> I was a good monk, and kept my rule so strictly that I could say that if ever a monk could get to heaven through monastic discipline I was that monk.... [But t]he more I tried to remedy an uncertain, weak and troubled conscience

with human traditions, the more I daily found it more uncertain, weaker and more troubled.[51]

Whoever does *quod in se est*, concluded Luther, is one who sins.[52]

"Pelagianism [was]," for Luther, "the one perennial heresy of Christian history, which had never been fully exterminated and which, under the patronage of the church of Rome, had now become dominant."[53] The cancer of Pelagianism had developed because "Augustine's doctrine of [salvation by] 'grace alone' ... [had] not been accepted by the church of Rome."[54] Man's justification, insisted Luther, is "purely passive."[55] Behind all Rome's follies about human works lurks the *facienti*, an error against the Gospel to be overcome only by the frankest admission that "man without grace can, strictly speaking, do nothing of the slightest value for salvation. He can neither dispose himself for it, nor work for it in any independent fashion. Even his acceptance of grace is the work of grace."[56] The Roman conceit that man is active in the process of salvation—and even the hope to salvage free will (an impulse Augustine himself had shared)—must now be abandoned: "We do everything by necessity and nothing by our free will, since the power of the free will is nothing and neither does the good nor is capable of it in the absence of grace."[57]

Man's actual state of wretchedness comes exactly from his inability to help save himself, while the good news of the Gospel is that God does for humans—or at least for some humans—what they cannot do for themselves. But Luther rejected Augustine's teaching that God graciously transforms man. All righteousness is properly Christ's; if a person is justified, it is because the "alien" righteousness of Christ is *imputed* to him by God. For Luther, henceforth, "man is, and will remain, a sinner, despite being extrinsically righteous."[58] Man is saved by faith alone—*sola fide*—but this faith is not man's free act. Man is justified *through* faith but not because of his faith. The cause of man's justification is Christ alone.[59]

> This is the reason why our theology is certain: it snatches us away from ourselves and places us outside ourselves, so that we do not depend on our own strength, conscience, experience, person, or works, but depend on that which is outside ourselves, that is, on the promise and truth of God.[60]

This preempts equality, because man retains nothing positive in respect of which he can be meaningfully equal. For equality, faith must be man's own free (if divinely empowered) achievement. And to the extent that the free act requires God's sustaining grace, that grace must be available—somehow—to all.

Luther's embrace of double predestination was implicit but unenthusiastic.[61] It was John Calvin (1504–1564) who unflinchingly affirmed that the dread sentence issues from the very idea of divine sovereignty and grace. Whereas for Luther, and even more so for his followers, God predestinated according to the faith he foreknew man would possess, for Calvin, God's electing will—his *decretum absolutum*—is the sole basis of salvation.[62] Man himself makes no contribution in God's plan. "Those whom God passes over, he condemns, and this he does for no other reason than that he wills to exclude them from the inheritance that he predestines for his own children."[63] Calvin's God, though "the necessity of [all] things,"[64] is "not promiscuous with His love,"[65] capriciously saving some and damning others. According to Calvin, "all are not created on equal terms, but some are preordained to eternal life, others to eternal damnation."[66]

The Reformation had at last produced "the complete Augustine."[67] But even in their own day, by taking the doctrine of grace to this extreme, the reformers unwittingly did freedom a favor. Sharing the complete Augustine meant also sharing the criticisms of his doctrine, particularly its rejection as fatalistic.

The Catholic Response at Trent; with a Parenthesis on Baptism and the Other Sacraments

Convening in a drawn-out and interrupted ecumenical council at Trent between 1545 and 1563, the bishops and other leaders of the Catholic Church undertook a thoroughgoing clarification of the Catholic doctrine of justification. "The Tridentine decree on justification was the most significant statement on the matter ever to have been made by the Christian church."[68] The *Decree* is significant for what it says, but even more for what it leaves unsaid.

Trent conceded important aspects of the reformers' theology: "We are . . . justified gratuitously, because none of those things that precede justification, faith or works, *strictly* merits the grace of justification" (DS § 1533).[69] This passage and others have often been interpreted as a complete repudiation of the *facienti*. But as a leading historian has shown, the evidence comfortably allows another interpretation. Trent clearly ruled out the possibility that anyone could *absolutely* merit God's special grace—the implausible notion that God from all eternity had no alternative but to justify the sinner who does *quod in se est*. But by a tricky distinction negotiated by two different Latin verbs, the council seems to have left open the possibility that God has *chosen* to accept our best as meritorious. Perhaps with Biel, "grace is no reward but rather a gift on which man may count, since God has committed himself to give his grace 'facientibus quod in se est.' "[70] The pilgrim thus seems free to believe that God has chosen to treat his humble diligence as though it were golden. If so, Trent is a signal victory for human equality.

The apparent Catholic tolerance of the *facienti* is only the first bit of good news. Trent also explicitly recognized that man must *cooperate* in his own justification—first in preparation for, and then in the increase of, the grace of justification (DS §§ 1525, 1535). "To those who work well 'unto the end' and trust in God," teaches Trent, "eternal life is to be offered, both as grace mercifully promised to the sons of God through Christ Jesus, and 'as a reward' promised by God himself, to be faithfully given to their good works and merits" (DS § 1545).[71] Over and over the council condemns those who deny that man must cooperate in his own salvation (DS §§ 1528, 1559, 1574, 1582).

Perhaps to keep things in obscure balance, the council did add another wrinkle. Though Trent condemned the doctrine of double predestination, like Augustine it affirmed predestination for those who are saved (DS § 1567). But so long as justification requires free human cooperation, this is a toothless predestination preserving the role of a real choice and, so far, equality is satisfied (DS § 1525). The questions remaining are whether this is a freedom to which God graciously predestinates all people or just the lucky elect, and whether it is bestowed uniformly.

Consideration of the sacraments, and of baptism in particular, focused these problems. Echoing Augustine, Trent proclaims: "If anyone says that baptism is optional, that is, not necessary for salvation, let him be anathema" (DS § 1618). This is, after all, a requirement for which there is scriptural warrant: "Unless a man be born again of water and the Holy Ghost, he cannot enter into the kingdom of God."[72] And on the surface Trent seems to require sacramental baptism administered with water and the Trinitarian formula; it even anathematizes anyone who would suggest that the requirement of a baptism by *water* is mere metaphor (DS § 1615).

Such an economy of salvation obviously would be hostile to equality; many will neither receive baptism by water nor even hear it preached. Missionary zeal may have reached the ends of the earth, but not every Middlesex village, town, tribe, or tribesman on the way.[73] But here we witness Trent's final act on the theological high wire. Equality gets rescued by the doctrine of the Baptism of Desire;[74] those who are barred from liturgical baptism by some invincible obstacle can be saved by their desire for this sacrament. Trent makes the rescue difficult, because it has said that "this transformation [to the state of grace] cannot come about—now that the Gospel has been preached—without either the bath of regeneration or the desire for it" (DS § 1524). But this still left an opening, for everything turns on discovering the referent of the "it." If regeneration is the whole of what one must wish for, one need not even have heard of the Gospel. On the other hand, it could be that one must literally wish to *bathe*, having first heard that such a bath is necessary. This more restrictive reading receives support elsewhere in the council's declaration on justification.[75] Trent left equality's fate as unclear as the water metaphor—if metaphor it was.

This obscurity was to endure for several centuries. Even today the Catholic Church continues to insist—on the same scriptural ground—that "baptism is necessary for salvation."[76] However, by an evolution too subtle for our discovery, the meaning has become utterly transformed:

> Every man who is ignorant of the Gospel of Christ and of his Church, but seeks the truth and does the will of God in accordance with his understanding of it, can be saved. It may be supposed that such persons would have *desired Baptism explicitly* if they had known its necessity.[77]

This 1992 pronouncement obviously baptizes those who do their best, leaving the requirement of liturgical baptism no obstacle to equality. What does remain in question is whether those effectively baptized have the capacity to do whatever else is necessary. Will moral diligence assure salvation even to one who mistakes the real good? And will the capacity to make the necessary commitment be uniformly distributed? These are questions still to be faced in this chapter and its sequel. In any case, to equality's advantage, no sacrament other than baptism seems ever to have been understood by the Catholics as being strictly *necessary* in its liturgical form.[78] Though each is thought to work an important change in the person, the salvific grace is *somehow* available to all. Equality may be possible.

Jansenism and the Persistence of Freedom

When it ended in 1563 the Council of Trent had not snuffed the Pelagian possibility.[79] The council had affirmed the reality of both free will and the necessity of grace without specifying their precise relationship. Even before its adjournment, its own members were busy peddling conflicting interpretations of the decrees. In 1582 the debate rekindled when Luis de Molina (1535–1600), a Spanish Jesuit, published *The Harmony of the Free Will with the Gifts of Grace*, maintaining that "sufficient" grace had its efficacy from divinely foreknown, free human cooperation with this gift.[80] For Molina the *facienti* meant that God gives the grace necessary for salvation to the man who does what he can with his natural abilities. Grace is not bestowed for man's merit but rather for the merits of Christ; but one necessary condition of salvation is the correct exercise of the free will that is a natural capacity. It was in reaction to this affirmation of the efficacy of free human action (known as Molinism) that the pejorative term "semi-Pelagianism" was coined.[81]

In response to Molinism a papal congregation was convened. Though at first disposed to censure the propositions, the congregation ultimately permitted the Jesuits to defend them, and the Dominicans (heirs to the theology of Aquinas) to oppose—pending a final resolution of the controversy. No such resolution ever has issued. The Jesuits had succeeded in preventing the censure of Molina's views; but, at least for the ensuing generation, that victory for "devout humanism" only raised the stakes in the continuing debate about free will and grace.

The opposition to Molinist semi-Pelagianism exploded into the *Augustinus* of Cornelius Jansen (1585–1638).[82] Jansen maintained that man cannot resist the grace of God. God's gift of grace to man is always "efficacious"; in no way does it depend on free human cooperation. God's infusion of grace, moreover, is not universal, nor must God bestow it on the man who does his best.[83] This position of Jansen was condemned by Pope Alexander VII in 1656 (DS § 2012). Nearly half a century later, nonetheless, that indefatigable Jansenist Antoine Arnault (1612–1694) thought he was advancing orthodoxy in declaring that "only within the Pelagian heresy could one question the damnation of all these Americans before they were illuminated by the light of the gospel."[84]

The arcane details of this dispute are not our concern. The Catholic Church was able to maintain an irenic truce between these irreconcilable enemies.[85] "On this narrow ridge between Semi-Pelagianism and Calvinism, Jesuit and Jansenist were both trying to fix the boundary of Catholic faith."[86] Where Augustinian truth ends and Pelagian error begins the Catholic Church decided to keep obscure.[87] It did, however, clearly interdict the temptation to annihilate ourselves before God. By affirming man's essential, free cooperation in salvation, the Church had preserved the life of the Pelagian plant, and it was to sprout anew, perennially pruned but never uprooted.

Rome and Pelagius Today

Before resuming the complicated Protestant half of the story about the division of labor in salvation, we can succinctly bring this Catholic development to its modern conclusion. On the Pelagian issues, equality has a clear ally in the modern Roman magisterium. The *Catechism of the Catholic Church*, published in 1992, was described by the Pope as "a statement of the Church's faith and of catholic doctrine."[88] Its theology of justification recently was characterized—by a sensitive observer—as "semi-Pelagian rather than Augustinian."[89]

The relevant propositions of the *Catechism* are in the form traditional since Trent. Man is invited to beatitude with God; but wounded by sin, he cannot accept the invitation. He "stands in need of salvation from God" (§ 1949). Salvation is possible, because Christ has merited man's justification. Man is thereby rendered *capable* of being cleansed from sin and restored to righteousness through (1) faith in Jesus Christ, and (2) baptism. The need for baptism, as we observed earlier, is not an obstacle to equality, because in one form or another it is available to everyone, and, as chapter 8 will show, faith too may be an unconscious thing that harbors within the good will even of unbelievers. In any case, however, it is not a mere passivity. Though it is a gift from God (§ 153), it is also "an authentically human act" (§ 154). "In faith, the human intellect and will cooperate with divine grace" (§ 155).[90] The need for human cooperation is out in the open. "God's free initiative demands *man's free response*" (§ 2002).[91]

By his cooperation man "merits" justification and sanctification. To be sure, here, as with Biel and Trent, "merit" is understood in terms of the divine economy of salvation; God is necessary throughout. But although "merit is to be ascribed in the first place to the grace of God," it is ascribed "in the second place to man's collaboration."[92] While the exact meaning of this distinction is no clearer than in the documents of Trent, it is sufficient to confirm the respective roles of God and man. Man cannot strictly merit salvation; but considered in light of God's gracious promise to accept man's conduct as a part of the salvation process, man's acts become meritorious.

But is the essential grace dispensed in a manner allowing everyone to accept the invitation? "Redeemed by the sacrifice of Christ, all are called to participate in the same divine beatitude" (§ 1934). We find no indication in the *Catechism* that anyone is out of the running. Predestination receives only passing mention, and no substantive development whatever, in the *Catechism* (§§ 257, 600, 1007, 2012, 2782, 2823).[93] God "wants all men to be saved" (§ 843).[94] That old enemy of inclusivism, the "*extra ecclesiam*" is not, it turns out, "aimed at those who, through no fault of their own, do not know Christ and his Church" (§ 847). The *Catechism* explains that "in ways known to himself God can lead those who, through no fault of their own, are ignorant of the Gospel, to that faith without which it is impossible to please him" (§ 848).[95] Catholic theology has finally freed God to be God, and the ignorant are the first beneficiaries of the extinction of the Augustinian impulse to trace and limit God's saving will.[96]

On the crucial issue of whether all men have grace and freedom sufficient to satisfy the conditions of salvation, the *Catechism* is in equality's court.[97] Whether this alliance entails the efficacy and uniformity of *good intention* will be a more slippery question. We turn to it in chapter 8, but first we conclude our canvass of the Protestants' foreign relations with semi-Pelagius.

How Pelagius Played in Plymouth;
the Gnostic Penumbra

While Pascal was converting the Jansenist controversy into literature, Puritan men and women of the seventeenth century had been working hard at their own solutions—first in old, then in New England. Eventually their colonies gave us that "peculiar religion" that avowed Jansenism but would ultimately help to inspire the politics of human equality. It is a very American story.

Puritanism had its beginnings in the sixteenth-century efforts of English Protestants to reform the Church of England.[98] Although the visible church could not hope to reach the unblemished purity of the invisible, it ought at least to be a group of saints set apart from the wicked. To achieve this society of discernible saints the Puritans were to a degree willing to repudiate even Calvin, who, like Augustine, had deplored the ambition of fashioning in this world a church as spotless as possible. The Puritans aimed higher, insisting that "professing Christians must separate from the wicked and form true churches."[99]

And separate they did. But formation of this ostensible community only intensified the question of who was really to be reckoned on the inside. Believing that man is saved by faith alone, these early Calvinists judged authentic membership by evidence other than works.[100] Even in those earliest days, however, the profession of faith required not only a statement of belief but also a *demonstration* of the candidate's *understanding* of the doctrines he professed.[101] In that modest hurdle an inchoate test of orthodoxy was already emerging, taking an intellectual form. Among the Pilgrims who landed at Plymouth, membership in the church visible would come by degrees to depend upon an essentially gnostic criterion.

Those Puritans who later settled in Massachusetts Bay, New Haven, and elsewhere in Connecticut were more wary of such cognitive tests of perfection. Unlike the Plymouth Puritans, they had not separated from the Church of England and still hoped to reform it. They had already concluded that membership in the community at Plymouth required much too external a standard. The profession and explanation of the faith, and even the leading of a holy life, were too easily feigned; by these criteria even the internally unregenerate could qualify for church membership.[102] These later groups never approached fanaticism; they recognized that the presence of saving faith was difficult to discern and that delusion about its whereabouts always threatened.

Nevertheless, even among these moderates, the impulse to seek signs was irresistible. Sometimes after attendance upon the preaching of the Word—

perhaps after a period of doubt and despair—God's elect might find God "kindl[ing] . . . a spark of faith in their hearts."[103]

> If then, faith could be recognized, not with absolute certainty, but with a high degree of probability, why should not a man seeking admission to the company of the faithful demonstrate his worthiness not merely by a formal profession, by covenant, by good behaviour, but also by showing that he had received true saving faith according to the established pattern by which faith had been shown to come?[104]

By itself, this theological craving for signs of faith cannot reconcile the Calvinist trimmer to equality, for—says he—God still does it all; God alone produces the saving faith. Nevertheless, the Pelagian virus was there; indeed, this first shift was accompanied (and perhaps motivated) by a second. Looking at their own hearts for evidence of saving faith, the Puritans were tempted to wonder whether there was something they might do to help it along—to *prepare* themselves for the coming of God's saving grace. "From the earliest settlement sound conversions had been few; and as piety seemed to wane, all were exhorted to prepare."[105] The possibility of preparation was a clear departure from the "blunt language of Calvin" that treated regeneration "as a forcible seizure, a rape of the surprised will."[106] It was, nonetheless, a development of Calvinist theology that made sense of how most of the Puritans had themselves experienced regeneration—not all at once, as in the case of St. Paul, but in a series of movements that might be assisted.[107]

This encouragement of preparation is technically irrelevant in a scheme of hard rock predestination. In the core conception God saves or condemns a person without regard to what he or she does—including preparation. But the doctrine of preparation vaguely impelled people to *do* something, and enthusiasm for its possibilities quickly spread. Inevitably it set people thinking in terms of an active relationship with God. The Puritans remembered that they were people of the covenant that God had made with Abraham. God had, to the Puritan mind, made a contract with man.

> If election be a flash of lightning which strikes without warning, men cannot place themselves in its path, nor cultivate anticipatory attitudes, but when it comes as a chance to take up a contract, they must first of all learn what is to be contracted.[108]

Justification remained an unmerited gift from God, not a human achievement. But the contractual framework and imagery (reminiscent of the "pact" by which Biel had God valuing man's efforts to do *quod in se est*) encouraged the Puritans to think of justification in terms of mutuality. The limits of natural ability were "expanding."[109]

This expansion was possible only because it was carried on behind the veil of a staunch resistance to creeping Pelagianism, known most often in the

seventeenth century as Arminianism.[110] Jacobus Arminius (1560–1609)—
though a Protestant—notoriously supposed that the efficacy of God's saving
grace depends upon a free human decision; Arminius even deployed the
facienti in his theology.[111] Accusing them of "summoning the Pelagian error
back up out of hell," the Puritans condemned Arminius and his followers
at the Synod of Dort (1618–19).[112] To the Puritan mind, it was clear Pelagianism to suppose that man of his own power disposes himself for the coming
of grace. Nevertheless, freedom stood in the wings. "The soul cannot choose
Christ 'out of the power of nature'—but an inn must be prepared to receive
the guest, else He will go to another lodging!"[113]

> Let predestination be what it may, the world calls him mad who argues, "I can
> do nothing for my self, therefore I will take a course that no man shall do any
> thing for me." . . . It may not be in your power to make the Gospel "effectual"—
> but "it is your power to doe more than you doe, your legs may as well carry
> you to the word, as to an Ale-house."[114]

Gradually the deeds of preparation became endlessly elaborated. John
Norton, for example, divided preparation into five steps.[115] While Norton
insisted that none of these exercises was a slip into Pelagian synergism, Perry
Miller can only wonder: "All these actions, mind you, while remaining passive! . . . Arminians and Pelagians allow too much to preparation—we may
wonder what more they could allow!"[116] For Miller, "the moral is clear,"[117]
as Norton's very words demonstrate: "It is the duty of every one that hears
the Gospel to believe, and that whosoever believeth shall be saved; but also
it ministers *equal hope unto all* (answerable to their preparatory proceeding)
of believing and being saved."[118]

By the tortured route of preparationism much of the Puritan leadership
thus approached the equality of access to salvation by resting it upon human
effort.[119] We would not overstate the case. Puritan religion never yet has
been cast as a free choice to accept or reject God's invitation to salvation.
This is a theology of preparation, and man's active cooperation enters only
by the back door. But enter it does. While Pelagius—now Arminius—remained officially the enemy, silently he was all but absorbed into the doctrine of preparation worked out as a part of the covenant theology.[120] What
man does is mere preparation; but upon man's doing his share, God has
contracted to do his. "The result was this conception, not of conditional
election, but of conditional covenant, set up by the absolute decree of God
and yet requiring the self-directed activity of man."[121] The language has
changed some, but the concepts are Biel's.

In the extreme version of Calvinism that earned him his name, the Puritan
seems a distant historical figure. But as a practitioner of the distinctly American Calvinism, founded on a bilateral covenant and the practical possibility
of preparation for justification, the Puritan is very much with us. By the

rigor he accords the process of preparation the Puritan today rightly "symbolizes those ideas of individual integrity and responsibility and of personal dignity and destiny to which the American mind has so persistently clung through all its phases of historical change."[122]

The Puritan is not merely the practitioner of an antique religious reform; he is the embodiment of an attitude that suffuses contemporary culture and has a primary significance for equality. Indeed, living out his capitalist destiny, the Puritan among us remains a palpable moral force. Max Weber saw that capitalism grew in significant part from this Puritan need to prove the authenticity of faith through activity in the world.[123] "The God of Calvinism demanded of his believers not single good works, but a life of good works combined into a unified system,"[124] which Weber identified as capitalism.

If capitalism is informed by a general consciousness of man's preinstitutional obligation to perfect himself by correcting his lateral relations, this ratifies a necessary element of the conventional meaning of equality.[125] But this unchosen universal obligation of the capitalist could be grounded as well in nature as in religion; either would suffice as the foundation of the relation of equality. Although we welcome this confirmation of our interpretation of the convention, in this chapter our specific and narrower interest remains whether there be harmony between this interpretation of equality and the tenets of Christianity. Thus we focus only upon the insight that, for the Puritan, *preparation* became the forerunner of *cooperation* with God in the covenant. If this is the legacy of the Puritan—and if American Protestant religion remains broadly puritan—equality and Christianity can, to this extent, join hands. For our part, this picture of a diffused Puritanism seems a fair approximation of the vector of religious forces that surge around us.

An American Gnosis?

There is, however, a competing contemporary view of Protestant Christianity that is both plausible and wholly poisonous to equality. It locates the roots of modern American religion not in the Puritans but in various religious enthusiasts of the last two and a half centuries and their present descendants. This thesis is argued by sources as diverse as Harold Bloom, a Yale professor and self-proclaimed Gnostic Jew, and Philip Lee, a theologian and Presbyterian pastor. The core of their claim is that American Protestant sects have managed over time to convert what had been a thriving and godly Puritan citizenry into a mass of largely unwitting gnostics. Our own interpretation of conventional human equality requires that the highest kind of human worth be determined not by what or how much one knows but by whether one seeks the good. By contrast, the classical gnostic understanding of human moral achievement takes ignorance to be the fundamental human problem. *Mea culpa* becomes *mea ignorantia*.[126]

For the gnostic who is also a religious believer, another proposition quickly follows. Salvation comes, not by repentance and grace, but by apprehension of his own true self that preexisted, and will survive, this transitory world. The gnostic escapes into the self. There is indeed an " 'identity or consubstantiality of man's innermost self with the supreme and transmundane God, himself often called "Man." ' The search for God and the search for self, because of this ontological identification, become synonymous."[127] The final and predictable tenet of this form of gnosticism (as of its classical forebears) is that not everyone is capable of this knowledge. Only an elite— the *gnostikoi*—are saved because they know themselves/God.[128] Strange as it may seem, this bizarre knowledge is the boast of contemporary gnostics.[129]

The early Christians quickly made gnosticism a heresy. They most despised gnosticism's recognition of an elite corps, saved not by seeking the Kingdom of God but by their own knowledge.[130] This original complaint endures as we pick up the contemporary debate. In his *Against the Protestant Gnostics*, Philip Lee argues that religious knowledge plays a role in the theology of contemporary North American Protestants that it utterly lacked for Calvin and Luther. For the great reformers, religious knowledge was merely a consoling by-product of the redemption that God works through Christ. By contrast, for many contemporary Protestants, says Lee, such knowledge has itself become the cause of salvation. Christ is now more a bearer of saving knowledge than he is savior.[131]

A shift toward a Protestant gnosticism might, we concede, be one stage in the evolution of the Puritan mind. It would be an easy slide from a semipassive Puritan "preparation" to a distinctly active cooperation in which one comes to recognize one's own election. Perhaps the next stage in self-delusion is to transmute the knowledge of election into the knowledge that elects. Salvation by knowledge alone can be a quick and inexpensive religious experience—sometimes being accomplished in the course of an exciting evening. Lee is credible when he returns to the 1740s to find that in the Great Awakening's insistence on individual experience and knowledge of salvation, there was born a distinctly American gnosticism.[132]

So is Harold Bloom. He thinks that American Protestantism (and even Catholicism) has developed symptoms of gnosticism. He has postulated "The American Religion," the still unacknowledged and unanalyzed essence of the properly American religions such as Mormonism, Seventh-Day Adventism, Christian Science, Jehovah's Witnesses, Pentecostalism, New Ageism, and Southern Baptism. It may be that "so creedless is the American Religion that it needs to be tracked by particles rather than by principles."[133]

Nevertheless, for all their differences, Bloom sees these religions to share the ancient fascination of gnosticism: "The American Religion . . . seems to me irretrievably Gnostic. It is a knowing, by and of an uncreated self, or self-within-the-self, and the knowledge leads to freedom, a dangerous and doom-eager freedom: from nature, time, history, community, other selves."[134] Bloom has made a case that the American Religion exists and that it is gnostic—that salvation is by a knowledge which only some can have. Indeed, we shall assume that both Bloom and Lee are correct—that gnosticism is thriving at least in certain sectors of our culture. The question for us, then, is what this means for equality.

Again, our specific task is to assess the compatibility of *Christianity* and human equality. To the extent that particular churches are Christian merely in name and not in theological substance they become irrelevant to the immediate inquiry. While we expressly avoided any crisp definition, there are limits to what could pass as Christian, and gnosticism plainly exceeds them. Harold Bloom would exclude Mormons plus even the Southern Baptists; if his description of their beliefs is accurate, he is correct to do so. On such grounds we could declare these groups to be of no immediate concern.

Eventually, of course, we need to deal with the presence of these gnostic clusters within the civil order, for, Christian or not, they deny equality. For them the human capacity for self-perfection and salvation varies in degree from person to person according to individual religious insight. This threat is vivid, but, for at least four reasons, not especially intimidating. First, the efforts of these critics to quantify the gnostic penetration of Christianity rest so far upon the boldest deployment of social-psychological evidence. Bloom and Lee are right to name the thing, but in their enthusiasm they could easily have overstated its penetration of the "real" Christian churches; our own experience suggests that this may be the case. Second, if the gnostic drift is largely a phenomenon of the collective unconscious, its vivid exposure—in credited works such as those of Lee and Bloom—will generate second thoughts, at least among renegades of the Baptist label who cherish their credentials as Christians. In short, the warning may be heeded. Third, whatever numbers it may legitimately claim, there is no reason to suppose that believers in the American Religion reject the *definition* of human equality which we have argued to be conventional. They may merely deny that such an equality exists. In that event, our discourse on equality remains intelligible at the level both of language and metaphysics. A fair fight on the issue of its credibility as truth is all anyone could ask.

Fourth, and finally, there is a very large sector of organized religion in America that remains theologically and culturally outside the gnostic maelstrom Lee and Bloom described on the basis of evidence they drew primarily from the evangelical sects. Bloom would extend the gnostic diagnosis to mainline Protestants, even to American Catholics. We think that both cases remain to be made. We have assessed the state of the Catholic mind on the question. Perhaps we can push the inquiry a bit further by scanning the traditional Lutherans and Calvinists as we find them today.

Barth, Thielicke, and the Protestant Problem with Equality

The Puritan part of the Protestant heritage may, in practice and outlook, verge upon a divine-human synergy sufficient to human equality. However, the traditional—at least the more bookish—Protestants hold fast to Augustine.

The leading Protestant theologian since Calvin is Karl Barth (1886–1968). God's election of man is the core of Barth's theology, indeed "the sum of the Gospel."[135] That God—not man—does the electing is not novel; on that, Calvin was clear. Barth, however, outstrips Calvin in holding that electing is not something God does (or did) but something God *is*.[136] But that is only the first of Barth's intensifications of the old theme.

Luther, as we saw, has God electing those whose faith he foreknew. But, says Barth, even though Luther is resolute that God does the electing and does it without dependence upon any properly human merit, election based on foreknown faith compromises God's absolute freedom.[137] If the Lutheran premise is accepted, wonders Barth, "is it not inevitable that God knows from all eternity that in certain men there will not be any opposition, and that because He knows these men He elects them?"[138] This consequence was not intended by the Lutherans; indeed, they denied it. "But," insists Barth, "it could hardly be evaded."[139] Foreknown faith ineluctably preserves a last visible Pelagian fiber. "The Lutheran doctrine could very well become the entrance-gate for a new Pelagianism"[140]—as it had in Arminianism (and then again in the Puritan's infatuation with preparation).

> Why was it . . . that at this decisive point the Lutherans allowed the will of God to be conditioned by the knowledge or prescience of God, why was it that they thought it necessary to introduce the concept of [foreknown faith], if they had no wish to compromise this basic interest, the defence of the free grace of God against every form of Pelagianism?[141]

To avoid the Pelagianism latent in Luther's doctrine, Calvin had insisted that God elects according to his inscrutable pleasure—the *decretum absolutum*. But this, too, is to be avoided, according to Barth, because it flies in the face of the revelation of Jesus Christ, a revelation that makes clear that God's decision to elect is not abstract or hidden in the depths of the Godhead. "[Election] is precisely the *revelation* of God's . . . love and grace for sinners."[142]

Election now is *revealed*, and the darkness of the Calvinist election dispelled. That revelation occurs in Jesus Christ. But Jesus Christ is not merely a revelation *about* an election: he *is* that election.[143] Jesus is the electing God; he is also elected man. From the beginning God chose Jesus Christ as the elect, as *the* elect of God. But because this elected man is at the same time the electing God, he does what no merely creaturely elect could do: he elects the rest—us—*in* himself.[144]

> From the very beginning . . . there are no other elect together with or apart from Him, but . . . only "in" Him. . . . "In Him" means in His person, in His will, in His own divine choice, in the basic decision of God which He fulfills over against every man. . . . Of none other of the elect can it be said that his election carries in it and with it the election of the rest. But that is what we must say of Jesus Christ."[145]

Barth is in high gear. Because Jesus Christ is the elect of God, predestination must be understood in a new way. It is Jesus Christ that is elected and predestinated. Yet that predestination is still a *double* predestination. In *Christ*, God has given to man election, salvation, and life; for himself, however, God has chosen rejection, damnation, and death.[146] In *this* form of double predestination, man can only win.[147]

> We are no longer free . . . to think of God's eternal election as bifurcating into a rightward and a leftward election. There is a leftward election. But God willed that the object of this election should be Himself and not man. . . . He has given away Himself and all the prerogatives of his Godhead. He has given them to the man Jesus, and in Him to the creature. . . . The thought of God's predestination . . . can awaken only joy, pure joy.[148]

This, then, is the basis of what is often described as Barth's universal salvation. It proceeds directly from his doctrine of election—from God himself bearing the rejection. "What we have to consider in the elected man Jesus is, then, the destiny of *human nature*."[149] No longer rejected, man is elevated in Christ's election. The grace of election is thus a comfort to man.

Despite its inclusivism, however, Barthean universal salvation prevents equality. For as we interpret it, human equality requires that a person not simply "be saved." The issue is not just whether, but *how* one gets there. Equality is not satisfied by mere passivity; human equality requires that God allow man to cooperate.[150] The person must make some contribution to his salvation, even if only receiving, by God's original grace, his invitation, and the capacity to accept—and then accepting. For Barth, however,

> the inevitability of faith exists "objectively, really ontologically for all men." . . . In God's [election] "the root of man's unbelief, the man of sin, has been destroyed," so that unbelief has become "an objective, real, ontological impossibil-

ity; faith, however, has become an objective, real, ontological inevitability for *all*, for *every* man."[151]

With this doctrine Barth successfully uproots the last residuum of Pelagianism, and with it the possibility of equality. God's grace triumphs all right, but by swamping and submerging freedom and responsibility.[152] It may be that "when we stand unequivocally and definitively before . . . the electing God, all [Pelagian] longings . . . are at an end,"[153] but then so too is the hope of human equality.[154]

Things may go even worse for equality, depending upon how we interpret another aspect of Barth's theology. God's grace has triumphed, and man is powerless to cancel God's victory. All people are indeed elected in Jesus Christ, but—Barth now adds—the elect differ in respect of their knowledge of this election. "The covenant embraces all. Only, there is yet a difference among men with respect to the *knowledge* of this saving fact."[155] Lack of knowledge (or unbelief) is both impotent to undo God's triumph, *and* a "deathly danger."[156]

We (the authors) cannot pretend to understand this apparent contradiction—this lapse into gnosticism. This perilous doctrine seems an interloper in Barth's theology.[157] The way Barth understands election, no subsequent human act could matter in any case; that much was necessary to suppress the last spasm of Pelagius and to avoid making salvation a form of divine-human cooperation.[158]

While trying to keep Barth consistent, some interpreters still insist that Barth is committed to a doctrine of universal salvation;[159] taken by itself Barth's doctrine of election does *point* unambiguously in that direction. But to claim that Barth in the end taught universal salvation is false, because— inconsistency to one side—Barth decidedly denies that we know of a universal salvation.[160] It is not difficult to discern why Barth was reluctant to follow his doctrine of grace to its conclusion. If men were elected and then saved in a purely "automatic" way, preaching would be for naught. But God's revelation cannot be pointless; the proclamation and reception of God's saving mercy are therefore necessary for salvation.[161] Thus salvation takes on a "cognitive character."[162] At the end of the day, "man's dilemma concerns his knowledge of God, rather than his bondage to sin or evil."[163] We would venture that, paradoxically, we behold a *cognitive* Pelagianism—yet another gnosticism.[164]

Equality loses either way. Either all men are saved without making any contribution of their own; or, if they make one, it is by receiving, believing, and responding to the Christian message *known* to be such. Equality is stymied first by passivity, then by gnosticism. Notwithstanding the beguiling openness of his doctrine of election, Barth is no friend of human equality.

Furthermore, his resonance with the Lutheran as well as the Calvinist side of the Reformation is evident and significant.

We see this most dramatically in the theological ethics of Helmut Thielicke (1908–1986), whom we have selected as our final exemplar of the Protestant commitments against human equality. Luther, readers will recall, threw off the *facienti* exactly to rout the moral athlete's hope that by his works he could help to save himself. Man is justified by faith alone, and when he is justified, it is because the *alien* righteousness of Christ is imputed to him. Thielicke remains completely on Luther's side. "When we seek self-perfection what we end up with is only the sublimated self-adoration of the superman. . . . Man's co-operation is quite impossible."[165] Self-perfection is a false idol, cooperation absurd. There can be no progress in holiness, no process of sanctification, no possibility of pilgrimage. The good news of the Gospel is that we have already been justified.

Yet man is not, for that reason, good. Penetrating the darkness of the fallen world, God has inaugurated the new, redeemed, and final age; he has irradiated the darkness in the radical summons of the Sermon on the Mount. But the demands are the contours of a mountain much too steep for man to climb. "There is no ontically righteous form of conduct. Conduct is *de facto* a compromise between the divine requirement and what is permitted by the form of this [fallen] world."[166] Man cannot avoid deciding and acting in compromise.[167] But even the ineluctability of compromise can be no balm for the troubled conscience.[168] Human failure is not quantitative or occasional. Failure is qualitative and inevitable. Man's moral endeavors are doomed to be sinful. Men's acts don't simply miss the mark; they cry out for forgiveness. "We are both channels and perpetrators of cosmic guilt. Our own action needs forgiveness, but so too does the situation within which it occurs."[169]

Thielicke surpasses even Greek tragedy in the double-bind to which he commits man. Thielicke objects that in "tragedy there is an implicit exculpation of guilt."[170] It was bad luck that caused Oedipus to behave abominably as he did. But the well-intentioned hero of Thielicke's drama is personally guilty. The implicit exculpation Thielicke finds in tragedy is not possible, for "freedom and necessity, volition and ineluctability, are all wrapped up in a single package labeled, not 'tragedy,' but 'original sin.' "[171] What this sin requires is neither more or less than divine forgiveness.

The necessary forgiveness, of course, already has been won by Christ, with the result that man's "action is of no avail."[172] Those who have been justified in Christ are forgiven and are "right before God" without regard to what they do.[173] With this we have come full circle to the query with which we began in the preceding chapters, namely, whether what man does matters to his destiny. Thielicke's answer is plainly negative. It is God who "refus[es] to let man fall."[174] The very point of the doctrine of justification is that man must look away from himself, his habits and his actions, and to look, instead, to Christ's righteousness. Thielicke's doctrine of justification, like Luther's, "snatches us away from ourselves."

For the Lutheran, man may do what he can to respond to the invitation, but God already has responded to the invitation on man's behalf.[175] Man's illusory contribution to self-perfection is, instead, man's justification solely by God. The setting out on pilgrimage is of only symbolic importance, for God in Christ has obviated the journey. This is Thielicke's Lutheran theology, and it drains the human struggle of any real salvific consequence.

To those who share his view, or Barth's, human equality must appear as the trivial confection of a gang of ego-subjectivists—and Pelagians to boot. But do these men state the conviction of the critical mass of Protestants whose opinion might establish or demolish the convention about equality?[176] With Harold Bloom we find it difficult to locate any articulated common Protestant belief on the crucial subquestions. The reason we chose to feature these thinkers is that on our chosen issues they are definite in their beliefs. They may also be rare; indeed, for every Thielicke we seem to encounter more than one Billy Graham and Norman Vincent Peale whose specific mission is to instruct man to strive to choose rightly and thus to merit what God intended for us all. It may of course be that the respective constituencies of Pelagius and Augustine are territorial, as the Protestant theologian Paul Tillich (1886–1965) urges: "America is very much in favor of this Pelagian idea that every individual can always make a new beginning, that he is able by his individual freedom to make decisions for or against the divine. The tragic element, on the other hand, is very much known in Europe, and is not so near to the heart of Americans."[177]

Conceding the importance of giants such as Barth and Thielicke, we wonder the extent to which they are heard, understood, and accepted by those who transmit the Christian message to the rank and file. These are not ideas we encounter in the ordinary religious traffic, here or in Europe. Our interpretation of the convention about equality could benefit from clearer Protestant support for man's created capacity for self-help; as it is, the most learned among their theologians oppose the premises of human equality. But weighing their voices against the *vox populi*, we feel satisfied to call the outcome a draw. At least we are confident that the efficacy of sheer human effort toward salvation is a thriving Protestant heresy.

Conclusion

Pelagius remains a nominal enemy of the Christian economy of salvation. In certain quarters—even among Catholics—the idea that man has been empowered freely to choose or reject Christ remains a Pelagian heresy. However, there is no solid Christian front for Augustine and against the human capacity for moral self-perfection. Protestants are quicker than Romans to discover Pelagian error,[178] but even Barth—not to mention Arminius—stops short of denying all effect to human initiative. Those who would be true to the Reformation—and to Augustine—will reject the theological propositions necessary to equality, but outside the theological academy these appear to be few in number. Most Christians, with various degrees of candor, agree that people have a role to play in forging their own eternal destiny.

The questions remaining for us, then, are, first, whether this self-perfection occurs simply by one's diligent search for correct behaviors or only by actually finding and attempting them; and, second, whether the capacity for this perfection could be uniform in degree. The "Christian" answers to these two questions are next on the agenda.

8

THE REPAVING PROJECT, PART II:

AN EQUAL-OPPORTUNITY CREATOR

Gnostic: I have the saving knowledge.
Christian: Who doesn't?

GENESIS HAS SCARCELY reported the flood when the question arises whether God counts good intention. Abraham, to avoid personal risk, pretends that his wife Sarah is his sister. Misled by this fib, King Abimelech plans what objectively would be adultery with Sarah. Observing the impending shame, God first tells Abimelech that his life is forfeit, then relents, being persuaded that the king's innocent intent ought to count. God's resolution leaves the final lesson in doubt: "I know that thou hast acted with a clear conscience; that is why I preserved thee from sinning against me, and would not let thee have intercourse with her" (*Genesis* 20:6).

We can only guess how Abimelech's case would have stood had God not warned him of the facts and allowed him to know Sarah. Would the amnesty have extended beyond the unfulfilled intention to include the objective act? At least the relevance of a good will has been established, and the scope of its benign effect has been put at issue.

Later in *Genesis* the credulous Abimelech nearly falls for the identical ploy at the hands of Abraham's son Isaac and his wife Rebekah. This time God stays out of the ensuing argument, but Abimelech is by no means reassured—had Rebekah actually submitted—that good intention by itself would have protected him from God's wrath: "Why didst thou pretend that she was thy sister? . . . One of my people might easily have dishonored thy wife and so thou wouldst have led us into grievous fault" (*Genesis* 26:9–11).

A third story—the favorite among the Abraham tales—also focuses upon the subjective. It lionizes the more punctilious Abraham who was prepared to sacrifice his only son at God's direction (*Genesis* 22). This story has been read in different ways. For many, Abraham's intended homicide makes him a great religious hero; sages from St. Paul (*Romans* 4) to Kierkegaard[1] celebrate his choice as the triumph of obedient faith over the law—both natural and revealed—against the killing of innocents. A more traditional interpretation, however, domesticates the story; assuming that the will of God defines the good, his mandate to Abraham simply transmutes what would be murder into correct behavior for this one occasion. From this angle Abraham is reduced to an exceptionally zealous supporter of conventional morality.[2]

We are interested in a third possibility suggested by the fact, obvious in retrospect, that God never actually willed the act of killing. What he wanted—according to scripture—was a particular manifestation of his servant's love, and he deceived Abraham in order to obtain it. Abraham committed himself to this act of objective horror because he supposed he knew God's will. In doing so he had the best of intentions; *but he was entirely mistaken.* Isaac's death was "a demand which God did not intend to take seriously."[3] Only Abraham was to do so. The "real" message of the story could therefore be that God favors and rewards the good intention even of those who mistake his will.[4] Thus comes the answer to Kierkegaard's question: "If the individual had misunderstood the deity—what can save him?"[5]

These scraps from scripture do not constitute an endorsement of an obtensional morality. But there is enough in all this to assure us that the issue we pursue here is primordial; indeed, our final example of it is older even than Abraham, having appeared in the Garden itself, as the fallen couple scrambled to excuse their highly objective error. By intuition Adam grasps the basic principle and makes his only possible defense:

> The woman . . . whom thou gavest me to be my companion, she it was who offered me fruit from the tree, and so I came to eat it. (*Genesis* 3:12)

The improvisation is clever: I was confused by the source of the temptation. After all, you imposed her upon me. Naturally I supposed it was OK. My heart was pure.

> Then the Lord God said to the woman, What made thee do this? The serpent, she said, beguiled me.[6] (*Genesis* 3:13)

Eve is equally nimble: How was I to know? I'm just a poor ignorant girl, and the snake was so intelligent.[7] I meant well.

Abimelech had a much better case than either of these hypocrites; nevertheless, the inventions of Adam and Eve confirm that the effect of intention already was an issue. Instinctively each grasped the primary theory for the defense. An honest mistake was, in principle, an excuse; their arguments lacked nothing but the truth. Suppose the facts had been slightly different— that, in the case of *God v. Adam*, Eve had offered the man the fruit without revealing its source. Could Adam even have sinned? Or suppose she pretended that a communication from God had repealed the prohibition; could Adam safely have taken this license at face value?

God v. Eve might also have come out differently had the tempter purported to represent God, declaring that the constraint had been converted to a duty to consume the fruit. Would there be no exception for the innocently misinformed or for the invincibly stupid? How careful, in fact, must the defendant have been in order to convert the act to one of self-perfection? Much of the history of the Christian doctrines of salvation, from the Garden to the Bomb, could be understood as a debate on these and related questions.

Still—with the powerful exception of Abraham and Isaac—these examples are but marginal support for the principle on which equality must rest. For the relevant question about good intention is not simply whether an actor was excused but whether he was positively justified. Did honest ignorance make Saul's homicidal career the saving choice for him? Saul believed he *should* be interdicting Christ; was he actually perfecting himself by acting on his mistaken belief? Does his case differ from Abraham's? Not if doing one's best is (literally) the best one can do. For Christians, a hard-won misapprehension of God's will may be a wholly effective key to salvation.

Saul himself later provides an answer. Now bearing the name Paul, he embellishes his account in words that encourage an obtensionalist interpretation of his experience. To Timothy, he says: "I had acted ignorantly in unbelief, and the grace of our Lord overflowed for me" (1 *Timothy* 1:13–14).[8] It is tempting to interpret the word "and" to mean "therefore"—a rendering assisted by other translations.[9] In such an interpretation Saul's own good intention would contribute decisively to his justification; even in his destructive ignorance he was actively answering God's invitation. This, however, puts too much weight on these ambiguous passages. We find no explicit scriptural commitment to obtensionalism.[10] Our inquiry must focus on the later history of the idea, and this chapter tries to discover whether historical Christianity has recognized mistaken good intention—thanks to God's grace—as sufficient to salvation.

The many languages and voices of the Christian tradition make it mercilessly difficult to detect what answers there are. Tantalizing clues nonetheless abound in the complex history and structure of Christian theology, and one can trace at least the skeleton of the story.[11] In fits and starts the Christians have hammered out a rough harmony among faith and works, intentions and acts, that might accommodate the premises of human equality.[12]

Abelard and Intention

Again it is Augustine who gets the ball rolling, and this time, too, in a direction hostile to human equality. For Augustine, of course, human actions have no worth of their own; all is grace, of the coercive predestinating sort. But Augustine was not content to leave it at that. He supposed that our behaviors serve as reliable signs of whether God's grace is operating in us. Thus one finds in Augustine's writings frequent inferences from what a person is doing to whether he or she is among the elect.[13] Even when Augustine exhorted his hearers, "Love, and do what you will,"[14] he was assuming that God gives true understanding of correct behavior to those he graciously moves to love him.[15] Further, Augustine's delphic assurance that "God does not require the impossible"[16] is consistent with his anti-Pelagian premise only on the assumption that God through grace makes us meet his own requirements. Augustine blithely assumed that the saved always are made to do the good. Once we step outside this context of coercive grace, the requirement of correct acts becomes the stopper to human equality.[17]

Perhaps it is not surprising that it was a medieval misfit, Peter Abelard (1079–1142), who first approached the form of moral intentionalism that is necessary to equality. Believing (with Augustine) that God providently orders all things, Abelard concluded that even states of affairs we call evil must in some sense be "good." Yet Abelard found this insufficient to make all human acts good. "Works in fact, which . . . are common to the damned and the elect alike, are all indifferent in themselves and should be called good or bad only on account of the intention of the agent."[18] Abelard distinguished between nonmoral and moral goodness and concluded that it is the intention with which an act is carried out that works moral goodness or evil. Goodness or evil is imputed to a man not because of what he does but because of his intention.

So far we witness a moral intentionalism approaching a pure subjectivism. In the end, however, Abelard's ethics is neither. In a peculiar about-face, Abelard declares that the goodness of intention is determined by its conformity to the will of God: "And so an intention should not be called good because it seems to be good but because in addition it is just as it is thought to be, that is, when, believing that one's objective is pleasing to God, one is in no way deceived in one's own estimation."[19] Abelard posits the existence of right and wrong answers about deeds, and requires correct apprehension of their rectitude by the actor. "Our intentions determine the morality of our actions but our intentions should be informed with the standards of divine law."[20] It seems the individual must both want to be correct—and to succeed in seeing what is correct.

Abelard's intentionalism is as incompatible with human equality as the objectivisms of Aristotle and Martha Nussbaum. A certain internal commitment determines our moral state. But if that commitment must have as its object the specific correct solution, it is hard to appreciate the difference for the individual. Nevertheless, many commentators on Abelard have taken him either to be a thoroughgoing subjectivist[21] (clearly this is wrong) or an intentionalist who holds that at least ignorance and sin cannot go together.

The second possibility makes some sense, as a famous incident in the history of theology illustrates. Abelard took the inflammatory position that those who crucified Christ were faultless (sinless). Assuming that they did not conform their intentions to God's will, why did they not sin in crucifying

Christ? His answer is that consent is the only source of sin, and consent is possible only to what we know; what we do not know, and therefore do not consent to, cannot hurt us. To sin, therefore, Christ's crucifiers had to know both something of what they were doing and that the act in fact was contrary to God's will. Somehow, says Abelard, echoing Christ, they knew not what they did; hence they could not consent and sin. It has been said that Abelard "underline[s] the faultlessness of the mind that consents to a wrong which it does not truly know."[22]

It does not follow from this, however, that Christ's crucifiers acquired merit on account of their intentions.[23] Abelard's position implies a third category of acts that are neither sinful nor meritorious—that neither perfect nor injure the actor. The crucifixion provides the example. This act was not informed by any true consent to good or evil. Stunted by ignorance, these choices earn neither merit nor damnation and should be labeled indifferent. This tripartite structure becomes plainer when Abelard discusses the fate of those who live by the natural law but do not believe in Christ. He denies that they thereby deserve to be damned, but neither will he say that they can earn merit without belief.[24] The ignorant neither advance nor regress.[25] By conditioning moral perfection upon correct understanding, Abelard puts himself at odds with human equality.

Abelard's new emphasis on the internal forum nevertheless strongly encouraged the sort of moral theory for which we are seeking evidence. He was the first to maintain that acts themselves *never* contribute to the moral goodness or evil of the actor.[26] In suggesting that all acts are morally indifferent and that intention is what makes men good or evil Abelard stood alone, and alone he was condemned.[27] But the possibility of a Christian obtensionalism had been broached, and it would not go away.

Aquinas Gives the Question Its Canonical Form: Excuse

Prestigious moralists continued to teach that the only way to avoid sin is to act correctly. St. Bernard of Clairvaux (1090–1153) insisted simply that those who do bad acts in good faith commit sin.[28] And Aquinas's own contemporary, St. Bonaventure (1217–1274), the Franciscan cardinal and bishop, agreed with Bernard and drew the hardrock conclusion reported (and apparently approved) only yesterday by Etienne Gilson:

> Where conscience prescribes some act contrary to the law of God, conscience does not oblige a man to act upon it but to reform it. In fact, so long as it imposes its erroneous rule upon his will, it puts him in a situation in which he cannot attain salvation, since whether he follows his conscience or not he will be in mortal sin"[29]

The mistaken individual is literally damned if he does the deed and damned if he does not. Of course he can reform his conscience; but how can he know that he stands in need of reformation? There is apparently an ineluctable duty to be correct. Diligence does not suffice.

The tendency to overlook the intentional aspect of the Christian life in favor of its objective components received unexpected fortification in 1215. In that year the Fourth Lateran Council mandated that every Christian make a private confession to a priest at least once a year. The idea of private confession was by no means new; monks had been going to confession from early Christian times, and by the seventh century the practice had spread outward from the monasteries, gradually becoming an ordinary part of Christian observance. But popularity created a problem whose solution shaped subsequent Catholic moral theology. When the uneducated secular clergy found themselves faced with complex cases and the hard business of giving spiritual direction, they looked to the experienced monasteries for help. The answer came in the form of the "penitentials," or confession manuals, which carved up the spiritual world into categories and assigned the precise penances for each of the myriad of sins a confessor might hear.[30] These books apparently had the salutary effect of helping unsophisticated clergy do a fair job in the confessional; at the same time, however, they routinized confession and, in practice, reduced the scrutiny to be given to intentions and diligence. Confession controlled by the penitentials led "to an approach to the moral life as discontinuous; 'freezing' the film in a jerky succession of individual 'stills' to be analysed, and ignoring the plot."[31]

When Lateran IV promoted confession from a permissive to a compulsory practice, the need for more sophisticated and spiritually sensitive guidance was felt. St. Thomas Aquinas was among those who contributed to the solution. His *Summa theologiae*, widely regarded by Catholics as *the* gothic cathedral of theology, was written to teach young confessors how to understand the tales of virtue and vice they were called upon to judge in the confessional. In the process he fixed the vocabulary for nearly all subsequent discussion of the efficacy of sincere conscience, giving it an answer somewhat more moderate than Bernard's—if not our own.

Aquinas rested on the authority of the revelation that man is God's image and likeness, an intelligent being who has control of his own actions.[32] Human actions are capable of *moral* evaluation, insisted Aquinas, exactly because they are free or voluntary. But to act voluntarily, man must act with knowledge of what he does. Ignorance of an important fact (or, in theory, even a rule of behavior) can deprive an act of voluntariness. Of course, where ignorance is merely affected, or where one does not trouble to acquire accessible knowledge of facts or rules, the defect and the subsequent act are truly voluntary and thus sinful. But where the ignorance is genuinely unchosen, the act is involuntary:

Thus a man may be ignorant of some circumstance of his act, which he was not bound to know, the result being that he does that which he would not do, if he knew of that circumstance; for instance, a man, after taking proper precaution, may not know that someone is coming along the road, so that he shoots an arrow and slays a passer-by. Such ignorance causes involuntariness simply.[33]

Those who know not what they do (and have not earlier opted to remain in the dark) act involuntarily and are delivered from the inevitable sin to which moralists such as Bernard had committed them.[34]

But is the honest bungler *perfected*? Thomas's answer comes in his treatment of conscience, which he respects because it is a dictate of reason whose ultimate source is God himself. Whatever a sincere conscience proposes, then, is proposed to oneself as ordained by God. Thomas knows what this entails: "When erring reason proposes something as being commanded by God, then to scorn the dictate of reason is to scorn the commandment of God."[35] An involuntarily erring conscience is binding because its (mistaken) judgment is understood to be God's will.

Aquinas then faces what is logically the next question: Is the will *good* when it abides by erring reason? That would be obtensionalism. Again insisting that the ignorance must be involuntary, Aquinas finally answers: "If the error arise from the ignorance of some circumstance, and without any negligence, so that it cause the act to be involuntary, then that error of reason or conscience excuses the will, that abides by that erring reason, from being evil."[36] The answer has been rendered, and it is a nonanswer. As with Abelard, those who act from invincible ignorance of an important circumstance are neither morally improved nor diminished, only acquitted. Advancing neither in good nor evil, they are dispatched to the moral Limbo of the excused.[37]

In fact things are now worse; for note that in the passage just quoted, Aquinas implies an important distinction among those cases where the actor follows his erring conscience. In only one set of cases is the actor excused; this is the sort we just saw: ignorance of a specific circumstance.[38] Where, by contrast, he is ignorant of the relevant *rule* of correct behavior, the actor is condemned: "If erring reason tell a man that he should go to another man's wife, the will that abides by that erring reason is evil; since this error arises from ignorance of the Divine Law, which he is bound to know."[39] If the human actor is "bound to know" God's law in all cases, innocent ignorance might in theory excuse—but there would be no such cases. It is assumed—not only by Aquinas but by Augustine before him, and by most moral theologians after him—that the moral code is knowable;[40] it is taken for granted that ordinary people always have the time, training, and intelligence to grasp and apply the rules correctly.[41] The implication is left that cases of apparent ignorance of the governing rule typically involve moral indolence or culpable self-delusion. The moralist concedes that sin requires "sufficient reflection," but in the moral analysis of specific acts he seldom gives much attention to the practical problem of sufficiency. Aquinas finessed the real problem by taking adultery as his easy example.[42]

But even had he conceded the obscurity of the moral law, we doubt that Aquinas would have come closer to obtensionalism. Such a concession would have committed Aquinas to "excusing" more people, but not to judging them morally good and perfected. For Aquinas believed, like most of the natural lawyers we considered in chapter 5, that man's goodness comes *exactly* from doing acts that are fitting for him, that is, acts that are in accord with right reason and the moral law. Man is *made* good by doing acts that *are* good; they alone can contribute to his perfection and happiness:

> Both [Aristotle and Aquinas] believe that people in this life are good insofar as they do what is perfective or fulfilling from a human point of view. . . . [Humans] have particular needs. . . . Reason can perceive these needs and, insofar as people find and act in the light of reason so as to satisfy them, they act well and are good. Insofar as their reason is impaired, insofar as they neglect these needs, they are diminished or thwarted and, therefore, bad in some respect.[43]

To do what is good, the actor must do the right act, with the right intention, in the right circumstances. All three of these conditions must be met for the act to be correct and thus perfective of the agent. The man who intends the good is good only inasmuch as he does what is good, that is, correct.

In judging good and evil, then, it is to acts that Thomas looks. Thomas's most basic concepts and vocabulary are simply different from our own, never separating right conduct from personal goodness.[44] The question of whether the *person* can be made good by striving for good acts simply does not arise. There is no category of moral goodness that can consist with bad (incorrect) acts and choices. The effort with which people seek the good is never itself recognized as making the person (morally) good.[45] Human equality is utterly out of the question.[46]

Pace Professor Porter

Our conclusion that Aquinas makes human moral capacity inevitably disuniform is contradicted by Professor Jean Porter. Being confined, as it is, to the interpretation of Aquinas, our disagreement with her would hardly be noteworthy except that her study was motivated by our very question: Can St. Thomas be read to support a descriptive equality based upon uniform moral capacity? Egalitarian in her social policy, Porter wanted a descriptive equality from Thomas as the factual premise for the good society.[47] Unlike Martha Nussbaum who celebrates the Aristotelian hierarchy, Porter objects to a moral perfection driven by luck; rightly she understands that it must be overcome if descriptive human equality is to be a possibility. Thomism, we fear, is not the remedy.[48]

The problem for Porter, as it was for us, is that Aquinas appropriated much of what—from equality's point of view—is wrong with Aristotelian morality. As Porter recognizes, Aquinas holds with Aristotle that goodness is achieved exactly by actions that contribute to man's natural end. And "if a particular action is to promote the attainment of the agent's true good . . ., [h]e must . . . be able to apply that knowledge effectively to this particular instance of choice."[49] From this Porter rightly concludes: "Aquinas's metaphysics demands that he offer a view of the moral life that is intellectualist."[50] "If [Aquinas] followed the logic of his theory of the virtues . . ., he would be forced to conclude that not everyone is capable of attaining true moral virtue, as Aristotle before him did not hesitate to say."[51] To that point Porter's reading of Aquinas matches our own and is nothing but bad news.

It is Porter's attempted theological rescue of equality that separates us. She thinks that when Thomas superimposed his doctrine of grace and the infused virtues upon the Aristotelian substructure, he eluded the luck trap. Indeed, Porter avers that Aquinas did not "follow the logic" of the theory he took from Aristotle because his Christianity committed him antecedently to an essential equality of persons.[52] Now we concede that Christ's celebration of the lowly rejects Aristotle's morality of civic success; but love of the poor does not entail a natural state of human equality (the poor indeed might be privileged).

Nor, so far as we can detect, did Aquinas on some other religious ground conclude that God made us uniform in our moral perfectibility. Indeed, Aquinas's doctrine of grace that Porter supposed to be a solution is but a further obstacle to equality. As we heard from an even sterner Aquinas in chapter 7, God predestinates to perdition without regard to any human merit. The whole of it is only slightly weaker than Augustine and sufficiently unpleasant to prompt Aquinas to the following rehabilitation of its author:

> Neither on this account can there be said to be injustice in God, if He prepares unequal lots for not unequal things. This would be altogether contrary to the notion of justice, if the effect of predestination were granted as a debt, and not gratuitously. In things which are given gratuitously a person can give more or less, just as he pleases (provided he deprives nobody of his due), without any infringement of justice.[53]

Before God's predestinating work, then, men were "not unequal." But can they be said to remain so even after they have received from God's goodness—as they have from all eternity—consignments to polar destinations? Porter perceives that salvation is, for Aquinas, a gracious gift from God to man,[54] but she fails to reck that it is a gift imposed only upon some.

Porter's conclusion that differential endowments of intellect do not prevent human equality is more understandable. In judging all people capable of reason sufficient for plenary moral perfection, Porter was buoyed by the current of ingenuous Christian thought that we introduced in chapter 1. Stoic ideas current in the early days of Christianity celebrated mankind's common possession of reason, and often enough this was said to show a human equality. Early Christian thought assimilated the core Stoic ideas regarding human reason and its capacity to know nature, and, sure enough, Christians have plausibly been said to believe in a descriptive equality. A. J. Carlyle's statement of the Stoic position that was absorbed by the early Christian church is familiar from chapter 1: "There is only one possible definition for all mankind, reason is common to all; men differ indeed in learning, but are equal in the capacity for learning."[55] Porter imputes acceptance of this tradition to Aquinas and concludes: "All people are equally capable of moral virtue, because they possess those capacities of knowledge and will that are proper to humanity as a specific kind."[56]

Carlyle strains credulity, and Porter happily does not join him in assuming that human intellectual capacities are uniform. But, though wisely foregoing the insupportable claim of a double equality, she backtracks and—in bits and pieces—quietly abandons the whole point. First, the question about *the fact* of equal capacity for learning gets transmuted to one concerning the "*belief* that some people are in fact more intelligent than others." Next, the issue of variation ceases even to be germane. "Being more or less bright . . . is not directly relevant to the attainment of moral virtue, on which human happiness depends. In other words, in order to be a morally good person, it is only necessary that one be able to reason and to will the good accordingly. One need not be capable of an especially high quality of reasoning."[57] Porter thus supports an equality of moral capacity on the ground that the reasoning required for moral virtue is, in all cases, within everyone's grasp. Properly understood, this could be a promising turn. But even this device fails as Porter asserts that the capacity for low-level reasoning itself generates not a real equality but only a similarity: "Human beings . . . share essentially similar capacities for reason, and therefore for moral judgment."[58] Even assuming the truth of this vague claim, it entails *unequal* capacity. Abandoning equality, Porter has settled for something like the "range property" of John Rawls.

The question for Thomas, as Porter herself concedes, is whether an act contributes to the agent's final cause. Given this, the nail is only driven deeper when she says that the "goodness of action in which human perfection consists . . . requires that the person acts and sustains activities in accordance with a (roughly) correct understanding of what it means to be a good human being."[59] And what is this new category of *rough* correctness but a strategy that smuggles a descriptive equality (similarity) into a morality where only correct acts count for moral goodness. We agree with Porter that a person can only "choos[e] as best she can in the confusion of her life."[60] But if equality is at stake, even a "roughly" successful intellectual effort cannot be a condition of a person's attaining moral perfection.[61]

An Aquinas who has God predestinating only some persons and favoring only correct acts cannot be reckoned a believer in an "essential equality of all persons."[62] We proceed now to a series of post-Thomistic changes that culminate in an equalizing reinterpretation of grace and in God's counting good intention.

Liguori: Vatican II Prepared

Thomas's judgment of the innocently mistaken actor had staying power. Even today, otherwise credible Catholic moralists think orthodoxy to demand the belief that errors about what is correct are corrupting for even the most invincibly ignorant person. Shortly we shall ask whether these moralists are in harmony with the verdict of their church. First, however, we note the perplexing neglect by Catholic scholars and the Church herself of a post-Thomistic and very respected voice on this question, a thinker recently described as the Catholic Church's "premier moral theologian."[63]

The reference is to Alphonsus Liguori (1698–1787), saint and doctor of the Catholic Church; his opinion on our issue was rendered more than two centuries ago, curiously invoking the authority of Aquinas himself. Liguori's conclusion is on all fours with our own; we can report it almost as simply as he wrote it, marveling only that Catholic moral theology seems in the meantime largely to have forgotten him.

Liguori's starting point is the proposition made standard by Aquinas (and already considered above) that humans are morally obligated to follow an informed conscience even where it is erroneous regarding the correct behavior for the particular case. For the actor to flout what appears to her as right reason would be to reject God, the very author of our reasoning powers. For Aquinas this meant that the actor who mistakes the rule that governs a specific case is in a double bind; she sins whether she follows or rejects her own conscience.[64]

Liguori cuts this knot. It is exactly because the diligent person who follows his conscience acts from reason (rather than from ego or caprice) that he not only avoids sin but, in Liguori's own view, "probably acquires merit." A person who honors reason by choosing the goods that it proposes "ought to be meritorious on account of the good end by which he acts."[65]

That the good of the chosen act itself is merely apparent (and objectively evil) is no stopper. When one comes to judging human goodness, it is not some conceptual perspective that counts but rather what Liguori calls the "proximate" perspective—specifically, whether *this* diligent conscience apprehends the act as good.[66] "Alphonsus saw a complex process behind the phenomenon termed 'a blameless erroneous conscience.' It is a matter not only of ignorance of the intellect but of an existential inability to perceive an obligation. There is question of things which a person at a certain stage of development is unable to grasp."[67] In support of his position, Alphonsus cites Thomas's own early (and later repudiated) determination that "a human act is judged virtuous or vicious according to the apprehended good toward which the will tends, not according to the act's material object."[68]

Alphonsus does not make the modern distinction between persons and acts. Purporting still to follow Aquinas, he deems the (concrete, not abstract) act itself good if, when "proximately" viewed, we find it apprehended as good by the diligent conscience. Abstractly it is wrong; proximately it is good. Liguori does not specifically say that the performer of the proximately good act is himself made good or self-perfected; but he "acquires merit."

There is confusion here, but Liguori's brief conclusion on our specific question is clear and sufficient. (Clear enough in his own day to catch the attention of the censors in Liguori's Naples, driving him to publish under the less vigilant—or wiser—scrutiny of the Venetian censors.)[69] Following one's diligently informed conscience is the cause of personal merit and not at all self-corrupting nor even merely excusing; it is the best thing that can be done in this world.[70] We witness here the potential satisfaction of the criteria of conventional human equality, two centuries before Vatican II.[71]

Newman, Modernity, and Vatican II

One modern hero of obtensionalism is John Henry Newman, who captured the authority of conscience in his quip that if he were *forced* to bring religion into after-dinner conversation, he would drink first to conscience, then to the Pope.[72] Newman, who later was made a cardinal of the Catholic Church and who today is under consideration for canonization, was no laxist. Rather, a convert to Catholicism himself, he appreciated each person's supreme responsibility to seek the truth. With unprecedented sensitivity, however, Newman appreciated the difficulty of genuine human knowing and choosing. Whereas Aquinas and the broader Catholic tradition generally assumed the availability of the moral knowledge that conscience must apply, Newman apprehended the practical limits of such knowledge and of the individual's own responsibility in ferreting it out: "The philosopher refers us to no code of laws, to no moral treatise, because no science of life, applicable to the case of an individual, has been or can be written. . . . The authoritative oracle . . . is seated in the mind of the individual, who is thus his own law, his own teacher, and his own judge."[73] How does the individual go about deciding? "Who can so sin against modesty and sobriety of mind, as not to be content with probability, as the true guide of life.[74] [T]he real and necessary method is . . . the cumulation of probabilities."[75] One popular edition of Newman's *Grammar of Assent* has an introduction written by Gilson. As one might expect, it betrays a measure of anxiety. Gilson put the brakes on Newman through the narrowest possible interpretation:

> The third and last mistake . . . is to see [Newman's doctrine] as a rational probabilism redeemed by a belated appeal to religious faith.[76]

> Attempts have been made to present the *Grammar of Assent* as exalting the inner faith of the believer at the expense of the objective truth of dogma. This . . . is about the worst misrepresentation.[77]

Maybe Gilson was right. In certain of his works Newman appears to give little quarter to those who encounter the divine word but reject any part of it, whether the subject be faith or morals.[78] The domain of his probabilism, then, may be confined to the single dominating probability that the Church's view of disputable questions is the correct one; to Newman it may have seemed sufficiently plain that the conscience of a Catholic in good faith will generally conform to the opinion of the ecclesiastical authority.[79] Newman's moral assessments might thus appear relatively rigid simply because of his estimate of the odds of a believer's being mistaken in good faith. We mean only that Newman can be read that way; Gilson, of course, cannot.

However narrow the window Newman opened, it has helped Catholic theology—or at least some of it—virtually to eliminate the practical prejudice against the honestly mistaken moral actor (whether Christian or pagan). Newman never applied his understanding of the development of doctrine to *moral* doctrine, but his general approach made this inevitable. It is now possible for a historian to write: "That the moral teachings of the Catholic church have changed over time will, I suppose, be denied by almost no one today."[80] The claim that the good is always perspicuous to the honest seeker ceases to convince. If the Church, with her rich experience, must revise her moral judgments, how can individuals, even at the end of the longest life, be expected to grasp what to do in every case?[81] For Newman and, increasingly, for those who have followed, the intellectual fragility of personal moral goodness no longer could be blinked, and eventually the Catholic magisterium yielded at the Second Vatican Council (1962–65).[82]

This new appreciation of moral fallibility and of its potential innocence began to coalesce in the 1950s with an emergent resolve among Catholics—especially Americans—to put the coup de grâce to mischievous old assertions that external membership in the Church was necessary for salvation. Such extreme claims had never prevailed. Dante was wholly orthodox when he admitted various pre-Christians, and even a few post-Christian pagans, to paradise; these people were saved in large part by their good lives conducted in accord with nature.[83] Nevertheless, even in America at mid-century, the audacious claim that salvation required Church membership was dying hard. In Boston during the 1940s Father Leonard Feeney was insisting—at Harvard and Boston College—that only believing Roman Catholics were saved. Feeney's weapon was the old "*extra ecclesiam*," taken literally and sharpened now to a narrow point unknown to Dante's time. Feeney's Jesuit superiors urged a more inclusive reading. But when all diplomatic efforts failed, Feeney ironically found himself excommunicated from the very church he deemed necessary for salvation.

The Feeney affair produced an unexpected bonus for human equality in the form of a clarification of the accessibility of salvation. In 1949 the Vatican of Pope Pius XII wrote to Archbishop Cushing of Boston instructing him regarding the true meaning of the maxim. Explicit membership in the Church, insisted the Vatican, was a help to salvation and a necessity for those "knowing" that it was founded by Christ. But contra Feeney, those can be saved whose invincible ignorance prevents their knowing the reality. God accepts their "implicit desire" for membership in the Church "because that wish is held within that good disposition of the soul by which man desires that his will be conformed to the will of God."[84] This formula would not, of course, satisfy the criteria of human equality because official members of the Church were seen to have an advantage; but here were genuine respect and hope for all in a universal economy of salvation.

A position closer to equality was simultaneously being developed by John Courtney Murray, another American Jesuit. Murray had labored over the proper relationship between the Church and civil government, concluding that the state's role was not to coerce religious belief but to preserve the environment in which people might freely choose. Murray contradicted the tradition that it was good for the state to privilege the Catholic faith; at the time his ideal of religious liberty exceeded the magisterially approved version of "tolerance." The latter maintained that if the practice of other creeds should be permitted (as it was in most Catholic nations), it was only because suppression of non-Catholic practice would destroy the public order that was itself a good.[85] In 1954 the Jesuit censors in Rome acted: Murray was not to publish on Church and state.

Four years later Angelo Roncalli became Pope John XXIII and soon thereafter convened the Second Vatican Council. The world's bishops were canvassed regarding the agenda, disclosing wide support for reconsideration of the proper role of the state regarding religion. Eventually Murray was summoned to Rome as an "expert." Resolution of the question provoked one of the fiercest contests of the council, a story of international cooperation and internecine conflict.

In the end, by a vote of 2,308 to 70, the bishops passed "The Declaration on Religious Liberty," *Dignitatis humanae*. It concedes and celebrates the plenary power of conscience in the order of salvation:

> It is in accordance with their dignity that all men, because they are persons, that is, beings endowed with reason and free will and therefore bearing personal responsibility, are both impelled by their nature and bound by a moral obligation to seek the truth, especially religious truth. They are also bound to adhere to the truth once they come to know it. . . . It is through his conscience that man sees and recognizes the demands of the divine law. He is bound to follow this conscience faithfully in all his activity so that he may come to God, who is his last end. Therefore he must not be forced to act contrary to his conscience. . . . God calls men to serve him in spirit and in truth. Consequently they are bound to him in conscience. . . . [T]he human person is to be guided by his own judgment and to enjoy freedom.[86]

The dignity of a person and of his conscience does not depend upon his conscience's being correct. The council fathers made this clear in the "Pastoral Constitution on the Church in the Modern World," *Gaudium et spes*, whose publication accompanied that of *Dignitatis humanae*; the relevant section was drafted by priests of the Redemptorist order, founded by none other than Alphonsus Liguori:[87]

> Through loyalty to conscience Christians are joined to other men in the search for truth and for the right solution to so many moral problems. . . . Hence, the more a correct conscience prevails, the more do persons and groups turn aside from blind choice and try to be guided by the objective standards of moral conduct. *Yet it often happens that conscience goes astray through ignorance which it is unable to avoid, without thereby losing its dignity.*[88]

The question is not whether a person is right but whether he has sought truth:

> Those who, through no fault of their own, do not know the Gospel . . . but who nevertheless seek God with a sincere heart, and, moved by grace, try in their actions to do his will as they know it through the dictates of their conscience—those too [may attain] eternal salvation.[89]

Every person can be saved by seeking as best he or she can to find and submit to the will of God, and no involuntary ignorance will affect the process of winning salvation through obedience to conscience.[90] "In ways known to himself God can lead those who, through no fault of their own, are ignorant of the Gospel to that faith without which it is impossible to please him."[91] Salvation still is by faith, and faith still requires God's grace; but finally the theologians have freed God to save even the bunglers. The "all men" of 1 *Timothy* 2:4 once again meant everybody, not merely "all the elect."[92]

From all this theological good news the Second Vatican Council educed an endorsement of human equality: "All men are endowed with . . . the same divine calling and destiny; there is here a basic equality between all men."[93] Though this warm embrace of "a basic equality" is cheering, strictly speaking it is a non sequitur. Even a universal "calling" satisfied by a sincere search does not entail a uniform capacity to commit to that search. It still could be wondered—and in due course we will inquire—whether, even in this Catholic commitment to the plenary power of conscience, the very capacity to will the necessary submission might vary among individuals.

But here we would underline the silent revolution wrought in the quoted words, and even more in the verbal omissions, of Vatican II. The authors of the council's documents set out to avoid the old scholastic categories in favor of a simpler and more biblical presentation. Thus we read about faith and conscience, not about final causes, acts, and intentions. The change in vocabulary was in the service of a theological shift. Rather than parsing and evaluating every isolated act, Vatican II looked to the underlying basic act of commitment to God in faith and thus made room for the *person* who would become moral by trying to live his or her faith. Vatican II restored to the foreground the "plot" of personal moral development that Lateran IV had by chance demoted by its emphasis on confession and on specific acts evaluated in isolation.

This brings us to a final observation about what happened at the council.[94] Bernard Lonergan was a Canadian; in chapter 5 we had to infer his commitment to equality from his deepest beliefs about the moral function of reason. In the case of Murray, the American, no such inference is necessary. Murray explicated his own commitment to descriptive human equality in canonical Jeffersonian terms. In the book of essays entitled *We Hold These Truths*, published during the 1960 presidential campaign, Murray had this to say about the classic formulation of our hypothesis that "all men are created equal": it is an "utterance, at once declaratory and imperative."[95] Equality is not simply a project (imperative) but also—and distinctly—a present truth to be *declared*. In celebrating equality Murray feared isolation neither from church nor countrymen. Equality was a basic element of what Lincoln knew as the American Proposition. "There are truths, and we hold them . . ."[96]

So far as we have been able to detect, Murray never paused to parse the host property of his equality (hence he does not note the need for uniformity both in possession and degree). Nevertheless, the ballast of his thirty years' project—including Lonergan's contribution—can leave little doubt about that property's identity. It is the personal capacity to search for and submit to the truth of moral obligation as one discovers it. This very American notion did its work of reconciliation at Vatican II. When the Catholic Church converted to descriptive equality, Jefferson was there.

Karl Rahner and the "Anonymous Christian"

The inclusiveness taught by Vatican II had other, more specifically theological sources. The most prominent and profound is the theological anthropology of the German Jesuit Karl Rahner (1904–1984). Rahner has been called the "chief engineer" of the glacial theological shift that occurred at Vatican II.[97] If the details of his theology have never been officially approved by Rome, still they help to explain the teachings of Vatican II.[98]

Rahner's theological agenda was to reconcile the two principles that have shaped our review of the Christian prospects for human equality: "We have to keep in mind both principles together, namely the necessity of Christian faith and the universal salvific will of God's love and omnipotence."[99] Rahner had read 1 *Timothy* 2:4 and believed it: "The scriptures tell [the Christian] expressly that God wants everyone to be saved (1 *Timothy* 2:4)."[100] At the same time he refused to ignore or dilute scripture's unwavering teaching that salvation comes only through faith: "This faith is in itself necessary . . . not merely as a commandment but as the only possible means."[101] The question for Rahner, then, as it has been for us, is how the grace necessary to such faith is communicated to all men, even those who know neither preacher nor sacrament (or, in good conscience, reject either or both). In our own terms, the question is how the invitation is extended and what counts as an acceptance.

Rahner starts by turning to the person, rather than to his acts. In his rational self-consciousness, according to Rahner, every person can discover that he already has been *called* out of himself to what is absolute. From the moment man becomes rationally conscious, the invitation already has occurred. The invitation does not arrive as discrete, ad hoc messages. The capacity to receive God is given in the dynamic constitution of the self. The person is not first oriented toward nature and only subsequently and contingently, through some addition or change, graced with an invitation to union with God. God's gracious offer of himself to man is communicated from within the subject.[102] In our own terms, original grace itself bears the special grace of the invitation. Rahner has no fear that grace will cease to be grace if God becomes too free with it.[103] "According to Rahner grace, at least as offer, is constant and universal. God elevates and supernaturalizes the immanent dynamism of human nature and therefore makes grace available to everyone all the time."[104] Grace is no longer episodic or occasional but constant. Rahner's God suffuses human nature with the grace Augustine's God administered a drop at a time.

If God's gracious invitation comes at this most basic level, so must man's acceptance. Faith, then, is not specifically in man's assent to a body of determinate truths but, rather, his trusting surrender to the reality present in the depths of one's being by which he already has been summoned to absolute mystery—with all that entails:

> If a person by a free act in which he accepts himself unconditionally in his radical reference to God raised up by grace, also accepts the basic finality of this movement of his spirit, even if without reflection, then he is making a genuine act of faith, for this finality already means revelation.[105]

Faith is an act everyone is empowered to make. Even an atheist can be an "anonymous theist" or, in Rahner's famous phrase, an "anonymous Christian," exactly by fidelity to the inner call to responsibility.[106] "[Faith] can be found in people who . . . accept themselves unconditionally, without self-rejection, fulfilling that primordial capacity of freedom which involves the subject as a whole."[107]

That man already lives and chooses within a graced nature does not entail that there are no correct behaviors, that one cannot mistake them, or that a throw-away "good intention" suffices for salvation. Rahner posits an objective order which one is called from the depths of one's being to seek. That call is not satisfied with a passing reference to the needs of one's neighbor nor by abstract benignity. "One should allow oneself to be educated to the right intention by the thing itself that is to be done."[108] Yet even where a person is mistaken about what is to be done, his obligation is to respect both his call to search and the results of that search and therefore to follow his conscience.

> Where freedom of conscience is respected as *such*, even when it—i.e., obeying the dictum of conscience—realizes itself in the wrong object and yet exists as freedom of conscience itself, *it would be more correct not to speak of tolerance or "toleration" but of active esteem and respectful deference before the conscience of another.*[109]

Rahner's formulation of moral experience makes it hard for the actor to say no to the invitation. Simply by taking oneself seriously, that is, by treating oneself as a person called to responsibility before the absolute, one accepts the invitation—even if the name of God never enters one's head. In some quarters this result has earned Rahner's theology a reputation for being saccharine and morally slack. The response to this criticism is that Rahner's understanding of man as called to God from the depths of his being (and not just from the pulpit on Sunday) is that man is forever being called—even nagged—to seek the fullness of being that alone will satisfy him. Rahner is demanding: "It is better to try to purify and refine one's motives by looking away from oneself to things and by letting oneself be occupied by life, others and their needs."[110]

Augustine's God issued the necessary supernatural equipment to a chosen few. By pouring his grace into human nature, Rahner's God equips all rational people to accept an invitation given in their very constitution. The RSVP consists in the trusting commitment to seek and follow in faith, not in specific behaviors. If the result were a *uniform* capacity to accept, Rahner's theology would reverse Augustine's, creating human equality where Augustine wrought hierarchy.

Veritatis splendor and the Catechism of the Catholic Church: Persons or Acts?

The conception of a graced human nature provides an explanation for Vatican II's inclusion of all human actors (including good faith bunglers) among the redeemed. We perceive no official Catholic obstacle to Rahnerian theology; many of Rahner's books received the censor's declaration that they were free from doctrinal error.[111] Whatever their status when published, however, at least some of their central theses now appear less favored at Rome and in its provinces. As we read them, recent restatements of moral theology from official sources raise real problems as to the status of those non-Christians (and Christians alike) who make honest mistakes. Contemporary magisterial moral theology has reverted to the scholastic categories Vatican II abandoned in order to make room for God to save the honest bungler.

As we saw in chapter 7, the *Catechism of the Catholic Church* continues to preach Vatican II's good news that God wills all men to be saved; the net of salvation is wider than the visible Church. We had expected that the *Catechism* would join Vatican II in describing a diligent but erroneous conscience as good and saving. But there is in the *Catechism* no moral analysis of the person. *Acts* are good or evil, but of *persons* we are left to wonder (§§ 1749–61). A morally good act requires the goodness of its object, of the intention with which it is performed, and of the circumstances (§1760). An involuntarily erroneous conscience must be followed (§1790), but the person who does so never is specifically celebrated. "If . . . the ignorance is invincible, or the moral subject is not responsible for his erroneous judgment, the evil committed by the person cannot be imputed to him. It remains no less an evil, a privation, a disorder" (§1793). Thomas's Limbo of the "excused" has become the land of "unimputed evil."

As we read the *Catechism*, then, those who (according to Vatican II) do not lose the dignity of their conscience do evil that is not imputed to them. Period. Conventional human equality, of course, would agree with the *Catechism* that a good intention does not make a disordered *act* good (§§ 1753, 1756), but the proposition—crucial to equality—is that such a good intention (which, the *Catechism* acknowledges, "can orient one's whole life toward its ultimate end" (§ 1752)) will make a *person* good. Of this we hear nothing. In racket sports this would be called a lack of follow-through.[112]

Pope John Paul II's 1993 encyclical, *Veritatis splendor*, likewise adopts a posture less warm to the premises of equality than that of Vatican II. In it the Pope undertakes a reflection on the foundations of Catholic moral theology, seeking in particular to check those theologies—known by such jawbreaking labels as proportionalism, consequentialism, and teleologism—that are said to deny the objectivity of morality. The Pope's insistence that the good or evil of humans acts is objective affirms an essential tenet of obtensionalism. But its other precept, that a *person* is made morally good simply by his or her search for correct acts, seems at first to be ruled out by the encyclical, and then to receive only an ambiguous endorsement.

First the apparent condemnation:

> To the extent that [the object of an act of willing] is in conformity with the order of reason, it is the cause of the goodness of the will; it perfects us morally.... "[T]here are certain specific kinds of behavior that are always wrong to choose, because choosing them involves *a disorder of the will*, that is, *a moral evil*."[113]

Nor is this hard-boiled morality of acts an aberration within the encyclical, which insists that "a correct choice of actions is . . . needed"[114] to bring about the perfection of the person. The person who with the best intention errs and does moral evil fails to reach his or her moral fulfillment.

Second, however, we encounter the possible endorsement of the sufficiency of a diligent conscience:

> Not infrequently conscience can be mistaken as a result of invincible ignorance, although it does not on that account forfeit its dignity; but this cannot be said when a man shows little concern for seeking what is true and good. . . . It is possible that the evil done as the result of invincible ignorance or a non-culpable error of judgment may not be imputable to the agent; but even in this case it does not cease to be an evil, a disorder in relation to the truth about the good. . . . Conscience, as the ultimate concrete judgment, compromises its dignity when it is *culpably erroneous*, that is to say, "when man shows little concern for seeking what is true and good."[115]

Had the Pope not been so direct and clear in upholding the plenary efficacy of conscience, we might have left *Veritatis splendor* holding little hope for human equality. But in the end we locate that hope in the very dissonance that echoes through the encyclical, as through the *Catechism*. On the one hand, he who does wrong (evil) actions does not advance toward moral perfection; but, on the other, the person who follows his involuntarily erroneous conscience does what he must and thereby preserves his dignity as a free moral agent.[116] This is less of an endorsement of obtensional perfections than Vatican II had given us reason to expect.[117] Nevertheless, we are content to rest upon the language of an ecumenical council and leave to others the task of harmonizing statements of the ordinary Roman magisterium.[118]

Certain theologians have wondered publicly whether the recent pronouncements are consistent with Vatican II. Prominent among them is Josef Fuchs, S.J., who has been perceived by some contemporary Vatican sources as imprudently relativistic and subjective. The charge is a curious one. Though Fuchs has focused less than is traditional upon sins of the flesh, he insists that the rational human is called to *correct* action in the world, action that is specified by the moral law.[119] In Fuchs one finds no reduction of the moral actor's obligation to seek and perform correct actions, but instead the resounding reaffirmation that "the burden of responsibly discovering correct conduct rests on the shoulders of the one who makes the decision to act. . . . Ultimately, every search for objectively correct solutions to problems is carried out by persons who ought to aim at objectivity."[120]

But the measure of the *person* and of his or her moral search, Fuchs insists, is not the success he or she has in reaching objectively correct solutions. It is Fuchs's observation that

> Jesus aims in the first place at the moral goodness and salvation of the person, and only as a consequence of this, rather indirectly, does he aim to teach about the rightness of the behavior of the person in his world. . . . He . . . admonishes us to be personally and morally good and consequently not to forget or rather, not to betray—the due rightness of human social . . . life.[121]

Fuchs finds that Vatican II emphasized this distinction between the person's correctness and moral goodness:

> When the Council speaks of human conduct in the world, it does not deal formally with morality in the truest sense, but with the problem of the rightness of the active shaping of man's world by man. . . . [M]oral goodness and moral rightness are to be distinguished; in its remarks on moral goodness, the Council therefore, repeatedly drew attention to fidelity to the inner word of conscience, not to the moral rightness or wrongness of actions as such.[122]

Thus instructed by the New Testament and the council, Fuchs teaches that a person's moral goodness derives from his laboring to find the truth and to adhere to it—not from what luck he happens to have in finding it.

Fuchs pointedly acknowledges that in the history of Catholic moral theology it has "proved difficult . . . to perceive that rightness of conduct is not directly related to the personal morality of the human person, i.e., to his moral goodness, but refers as such to the good of the human being (of mankind) in his horizontal dimension."[123] Yet Fuchs insists it is the *central* message of Christian morality that the Christian's first obligation is to make himself good, for it is "precisely when a personal human being is morally good and, therefore, a man of the grace of salvation, [that] he accordingly takes care that his particular self-manifestation in its effect in the world can be integrated into . . . the world of . . . humanity."[124] A person becomes good precisely by deciding to search for right human behavior and, to the extent possible, to realize it in the world.[125] One's hope for goodness and salvation is not left to the lottery of luck and brains. "Personal moral goodness is always possible. Not so the identification of the rightness of conduct in our world, and the realization of such rightness."[126]

Personal moral goodness is always possible. As with Rahner, it is unclear that this entails the necessary uniformity of the capacity to commit to the search. Apart from this gap, we are satisfied that Fuchs endorses equality. But of course the final question, from the point of view voiced in this chapter, is whether we can call this view Catholic.[127] Catholic moral theology seems true to Vatican II's understanding of the dignity of the inculpably erroneous conscience if it holds that, though most morally good persons may tend consistently to perform correct acts, the moral goodness of the actor depends only upon his or her search for correct acts and is not diminished by unchosen error even when it is systematic. Equality would be consistent with such a formula, and the highest kind of human worth finally would have been freed—for Catholics at least—from the gnostic misunderstanding.

A parenthesis: We need not take up here the attitudes of the leading Protestant authorities toward the moral efficacy of good intention. Their general position is dictated by the Augustinian victory in the Reformation. If God does all—if human choice is illusory—the questions raised in this chapter do not arise. Paul Tillich gets it exactly right: for "all of [those] who teach predestination, . . . there is a selective and not an equalitarian principle effective in life."[128] Conversely, to the extent that Protestants do allow self-perfection by obtension, they have decamped from Augustine toward Rome, and of Rome we have said enough. We regret that social science tells us so little of how ordinary Protestants line up on these crucial questions. We can go no further than the rough guess we offered in chapter 7 that the Protestant-in-the-pew leans more toward the premises of equality than his principal theologians would allow.[129] Pufendorf spoke for such people, not their theologians, when he affirmed—ushering in human equality—that it is by the sincerity of their piety that God will judge men and women.

The Uniformity Issue

If Christianity allows self-perfection by obtension as a universal possibility, the remaining question for Christianity—or any other belief system that comes this far—concerns uniformity. We may all have the capacity, but do we have it in the same degree? In the religious context this reduces to a question about the distribution of grace. There are, however, right and wrong ways of stating this issue. One wrong way is to ask whether Christians believe that God has given "equal promise of divine grace."[130] Arguably, such a promise could be kept by a universal dispensation that differed radically in degree from person to person. Its practical effect would seem to be not equality but inequality.

It would be nearer the mark to ask whether there is divine promise of equal grace. But this, too, could mislead. A dollop of grace for every person regardless of natural endowment or circumstance would not produce a uniform capacity. And that brings us to the real question: Does God do whatever is necessary to produce for all persons, whatever their situation, a uniform capacity for salvation?

Having come so far toward human equality, Christianity has no obvious remaining principle that would require either a yes or no answer to the uniformity question. On the whole, the traditions of theodicy appear to favor uniformity;[131] a sense of cosmic "fairness" drives many Christians to conclude (in curious concert with an unsuspecting Bernard Williams) that there would be something odd about God's issuing invitations to the banquet in a form that either makes it harder for some to accept or that gets some invitees no farther than the front hall. Christians have it on the authority of 1 *Timothy* 2:4 that it is God's will that all men be saved. It was the achievement of such as Rahner, Barth, and Vatican II to make it thoroughly Christian to think of grace in a systemic way—as more than the bestowal of private favors.

> In the light of Biblical theology and a deeper appreciation of the history of theology, a much larger perspective has been given. In it the term grace is seen not only as a personal gift but as a whole economy. Seen in this perspective, the various aspects stressed as a result of particular historical situations are judged to be derivative and secondary. Grace, then, rather comprises the whole history of God's saving dealing with man. It signifies essentially an economy of love.[132]

To insist upon a cosmic symmetry, however, would be merely to impose human standards without even the warrant of a testable human consensus. In fact, many good Christians do reject this picture of what "justice" requires. Since God owes nothing to anyone, it would not be surprising if he discriminated among us. Hence it is not altogether clear where theodicy takes us. Christian writers often have spoken of grace in terms that could eliminate equality. From Augustine to Calvin, God's saving grace "from above" advantaged only a select bunch; the magisterial Aquinas supposed that God's "consequent will" is that some be saved, others lost.

Nonetheless, all agree on the two necessary points: no human knows God's mind, and—above all—God is free to do as he chooses. And that is quite enough to establish the possibility of uniformity; at the very least it means that Christian writers could never commit against it. There may be tales galore of special divine intervention, but no final calculus can claim that God gives St. Cuthbert easier access to salvation than the least of us. For all we know the dear man needed divine intervention merely to keep even.

We propose this test of plausibility: If belief in an equality of capacity for salvation seems a bit of a stretch, one should compare it for hubris with the claims about grace that are made by modern theologians of the first rank. Karl Barth replaced the dark mystery of Calvinist double predestination with the joyous announcement that all are elected in Christ—a doctrine which virtually assures that grace sweeps everybody into the net of salvation.[133] And according to Karl Rahner, though we act freely, it is virtually certain that in the end no one is lost; we may say no ever so stridently, but, at the core of our being, no really means yes.[134] By comparison, our diffident suggestion that all humans just might share a uniform capacity to choose between God and self requires but a paltry adjustment of the most traditional and conservative perspective. Far from requiring the uniform outcome imagined by Barth or Rahner, human equality entails only the sameness of opportunity. And that opportunity includes the free choice of eternal separation from God. As Josef Fuchs says, moral goodness is always possible, but it is by no means certain. Salvation by obtension stands within the inner circle of Christian possibilities. If universal salvation is a legitimate Christian belief of theological explorers like Barth, uniformity of capacity for salvation is the faith of moderates. It is one of history's little jokes that what turned out to be at the moral center of a living Christianity looks more like Pelagius than Augustine.

A Conclusion about Christianity and the Convention

All these questions should be put separately to the various confessions by scholars who are sophisticated in and sensitive to their distinctive theologies. We exit satisfied that there is considerable room for descriptive human equality within many (or even most) forms of mainstream Christianity.

Our overall judgment about the commitment of the West to our interpretation of the convention remains about as we gave it in preliminary form in chapter 3. The individualists have rejected human equality, Kant is promising, the naturalists are divided, a good many of the Christians are friendly—and the rest we have yet to hear from. Our hope is that some will find it worthwhile to assume the necessary criteria, or to correct them, and then to address the question to themselves. The belief in and possible fact of human equality are too important for the West to leave unexamined.

PART IV

GOOD PERSONS AND THE COMMON GOOD

God will not love you any the less, or have less use for you, if
you happen to have been born with a very second-rate brain.
He has room for people with very little sense, but He wants
every one to use what sense they have. The proper motto is not
"Be good, sweet maid, and let who can be clever," but "Be
good, sweet maid, and don't forget that this involves being as
clever as you can." God is no fonder of intellectual slackers
than of any other slackers.

(C. S. Lewis, *Mere Christianity*)

INTRODUCTION TO PART IV

*A man and a woman cannot live together without having
against each other a kind of everlasting joke. Each
has discovered that the other is a fool, but a great fool.*
(G. K. Chesterton, *Charles Dickens*)

WHATEVER THE PHILOSOPHERS and theologians may conclude, it is the popular belief and our own that human equality is not only true but benign. But in what could its excellence consist? Why is this peculiar reality a blessing for the race? For our own part, it is sufficient that equality rescues us from the dispiriting assertion "that the achievement of moral worth should depend on natural capacities, unequally and fortuitously distributed."[1] We grasp the plausible alternative; if one's moral potential is distinct from one's gifts, intelligence, and luck, self-perfection becomes a matter of honest effort. The primary form of excellence stands open to all. To us that is good news.

This reaction, however, could be mere prejudice. What the authors find absurd about inequality of moral endowment, others think indifferent or even positive. Nor is their attitude aesthetic only. We have frequently heard the claim that the belief in perfection by obtension encourages carelessness in moral judgment, threatening the common good. The descent into subjectivity may have been necessary to assure uniformity of opportunity, but, says the critic, this was too cosmic a price. The world needs its citizens to believe that self-perfection requires correct performance; if this belief cancels human equality, no matter, for it is not difference but sameness in moral capacity that is absurd.

The aesthetic issue about equality is too elusive for argument, but we can explore the practical question of whether a belief in self-perfection by obtension encourages a soft morality. We do so briefly in chapter 9, adding that the material content of obtensional morality is best expressed in the language of fraternity. Finally, in chapter 10 we specify how this belief in equal access to personal goodness throws modern assumptions about the human condition into what is either a new or very old light.

9

HARMONIES OF THE MORAL SPHERES

CHARLES. Your mother and brothers have sued the courts to have
your case tried over again. And the courts have declared that
your judges were full of corruption and cozenage, fraud and
malice.

JOAN. Not they. They were as honest a lot of poor fools as ever
burned their betters.

(Shaw, *St. Joan*)

BELIEF IN HUMAN EQUALITY lodges each of us simultaneously in
two spheres that we label the first and second kingdoms. The *first* is
the interior realm in which the self exercises that capacity for moral
choice that is the ground of the relation of equality. The *second* is the world
of the Other whose practical good we are obligated to seek. Moral decision
affects these two spheres in related but distinctive ways. When I make my
subjective choice whether to shoulder (or ignore) lateral obligation, this
works my own moral perfection (or regression). By contrast, in the second
kingdom my submission to authority does not automatically achieve the
material good that I seek; for two independent reasons the material outcome
of any act of obtention is radically contingent. One is that the impact of our
decisions upon the external world is unpredictable; a particular attempt may
achieve the effect intended, the opposite effect, or none at all.[1] The other
reason is that the subjective choice to honor obligation may mistake the
specific terms of the practical good that is its ideal object.

In the second kingdom we are judged primarily by our measurable effects.
Here is the realm of justice and social ethics, where theories of the common
good and personal rights abound. These theories about good deeds may
conflict, but all of them agree upon the secondary role assigned to the actor's
subjective state. The good peculiar to this realm consists in correct *treatments* meted out to persons. Only certain *behaviors* toward other individuals
and society are appropriate.

Here, then, looms the basic problem: Were we all well-intending saints,
this second kingdom might remain empty of its own proper good. Like Don
Quixote we might seek our duty but never accomplish or even recognize
its behavioral terms. If the morality of self-perfection is obtensional, it allows
the possibility that one will *be* good without *doing* good. Nor is this problem
one of theory only; practically speaking, mismatches are inevitable. The fol-

lowing examples illustrate the possible disjunction between these two spheres.[2]

Tough love. The prodigal son wants to return. His father painfully and very deliberately concludes that his own duty is to administer "tough love." Accordingly, he closes the door to the child he wants to help. Let us suppose that in fact he should have given the son loving acceptance; his decision was not only unscriptural but stupid and destructive. As a consequence the son (and maybe the rest of the human community) are worse off. The father, nonetheless, is better off for having followed his conscience. Because he was honestly mistaken, the good of the first kingdom—his own moral good—was achieved, but only while frustrating that of the second.

Correct politics. In order to favor a political contributor, a legislator votes against the regulation of an apparently dangerous substance that later is proved to be safe and beneficial. The perfection of the second kingdom has been advanced by his choice, but the legislator is morally diminished.

Knowing best. At personal risk, by lying and concealment, Brian helps his drug-dealing friend to avoid capture. Brian considers his friend a genius whom he alone can reform and turn to positive pursuits. Whether Brian's behavior improves or injures the common good depends upon which of various conflicting theories of that good is applied. The internal moral effect on Brian himself, however, depends only on whether he has acted with the intention to do his lateral duty or, instead, is culpably deluding himself.

True charity. Long neglected by a cold and unfaithful husband, Anna decides it is an obligation of charity to share her love with a generous and lonely man whom she supposes to need her in his important work. Whether her choice is morally self-perfecting depends upon the intensity and honesty of her effort to determine the lateral good in these circumstances.

Helping the state. Zöe lives in a country with an inefficient welfare system. She makes generous and anonymous donations of cash directly to families whom she knows to be in real need (as opposed to welfare cheaters). She reports these on her income tax return as gifts to exempt charities. This is a violation of law, but she has carefully concluded that this behavior is the best way to realize the underlying objective of the law, for it allows society to support a larger number of truly needy families.

Protecting the ignorant. Thomas Aquinas was a generous and kindly man. He conscientiously supported the burning of heretics. This was injurious to justice and beneficial to Thomas.

Goodness my way. A philosopher tells his audience that Gaugin's desertion of his children was to his moral credit if he thereby succeeded as an artist. This is a corrupting message. The audience may be the worse off but the philosopher will be morally better off for having said it, if his conviction derives from honest struggle to find the real good.

Tender treason. Out of concern for his demoralized men, the commanding officer of a captured British unit cooperates in the building of a bridge of military importance to the enemy. Both the correctness of the deed and the moral consequence for the officer are in doubt.

However one judges these cases, clearly the well-intending person is not necessarily the ideal citizen (or neighbor). The two roles are distinct, and each entails a perfection of its own. The good citizen of the second kingdom is defined less by his heart than his behavior. He is one who acts according to the protocols of justice. Making consistently correct choices in his treatment of others, he realizes as much of this true good as he can within the boundaries of prudence. (He cannot do everything, and sometimes he has conflicting responsibilities or even dilemmas.) Observing his good deeds, the rest of us assume his motivation to be proper. We honor and reward such a person simply for accomplishing the common good (as we define it). He may be a pious hypocrite. If so, he is producing good works without becoming one. Meanwhile, the conscientious bungler injures others but saves himself. While awaiting a happier label, we could call this "obtensional disjunction."

How should this potential discord between moral self-perfection and the lateral good be understood?[3] First, it could be thought of merely as a precondition of personal morality.[4] The capacity to perfect ourselves requires that we remain fallible concerning the details of good behavior; a full grasp of the truth in specific cases would end the individual's freedom to choose. If this "defect" in knowledge causes an increment of social disorder, that is the small price we pay for the chance to be fulfilled as individual moral beings. Call this outlook cosmic resignation. We think it concedes too much. There is no reason to suppose that belief in obtensional perfection diminishes the common good in the slightest.[5] For all its injurious effects in particular instances, the coronation of conscience exacts no net social price of injustice or unhappiness.

The precise question here concerns the effects of belief: Would society be worse off if Jones believed himself better off for his own well-intended errors of behavior? Our answer is no; this belief nourishes both the common good *and* individual moral perfection. Subjective self-fulfillment operates in *practical* harmony with the purposes of the second kingdom.[6] But to argue for that conclusion requires some conception of the content of the good that is characteristic of this objective world. Considering our emphasis upon moral fallibility, this might seem self-conflicted, but things are not so bad. We have not argued that nothing useful can be said about the substance of lateral morality, but only that knowledge of correct acts is never so clear as to force the submission of the individual or to cancel his capacity to delude himself. Reason retains its role. Whatever the various traditions of morality have said of justice and the good society remains as relevant as ever to the judgments that conscience must reach. In an obtensional world the only irrelevant moral theory is one that defines the good as the will of the sovereign individual.[7]

The Common Good as the Ideal Object

Obtension seeks the content of the true common good. It rewards honest effort even when that effort misfires; but it insists that the common good be one's ideal object. The practical meaning of that obligation is to be sought in the circumstances and needs of other humans as they stand in relation to ourselves. The Other, in his needs and his deserts, is fully present to the obtending subject, for it is only within the encounter—and not abstractly— that the self seeks to grasp the particulars of obligation. In the discovery and appreciation of the Other lie the clues to concrete answers; this holds for the natural lawyer, the religious believer, and whoever else goes in search of the practical moral truth. The signals may be faint, but, for the attentive subject, they reinforce, clarify, organize, and extend the familiar precepts of natural and religious moralities. To be more specific, tucked within the experience we have called recognition is the insight that the Other is not a self-defining being; the perception that her nature generates my obligation is one that implicates a defining and authoritative source. Obligation arises precisely because that source, whatever *it* is, has made her—whatever *she* is. It has cast her in this form that utters the message of mutuality.

While it fixes the terms of our moral possibility, this symmetrical cast of our natures leaves unscathed the antecedent liberty to behave as I will. If ever I had that choice, it is still mine. The disclosure that duty exists is but an invitation; it leaves the individual the same old menu of decisions. He can either subordinate or bless the Other; all that he lacks (and never had) is the sovereign power to define the moral consequence of this choice. If he had wrongly supposed himself the reigning authority over the significance of his own actions, it is in the encounter that he sees his error. And here it is that the moral meaning of choice becomes defined for him. The freedom of the self has been limited to the embrace or rejection of an order of obligation not of our own design, except to the extent that our creative participation has been *invited*. (Of course, this is an important qualification; in the process of practical choice the encouragement to invention often is what we experience. Nevertheless the scope of that invitation, however generous, has already been fixed.)

Whether the source behind the duty is taken to be natural or supernatural, it has manifested itself in this very particular sort of object-creature that is the Other. The experience of the encounter is the epiphany of authority. But the invitation to obey arrives simultaneously with the consciousness that the obligation is to be exercised laterally. Thus the content of the obligation must be sought within this relation. Obligation is *about* the Other. At first we may be unclear that it is also *to* the Other, for this is not a necessary inference;[8] though my obligation concerns her, it could be owed exclusively to the natural or religious source[9] which indeed could command that I enslave, dominate, or injure the Other. Occasionally people take nasty ideas of that sort very seriously. The West, however, has seldom done so,[10] nor do we. Whatever obligation arises in the course of the encounter is benign in regard to the Other. Only when so interpreted does the experience of obligation become fully intelligible; the invitation to a free obedience makes sense only when acceptance comes *in service* of the intended beneficiary.[11] The duty, then, is owed to *both* source *and* Other.

This all seems relatively easy so long as one accepts the disputed premise that in the first place there is obligation real and discernible. Again, this was, and remains, the Western presumption; duty is a preinstitutional work of God or nature. For reasons of its own, the Enlightenment hoped to discard this presumption. It advertised three counter propositions: First, no obligation to others arises from God or nature; second, we legislate obligation for ourselves; and third, implicitly, each of us may (even ought to) continue in unwavering pursuit of self-interest as that interest becomes identified to us by our untrammeled will.

Consider the magnitude of the task that Hobbes and company thus set themselves. It is exactly this inward-turning spirit of radical individualism that has made it so difficult for moderns to sustain a believable ethic of benevolence. The crucial premise at the threshold of individualism is competition; we are at war. It has been the Herculean job of moral philosophy to carry the burden imposed by this anarchic presumption—to convert mutually malevolent individuals into seekers of justice. The end is noble; we admire these philosophical heroics that sometimes produce practical ideas. But the individualist assumption makes it difficult to identify just how obligation ever begins at all. By comparison, conventional ("naive") moral realism makes the case for human reciprocity look ridiculously easy. Of course these traditional notions may fail to convince just as individualism has failed; deconstructionism would dish both as nonsense. Nonetheless, it is the assumption of a real common morality that most easily sustains a society we can perceive as broadly fraternal.

Obtension respects all the competing versions of this preinstitutional lateral good. No argument drawn from realist sources is irrelevant, though of course each must succeed on its own merits in persuading the individual conscience. Systems of duty may be grounded in nature or religion; they may be intuitional or rationalistic. The self uses whichever of these tools falls to its hand; its selection among moral systems is mostly a gestalt affair. At decision time people seldom resort consciously to theories. But, especially when there is time to reflect or where the question is one of a long-term commitment, the authority of moral principle plays its part. One deploys ideas already encountered, seeks new ones, or, most frequently, consults somebody one trusts in practical moral affairs. This confidant could even be some off-duty individualist who—forsaking theory—recognizes (and insists upon) the real good in practical matters.

So the personal search for the content of the common good goes well or badly—but it goes. Particular moral questions get framed differently for the individual depending upon whether she is an orthodox Jew, a Southern Baptist, a natural lawyer, a Buddhist, or a Theosophist. Much depends upon education, intelligence, and other circumstances. A person can work only with those ideas he or she knows, judging and applying them and remaining open to insight. Else we are not well-intending. The answers reached on any given issue—should I take the money, join the Peace Corps, have an abortion, leave Jimmy?—will be affected by the traditions and premises of the particular system the actor embraces. Some will be more persuasive than others, but none will be coercive in its clarity. To the honest seeker there are glimpses of specific good solutions, but no conception of moral truth can wholly capture what one is to do here and now. At their best, theories help clarify the options;[12] at some point the self must choose the particular course of action. I *will* break off this relation; I *will not* contribute to this cause.

Many would call this subjective event "an act of moral faith," and that phrase may suggest that the "source of obligation" is a person—as typically it is for religious believers. Poised at the brink of choice, they take their moral leap into the arms of God. Nonbelievers must close this gap between knowledge and decision on some other basis; respecting this difference, we prefer the more neutral metaphor "a leap in the dark." The necessity for this leap does not mean that ideas about correct outcomes in the end prove useless nor that all systems for discovering practical wisdom are equally efficacious. Among the Tao, the Koran, the dozen versions of natural law, the Commandments, and the Sermon on the Mount, some prepare us better to vault the gap between our understanding of the options and our decision. But in preparation for every act of choice, the obtending individual has no alternative but to search for the right behavior under whichever conceptions of the real good have gained ascendancy in his or her own active conscience.

Parenthetically, it is the further strength of obtensional morality that the pursuit of practical benevolence simultaneously effects the moral self-fulfillment of the actor; indeed, this fulfillment is itself a corollary *obligation*. "Do what is good for yourself" stands as an authoritative command (or invitation). "To thine own self be true" becomes a mandate of the gods, not merely a piece of egomania.

Is Obtension an Easy Morality?

Every actor must seek the correct answers of the second kingdom, but will the obtensionalist be efficient at this search? We must compare the incentives that are generated by competing beliefs about the process of moral self-perfection. Our assumption will be that the more diligently one searches for the correct answer, *the more likely* one is to find it and thereby serve the common good. We must, then, predict the level of moral effort of those who believe in perfection by obtension and compare it to the predicted effort of those who believe that self-perfection requires correct answers. Neither view being provable as truth, whichever stimulates greater diligence will contribute more to the common good, and its belief may legitimately be encouraged.[13]

How efficiently does obtensional belief drive us to seek the lateral good? Its critics think it "too easy" to be properly stimulating.[14] We share with them the common concern that too soft a morality somehow tends to corrupt; however, we deny that the obtensional imperative is in any sense soft. To get the problem into focus, recall Etienne Gilson's advice to the well-intending bungler who breaks the rules: Get it straight, or perish.[15] Now ask these questions: Is Gilson's threat psychologically "useful"? Does it stimulate greater moral effort? Would the bungler's incentives be diminished if we told him that salvation lay in doing his best to get it straight?

We see no reason to think so. Whether a Gilsonian or an obtensionalist, the moral actor *can* do no more than his best to discover correct behavior. And he *may* do no less. The regimen of good intent binds us to search at least as diligently as the objectivist himself could wish.[16] We are bound on pain of our own corruption to avoid self-delusion. The objectivist would penalize the actor for honest mistakes; but will this threat improve the efficiency of that quest for the lateral good he is already obligated to make?

We suspect that those who believe so confuse obtension with probabilism, a notion long-disputed, especially among Catholic moralists. For the probabilist the question has been whether, in cases of authentic difficulty, it is permissible for the actor to choose freely among alternative courses whose chances of being correct meet a certain (or uncertain) standard.[17] Obtensionalism, by contrast, is not a resort to probabilities as a way of identifying alternatives. It is the duty to *seek* the *good* as the price of one's own moral perfection. Granted, in any given case our only evidence of the good solution may be a probability; on occasion there may be "ties." The obtensional enterprise is, nevertheless, entirely different from that of the probabilist. There is nothing in it to excuse the actor from the most diligent pursuit of the correct answer; in no sense is it a latitudinarian menu of conflicting but allowable acts. Of course, any actor can allow phantasms of his own good intention to lull him into self-delusion. But this capacity to avoid the search for moral truth remains available to us whether we take a subjective or an objective stance on moral self-perfection. In every hard choice one's reason may conspire with one's will in the subtle decision to look away.

Finally, insofar as there is anything like a history of this issue about a possible *self*-corrupting effect of believing in goodness by intention, the evidence seems to go the other way. Earlier we noted the anguish of Gabriel Biel and others around the time of the Reformation who took their leave of any rule-dominated approach to personal salvation. For them, moral judgment, once liberated from formulas, became an intense challenge. While accepting the *facienti*, Biel and company were less reassured than driven.[18] The news that God guarantees grace if you do what is in you was for them not a message of consolation. They would have agreed with Grantland Rice that nothing matters except how you play the game; but this would only remind them that to score early is no ultimate advantage. Even if you get right moral answers, you must still do your best, or you lose. There is no rest for the good.

Put another way, the morality of good intention is a discipline of pure diligence. Given the obscurity in which we must seek the common good, the honest actor will have to strive for it. What an adequate description of diligence would be, we cannot say; the question—as we observed in chapter 3—is strangely neglected by the moral theologians, who instead have emphasized the supposed clarity of the obligating rules. Perhaps fidelity to Lonergan's transcendental precepts is as close as one can come. In any case, the obtensionalist cannot avoid confronting the diligence question in his own life, because for him there is no resting even in the good behavior commanded by the rule. Rules can be anesthetic, sealing off areas of practical inquiry and letting us get on with life;[19] for some this is enough. But for the obtensionalist, moral life is an uninterrupted search for the best; to close off the consideration of possibilities is an act of moral insolvency.

One does not have to be a zealot to share the hope for something beyond minimalism in collective life. Even lawyers can prefer a "morality of aspiration" that seeks behavioral outcomes superior to what the law commands.[20] Anyone who takes the good of the Other seriously embarks upon an inquiry that extends indefinitely beyond the rule. If we can improve our neighbor's lot by "supererogation"—by exceeding our duty—so much the better in light of the benign purposes implied in the rule itself. If our neighbor needs a shirt, it could be good to give him shoes as well.

This open-endedness represents a vital difference between those who rest on the rule and those who focus on diligence. The latter tend, in practice, to exceed the minimum. Consider the problem facing the person who would be well-intending. Satisfaction of the rule—honesty, fairness in dealing, respect for others' feelings, paying taxes, work—remains problematic as the perfecting instrument of his own moral state. The very conception of a minimum invites his concern that the all-important intention never gets beyond mere behavioral conformity. Since what obtension requires is a certain mental state, even the careful selection of a particular behavior allows the doubt to endure. Where the chosen act achieves exactly what the law prescribes, this may even exacerbate the actor's problem. Can a well-intending person like me rest content with the minimum? My reflective decision to do so may itself constitute the surest signal of imperfect intention. Like the rebellious employee, I could be merely "working to rule."

The real challenge to the obtensionalist is that he lacks a conclusive set of particularistic duties. He has instead a vocation—a calling. As a calling, good intention not only leaves us uneasy about resting at the minimum but provides no secure grasp of where to stop. Its potential unboundedness is further magnified by its being specifically an order of duty and not of rights. Good intention consists purely of assent to responsibility. At the level of the minimum—the level of law—there may also exist a reciprocal order of individual rights against the Other; but, if so, that is never a proper concern for the perfecting self.

Thus the morality of obtension can be expressed only as the obligation to probe beyond the objective minimum. Rules of conduct must be honored; but they neither limit the possible range of obligation nor prescribe the manner of the search. The duty to explore is the invitation to transcend.[21] Above the minimum its specific call will vary according to what a diligent search reveals. Out of his or her unique endowments each is to cooperate with the source of obligation in the design of an embodied good.[22] If we decline to participate as creators, we initiate entropy and disorder. As a general moral strategy, minimalism is the impulse to nonbeing, and its end is disintegration both in society and self.

Belief in the obligation to probe beyond the objective minimum is society's best assurance that the citizen will avoid an unreflecting passivity and acceptance of what is. Not everyone will agree that the moral restlessness this implies is a good thing, and the authors reject the absurd notion that change is desirable for its own sake. We see little harm, however, in maintaining a strong incentive to unceasing moral education of the self. The well-intending person has the best of reasons to search with care among the competing notions of a real good.[23] Moral identity depends upon the dedication with which that inquiry is conducted.

So understood, obtension is our highest vocation as citizen—whether of the family, neighborhood, nation, or world. In our fallibility we will sometimes mistake the higher good, just as we mistake the minimum. But it is our primary obligation to go on seeking both.

Liberty, Equality, Fraternity

We conclude that the experience of obtensional morality is not another Snark hunt in which each of us seeks the real good without a clue. Our moral map is as clear as that available to Columbus. His world provided him the limiting principles; he had only to keep his craft moving in a general direction and maintain his purpose and concentration. He explored terra incognita; but he had his ship, a compass, and a reason to sail. The good citizen likewise begins with the familiar minima and, committed to doing her best, tacks her way toward the ideal.

What shall we call this ideal? Words are inadequate but all we have. Labels such as "obtension," if graceless, are necessary. Still, we can hope for words both more familiar and more inviting. Before leaving this second kingdom we will try to restore one part of its heraldry that for two centuries has survived as a happy slogan. The idea of a descriptive human equality in a remarkable way completes the moral epic that began in Paris as "*liberté, egalité, fraternité.*"

Whatever became of this late-eighteenth-century enthusiasm for *fraternity*? "Remarkably little attention has been paid to fraternity compared to liberty and equality."[24] The revolutionary slogan gave the three concepts equal billing, but fraternity was unable to maintain its place in the succeeding ideological competition. Commentators on the revolution have exhausted their ammunition approving and deploring the other two branches; most, in practice, reduce the French jingle to "liberty and equality."

Friends of the revolution construed liberty broadly as the Hobbesian assertion that we are born without obligation and acquire it only by consent. Liberty thus became a claim partly of anthropological fact, partly of rights. Equality, by contrast, has been a claim exclusively about rights—that is, about those rights in addition to liberty itself that accrue to these naturally free individuals. The identity of these nonliberty rights continues to be a matter of dispute and contradiction, but, in any case, equality taken in this sense plainly remains a claim about the good society; Bentham, Mill, Tocqueville, Nietzsche, and virtually all the modern commentators we canvassed in chapter 1 have seen equality almost exclusively as an inchoate theory of the social good and only rarely as the human fact that supports these egalitarian visions. Jefferson's descriptive declaration of equality has never really made it into the philosophical dialogue.

Nor has fraternity. The revolutionary slogan announcing it arrived a bit late on the Paris scene. The *Declaration of the Rights of Man* in August 1789 had ignored fraternity altogether, being preoccupied with repetitions of liberty and equality as *rights* to be protected by the state.[25] The origin of the three-word phrase is apparently unknown; its earliest recorded appearance is June 1793.[26] Fraternity was to be yet another prescriptive term—some manner of good that was to come out of the revolution. It had, at least potentially, an identifiable content of its own. By the time it arrived, however, the available moral space was already occupied by the expansive claims of the regnant egalitarians. These proved to be of a thoroughly unfraternal sort, aspiring more to separate individuals from their wealth (or heads) than to affirm their common humanity. The spirit of a human—or even a Gallic—fraternity did not easily fit this scene.

Confined to cramped moral quarters during these early struggles of liberalism, fraternity remained a largely ineffectual weapon. The problem was more than tardiness. Apprehensive of its conservative, Masonic, and Christian roots, even communism gave it only a modest part. Despising it for its etymological connection to the family, the Left transformed fraternity into the fatherless, motherless—and thoroughly secular—"comrade." Before 1848 Marx and Engels had helped direct the socialist League of the Just which took as its motto "All Men Are Brothers."[27] In the drafting of the *Manifesto* they carefully avoided such sibling sentimentality, substituting class for family.[28]

Bowdlerized and largely lost among the Left,[29] fraternity was unappealing as well to the Right. Even when taken seriously (as by James Stephen), it was treated as a vague appendage of egalitarian politics.[30] Too often it went unobserved that when both equality and fraternity are understood as prescriptive ideas, they turn competitive. Class theorists who stump for equality tend to depict humans outside their own client group not as lost brothers but as victimizers. As with Marx, they write "less to move us to fellow-feeling with the workers than to destroy the human aspect of their masters."[31] Much of the literature of race and feminism oscillates between the themes of human solidarity, on the one hand, and the division between "us" and "them," on the other.

This conflict between normative principles of equality and fraternity is structural. The socialist prophet who would impose sameness must first steel himself against the vivid claims of individual difference among his clientele. His square trap will catch decent people of all shapes whose anomalies he must then lop or stretch. Only parents, sisters, friends, and lovers—people less committed to symmetry in human affairs—can value the eccentricities that are a scandal to the egalitarian enterprise. And, if the collectivists are rightly wary of such loyalties, the individualists would strangle them in their cradle. Hobbes and his descendants have opposed the notion of fraternity in any of its forms because every version of it recognizes preinstitutional responsibilities—and these come in protean and unpredictable forms. Fraternity is sloppy, pluralistic, and entangling. It celebrates "mediating structures"—families, clubs, trade unions, political parties, cooperatives, and even the churches into which one is born. It is quite capable of extension to the whole of the human race (viz., the "brotherhood of man") but its penchant for lumpy affinities at all levels makes it dangerous competition to the simplicities of radical individualism at one political pole and totalitarian democracy at the other.

As a standard of justice—or even of love—fraternity, too, has its limitations; but it has two plain and important advantages over egalitarianism. First, fraternity has no interest in sameness of treatment simply for its own sake. If it is good for every baby to be inoculated, let us proceed without exception; but let us do so because it happens to be correct in each case and not because there is any virtue in treating all the same. If there is one child who does not need it, pass her by; she has neither right nor duty. Fraternity is no imperative for mathematical symmetry in human intercourse.

Second, fraternity is an affirmative that replaces egalitarian arithmetic with an ideal specifically human. It is the natural political metaphor for the radiating web of mutuality of which family is our first experience, challenging the impulse of egoism with another of loyalty both to one another and to a common good.[32] The question becomes unavoidable for the moral actor; where does my duty lie within this real order of reciprocity? If the word fraternity by itself gives few specific answers to moral questions, it invites the diligent search. It is another name—perhaps the best—for that real good of the social order whose pursuit works our moral self-perfection.

This has a structural significance whose appreciation requires a shift in our historical perspective. For one moment let us suspend belief in equality as an appropriate *end* of politics. Accept the possibility that human equality is not a goal at all but a pure *fact* of human nature—a relation springing from a trait that is uniform in degree among all rational persons. When so viewed, equality may cease to compete with fraternity and become instead one of its explanatory principles. In this spirit, return to 1793 and celebrate equality as a pure fact. Next, perform a similar intellectual exercise with the concept *liberté*: For the moment forget that liberty is also a name for certain types of protectable rights; remember only that liberty is a real property of the natural self.[33] We have the capacity for moral choice; we *are* free.

Observe the consequence of viewing liberty and equality in this way, as descriptions of the human person. The three terms of the revolutionary slogan now constitute an interesting progression from fact to aspiration. Liberty reigns as the distinct and active element of the moral self. Part reason, part will, and part mystery, liberty is the personal power to respond to all claims of obligation, whatever their source. When these claims arise from human encounter, liberty becomes the dynamic of a lateral morality; the self receives its invitation to embrace or reject obligation to others. But the encounter simultaneously generates the relation of human equality, and in making lateral choices liberty must take that fact into account. Equality is a reality of every environment in which moral liberty is to be exercised. The option is

Fraternity

Liberty　　　　　　　　　　　　Equality

inescapably to accept or reject a responsibility to our moral peers; it is their nature and their needs that limit the possible forms of our chosen behavior as we undertake the journey toward—or the flight from—moral self-perfection. Liberty's world is a world of moral equals.

Earlier we labeled the practical details of this bilateral responsibility vaguely and variously as "reciprocity," "lateral morality," "the good of others," "the common good," and so forth. Now we see that the behavioral content of this order might be more clearly specified by attaching the elegant Paris label so long obscured by the obsession to homogenize. *Fraternité* is the plausible name for the behavioral ideal that is peculiar to free and equal beings. It is a word that highlights the real differences among the three terms. Understood as the *hope* of a just revolution, fraternity makes the twin *facts* of liberty and human equality fully coherent. The true relation of the three can be represented by a simple pyramid in which the descriptive elements of the self provide the base for the moral apex that is fraternity.

Equality abandons its career as an ideal, satisfied instead to be the relation within which liberty gains access to the real lateral obligation that holds among humans; that is, liberty retains its preeminence as the dynamic factual element of every form of morality, the indispensable ground of human dignity, and the architect of moral self-perfection. It also constitutes the decisive descriptive element in the host property of the relation of human equality. We are equal precisely in our freedom to commit to the search for the lateral good.

This power freely to choose or refuse the good is an awesome and dangerous gift. And only in its marriage to descriptive equality does liberty shed its menacing tendency toward hierarchy. Cut adrift from equality, liberty's unvarying function is to convert knowledge into forms of personal power;

all combinations of knowledge and freedom constitute greater control for the individual over a contingent world. If this synergy of brains and choice were to hold even in respect of the power to achieve moral self-fulfillment, the human race would be a gnostic aristocracy. It is equality that prevents this; it rescues us from hierarchy, withholding from knowledge the power to vary our capacity for moral self-perfection. It is the limited but crucial function of descriptive equality to forestall the lapse into gnosticism. In respect to *every human aspiration other than moral self-perfection*, knowledge remains unrestrained as a source of differentiating power. But all rational persons have the same capacity simply to be good.

Understanding liberty and equality thus as facts of nature invites us to express the content of lateral duty as "fraternity." This label may not help a great deal in the search for answers to particular cases of practical difficulty; fraternity is no great analytical advance upon natural law, the categorical imperative, equal concern and respect, or love thy neighbor. Nor does it point clearly to social policy.[34] What it does represent is the hope, first, to resurrect and then to rectify the long-corrupted revolutionary motto. If the *fraternité* of the Cordeliers could reemerge as the intelligible symbol of humane purpose, the effort would be psychologically and politically worthwhile. Western society needs access to a social purpose more ennobling than an exhausted and meaningless equality; but it needs also to preserve and relegitimate the authority of its basic symbols—of which equality is surely one. Descriptive equality presents the opportunity to move almost imperceptibly from the frozen abstraction of social sameness toward a warmer conception of our mutual responsibility to one another as members of a family. Societies tend to sink or rise to the level of their symbols. A fraternal ideal emergent from a descriptive human equality is a symbol to which the West might, with profit, rise.[35]

Some perceive the symbol of fraternity as a gender-specific instrument of male dominance.[36] We take the point and concede that fraternity has, on occasion, been misconstrued. Whether that risk justifies the abandonment of what most believe to be an important symbol of human unity is another question; its surrender could be consequential. We leave this to those more sensitive to such matters.[37] In any case, if fraternity is out, the twin facts of liberty and equality deserve some companion ethical symbol capable of redeeming the humane element in the old revolutionary aspiration.[38] Among the obvious candidates are friendship, family—and, simply, responsibility. "*Liberté, egalité, responsabilité*" constitute a triangle the world could live with.[39]

10

HARVESTS OF EQUALITY

The closure of the soul in modern gnosticism can
repress the truth . . . but it cannot remove the soul and
its transcendence from the structure of reality.
(Eric Voegelin, *The New Science of Politics*)

WE HAVE ARGUED that the *subjectivity* of our power to work our moral self-perfection has a positive, practical implication; it is in harmony with the common good. Now we must ask the same about its *uniformity*. Does it matter for good or ill that humans possess this capacity for moral fulfillment in the same degree? This is the final question about human equality.

Recall our assumption that the capacity for moral self-perfection *could* differ in degree from person to person; uniformity is not part of its definition.[1] Nevertheless, if human equality is to be, this variable capacity must be uniform in fact. Otherwise our equality would consist merely in its common possession; insofar as it varied among us in degree, we would be decisively disequal in respect to this crucial characteristic.

This sameness in both possession and degree—what we have called double equality—is anything but obvious. Indeed, the only thing self-evident is that equality is neither self-evident nor demonstrable. It is precisely plausible, hence a matter for individual belief—possibly an important belief. This chapter assumes the existence of the necessary uniformity and asks—so what? Are humans better off for having this capacity for moral self-perfection in the same degree? Our answer is an emphatic yes. Besides satisfying a necessary criterion of equality, it is this double uniformity that makes human community a possibility. Conversely, inequality of moral endowment is a principle of division; the mere belief in moral hierarchy is a source of both individual anxiety and social discord. Uniformity of capacity does not of course imply homogeneity in actual intent or behavior; the equality at stake here concerns only what we are. With respect to those choices we must make, we should expect and even cherish disuniformity. It is part of the rich harvest of our human liberty, and equality itself blesses and civilizes the diversity.

We approach the question about the practical effects of uniformity in a manner already familiar; we play it off against the (also plausible) gnostic worldview, highlighting the conflicts. The gnostic supposes that the capacity for moral self-perfection varies in degree by intellect. Often he is unaware that his position is parochial. A prolonged immersion in the attitudes of school, university, profession, and media blocks his view of the alternative and broader vision of individual excellence. We hope to give the gnostic a fresh look at the good life through the prism of equality. If he will suspend his prejudice, he may manage a perception of human possibility that still embraces intellect while lodging it in a larger world—one in which intelligence serves purposes that are splendid but less ultimate for individual self-perfection.

In this final chapter we show how human equality entails answers to six specific questions that are of special concern to educated Westerners. For convenience we name these broad themes "human dignity," "individual greatness," "community," "racial prejudice," "progress," and "world society." The fundamental meaning of each is radically affected by belief in the uniformity of the capacity for moral self-perfection.

Uniformity and Dignity

That unique capacity for moral self-perfection is the locus of human worth. Persons do not have value principally as worker, owner, consumer, or athlete but as free moral agents able to say yes or no to the call of conscience. It is in this personal capacity that philosophers and bus drivers locate "human dignity." This term implies the presence of the "host property" of the relation of equality; for dignity, too, rests upon the capacity for moral self-perfection. Dignity, however, is not identical to human equality because it could be unevenly distributed without losing its identity. If our individual capacities for moral self-perfection were different in degree, equality would perish but dignity would remain. Every person would have it; but it would be relativized. Some would have it more than others. That is a problem for which equality is the only answer.[2]

The Idea of Dignity

Contemporary accounts of dignity seldom seem conscious of its antiquity. Two thousand years before Christianity, *Genesis* had already announced the astonishing news that the entire race had been designed as *imago Dei*. Every half-blind, tergiversating descendant of Adam represents, manifests, constitutes—indeed, somehow *is*—"the image and likeness of God."[3] Thus, from the beginning of history, human dignity has had its foundation in the godly stuff that is infused into our flesh and spirit. Or so the Jews believed, and the West as a whole came to agree. From Christian Rome until the seventeenth century this idea was accepted as the fundamental expression of our worth and the ground of our obligation to one another. Doubtless, familiarity has robbed this remarkable revelation of some of its radical panache, but to us this old report of Moses is still sufficiently startling to make the twentieth-century rediscoveries of dignity seem rather weak tea.

The history of "*dignitas*" is exceedingly rich on both its theological and classical sides. Its religious streams were several and distinctive, being represented variously in Jewish, early Christian (both Greek and Latin), and eventually medieval thought.[4] Though discrete, these ideological strains were essentially in agreement with one another; God had produced one species that enjoyed those specific properties which, in their infinite form, constitute divinity itself. In a humble, finite—but very real—manner, all humans participate in will and intellect.[5]

This location of dignity within our moral and cognitive life had its non-theological parallel in Greek and Stoic philosophy; humans held their exalted place in the universe by their peculiar power to originate good and evil.[6] Gradually all these religious and classical tributaries were to merge in Renaissance figures such as Pico and Ficino. United as a single theme, human dignity debouched from the Middle Ages prepared to become and remain a common part of modern discourse. There is no covenant for the United Nations, no constitution for Somalia, no papal encyclical, no charter for the Young Democrats of Yolo County that does not remind us all of our dignity.[7]

At the same time modern discourse about dignity has become progressively unclear about its source and nature. Antiquity saw dignity as something real; it was an aspect of what humans are. Springing from constitutive elements of the person, it came as an endowment from either God or nature. Contemporary writers seem uncertain about all this; for them dignity sometimes obtains not as a necessary inference from our makeup but as a concession of our fellow citizens. The general counsel of the United Nations describes it as merely an "ideal" or "goal" of human society, oblivious to its intellectual history as a claim of fact.[8] So viewed, dignity is reduced to an aspect of the treatment other people bestow upon us. If they show you respect, you have it; if they do not, perhaps you lack it altogether. Its status is in doubt.[9]

Enforceable legal rights including "human rights" are important, but to conceive of dignity as a sort of social or juridical supplement to our nature would miss the point made by Moses and Cicero. Hobbes himself might have hesitated to reduce dignity to a social artifact. Even in his mythic savage condition, man's cognitive life had a certain center and essence that justified all the effort Hobbes poured into the *Leviathan*. However quickly the individual yields his moral autonomy, it was truly his by nature, and Hobbes supposed its surrender to society to be voluntary and real. The Enlightenment tried very hard to make something of this idea, picturing the self-legislating autonomy of each self as a kind of proxy for the dignity that formerly was said to be infused by God. Hobbes would have agreed with this intellectual campaign. He wanted to subordinate religious authority and moral tradition, but he hoped to escape with his soul intact.

Were the authors sufficiently modern in outlook we might embrace Hobbes as the best hope for human dignity. At least his lonesome uncommitted selves did not have to get theirs from the neighbors. Gifted naturally with intelligence and will, the human person could view himself in the mirror and declare his own worth. But though this notion might qualify as modern, the authors sadly cannot; we consider this Hobbesian version of dignity to be a caricature and a forfeiture of the real thing. To crown each person a sovereign source of good and evil leaves dignity anemic and rootless. There is something essentially silly about my claiming dignity on the ground of my own ability to prefer one thing to another. The problem is not that this claim glorifies free will; that is as it should be. The rub is that if my will makes every possibility into a potential good, good itself ceases to be an intelligible concept, and dignity along with it. To make dignity self-referential is an indignity.

Only when it derives from a real source and is anchored in a real good does dignity become a thing of consequence and a spark of nobility. We need not elaborate all the arguments for this; in essence we have already done so. Dignity arises essentially from the assembly of elements that constitute the host property of the relation of human equality. It is the capacity for self-perfection viewed in one of its consequences. The criteria we propose for dignity will thus sound familiar.

What an Authentic Dignity Would Require

The requirements of human dignity are five. First, some sort of capacity is implied, not a passive quality but a fitness for participation in activity. From *Genesis* to Ronald Dworkin there is agreement on this. More specifically, human dignity issues from our liberty and free creativity. Determinism is its antithesis; as a rigid behaviorist, Skinner was quite correct to dissociate himself from dignity.[10] The *Imago* is someone who is able to do something meaningful.

Second, as already noted, in order to generate dignity, this autonomy must be something received. A dignity self-bestowed is the laurel of the posturing crackpot who supposes himself the emperor. As the gift of God or nature, dignity cannot be grasped or even achieved, for it is already present in the one who would grasp or achieve it. Contemplating my own dignity, the only appropriate response is gratitude.

Third, this germinal moral autonomy is itself a thing of structure and of limits that are fixed and determined by its source. Our freedom endures only because it is sustained and anchored; we discern trace elements of its ancestry as we experience the invitation to seek the good. Granted, just how our response can avoid being determined by that source is more easily experienced than explained. In any case, dignity rests upon this free capacity to commit ourselves; the decision somehow is ours. This freedom is itself the transmitted structure, and through it we confront the option to say either yes or no to a good that is real and not merely to the outcomes we would prefer. We have been thrown into a game of seek-the-good. Victory requires only that we play as well as we can with the equipment we have been issued. The only defeat is the refusal to play.

Fourth (and related), dignity is not only a reference back to the metaphysical root of our moral capacity but, by reason of our social nature, is also a reference forward to our fellow humans whose presence and behavior set the external conditions of our choices. Thus we *experience* dignity within a *relation*. As humans we share a medium in which we all are mutually vulnerable, thereby creating the possibility of lateral moral choice. *Human* dignity cannot work as an idea, unless it captures this engagement in a common activity and purpose. The game is played by all and with all. The recognition of dignity depends upon our state of potential reciprocity; it is by being in the game that we confront dignity in one another.[11]

Fifth, and finally, human dignity must be a quality invulnerable to all contingency save the total and permanent loss of rationality. While we can choose, we can play.[12]

In short, dignity is the worth we possess because of our freedom to accept real obligation and to participate thereby in the universal possibility of moral self-fulfillment. We are dignified as potentially self-perfecting moral agents responsible to and for others.

The Problem: Dignity Is a Variable

However, if dignity depends upon our capacity for moral fulfillment, it could in theory be disuniform in degree from person to person; that is, if the capacity varied in fact, not only would equality fail completely but human dignity would simultaneously become relativized and hierarchical.[13] Individual persons would possess varying endowments of the very property from which their dignity proceeds. Thus there are practical social consequences to the position one takes on the possibility of goodness. The interpretation of moral structure fixes one's understanding of one's relation to others; this picture in turn affects the terms of our common life. Fundamental attitudes toward obligation and morality are at stake.

A relativized dignity is logically possible. The capacity for moral self-perfection could vary; it could do so, for example, by disparate dispensations of divine grace. We have no proof to the contrary. We can show only that uniformity is plausible and then candidly accept this uniformity as our un-proved premise. This, however, gives us a great advantage over the gnostic. Self-perfection is for us a wholly subjective activity that *permits* uniformity of moral capacity as a logical possibility. The human ability to accept or reject the responsibility to search for the content of ideal behavior *could* be uniform in degree.

By contrast, the gnostic view of the self's capacity for moral choice forbids uniformity and thus requires that dignity be relativized.[14] Intellectual power varies among us, and variations in our individual opportunities for a per-fected moral self would be inevitable. Though the two chief versions of moral gnosticism contradict each other regarding the source and nature of moral obligation, both implicitly agree on the disuniformity of dignity. To clarify this point we briefly revisit these opposing schools.

The first of the two gnostic perspectives we shall call "objective"—using the term in its *traditional* sense. We have seen it before; it is the stand of certain mainline philosophers including Socrates and Thomas Aquinas.[15] For both of them, the capacity for moral self-fulfillment is either defined as, or deeply affected by, the ability of the individual person to discern the objectively correct answer to moral questions. Moral self-perfection is fore-most an intellectual achievement, and the knack for it is directly propor-tional to one's cognitive horsepower. Uniformity of capacity is therefore out of the question. The human race is a hierarchy composed of persons arrayed principally by their moral acumen. None is wholly without dignity; but (though this is discreetly left unsaid) to have this dignity in inferior degree is necessarily negative in consequence, for one thereby has less of what it takes to attempt the supreme human achievement.

The opposite version of gnosticism is also familiar from our discussion of Hobbes.[16] For convenience we can call his view either "subjectivist" dignity or, more simply, the dignity of Hobbes. It was Hobbes who taught that by nature the individual is sovereign of the good. The value of any choice is man's autonomous creation, wrought of his own will from alternatives iden-tified by will's servant—reason. Such radical autonomy could perhaps be the seat of dignity; indeed, some would say, the more radical the more dignified. Hobbes merits the label gnostic because for him the effective range of this moral autonomy of the person is a direct function of his intelligence, train-ing, and circumstances. The savant has the scope and power of Faust to declare the good; the sweep of his will is coextensive with the vastness of his intellect.[17] The same principle governs the high school dropout; his will ranges over whatever options his reason is able to report, and—sooner than Faust and Hobbes—he encounters the boundary of his moral possibility.[18] Once again, the gnostic would array us on the ladder of worth according to brain function; in doing so, paradoxically he transmutes dignity itself into the medium of indignity.

Note once more that—compared to Hobbes and company—both natural law and Christianity are less committed and more ambiguous on this question of the uniformity of our capacity for moral self-perfection. As we saw, either could be interpreted as an objective gnosticism in which moral advance requires the individual to grasp the correct answers. On this view, the degrees of individual acumen would mean disuniformity in dignity. But the opposite interpretation is also available. Both natural law and Christianity (and the latter more easily) can accommodate the view that degrees of intellectual power are irrelevant to subjective moral achievement. And each has absorbed a good deal of Kant who (as we argued in chapter 4) rescues dignity from relativization by connecting it to a capacity that is invulnerable to empirical variation. Leszek Kolakowski catches this in his essay on why we need Kant:

> Even though the idea of human dignity, conferring the same equality on every human being, is older than Kant and actually of biblical origin, we owe Kant not only the attempt to establish it independently of revealed religion, but also the clear distinction of this idea from everything that may ever be discovered in anthropological, historical, and psychological research.[19]

Gnostic Anxiety

Wherever it is made a function of an empirically variable power such as intellect, dignity thus faces self-cancellation. Nowhere is this better understood than at the top of the gnostic moral heap, a realm we can locate vaguely in the academy, the arts, the professions, and the media.[20] No one fears the decline of cognitive power more than the one to whom dignity appears to consist primarily in brains. And decline it can and will even in this life; intellect is contingent and fleeting. Hence the gnostic individual experiences dignity as something threatened and ephemeral. Even if he or she becomes resigned to its anticipated erosion by age, accident, or illness, there remains the insufferable displacement by superior intellect. Consider the case of the East German academics formerly prominent in fields such as law, history, and economics. Many of these men and women were simply discarded in the process of German reunification—and not merely in the sense of loosing their jobs. A major part of their intellectual identity simply evaporated; literally, their special knowledge of human good was knowledge no longer. Many no doubt took sufficient consolation in some alternate version of personal integrity. But for those accustomed to conceive of their own moral worth in cognitive terms, the experience was a crushing humiliation.[21]

East Germany, however, is only an extreme and spectacular example of a calamity familiar to every gnostic. It is the agony of the professional (or anyone) who must come to terms with cognitive competition on the staircase of dignity. Insofar as a person shares the gnostic interpretation of worth, the association and comparison with superior intellect can be pure torture. This is our observation of certain students and academics when they are confronted with higher intelligence among those who are nominally their peers. The gifted stranger who appears in their midst will seem a threat, even though he or she enhances the intellectual quality of the group. For some this fear can be understood in objective terms—for example, as job competition. For the gnostic, however, the pain is that of an implicit moral demotion. He is diminished in worth by inferiority of intellect: " 'This race we must suppose to have no other goal, no other garland, but being fore-most.' And in this race 'continually to be outgone is misery. Continually to outgo the next is felicity. And to foresake the course is to die.' "[22]

Given the elitist premise, this is entirely rational; hell for the gnostic con-sists in a descent to the existential lot of the stupid, a state defined in relative terms. And whether or not this descent occurs in fact, it looms always in anticipation; vicariously the gnostic experiences the degradation of the dull. The superior colleague may never actually appear, but he will always seem just around the corner.

This plague is not exclusive to academics or the sophisticated. The dullest working stiff can be morally marginalized by the real or imagined scorn or condescension of fellow gnostics. The sufferer may be able himself to iden-tify others who are still lower on the gnostic ladder, but he remains threat-ened in dignity by those above. The classic tormentor of the rube is the bully who secretly despises his own place in the cognitive pecking order.[23]

This purgatory of the modern gnostic is in certain respects a replay of the Calvinist experience. The world is composed of sheep and goats, and even those who by appearance seem most secure must ever live in constant anxi-ety about their own election. Max Weber saw nineteenth-century believers seeking confirmation of their salvation through activity and industry.[24] To-day's intellectual Calvinist is driven to parallel expedients such as erudition, the adoption of correct political attitudes, and other indicia of cognitive supremacy. Of course there are differences in the two cases. The old Calvinist election was utterly ascriptive; in the end you were simply saved or not, whatever your works. And election was essentially inscrutable regardless of the favored appearances one accumulated. By contrast, education truly elevates the modern secular gnostic a moral notch or three in his own terms, because election for him occurs here and now by an empirical and relativistic calculus. Because this chance to excel is so obviously real, it drives some moderns to cognitive exertions that a healthy Calvinist would have fore-sworn. In any case, for sheer moral futility it would be hard to choose be-tween the two.

Two clarifications are important. First, even in an "information society," most people do not experience gnostic anxiety to any significant extent;

for they do not confuse brains with moral possibility. The average person attributes no moral weight to superior intellect; until given reason to suppose otherwise, he presumes the janitor to be the moral equal of Einstein. The gnostic is most typically from the academy; the confusion of the best with the brightest is largely a self-generated pathology of the bright.

Second, none of this suggests anything at all about the personal moral state of individuals who are afflicted with this virus. Some of our best friends are gnostics, and they seem as likely as the janitor to be well intending. An obtending gnostic—one seeking the real good—is self-perfecting even if he is wrong about the moral importance of intellect. He sees moral hierarchies that do not exist, but his heart is pure and his virtue solid. This innocence, however, does not keep him from doing a special kind of harm in the Kingdom of the Other, a truth we illustrate first by briefly tracing the confusion gnostic writers have introduced into the simple idea of personal moral greatness. It is a disorder for which human equality is the specific remedy.

Uniformity and Greatness

One casualty of the current culture wars is the Great Man. The climate is no longer friendly to the hero who in some remote century drove history from its course and altered the consciousness and aspirations of our forebears, hence of ourselves. Adulation of these demigods of the Western past was a familiar feature of the late Enlightenment, swelling and ebbing as the culture turned seasonally toward, then away, from the romantic. The phenomenon was epitomized in the work of Thomas Carlyle who emerged in the mid-nineteenth century as chief hagiographer of these secular saints and of their fateful "callings."[25] Just who deserved to be in the top ten was a lively issue among the herophyles, but most, like Carlyle, recognized "men of action" alongside those of letters and arts. Frederick (the Great, naturally), Cromwell, and Dante were all favorites of Carlyle. Nietzsche took an equally eclectic view; moreover, he stretched the category of greatness by becoming a superstar himself. But every educated Victorian had his own gallery of the greats.

Today the whole concept is on the ropes, at least in the view of many who are paid to criticize literature and the arts.[26] According to them the problem is not merely that the established greats were mostly white males (though for some that is a reproach sufficient to dish the lot). Nor is it that moderns feel no need of greatness as a human possibility; to the contrary, the evident angst of many over the continued sovereignty of Shakespeare betrays a deep craving for a new model of Prometheus.[27] This craving unfortunately cannot be satisfied; that is the greatest misery of all. Greatness, it seems, is not rampant. At least for the moment there are no subs that can put Shakespeare and Dante on the bench.

The more politically conservative among the herophyles explain the dearth of contemporary greats as a pathology of overextended democracy, a kind of regression to the mean. We might call their concern "Carlyle's complaint." This syndrome involves a chronic confusion of two very different meanings of greatness. Understood as a classic objection to the cultural fruit of egalitarian politics, this concern over a general debasement makes some sense. Understood as a claim about the distribution of the capacity for moral greatness, it is a corruption, and that is our concern.

Greatness is a quality that can be ascribed either to a work or a worker. Obviously the two are distinct, and so are the justifications for assigning greatness to the one or the other—to the person or his deeds. What constitutes achievement in the realm of individual conscience has no necessary correspondence to the advancement of the objective good. This we said in chapter 9, and its application here is straightforward.

Carlyle identified his heroes by their specific impact upon Western civilization. The glory was less the worker than the work; it was the external achievement that deserved to be canonized. For this purpose, however, the persona of the actor was an indispensable literary instrument. Carlyle and his successors elevated military, philosophical, artistic, and political achievements by the common literary device of personification. In the process Dante became a role, and playing the part called Dante was deemed a very good thing to do. A certain man did it and was declared great.[28]

The literary habit of personification is unlikely to disappear. How else can there be a readable history or criticism? (Marx may have succeeded but only for readers of a peculiar taste.) Today this enterprise of Carlyle—at least in its literary mode—centers in the efforts of those, such as Harold Bloom, who defend the dead icons of the Western canon against the political enthusiasms of the hour.[29] Bloom's is a hard but useful vocation. It is useful because it affirms a real good. It is hard because of the intellectual collapse of the academy. How can it be asserted that a man or woman is great for some specific contribution, when there is no regnant measure of what could count as a contribution?

This lack of criteria is only partly explained by skepticism regarding the real good. There are plenty who do still believe in it; unfortunately they very often believe in conflicting goods. Some would canonize FDR for the very works that others abominate. Still, if conflict about substance were the only difficulty, the enterprise of finding models would go forward, at least haltingly. The really lethal element in the current scene is indeed the deep moral skepticism sprinkled among the writers and professors; many of them *do* regard the whole conception of an objective moral reality as nonsense.

As a consequence the modern academy is itself an occasion of Carlyle's complaint. In a world in which one invents the good for oneself, nobody can be great.

To this the obtensionalist can say, never mind. The personification of great works is itself but an act of obfuscation and would be so in any society—even one that has achieved consensus on the good life. This does not deny that some works deserve the label "great"—quite the opposite. What is unclear is that those who carry them out merit the same description. There is a vain and even comic confusion in our attribution of greatness to the person; for in fact these central achievements of the Western tradition—books, deeds, whatever—are, to an extent that is indeterminable, mere accidents.

By accident we mean that in some measure every great work is the consequence of having the opportunity—the brainpower, the health, the "being there"—that the rest of us lack. It is by the luck of the draw that you and I were never candidates for the role of Dante or Luther. Nor would Luther himself, had he been born stupid or phlegmatic or Chinese. Note that this does not counter the claim that Luther contributed indispensably to his "work" by his own conscious, voluntary commitment; after all, he could have stayed an Augustinian recluse. Certainly as a rational human Luther made personal choices to seek (or evade) the real good.[30] But of these we can know precisely nothing. And thus we encounter the radical disconnection between the greatness of a work and that of the worker. We may call Luther great, but we cannot know the one thing that would make him great; we call Shakespeare great, but we don't even know who he was.[31]

Is there anything intelligible to be said about personal greatness? There is this: If there were degrees of moral greatness to be achieved, this would be interesting only if every level were achievable by all. It is exactly because we are uniform in our capacity for moral self-perfection that the realization of that perfection becomes meaningful as a distinction among us. What could greatness signify if the opportunity for it were thrust upon the person in the manner of his height or the keenness of his sight? Greatness is and must be a thing to be achieved by free beings in hot pursuit of the good and starting from the same place. The real work for equality is to make personal greatness possible.

All this, however, is not only unprovable as a proposition but unavailable as a judgment upon any individual—even upon ourselves. "We do not know who are the major and who are the minor characters."[32] We cannot identify the Shakespeares of the subjective any more than we can find the one who wrote the sonnets. If personal moral greatness is worth believing in, it has become so in the manner of any other basic dogma; that is, it is plausible, and its reality is consequential to the environment of authentic democracy. Its very mystery is an invitation to execute our daily responsibilities with respect, reserve, and—above all—humility. The impenetrable possibility of greatness in every person is a primary datum to be freely grasped and cherished. To accept the fact that greatness is—but to wonder where it is—constitutes the first insight of democratic life.[33] And this in turn reminds us of the latent tension between gnosticism and the ideal of human community.

Uniformity and Community

The communitarian movement of the last decade has been struggling with mixed success to identify the subject of its own mission. The consensus so far is this: Whatever its other criteria, the term "community" connotes the benign elements of any human cluster; only insofar as a social aggregation entails the experience of morality could it be deemed communitarian. Thus one plausible candidate for inclusion in any definition is the claim that every true community—whether family, church, nation, or neighborhood—rests upon the mutual judgment that each member possesses in the same degree the capacity for moral self-perfection; every ignorant peasant and every Gandhi within the circle must be credited with the same opportunity for moral self-fulfillment. If the brahmin and the outcast differ in their access to perfection, they might still achieve coexistence or even society; but community would elude them. For community to hold, the most marginally rational person—the most wretched and disadvantaged—must have a capacity for moral and/or spiritual self-fulfillment that is as plenary as that of the most gifted and fortunate.[34]

This is, first of all, a linguistic claim about the legitimate uses of the word "community" as it is implicitly understood among those who deem it important. At the same time it is a claim about how this evocative word *should* be understood. Simply put, the belief that the capacity for moral self-perfection varies is one that cancels genuine community. Once again we would invoke Bernard Williams's denunciation of the "ultimate and outrageous absurdity in the idea that achievement of the highest kind of moral worth should depend on natural capacities, unequally and fortuitously distributed." This absurdity can be erased only if the capacity for moral self-perfection is uniform. What we now add to Williams's observation is that this uniformity is also a precondition of benign human solidarity.

This, however, takes us to the brink of a claim that could not be sustained as a linguistic convention; that is, we have nearly said that *no* community could exist whose members do not profess *universal* human equality. But that would violate common usage. Even self-defining moral elites are generally recognized as "communities," at least so long as they accept the equal capacity of their *own* members for self-perfection and, in addition, meet whatever other conditions of community may be imposed by those who use that term. Black Muslims, Hasidic Jews, and Hutterites might (or might not) be gnostic in their depreciation of the moral prospects of outsiders and still judge their own coreligionists as wholly equal to one another in their access to moral perfection and salvation. Many families (or racial groups) may have a similar view of outsiders and still qualify as "communities" in conventional discourse.

Thus the tactical aim of the communitarian—limited as he or she is to the vague coin of community—could not be to exclude every insular and exclusive group.[35] This practical necessity, however, does not interdict the communitarian's effort to clarify, preach, and advance the terms of a universal ideal of community. And for that larger end the descriptive moral equality of all rational persons would indeed be definitional. This conclusion would, as we have seen, be cordial to certain schools of natural law and to central versions of Christian moral theology. Indeed, we perceive that the present Catholic world (with considerable Protestant agreement) would constitute an interesting and important illustration—one very large example—of the interdependence of equality and community. To enlarge the point, let us assume that the population of believing Catholics satisfies whatever other criteria of community might be imposed by the communitarian. In that event, their belief in descriptive human equality makes Catholics a community in both senses identified—they are simultaneously exclusive and universal.

Put another way, they are, *first*, a community to and among themselves; their church claims authoritative access to correct moral rules, and recognition of that ecclesiastical authority is a criterion of membership. They are, then, an exclusive community—but a community indeed. And membership is no trivial matter, for orthodoxy triggers specific obligation. By their membership they are bound—and nonbelievers are not—to give the teaching authority of their community a presumption of correctness. When engaged in moral choice, this presumption operates as the practical threshold of that good intention upon which their salvation depends; the obtending believer cannot reject an ordinance of the Church merely because he or she has reservations.

Conversely, even the most well-considered and plausible apostasy on some serious moral matter sets the dissenting individual outside this exclusive ecclesial community. The dissenter emigrates from the cluster that upholds the moral authority of the Church. Because that authority is vaguely defined, there will be practical disputes about who is in and who is out. But the principle is clear enough: The doctrinal émigré asserts that the ecclesiastical authority can be wrong and—in this case—is wrong; in his eyes the exclusive community which accepts that authority is deluded about its reliability. The act of emigration is thus the invitation to a new and more discerning (but also exclusive) community. It initiates a plurality of exclusive communities (even though each may aspire to the old name). Either the Church was commissioned to define its own believing community or it was not, and individuals either belong to the community that believes this or they do not—in good faith or bad.

Second, however, the specific beliefs of this exclusive community of faithful Catholics confirm its solidarity with a second and universal moral community. This at first appears as a paradox. Here is an aggressive and exclusive ideological community that asserts the divine commission and responsibility to teach the rest of humankind the Catholic apprehension of truth which, by definition, the outsider lacks. If there is any element of community in this didactic relation between the outsider and the Catholic believer, at first it seems very thin.

On the other hand, when we recall its commitment to universal human moral equality, the Church's attitude toward the unbeliever becomes rather interesting in communitarian terms. In Catholic eyes the outsider is free—as the believer is not—to weigh the specific moral messages of the Church just as he does any other. His obligation is not to give priority to its claims; quite the contrary, the outsider, like every other human, is already obligated to seek the objective good wherever he can find it. The unbeliever or émigré thus has the duty—the natural duty—to consider Catholicism's moral answers along with the rest; but for him they can carry no special presumption of truth. Rome to him is but one of the world's many representatives of the Tao. Looked at from the Catholic perspective, there is here a relation of community between the outsiders and the believers, but curiously it is a one-way bridge; responsibility is all on the side of the believers. Their "exclusive" community has special duties respecting the outsider; the outsider has nothing of the sort toward them.

The Catholic presumably would drive the point even further, asserting what is ultimately a bilateral relation of a most arresting sort between believer and unbeliever. The Church's own commitment to human equality entails its communal message to the outsider that, if he concludes the Church is wrong (on whatever issue), he is not only bound in conscience to *reject* her but that, precisely by doing so, he achieves the very end the Church herself sought for him. Even amid the most intense ideological conflict, real human connection thereby remains possible. The unbeliever is recognized by the believer to exercise full membership in the one essential and universal moral community exactly at the point when in good faith the unbeliever conscientiously refuses what purports to be the authoritative message of the exclusive ecclesial community.

But this paradoxical relation between Catholics and their ideological competitors is merely one large and vivid example of the subsurface harmonies that are everywhere generated and sustained by assent to universal human equality. We have argued that, at least in the West, this crucial belief is a cultural reality in most communities—be they churches, families, home-towns, ethnic clubs, string quartets, or the United States of America. If we are correct in this, it is possible to view the frequent discord among the human tribes with this crucial consolation: The inevitable quarrels among such communities reduce in their deepest meaning to disputes within the human family. These convulsions, often so destructive in objective terms, never risk either the moral integrity of the individual or of the community that is mankind.

This limitation of group conflict to the objective or behavioral level has a positive and practical implication for contemporary Western societies en-gaged in "culture war" against competing ideologies. A full-throated public assent to the distinction between the goodness of persons and the correct-ness of acts would be a contribution to democratic peace. Specifically, the assertion that Europe has transmitted a superior culture should be under-stood by its friends and opponents alike as a limited and disinterested claim; it concerns specific rules of private and public life and the modes by which these are communicated as guides for individuals and institutions. (E.g., the Golden Rule is superior to xenophobia.) Anyone is free to criticize and reject these claims of truth, but rejection should come in a spirit of gratitude that the claims have been offered at all. To profess hard-won wisdom about the proper conduct of life is not an act of aggression but a loving invitation to dialogue. Offense is properly taken only when the claim of truth entails the implication that knowledge of the right rules is necessary to personal goodness. Unfortunately, that message has too often been conveyed by those apologists of the West who fail to distinguish the two forms of good.

It is the grave responsibility of moral leadership to disclaim any personal moral advantage accruing to the inheritors of the Western or any other tradi-tion. Particular cultures may in fact be superior (so we believe), but whether a particular person is superior is a discrete question. Indeed, human equality (that thoroughly Western insight) is precisely the claim that although the received wisdom can help identify correct behavior, the mastery of its con-tent is irrelevant to personal goodness. The least clever person who hails from the most ethically impoverished culture has the capacity of Albert Schweizer to achieve moral perfection. All of us are gifted in the same degree to succeed or fail at this one essential responsibility and opportunity to seek the right way as best we can.

There will always be cultural propagandists who by ignorance—or by an enfeebling envy of the West—either cling to relativism or claim superiority for what are in fact morally deficient ways. But when the Westerner imputes an inferior capacity for moral self-fulfillment to those who lack access to the higher standard, he only invites more such folly.

Uniformity and Race

There are two distinguishable aspects of the "race problem." The easier issue—though vexing enough—is what to do once we have identified acts of unjustified discrimination based upon race; should we pay reparations, bus school children, or engage in affirmative hiring practices? Choosing the right legal response is difficult because the outcomes of intervention can be quite unpredictable and destructive of other values. But at least the policy is ours to create; it is a political and moral decision, and, in due course, we make it and then live with it or change it.

The harder issue is the intellectual one: just what human fact is racial prejudice supposed to be about? What perception of difference drives the person whom we call "racist"?[36] There is clearly *something*—some fact he deems important, a reality he has prejudged about the particular race he deems inferior (or superior) to another; its members are different in some specific and significant way.

Pigmentation is not it; even the avowed racist concedes as much. Color, accent, and the like, are the merest proxies for some difference that really counts; racism is a judgment about this more ultimate fact. A race is deficient insofar as its members, on average, fall short in regard to whatever measures human worth. By definition, this is a human property that *could* vary in degree among races, and racism is the belief that it *does* vary.

Assuming truth to be the ultimate value, racism could in theory be a benign phenomenon. For races might in fact differ according to this standard—whatever it is—that grounds our worth. Of course, this would hold only if this criterion is the valid one. If relative wealth were the criterion of human merit and dignity, one would judge blacks as a group to be inferior; the problem would lie with the standard.

We cannot probe those individual, one-at-a-time evaluations that people make of persons of other races. Whichever standards of worth they employ, there must be a good deal of simple error in the specific applications. This is no concern of ours; these judgments are beyond scrutiny. We should add that in this area, as in others, even the accuracy of formal empirical judgments about persons (for example, estimations of intelligence by organized testing) is problematic. Social science is not always confident that it measures even what it tries to measure. We cannot hope to clarify this issue.

By contrast, something worthwhile might be said about the *standards* by which these judgments of individuals' worth are made. That question is not a technical one, and its engagement by ordinary people is important. Indeed, the respective standards of the commoner and the elite may be quite distinct; we have argued at length that there is an implicit popular consensus recognizing that human worth rests solely upon an individual's capacity for moral self-perfection through diligent intention of the good. This capacity is taken by the convention about equality to be uniformly distributed not merely among races but *universally* among rational individuals.[37] This view would altogether cancel racism.

Nonetheless, the plague persists and is properly denounced as the rotten fruit of human ignorance. However, this is not the classic case of proletarian prejudice. The poor may share in the problem, but the primary locus of the misunderstanding about human worth is not the unsophisticated but the intelligentsia; it flourishes there as the unconscious inheritance of the Enlightenment. Just as this false standard was accepted by many nineteenth-century missionaries, it has been unwittingly assimilated by a disproportionate number among our cognitive elites. This becomes most nearly explicit when it is embodied in formal testing instruments that are taken to register the "human potential" of individuals. But it is also observable in the tribal subtleties of the university as we choose our colleagues and our intellectual agenda. It rests upon a specific metaphysics—a philosophical interpretation of the moral self.[38] Racism *is* that parochial belief when, consciously or otherwise, it is applied to racial groups.

Its content is the familiar claim that moral self-perfection is essentially cognitive or intellectual. We have called it gnosticism. Except for spasmodic interludes of romanticism, it has been the message of the Enlightenment. Throughout the West it has been broadcast to the man in the street by the man in the tower. It is this insular philosophy that allows race to be a plausible moral category.

Still, confusing human worth with brains is an understandable—almost forgivable—quirk of our brahmins. Every modern society properly entrusts to gifted individuals those tasks that demand talent and training. In a technological culture these cerebral jobs have ever greater economic and political importance. In truth, we depend on smart people for our material progress and often for physical survival.

The intelligent and educated individual thus faces the temptations common to these decisive social roles. Why was I put here? Who are we noble few that provide the fire, the food, and the hope? Pride is still the most easily seductive of the deadly sins, and it whispers that we indispensables belong in this priesthood because we have more of what really counts as human beings. Call it the right stuff, or what you like. We have it. And essentially that stuff is brains. This is the gnostic creed. "He who knows the good does the good"—hence *is* the good.

Maybe this is the way things really are. Perhaps being born brainy and developing this particular gift is the authentic definition of human perfection. In any case, it is this view that invites the perception (true or false) that specific human groups are inferior in a morally meaningful way.[39] Idolatry of intelligence entails the catastrophic interpretation of the possibility of racial variation in moral capacity. In the alchemy of the Enlightenment, knowledge became the medium of virtue; it was then that inferiority became an empirical question about cognitive potential. There will always be evidence sufficient to fuel that issue with respect to some human cluster. Whatever the empirical reality, in a gnostic moral world the perception of hierarchy is ineradicable, and its embodiment in racial attitudes and practice is inevitable.

Happily, most of the world is less hypnotized by IQ. The moral supremacy of brains is largely the totem of the intellectuals; in spite of unrelenting propaganda from the academy—most of it naive and well-intended—the standard of human worth applied by ordinary people remains a good deal more ambiguous and humane. The idea of human equality has not yet been trained or bribed out of them; relatively few seem to believe that sophistication in itself has much to do with human worth. Their common view of the right stuff may be difficult to specify, but, at a minimum, it includes the anti-gnostic conviction that human fulfillment is fully available to everyone. For the philosopher of the street the perfecting act is simply that of doing the best one can to discover one's real obligations and honor them. Beyond the bare capacity to choose at all, intellectual strength is irrelevant to basic worth. Even getting the right answer is irrelevant (on condition that it be truly sought). This plebeian wisdom is the specific therapy for the thoroughly nasty hierarchy of gnosticism; it liberates the concept of human worth from every accident of birth or circumstance.[40] Kant gave this insight philosophical form.

To the extent that those who run the schools and the media treat intellectual power as the measure of the capacity for personal excellence, the question about who has it (and in what degree) is for them *the* moral question. Ethics is experienced as a cognitive "clarification"; what is noble subtly merges with what is Nobel. Paradoxically, this conflation of the brightest with the best explains the resolute (if subtle) censorship that has been imposed by the "scientific community" upon serious research concerning differences among the races. The academy may be gnostic, but it is equally "liberal," and these two cults can cohabit only if every group is as smart as every other. On this issue the safest course for the liberal gnostic has been not to inquire.[41] His contribution to racism thus remains subsurface, but it constitutes the sustaining mass of the iceberg; borne upon this ideological bulk, the obscene tip makes it to the media. Archie Bunker—that inveterate gnostic—observes all this and understands only too well why the academy polices serious inquiry. For Archie, the frown of the censors ratifies the very differences on which he takes his bigoted stand. By remaining historically mute, the academy has encouraged the attitude it claims to despise.[42] Afraid to defend explicitly its own gnostic standard, it has allowed no alternative account of human dignity to confront the racist. Prejudice claims the resulting vacuum.

Consider the ideal future the gnostic envisions. His hope is that a century or so of correct public policy will have two effects: (1) the brain-jobs will be filled from all population subgroups in correct proportions: in short, color will *appear* to be irrelevant; and (2) color will *in fact* be irrelevant, since by that time everyone will have achieved his or her position by merit. It will have turned out that the crucial human property really was distributed evenly among racial groups; an interim policy of affirmative action followed by a permanent policy of color-blind selection will have proved the contested point.

Current academic dogma holds this to be the recipe for the stable, just, and orderly society of the future. If such a program be honestly administered and the results indeed prove to be proportional, cognitive racial groupings will have been discredited; that will constitute a modest contribution to human knowledge. The problem is that this "neutral" society—to a disquieting degree—will have been fought for and achieved on the false premise that what really matters about an individual is his or her intellect. With our treasure and energy we will at last have enthroned the gnostic creed and identified those who are to be despised in the new order—the stupid of every race, culture, sex, and dialect.[43] For if it can be an insult to discern the intellectual potential of a racial group, this can be so only because it is an insult to do the same in regard to an individual.

There is some risk that the authors' rejection of gnostic perfection will be misunderstood as contempt for high intellectual achievement—that we have embraced a Mennonite mistrust of sophistication. And that misperception could be exacerbated by our insistence that the least-gifted person living in the most backward and unjust society can reach the moral perfection of any polymath from Princeton—that God's heroes could be the world's helots. But to say so is merely to reject cognitive idolatry; brains retain an immense importance as a perfecting instrument of our common life. Indeed, the first condition of moral fulfillment for the dull, as for the gifted, is the obligation to use what intellectual resources one has in pursuit of the good. The duty to harness reason as the path to good behavior belongs to every human with a scrap of rationality.

Nor does human equality imply anything specific about the proper distribution of jobs. Everyone, simply because he or she is bound to seek the common good, must encourage society to empower (and, to the extent necessary, reward) individuals at least roughly according to their intelligence, education, and skills. The efficient discharge of technological, artistic, political, and other objective functions is often inseparable from cultivated intellect. Society must establish roles and incentives accordingly. All that we need to see—and believe—is that recognition of this practical reality carries no implication about the moral worth either of individuals or the racial or cultural groups to which they belong.[44] To distribute worldly authority and responsibility according to intellect or skill is consistent with a relation of human equality that rests upon the capacity not to perfect the world but to perfect oneself. Neither president nor pope has superior access to the means of moral self-fulfillment. We could add, indeed, that their positions put them in a special relation of servitude to the rest of us. Leaders are given in trust the rights and authority necessary to discharge their stewardship, but servants they remain. This is an easy idea, and it takes considerable philosophical sophistication to avoid it.

It is fair, nonetheless, to wonder whether these propositions will be received everywhere with enthusiasm. Some will misconstrue them as a placebo designed for those groups who are not presently making it in the political or economic order; human equality is not accompanied by jobs and honors nor anything else tangible. And we concede that it may be especially difficult for gifted members of racial minorities to accept what for them could seem a revisionist measure of human worth.[45] So much has been invested in persuading them of perfectibility-through-intellect that they might be forgiven some skepticism regarding any competing system of moral accounting.

Nevertheless, deliverance from this false metric cannot be postponed, even if it begins only with the gentlest reproof to the gnostics themselves. The transformation called for among them is essentially moral, and in the radical sense of their redefining moral achievement. With Orwell we conclude: "It is not at all certain that a merely moral criticism of society may not be just as 'revolutionary' . . . as the politico-economic criticism which is fashionable at this moment."[46]

Uniformity and the Perfection of Mankind

In defining human excellence, the gnostic properly abandons the empty distinction of race; for it he substitutes the real distinction of intellectual power. This solution betrays his favorite metaphor of human ordering. Mankind for him is a queue of intelligences—the strong, the indifferent, the puny—each with its place in line determined by its capacity to achieve perfection.[47] Gnostics imagine their own intellectual heroes at the head of this queue; for one a cadre of distinguished Greeks, Socrates at the front; for another Luther and his illustrious contemporaries. Others (for whom time devalues knowledge) will prefer this year's squad of Nobel laureates.

Nor could it occur to them that the queue might be headed by some intellectual invalid—the simplest of minds, unsuspected of moral greatness even by his familiars. To the gnostic the greatness of a person implies greatness of gifts; the Unknown Soldier of the Good must be some undiscovered Prometheus—certainly not "The Man with the Hoe,"[48] or even "The Woman Who Was Poor."[49] In the moral queue of the Enlightenment the dull go to the end of the line.

On closer inspection we see that the line is not static. Places are traded as the relative intellectual capacities of individuals wax and wane; new persons join the line and others simply drop out when cognition ceases. But the line itself is also in motion. Our original metaphor was insufficient; this is not a queue but rather a column that constantly gains, loses, and reshuffles its members. It is an endless file of shifting selves plodding the Via Cognita—trudging toward some state of higher intelligence and perfection.

The gnostic metaphor is in fact one version—the moral version—of the idea of human progress. Though momentarily chastened by the colossal disappointments of the twentieth century, various images of progress are still very much with us. Some are, and some are not, threatening to equality; wrenching and tearing a bit, we can reduce them to four major forms—human power over things, natural selection, moral destiny, and fluctuation.

First, it is progress to make nature behave as one wants. Since Prometheus stole fire, man has struggled with at least limited success to turn the material world to his purposes. In itself, this is perfectly innocent. There are joy and wonder in watching nature yield—if just a bit—to our will. To create fire and music is to make love to a universe that without us would remain dark and dumb. Invention and material progress are, in principle, good clean fun. There are, of course, good and bad practices, and the risks one can pose to unborn generations are at last a recognized part of the moral calculus. Nor is this merely a collective responsibility; life invites each of us to promote the best outcomes we can conceive, and each accepts or declines as an individual. This first notion of progress is easily domesticated within the idea of human equality.

Nineteenth-century evolution provided the second meaning by turning the first conception of progress on its head. *Genesis* and the Enlightenment had set man in the saddle; but Darwin made things ride man. Far from controlling nature, he learned that nature had created and controls the species, converting man from *homo faber* to homo fabricated. In itself this "descent" had no great metaphysical implication. Man—in his sober moments—had always seen himself to be a crafted and dependent being. This part of Darwin's message was significant only to biblical literalists. So long as evolution was content to remain scientific, it was morally irrelevant. This, however, was not to be. Science promptly began to drift toward a third progress, one with a moral and gnostic genius.

Even Darwin himself had interpreted the physical evidence in moral terms. He announced the extinction of less improved forms, making "the survival of the fittest" shorthand for the "fatalistic optimism"[50] that some process, soon to be explained, was busy turning out beings—including humans—that were, by definition, superior to their ancestors.[51] The proposition that the fit survive is of course empty. If being fit means leaving descendants, it is no surprise that the fit are with us yet. There may be some other sense in which particular species deserve this label, but the scientists have yet to identify it except in lyrical form; it is the poets among them who have gradually transmogrified natural "fitness" and selection into its present form of secular evangelism. For a nineteenth-century academy already in revolt against religion this was understandable, but ironically these prophets themselves came to resemble nothing so much as a church. The fervor of Spencer, Wells, and the Huxleys became less and less about bodies and more and more about this new moral direction for the race. A canon of protected dogmatic truths gradually emerged as eschatology—a tale of ultimate human fulfillment. The best is ahead, and the best is wherever evolution is taking us within the higher life of the intellect.

This idea of straight-line moral improvement is distinct from our final, and more conventional, notion—one we hesitate even to identify as a version of progress; we refer to the prosaic view that in any historical period, there can be increase or decrease in the net quantum of moral good. This net good or fluctuating version simply supposes that in certain eras those people who have committed themselves to search for the good have actually found it with sufficient regularity to produce a temporary warming of global or regional morality in the sense of just and rational conduct. (There is a Miniver Cheevy in most of us that drives us to choose a favorite century selected in these terms.) By definition, however, such a perception also permits regress (viz., the twentieth century?). Most important, this net-good version of "progress" involves no substitution of standards. When good is on the increase, this is the same good we knew yesterday; otherwise, how could it be said to increase? And it is accomplished—or not—by the same sort of moral beings.

It becomes quite another matter when the meaning of good itself has altered; it is especially significant if the good alters in a way that makes the human capacity to achieve it in our own selves a function of the individual's relative sophistication. It is plausible that the sophistication of individual human beings is, as a whole, on the increase. At least it has long been widely believed that the next generation will "know more" than we. There may be serious problems in defining what counts as knowledge, and certainly in our own time there have been fearful intellectual setbacks;[52] nevertheless, for present purposes, let us assume an increase. What does this cognitive inflation portend, if the gnostic conception of the capacity for self-perfection is accepted as the locus of human progress?

By definition, it entails the moral ascendancy of the latest generation over its predecessor.[53] Constant progress in the gnostic sense implies a permanent system of castes. This is very different, however, from caste perceived (say, in Hindu terms) as a lifetime role; for moral progress implies that in an

average life span, each age cohort will pass through the entire set of roles—
but in descending order. From the onset of reason we proceed to regress in
dignity, for the person with the greatest potential is the one who has arrived
latest. He enjoys the greatest access to the expanding knowledge that is
constantly perfecting the race. His parents are encouraged to look up to him
as the locus of tomorrow's higher perfection, just as they are to look down
upon their own parents as the representatives of a puerile past. Of course,
each must anticipate his own descent to this state of relative moral obsolescence. We beget our betters and then pass on to become the well-meaning
barbarians that history and progress make of us all.

The ravages of gnostic obsolescence cancel the dignity of human beliefs
and practices. The moral progressive denies equal time to ideas that derive
from tradition or that naively claim a permanent validity.[54] For him their
survival is a kind of static primitivism, and those who profess them are
moral Luddites.[55] It is the destiny of the New Man to extirpate these notions
and, occasionally, those who hold them. The moral nonchalance with which
the nineteenth century nearly annihilated the American Indian is testimony
to the righteousness of the bright.[56] Hans Jonas has it about right:

> The resolute secular eschatology entails a conception of human events that radi-
> cally demotes to provisional status all that goes before, stripping it of its inde-
> pendent validity and at best making it the vehicle for reaching the promised
> state of things that is yet to come—a means to the future end which alone is
> worthy in itself.[57]

Gnostic Visions

Not all elements of this notion of moral progress are secular in origin;[58] the
gnostic filament itself is traceable to ancient religious roots and was real
enough to early Christianity to be declared a heresy.[59] From the beginning,
Christianity, as Judaism before it, floated up fevered visions of an end time.[60]
Inspired by ambiguous revelation and natural hope, Christians are to this
day tempted to say more than the evidence justifies about where the world
is going. Prophetic visions come like the seasons, and our century has in
the fullness of time produced its own Christian eschatology—a glimpse of
the final state of nature that is peculiarly modern. Christopher Lasch labeled
progress in this form "the last superstition."[61]

One would expect such a vision to be either pious or starkly scientific. It
is both. The best example is in the work of Pierre Teilhard de Chardin, a
French poet who also happened to be a major paleontologist and a Jesuit.
Its principal expression is his *Phenomenon of Man*, published posthumously
in accord with ecclesiastical restrictions and bearing an admiring introduction by Julian Huxley. Its influence has been enormous and, we think, gener-

ally baneful. It has gone far toward rehabilitating the battered progressive vision of an earthly Utopia in, of all places, the Christian churches.

Chardin himself is a prophet of human perfectibility. Drawing from a professional lifetime of fossil research, he unrolls a dramatic cinema of emergent life, intellect, and love—each unfolding in its appointed epoch at the beck of God. Up to a point it is scientific; beyond that point it becomes epic theology. For Chardin it was important to maintain not only the integrity of both science and traditional religion but also their mutual comfort. Material reality is drawn into transcendence by the power and love of an independent principle, "Omega," ultimately identified as God in the personal and Christian sense. God is immanent in—but also separate from—his creation, which he loves and saves. He draws it first into life, next into consciousness and intelligence, and, at the end, into love and unity.

Here, we are interested in those aspects of this notion of progress that might bear upon moral hierarchy. Chardin obliges us. In the evidence of continuing evolution he perceives the growth of a collective mind rich in love but (to us) problematic for human liberty. For all practical purposes he enters the determinist tradition when he asserts that "not necessarily, doubtless, but infallibly . . . [man] must reach the goal" of collective unity with God.[62] This curious and twisted expression suggests Chardin's recognition that perfected knowledge is a threat to liberty. Indeed, he effectively concedes that since mankind really must reach this goal, the reality is a de facto determinism.

As an escape from this, Chardin hypothesizes a final individual choice to be offered every human—a choice for or against union with "Omega." These decisions will effect a collective separation of the race which, in a biological metaphor, he calls "Ramification once again, for the last time."[63] It seems, after all, that only some may be saved. How this solution harmonizes with the "infallibility" of man's collective unity with God is unclear. Or perhaps it is all too clear: They are in flat opposition. And if one accepts the "ramification" hypothesis, there is nothing to suggest whether, in the final accounting, the history of man is to be progressive or degenerate. For this will depend entirely upon individual free choices. Lastly, if all these final choices are equally informed, how can they be both infallible and at the same time in conflict with one another? Chardin is ensnared in the deterministic confusion that threatens every "optimistic" morality.

The elitist theme in this is central. Transcendental progressives like Chardin see the human race at all times as harboring a number of individuals who have acquired, not merely through successful reproduction but through insight, the power to propel the race as a whole toward its higher moral destiny. Chardin specifically labels them "elite."[64] And Julian Huxley (no Jesuit he) puts the same idea this way: "I was searching to establish an ideological basis for man's further cultural evolution, and to define the position of the individual human personality in the process."[65] Huxley then gives this special evolutionary role to what he vaguely calls the "developed human being." In commenting on Chardin, he says:

> A developed human being . . . is not merely a more highly individualized individual. He has crossed the threshold of self-consciousness to a new mode of thought. . . . He is a person, an organism which has transcended individuality in personality. This attainment of personality was an essential element in man's past and present evolutionary success; accordingly its fuller achievement must be an essential aim for his evolutionary future.[66]

Finally, Huxley adds that in the "developed human being" we see "that the process of evolution on earth is itself now in the process of becoming cephalized."[67]

To the feverish confusions of Chardin and Huxley must be added Karl Rahner's surprising agreement expressed in passages such as the following: "In and through the corporeality of man . . . the cosmos really presses forward to this self-presence in spirit. [Those] beginnings of the self-presence of the cosmos in the spirit of individual persons has [sic] a history which is still going on."[68]

Moral progressives like these detect something extraordinary in the capacities of those gifted individuals who accomplish these "saltations"—or leaps forward—in human moral history. Only in the fullness of evolutionary time do these positive quirks of the individual prodigy become a common feature of the race. Plainly, therefore, in terms of the opportunity for individual moral fulfillment, it is for most humans advantageous to live in a time of higher consciousness—which means simply to live later in history.

Now, all these propositions for and against variation in the capacity of humans for moral self-perfection are quite unprovable, and in theory these prophets could be right.[69] We only wish to clarify that belief in this sort of "progress" eliminates equality, except perhaps at the eschaton. While waiting, convention recommends the rather different cosmos that would be entailed in human equality.

A Simple Man's View of Progress

This is no reveille for reactionaries but merely a more temperate view of progress—one for which lowercase is quite suitable. We accept the term in the prosaic sense first described above. It is simply the growth of the race in material power and sophistication. As we learn more we can do more; we climb on the shoulders of our predecessors to scan new material worlds. But this is the merest fact. It has no moral significance beyond providing the opportunity to commit the same deadly sins by more up-to-date means.[70] There is no law that people on the whole must perfect themselves. They might, but we do not see either that they must or even that in fact they do.

The world's quantum of moral self-fulfillment probably has its ups and downs (per the net-good version of progress), but, if so, this occurs according to the free commitments of human individuals.[71]

Progress is then useful only as a set of practical notions about increase of material goods and knowledge and about unpredictable oscillations in the achievement of justice. It is certainly a good thing whenever changes in technology provide a richer life experience to individual men and women over the advancing centuries, and whenever human actors successfully struggle for the common good of their own time. But, in whatever century, each actor will be identical to us in both moral dignity and corruptibility.[72] Some will choose to seek the good, others to avoid it. There will be pain, tragedy, and heroism entailed in their choices. Sometimes there will be net moral progress, but it will be unstable; when it occurs, some persons will still choose evil, and for them there will be degradation. As for the individual's capacity to go one way or the other, it will not matter whether one is born late, early, or—like us—yesterday.

Is this a dull world? Chardin thinks we would be bored literally to death:

> [Unless mankind] believes in . . . a perfecting of the world . . . all spiritual movement on earth would be brought to a stop . . . [M]ankind would soon stop inventing and constructing for a work it knew to be doomed in advance . . . [I]t would disintegrate from nausea or revolt and crumble into dust. Having once known the taste of a universal and durable progress, we can never banish it from our minds. . . . If progress is a myth, that is to say, if faced by the work involved we can say: 'What is the good of it all?' our efforts will flag. With that the whole of evolution will come to a halt—because we are evolution.[73]

It is curious what people find boring. Chardin offers us two contrasting experiences. In the first we participate as subjects of a collective, inevitable, and undefined perfection of the race through evolution. In the other we live, love, and sacrifice (or refuse to) not only for those who are at present our imperfect but very real neighbors but also for unborn generations for whose contingent and unpredictable future we hold the world in trust. Which is the more exciting story—that of the determined perfection of yet unborn masses—or that now being written in our own flesh-and-blood choices?[74] Perhaps both could be engaging, but ours has the signal advantage of being true. What is more, it is true to life. There is one dependable rule about good science fiction: Whenever and wherever the story takes place, it has to include vulnerable beings like us. It must be true not only to our strengths but to our weaknesses; a story about inevitably perfected beings is no story at all.

In our view there could be only one form of utopia worthy of the race, answering its need for challenge and excitement. This would be a world in which the decisions of individual men and women counted here and now, in which love was possible, in which desperate risks were normal, and in which there was a final point to it all that is settled separately for and by each of us individually in a lifetime. That would be exciting. As we understood it, that was the claim of Christianity. It held that such a world began, exists, and will continue at the will of its maker who evidently takes interest in the unique dramas that are freely lived by his creatures.[75] For them, as for Chaucer, the image of human life is "a pilgrimage not so much to Jerusalem as to judgment."[76]

If this be so, human nature is not moving to some new and better end state; that end state is here. The essence of utopia is not comfort, brilliance, or even a moral perfection bestowed by evolution but rather the chance here and now for each of us to choose for or against the life of conscience. This freedom is a good—the one truly attainable good; in a world dragged to its own perfection this good would be exterminated. Paradoxically, it is the perfect world of the evolutionists that would be the least humane. In *Candide* Voltaire portrayed Pangloss as a fool,[77] but the disgusting optimist was fundamentally right; ours may indeed be the best of all possible worlds, the one utopia a free spirit could unconditionally desire.

Once we give assent to such a world, things fall into place. I contemplate the needs of my luckless brother with no ambivalence about his place in the scheme of things. Not even for a dark instant can I imagine this warped, unappetizing, and unappreciative creature as the discard of a cosmic process of which I am the next and higher form. He is flawed; I am flawed. The mythology of "progress" melts away in the democracy of original sin.

The issue becomes the here and now. And whatever our relative circumstances, the duties of justice and love run in both directions. Here is no trace of noblesse oblige, for now we see that aristocracy is universal. Even the wretched of the earth carry the debt of reciprocal justice and love. Because all are free, all are responsible. Meanwhile, the form of the economic or political system which together we design to support human freedom remains a permanent but subordinate question. Human equality implies neither a static nor a dynamic economic and social order. No doubt our moral nature sets limits and demands for Caesar, who must constantly be pressed to sustain the practical conditions of justice; but he is a necessary and not merely dangerous evil. The details of those limits and demands are a matter for debate, but not here.

Uniformity and World Unity

Nor does human equality provide any particular reason either to struggle for (or to fear) a world society. Some do associate descriptive equality with vague ideas of this sort. They raise a question quite distinct from the one already posed by the moral evolutionist; the one-worlder asks not whether the moral stuff of which we are made is improving but whether the race is actually advancing to some form of solidarity by exercising the capacity it already has. This is a special form of the question of whether the net good of the world is being altered by the free choices of humans.

This question should not be reduced to a political issue about world government—a mere lawyer's problem about "human rights" that can be enforced by some global supreme court. Many do imagine such a juridical convergence, but that idea has no evident connection with human equality; each could exist with or without the other. World government could rule equal persons by disparate rules or unequal persons by uniform rules. These rules could be just or unjust; beyond providing the spirit of fraternity, the belief in a descriptive human equality would not imply particular rules that constitute the minimum or the ideal for the just society.

If there is a coherent question here at all, then, it must be one of an even larger order. It is perhaps Augustine's question about the City of God. In a certain sense Augustine was the first one-worlder. He took a highly inclusive view of what constitutes a human being:

> What is true for a Christian beyond the shadow of a doubt is that every real man, that is, every mortal animal that is rational, however unusual to us may be the shape of his body, or the color of his skin, or the way he walks, or the sound of his voice, and whatever the strength, portion or quality of his natural endowments, is descended from the single first-created man.[78]

In *The City of God* and his other works Augustine always stressed the unity of creation under God, rejecting the dualism of his enemies, the Manichaeans. But in this world that was united in its subordination to God, Augustine saw humanity itself as sundered; his tragic commitment to predestination split mankind into two cities from all eternity. He made us a race divided; at the start, and always, each inhabits either the City of God or the City of Man. This calamitous separation—so fateful in human history—is bridged and ended by equality. Humanity is not riven from all eternity but rather, as Jefferson supposed, we are one. It is in our shared and uniform capacity for moral self-perfection through free commitment to the real good that we constitute one world.

This unity of moral capacity is not, however, what the enthusiasts of twentieth-century globalism have had in mind. When they say "one world," they are not satisfied with the news that we have a common nature grounded upon the freedom to choose good or evil. Though they may vaguely believe in some such "intrinsic" or descriptive equality, what they have clearly wanted is for all people to act justly toward one another all the time and everywhere.[79] But that is not what human equality is about. It is not a state of society—either local or global, good or bad. It is a state of individual persons; its subject is not some world order to come but rather the constant possibility of individual fulfillment in any historic age.[80] For the common state into which we are born and remain—the only possible ground of our unity—is our freedom. Each of us retains the potential to contribute to the building of either city. These cities are different, however, from those of Augustine, for the division between them requires man's choice as well as God's. They might well be relabeled the City of Trust and the City of Self. The citizen of the one commits to the search for duty and trusts what he is able to find; the citizen of the other recognizes no authority but himself.

Those committed to Trust carry out their stewardship in the only way possible—by the exercise of whatever gifts nature and luck have provided. This is entirely sufficient for their own perfection, for theirs is a city that values every honest contribution—intellectual, intuitive, emotional. It is a gaudy affair, this city, celebrating even heroic mistakes conceived by bunglers in the worst of taste. The works of these irregulars cohabit peacefully with the beauty achieved by those who get things just right; as gargoyles that animate the Gothic, these prodigies somehow contribute to the effect of a living moral whole. By comparison, the other city is more orderly; all that it lacks is life.

If there is a unity in this tale, it is not that of a world tending inevitably to harmony. Indeed, neither city is stable, for we are always at liberty to switch allegiance. All of us remain both free and fallible, pursuing every imaginable course—good and bad—in the practical order. It turns out that the fact of human equality is consistent with any sort of world; indeed, it has produced the fantastic one we know. Contemplating that world, each of us is called to its constant, practical amendment. In that task few may succeed; there are no guarantees. But those who try shall have grasped the point of their own lives.

NOTES

NOTE TO EPIGRAPH

1. Bernard Williams, "The Idea of Equality" (1962), in Joel Feinberg, ed., *Moral Concepts* (London: Oxford University Press, 1970), 157–58.

INTRODUCTION
IN SEARCH OF A DESCRIPTIVE HUMAN EQUALITY

1. "Men are born and remain free and equal in rights." *Declaration of the Rights of Man and of the Citizen* (1789), art. 1.

2. Carl Becker, *The Declaration of Independence* (New York: Vintage, 1958), 142.

3. Pauline Maier remarks on both the influence of George Mason's draft of the Virginia Declaration of Rights and Jefferson's independence on this specific point (*American Scripture: Making the Declaration of Independence* [New York: Knopf, 1997], 133–34, 165–67).

4. Becker, *The Declaration*, 161. We assume that the drafters had intended a semi-colon after the word "equal." It was eventually reduced to a comma, probably to be consistent with the commas that were substituted for semicolons after "self-evident" and "rights."

5. There is no way to be absolutely certain that any particular set of words appeared intact at any given moment.

6. That is, assuming the semicolon to be the intended punctuation.

7. Nor did James Madison suggest otherwise in the First Congress in 1789, where he referred to the Declaration's proposition of equality as "an absolute truth." See Madison's speech (June 8, 1789), reprinted in Bernard Schwartz, *The Bill of Rights: A Documentary History* (New York: Chelsea House and McGraw-Hill, 1971), vol. 2, 1029. See Hadley Arkes, *First Things: An Inquiry into the First Principles of Morals and Justice* (Princeton, N.J.: Princeton University Press, 1986), 29–30. Building on Madison's claim, Arkes comments: "That kind of language would stir unease in the circles of the educated today, and yet Madison understood the Declaration to be stating a truth that had the properties of an apodictic truth" (id. at 29–30). Our own position differs from Madison's as interpreted by Arkes, inasmuch as we think human equality believable but not apodictically demonstrable. Our understanding of human equality harmonizes with Madison's rather deeply, however. Though his principal focus is the proffering of a juridical equality, the real equality among humans he perceives is rooted in their duty to act according to the dictate of conscience. See James Madison, "Memorial and Remonstrance against Religious Assessments," Gaillard Hunt, ed., *The Writings of James Madison* (New York: G. P. Putnam's Sons, 1901), vol. 2, 183–91; John T. Noonan, Jr., *The Lustre of Our Country: The American Experience of Religious Freedom* (Berkeley: University of California Press, 1998), 69–70, 79, 82.

8. In the debates with Douglas, Lincoln either missed or chose to obfuscate this point: "I think the authors of that notable instrument . . . defined with tolerable

distinctness in what respects they did consider all men created equal—equal with 'certain inalienable rights, among which are life, liberty, and the pursuit of happiness.' This they said, and this they meant" (Sanford Lakoff, *Equality in Political Philosophy* [Cambridge: Harvard University Press, 1964], 2). Lakoff declares this "an admirable display of clear thinking" (ibid).

9. Becker, *The Declaration of Independence*, xii.

10. J. R. Pole is perhaps typical in mistaking both the prima facie meaning and intent of Jefferson's words as they emerged in their edited final version. "Only in respect of certain rights could they [men] be thought of as equals" (*The Pursuit of Equality in American History* [Berkeley: University of California Press, 1978], 53). Pole is certain that the fact of equality is trivial nonsense, and (ignoring the actual words) he adds that Jefferson saw it so: "Jefferson's phrases . . . referred only to an equality of rights; if all men had been equal in other respects there would have been no cause to declare the fact, and little likelihood that anyone would do so" (id. at 55). Even the most recent and sophisticated treatments register no interest in the committee's oscillations between pure description and the egalitarian claim. See Maier, *American Scripture*.

11. Garry Wills, *Lincoln at Gettysburg* (New York: Simon and Schuster, 1992). Wills's very interesting speculation on Jefferson's own understanding of "created equal" is presented in his earlier work *Inventing America* (New York: Vintage, 1979). His historical thesis suggests important similarities between Jefferson's version of descriptive equality and that presented here. It is discussed infra at 94–98.

12. "It must be agreeable to have a casual superiority over those who are by nature equal with us" (James Boswell, *The Life of Samuel Johnson*, vol. 3 [New York: Heritage, 1963], 257). The same expression plays a more elaborated role for Hobbes (*Leviathan* [London: Collier-Macmillan, 1962], 98).

13. For Aristotle there is a form of being (X) that, when we know it, we necessarily know of some other beings (not X) that are related by it. This is part of the definition of relation. To know ownership (an instance of relation) is to know of property and an owner. To know equality is to know of at least two persons (or things) that are thus related.

Aristotle concluded his principal analysis of relation with the understatement that he had not settled the details of how relative being should be understood (*Categories* 7, 8b21–24). He had, however, made respectable the view that relation can be a part of the real world, not just a mental creation. One side of the tradition descending from him has developed and clarified his analysis, and it is this branch of the tradition that makes philosophically plausible the premise of conventional human equality that this relation among humans is real, not merely mental. The primary text with the deepest insight and clarity is John of St. Thomas, *Cursus Philosophicus Thomisticus* (1631–35) (Turin: Marietti, 1930), log. 2, p.q. 17, vol. 1, 573–608. For a good modern analysis of the tradition (but one that misunderstands John of St. Thomas's contribution), see A. Krempel, *La Doctrine De La Relation Chez Saint Thomas* (Paris: Vrin, 1952). For an acute, contemporary treatment, see John Deely's editorial contributions throughout *Tractatus de Signis: The Semiotic of John Poinsot*, ed. John Deely (Berkeley: University of California Press, 1985).

The other half of the tradition (of which our "Peter" was a partial representative in the colloquy with "Mary") claims in various ways that relation is always just mind-created and mind-dependent, never real being. This view is epitomized in the thought of William of Ockham, according to whom—in the words of a sympathetic modern commentator—"there is no such *thing* as relation" (Gordon Leff, *William of Ockham: The Metamorphosis of Scholastic Discourse* [Manchester: Manchester University Press, 1975], 215). See William of Ockham, *Expositio in Librum Praedicamentorum Aristotelis*, in G. Gal, *Guillelmi de Ockham Opera Philosophica et Theologica: Opera Philosophica*, vol. 2 (St. Bonaventure, N.Y.: Franciscan Institute, 1978), sections 12–13, 238–68. Good modern analyses of the relevant aspects of Ockham and his place in the tradition are Philotheus Böhner, "The Realistic Conceptualism of Wilhelm Ockham," in 4 *Traditio* 307–36, esp. 311 *et seq.* (1946); Gottfried Martin, *Wilhelm von Ockham: Untersuchungen Zur Ontologie Dur Ordnungen* (Berlin: De Gruyter, 1949), 99–182; Marilyn McCord Adams, *William Ockham* (Notre Dame: University of Notre Dame Press, 1987), vol. 1, 215–76. As Wallace Stevens would have it, even of persons:

> You were created of your name, the word
> Is that of which you were the personage.
> There is no life except in the word of it.
> ("Certain Phenomena of Sound," *The Collected Works*
> [New York: Vintage, 1990], 287)

Bernard Lonergan would forge a middle way here (between realists and nominalists) by affirming Ockham's judgment that relation is no "thing" and then proceeding to argue that "the real" is not limited to "things" but is coextensive with what can be affirmed in correct judgments. See Bernard J. F. Lonergan, *Insight: A Study of Human Understanding* (San Francisco: Harper Row, 1958), 490–97.

14. Peter Westen's searching study *Speaking of Equality: An Analysis of the Rhetorical Force of "Equality" in Moral and Legal Discourse* (Princeton, N.J.: Princeton University Press, 1990) is no exception. More than most, Westen has grasped that equality is a connective. But like the rest, he has chosen not to explicate the kind of being—real or mental—that constitutes relational being. He appears to assume that relations, including equality, always are merely mental artifacts with no real (i.e., extramental) reality; the mental act of an individual who measures by a common standard *constitutes* relations such as equality, similarity, and the rest. See, for example, id. at 41.

15. To be sure, the meaning of possession itself could stand a bit of analysis, but its ambiguity is harmless for present purposes.

16. In fact, however, the law is generally interested only in whether the description of the individual fits the applicable rule and not in his "equality" with others. See Westen, *Speaking of Equality*, supra.

It is not possible to demonstrate the background influence, if any, of beliefs about descriptive equality upon the shaping of legal rules; rules that could raise the issue—even those of constitutional status—can be, and generally are, justified exclusively in a pragmatic spirit by reference to empirical features of the case. A vivid example is the rule in *Payne v. Tennessee*, 501 U.S. 808 (1991), which allows death-penalty juries to hear surviving relatives' testimony about the victim's qualities. Justice John Paul Stevens (in dissent) finds this practice offensive to what is clearly a notion of descriptive equality:

Aspects of the character of the victim unforeseeable to the defendant at the time of his crime are irrelevant to the defendant's "personal responsibility and moral guilt" and therefore cannot justify a death sentence. . . . Evidence offered to prove such differences can only be intended to identify some victims as more worthy of protection than others.

(Id. at 860–61, 866)

Chief Justice Rehnquist, writing for the majority, did not deny Justice Stevens's premise of equal worth but concluded that the law was, nevertheless, permitted to value external differences among victims such as their place in the community (id. at 823–24).

An interesting exception to the lawyers' avoidance of human equality is the Model Penal Code's assertion that "in all ordinary circumstances lives in being must be assumed to be of equal value" (*Model Penal Code and Commentaries* [1985] 3.02, comm., p. 16). What the Code treats as an assumption we would describe as a conventional belief. It is, in any event, not given expression in *Payne*.

17. Mortimer Adler grasps the essence of this distinction in *Six Great Ideas* (New York: Macmillan, 1981), 33, 162, where he refers to equalities "in kind" and inequalities in degree. He seems, however, to forget the point when it becomes most germane. See infra at chap. 10 n. 13.

INTRODUCTION TO PART I

1. Edgar Bodenheimer, "A Neglected Theory of Legal Reasoning," 21 *Journal of Legal Education* 373, 378 (1969).

CHAPTER 1
WHAT HAS BEEN SAID?

1. Harry Frankfurt, "Equality as a Moral Ideal," *Ethics* 98 (1987): 21, 24.

2. Westen, *Speaking of Equality*, 285, 285 n. 1.

3. Albert Menne, "Identity, Equality, Similarity: A Logico-Philosophical Analysis," 4 *Ratio* 50, 57 (1961).

4. John Rawls, *A Theory of Justice* (Cambridge: Harvard University Press, 1971), 508.

5. A wise assessment of some of the reasons for this liberal hesitation is D. A. Lloyd Thomas, "Equality Within the Limits of Reason Alone," *Mind* 88 (1979): 538.

6. See Menne, "Identity, Equality, Similarity," supra.

7. Westen, *Speaking of Equality*, 39. (Mortimer Adler's version is similar; see Adler, *Six Great Ideas*, supra, 33). As noted supra, 263 n. 14, Westen may reject a descriptive equality that is "real" and not just mental.

8. Id. at 32–38.

9. Id. at 266 (quoting, in part, Williams, "The Idea of Equality," supra).

10. Id. at 266–67 (emphasis in original) (citation omitted); see also id. at 65–72.

11. The X chromosome example also shakes our confidence that Westen credits the importance of a double equality. All persons do possess chromosomes (single equality) but not all possess them in the same degree (double equality), this basic

factual difference being associated with sex. We doubt that Westen was suggesting that the egalitarian could found a prescriptive equality upon the basis of a descriptive double equality that attaches only to men *or* women.

12. A still larger category of "equality" literature would be the *irrelevant*—pure and simple. In such works equality is treated as a property of *groups*. This allows the observer to disregard the spectacular differences among individuals within each group. In this respect the Confused Jeffersonian is again typical. His first instinct is to emphasize plausibly measurable traits such as intelligence that vary widely among individuals; this drives him to make claims about averages for politically significant groups. And if these prove dissimilar, he next asserts (what could be true) that the cause lies in external influences such as racial discrimination. Alternatively, he may argue that other traits for which these socially isolated groups have superior average records should be upgraded in public perception; we should, for example, put more stress on artistic faculties or "caring." In some mystic calculus he supposes that a group's superiority in one trait will offset its shortfall in another, working a kind of overall equivalence of dignity. Both moves typify a certain kind of social science. The most familiar example is the endless debate over group performance on intelligence and achievement tests—a tussle wherein angry protagonists wrongly suppose human equality to be at stake. In the 1990s the heat has focused upon Richard Herrnstein and Charles Murray, *The Bell Curve: Intelligence and Class Structure in American Life* (New York: Free Press, 1994).

13. Williams, "The Idea of Equality," in Bernard Williams, *Problems of the Self* (Cambridge: Cambridge University Press, 1973), 230.

14. Id. at 231–32, 234.

15. Id. at 234.

16. Id. at 235. Williams was focusing on politics, not personal perfection. Even when doing character, however, Williams is at pains to establish, contra Kant, that "no human characteristic which is relevant to degrees of moral esteem can escape being an empirical characteristic, subject to empirical conditions, psychological history and individual variation, whether it be sensitivity, persistence, imaginativeness, intelligence, good sense; or sympathetic feeling; or strength of will" ("Morality and the Emotions," in *Problems of the Self*, 207, 228). We return to Williams at length in our treatment of Kant at the end of chapter 4, infra, at 120–21.

17. Ibid., 228.

18. More recently Williams has continued his campaign against Kant and equality with the oxymoron "moral luck," coined to popularize the idea that our access to even the highest form of value is indeed a function of fortune (Bernard Williams, "Moral Luck," in Daniel Statman, ed., *Moral Luck* [New York: SUNY Press, 1992], 35). He sees clearly that his old hope for equality would require him to grasp the nettle of metaphysics or religion, and to either prospect he prefers to continue rambling in the empirical world of moral "absurdity" (id. at 36; see infra chap. 4 at 120–21). Williams's original essay has nevertheless shown its canonical status in paradoxical ways that revive the issue of a descriptive equality. For example, in *The Moral Commonwealth* (Berkeley: University of California Press, 1992), Philip Selznick enlists Williams in aid of the descriptive equality that Williams himself rejects. Equality appears to emerge out of Selznick's rich harvest of social wisdom as a kind of intuition and is worthy of our independent comment. Sometimes conflating fact

and ideal, his principal focus is normative. Nevertheless, the brief bursts of description are promising. We hear of "equal moral competence" (482) and the claim that "persons are equal as moral actors" (483); indeed, we learn that they have "moral equality" (484, passim). Contrary to Williams (and ourselves), Selznick claims this as an "empirical" conclusion (484); elsewhere, however, it is said to come as the "leap of faith" (482) that Williams rejected. The result is largely unhelpful to our purpose because it is never clear that Selznick is describing anything more than a *single* equality (one based upon possession alone). Mere *possession* of the necessary trait would be insufficient, and Selznick concedes that people are only "roughly equal in moral competence" and that they have "much the same capacity" (484). What would count for him as a threatening difference in moral competence is left both unidentified and unquantified. Later we shall see that this resembles the treatment given to descriptive equality by John Rawls who makes the basic human trait into a "range property" (see infra at 32–33). Like Rawls, Selznick says that "although moral equality is a normative idea, it has a factual basis" (484). However, neither scholar ever suggests how this *varying* competence for morality could *deserve* the label equality.

19. Thomas Nagel, *Equality and Partiality* (Oxford: Oxford University Press, 1991), 5.

20. Id. at 3.

21. The occasion being a colloquium at Boalt Hall, School of Law, University of California, Berkeley, on April 10, 1992.

22. Nagel's thinking took a rather different turn in his essay "Moral Luck" (in Statman, *Moral Luck*, supra), where he essentially agrees with the conclusion in Williams's essay of the same name.

Nagel's initial insight that human equality somehow implicates the capacity for moral achievement seems to be shared by the Harvard economist Amartya Sen. Yet because he assumes that moral self-perfection requires the achievement of valuable "functionings" in the external order, what Sen actually concludes about descriptive equality is that people are "thoroughly diverse" (see Amartya Sen, *Inequality Reexamined* [Cambridge: Harvard University Press, 1992], 1). Not satisfied to leave the matter there, Sen proposes by policy to equalize people's freedom to achieve these "functionings." But conceding that such achievement inevitably will be unequal, Sen is left with no real descriptive equality, either natural or artificial, only the common political assertion that everyone equally deserves equal consideration—whatever that means.

23. It could be, however, that we attribute a theory of descriptive equality where there is none. On an earlier occasion, when his topic, "The Meaning of Equality," invited him to identify a descriptive meaning for equality, Nagel observed that "there are three kinds of equality that might be thought to be important" and thereupon rendered a tripartite division of *normative* equality ("The Meaning of Equality," *Washington University Law Quarterly* 25, 26 [1979]). However, that the occasion for this taxonomy was a symposium entitled "The Quest for Equality," probably meant as normative, prevents the inference that any descriptive equality would be unimportant to Nagel.

24. John Wilson, *Equality* (New York: Harcourt, Brace and World, 1966), 104.

25. H. Bedau, "Egalitarianism and the Idea of Equality," in J. R. Pennock and J. Chapman, eds., *NOMOS IX, EQUALITY* (New York: Atherton, 1967), 3, 17.

26. Wilson, *Equality*, 97.

27. Id. at 98.

28. Wilson's view may be prefigured in Gregory Vlastos, "Human Worth, Merit, and Equality," in Feinberg, *Moral Concepts*, 141. Vlastos asserts that "our legal system accords to all citizens an identical status" (id. at 146). For him this implies that humans have equal "worth." The descriptive property that generates this worth seems to be the capacity to experience value and to choose among alternatives. It is not clear, however, that value consists—as it does for Wilson—in whatever one chooses, for "we hope that all of them will make the best possible use of their freedom of choice" (id. at 150). This implication of an external standard of value is left unexplained but leaves some hope of accommodating Vlastos to our own view.

29. As Charles Taylor would have it: "Not just any new definition can be forced on us, nor can we force it on ourselves; and some which we do gladly take up can be judged inauthentic, in bad faith, or just wrongheaded" ("Interpretation and the Sciences of Man," *The Review of Metaphysics* 25 [1971]: 15–16).

30. Wilson, *Equality*, 129 (emphasis in original). Sanford Lakoff's interesting book slips into similar conflations, often just as he begins to distinguish fact from egalitarian hopes, for example, in his discussion of Locke. See Lakoff, *Equality in Political Philosophy*, 93–101; see also Lakoff, "Christianity and Equality," in Pennock and Chapman, *NOMOS IX*. This said, Lakoff provides an excellent historical panorama of relevant thought, which was his evident purpose.

31. See infra at 101–16.

32. Rawls, *A Theory of Justice*, 508.

33. Id. at 19.

34. Id. at 504–12.

35. Id. at 505.

36. Id. at 508.

37. The impression is confirmed when Rawls later adds that "the only contingency which is decisive is that of having or not having the capacity for a sense of justice" (id. at 511).

38. Harvard law professor Lloyd Weinreb, like Rawls, would identify a descriptive equality to act as a springboard to the good society. Not sharing Rawls's allergy to nonempirical reality, Weinreb credits the possibility that we share an "equal humanity." In the end, though, Weinreb's metaphysics proves too thin to yield more than a range property:

> Our common humanity is an abstraction that becomes concrete in characteristics that are not universal but endlessly various. The individual differences may be unimportant compared with the features that all have in common. If so, that is a conclusion that has to be reached, not a fact one can observe. Ignoring all our individual differences, the argument about common humanity is necessarily as abstract as its premises. (Lloyd Weinreb, *Natural Law and Justice* [Cambridge: Harvard University Press, 1987], 167)

Nor does Weinreb manage to locate a real and uniform common humanity in his later, related book, *Oedipus at Fenway Park: What Rights Are and Why There Are Any* (Cambridge: Harvard University Press, 1994).

39. "We hesitate to say what we mean [by equality], because we know that we do not mean what we say" (H. Schneider, *Three Dimensions of Public Morality* [Bloomington: Indiana University Press, 1956], 94).

40. Implicitly Rawls rejects the strategy of egalitarians such as R. H. Tawney who took inequality as the fact and equality as the ideal. For Tawney, natural equality was a piece of mythology against which biologists and psychologists had accumulated irresistible evidence. See R. H. Tawney, *Equality*, 4th rev. ed. (Totowa: Barnes and Noble, 1952).

41. See Thomas, "Equality within the Limits of Reason Alone," 549. Nothing in Rawls's later work asserts anything more than a "range property" as the basis of a relation of equality. If there is a descriptive human equality at all, it is a *single* equality based upon the mere possession of some trait in varying degrees. In his 1993 book he asserts that having two specific powers in common is what "makes persons equal"; each of these specified powers is a range property but need only be enjoyed to a "requisite minimum degree" (John Rawls, *Political Liberalism* [New York: Columbia, 1993], 19). The two capacities he identifies are those "for a sense of justice and . . . for a conception of the good" (ibid.). Recall that politics, not self-perfection, is Rawls's consuming interest; hence it is not surprising that he would settle for a minimal capacity (a range property) as a qualification for egalitarian rights. We think it a pity, however, that he so casually has relativized the personal capacity to be good. Moral choice is the one human power that is the most promising candidate for host property of a *real* relation of human equality—one that could hold both in possession and degree.

42. Ronald Dworkin, "What Is Equality?" part 1, "Equality of Welfare," *Philosophy and Public Affairs* 10, no. 3 (summer 1981) 185; "What Is Equality?" part 2, "Equality of Resources," *Philosophy and Public Affairs,* 10, no. 4 (fall 1981), 281; "What Is Equality?" part 3, "The Place of Liberty," 73 *Iowa Law Review* 1 (1987). To be sure, in the last cited article Dworkin does devote two sentences to dismissing the descriptive or "flat sense" of equality as irrelevant (id. at 5–6).

43. See Ronald Dworkin, *Taking Rights Seriously* (Cambridge: Harvard University Press, 1978), 227; and Stephen Guest, *Ronald Dworkin* (Stanford: Stanford University Press, 1991), 225–53. Michael White acutely captures the dilemma facing liberals who would justify normative equality with a descriptive equality: "In order to get the egalitarian consequences that liberalism wishes to obtain from a notion of human beings as equals with respect to fundamental, transempirical dignity, worth, or respect, liberalism requires a very special notion of such equal dignity, worth, or respect" (*Partisan or Neutral: The Futility of Public Political Theory* [New York: Rowman and Littlefield, 1997], 66, 39–79).

44. See, in general, Pennock and Chapman, *NOMOS IX*, part 2 of which (115–216) consists of five essays on "Egalitarian Implications and Consequences of Belief Systems."

45. See, for example, Lakoff, "Christianity and Equality," 115–19; and Hans Küng, *On Being a Christian* (Garden City, N.Y.: Doubleday, 1976), 482–83.

46. See, for example, Paul Sigmund, "Hierarchy, Equality, and Consent in Medieval Christian Thought" in Pennock and Chapman, *NOMOS IX*, 134, 138–40.

47. Even the inexhaustible Ernst Troeltsch is satisfied with the ambiguous observation that, to the Calvinists, "all men were equal on the basis of the equal possession

of reason and the power of exercising it" (*The Social Teachings of the Christian Churches* [New York: Harper, 1960], vol. 2, 620).

48. Emanuel Rackman, "Judaism and Equality," in Pennock and Chapman, *NOMOS IX*, 154, 155 (emphasis in original).

49. Samuel Pufendorf, *De jure naturae et gentium [1688]* (Oxford: Clarendon, 1934), vol. 2, 330.

50. Id. at 335.

51. For example, by the moral philosopher Jean Porter. For our analysis of Porter's contribution, see infra chap. 8 at 198–201.

52. A. J. Carlyle, *A History of Medieval Political Theory, from the Roman Lawyers of the Second Century to the Political Writers of the Ninth*, vol. 1 (Edinburgh: Blackwood, 1962), 9. For our discussion of the French understanding of equality as a part of the triadic revolutionary cry, see infra at 52, 227–31.

53. Id. at 8.

54. Carlyle does add that we are "equal in the capacity for learning" (ibid.), but he can only mean equal in *possession*; that we have it in uniform degree would be absurd.

55. Id. at 88.

56. A Catholic commentator gives the sibling metaphor a twist similar to Carlyle's:

All persons have been created by the same God, which means that they are brothers and sisters and are all of them equal before him. All people, without any distinction as to sex, race, or social position, can say that Genesis 1:26–27 speaks of them. . . . In the perspective of Genesis, this is the deep root of human dignity and the respect that is due to all human beings. (E. Hamel, "The Foundation of Human Rights in Biblical Theology Following the Orientations of *Gaudium et spes*," in R. Latourelle, ed., *Vatican II: Assessment and Perspectives* [New York: Paulist Press, 1989], vol. 2, 460, 463)

57. Jacques Maritain, *Redeeming the Time*, chap. 1, "Human Equality" (London: Bles, 1944).

58. Id. at 3, 15.

59. Id. at 15.

60. Id. at 19.

61. Id. at 1–28, passim.

62. Id. at 25.

63. Id. at 16. Specifically he says:

It is ontological and concrete, just as much as the likenesses and affinities which in the external world serve as bases for that positive unity which the species has within our mind. For the universality of our ideas is grounded *in re*, in things, and it would be necessary to have angelic vision to measure the depth of the real relations and the real solidarity connoted by that maxim of the schools.

The equality in nature among men consists of their concrete communion in the mystery of the human species; it does not lie in an idea, it is hidden in the heart of the individual and of the concrete, in the roots of the substance of each man. Obscure because residing on the level of substance and its root energies, primordial because it is bound up with the very sources of being, human equality reveals itself, like the nearness of our neighbour, to every one who practices it; indeed it is identical with that proximity of all to each, and of each to all. (Id. at 15)

64. A. Reck, "The Metaphysics of Equality," *The New Scholasticism* 34 (1960): 327, cites the Maritain chapter and devotes five pages to the proposition that "egalitarianism . . . presupposes a metaphysics of human nature"—specifically a continuing independent self and "the same essential humanity" (id. at 335). But Reck also sees, at least broadly, the need for sameness *in degree*—a double equality (id. at 338). Regrettably the discussion is sufficient only to whet our appetite.

65. In other contexts there is evidence that, for Maritain, this is an equality only of possession; humans vary in their capacity for moral perfection. See infra chap. 5 at 128 and 296 n. 21. Still, obviously this would be *a* theory of equality representing a descriptive or *ontological* analogy to Aristotle's *normative* or "proportional" equality, by which society distributes goods according to what a person deserves. (Westen has several excellent discussions; see *Speaking of Equality*, 52–57, 150–53, 156–57.) The descriptive analogy would be this: Equality is the relation based upon the (proportional) *capacity* of every person to reach that level of virtue of which one is capable. Would this be a tautology, all persons by definition having that capacity? As such it would seem to be another mere equality of possession. Further, it would constitute what we will call a "gnostic" concept; people who know more—though equal in *having* the capacity—could be better people. That this is not "human equality" is a point that will consume a good portion of this book.

66. Gene Outka, "Equality and Individuality: Thoughts on Two Themes in Kierkegaard," *Journal of Religious Ethics* 10, no. 2 (1982): 171–203, 182 (internal citation omitted). This insightful essay has received stunningly little attention from professional philosophers and theologians.

67. Id. at 188.

68. Id. at 184–85.

69. Id. at 184.

70. Id. at 172.

71. Arnold Brecht, *Political Theory* (Princeton, N.J.: Princeton University Press, 1959), 309–11.

CHAPTER 2
THE HOST PROPERTY

1. See Rawls, *A Theory of Justice*, 508.

2. Id. at 19.

3. Had we forgotten, we would be reminded of the intensity of the claims on both sides by the appearance of *The Bell Curve* in 1994.

4. "*Ens minimum, scilicet relatio*," Thomas Aquinas, 1 *Sent.* d. 26, q. 2, art. 2, *ad* 2.

5. Arnold Brecht, in his perceptive clarification of the convention of human equality, distinguishes between the possible fact of equality and the value ("or disvalue") of that fact (*Political Theory*, 306).

6. The classic analysis of envy is Max Scheler, *Ressentiment*, trans. W. Holdheim (Glencoe: Free Press, 1960). Thoughtful contemporary critiques are H. Schoeck, *Envy* (New York: Harcourt, Brace, 1970); Robert Nozick, *Anarchy, State, and Utopia* (New York: Basic Books, 1974), 239–49; and Jane Mansbridge, "Envy, Equal Respect, and the Pursuit of Equality" (1986; unpub. ms. in authors' possession). John Rawls defends his own egalitarian precepts against the charge of envy in *A Theory of Justice*, 537 *et seq.*

7. See Bruce Ackerman, *Social Justice in the Liberal State* (New Haven: Yale University Press, 1980). Actually Ackerman renders this chant incoherent by setting it in the form "I'm at least as good as you are" (id. at 15 *et seq.*). This piece of egomania appears to be a corruption of the innocent classical assertion (as by Pufendorf) that "I am . . . as much a man as you are" (*De jure naturae et gentium*, vol. 2, 330).

8. See Plato's *Gorgias*.

9. For example, Friedrich Nietzsche, "The Tarantula," in *Thus Spake Zarathustra* (Baltimore: Penguin, 1969), 123–26.

10. Nietzsche's tarantulas declare, "We shall raise outcry against everything that has power," thus enthroning an equality of *incapacity* (id. at 123).

11. Jefferson wrote that "it was intended to be an expression of the American Mind" (*The Writings of Thomas Jefferson*, 1869 ed., vol. 7, 304). Carl Becker adds that "the underlying preconceptions from which it is derived, were commonly taken for granted" (*The Declaration of Independence*, 26).

12. Richard D. Mohr recounts the reaction of a white southern granddame to her grandson's enrolling in Howard University: "If God made them equal, I hate God!" (*Gay Ideas: Outings and Other Controversies* [Boston: Beacon, 1992], 1).

13. Which is why, "when everybody is somebody, then no one's anybody" (W. Gilbert, *The Gondoliers*).

14. Reprinted in *The Responsive Community* 2 (Winter 1991/92): 4–20.

15. This problem is considered in more detail infra at 233–40.

16. For the place of free will in the cultural/legal conventions of the West, see Selznick, *The Moral Commonwealth*, 440.

17. On the other hand, the eighteenth-century convention could have contained an implicit recognition of some shared *variable* property that is *invariant in fact*. Defined a certain way, the concept of liberty itself could serve such a role. It could mean precisely the individual's capacity freely to accept or reject a lateral morality. And if that capacity were plausibly uniform and invariant in fact, we would have something very like the meaning asserted here for human equality.

18. See Richard Sorabji, *Animal Minds and Human Morals* (Ithaca: Cornell University Press, 1993), 122–33; see also id. at 134–57.

19. Hans Jonas cites our "deserved discomfort" for excluding animals (*The Imperative of Responsibility* [Chicago: University of Chicago Press, 1984], 63). Whitehead had a similar hesitation (*Modes of Thought* [New York: Macmillan, 1938], 39). T. Regan would go all the way in recognizing their "rights" ("The Nature and Possibility of an Environmental Ethics," *Environmental Ethics* 3, no. 1 [1981]: 19). Pope Pius IX, however, refused to permit the Society for the Prevention of Cruelty to Animals to operate in Rome, on the ground that it was a theological error that people have any duties to animals (W. R. Inge, *Christian Ethics and Modern Problems* [New York: Knickerbocker, 1930], 295).

20. Wilson, *Equality*, 99.

21. Rackman, "Judaism and Equality," 155. Rackman would find support in Pufendorf, *De Jure naturae et gentium*, vol. 2, 333. Pufendorf in turn invokes Boethius.

22. To invoke theology, of course, allows speculation regarding an interval of time in the afterlife in which rationality, hence choice, is extended to anyone who was *non compos* in his or her earthly sojourn. Cf. C. S. Lewis, *The Great Divorce* (New York: Macmillan, 1946).

23. We have no occasion in this essay to consider the rights of persons who have become permanently incapable of choice. There is, of course, a vast casuistry on this difficult subject. See, for example, Robert Spaemann, "Is Every Human Being a Person?" *The Thomist* 60 (1996): 463.

24.
      Hast thou not made me here thy substitute,
      And these inferior far beneath me set?
      Among unequals what society
      Can sort, what harmony or true delight?
      Which must be mutual, in proportion due
      Given and received . . .
      . . . Of fellowship I speak
      Such as I seek, fit to participate
      All rational delight wherein the brute
      Cannot be human consort . . .

                  (John Milton, *Paradise Lost*, book 8, verses 381–92
                  [New York: Viking, 1949] [*The Portable Milton*,
                  ed. D. Bush, 425–26])

25. This, as Henry Veatch tells us, is the point of Aristotle's well-known assertion that man is, by nature, a political animal: "Outside of a *polis* or of civil society, a human being could scarcely be conceived as being human" (Henry Veatch, *Human Rights: Fact or Fancy?* [Baton Rouge: Louisiana State University Press, 1985], 119).

26. One could prefer to identify the mental shift as consciousness itself. "If the world contained only one mind, there would be no consciousness. . . . [C]onsciousness is social in its very origin" (Berdyaev, *The Destiny of Man* [London: Bles, 1945], 69). Berdyaev elsewhere says that consciousness is a consequence of the Fall (id. at 38); this is hard to credit, since any "fall"—however conceived—entails a free choice in response to an already recognized duty.

27. This problem gets a more general treatment in A. Buchanan, "Justice as Reciprocity Versus Subject-Centered Justice," *Philosophy and Public Affairs* 19, no. 3 (1990): 227.

28. If they were also *free*, the possibility of animal obligation would arise. We have no logical objection to a descriptive "moral equality" broader than a "human equality." We merely disbelieve it.

29. At the very least he is "encumbered" by a "constitutive attachment" (Michael Sandel, "The Procedural Republic and the Unencumbered Self," *Political Theory* 12 [1984]: 81, 89–91, 94). Richard Schenk puts the point precisely: "Identity is attained only in tandem with relation. . . . The ideal of a meaningful identity prior to relation, apart from never being fully attainable, would prove destructive of identity itself to

the degree in which it was realized" ("Discretely Metaphysical: Refracting Metaphysical Light in Post-Metaphysical Prisms," *Listening* 30 [winter 1995]: 15).

30. If there were nonhuman creatures so constituted as to be obligated by a free morality of obedience to God, such a thin version of equality could also hold among humans and these responsible beasts. So long as the capacities of these creatures for free commitment to ascendant responsibility were equal to ours in degree, we could imagine, for example, a universal mammalian equality. Humans would relate to giraffes and to other humans as equals—but, still, only in the restricted and trivial sense noted in the text; that is, the relation would hold *between* humans and animals, but, the obligation being exclusively ascendant, it would not be *about* either humans or animals. This peculiar relation of equality would be morally empty. One thinks of the nativity scene in which sheep and shepherds share a nonlateral focus. Would it be an impiety to suppose that the sheep were ultimately eaten (or perhaps sacrificed)?

31. Karl Rahner, *Foundations of Christian Faith* (New York: Crossroad, 1992), 344; see also 350, 356, 395–96.

32. It is for this reason we have not adopted thoughtful suggestions that the host property be conceived as the awakened capacity for empathy or pity. The capacity to put oneself in the place of another or to feel pity is distinct from the capacity that awakens to lateral obligation. To experience empathy is one thing; to experience duty is quite another. Duty binds whether empathy is present or not and exists apart from any choice by the self. Its source is not in the ego. Without the consciousness of its authority, there can be no aspect of moral capacity that is distinct and real. In mere empathy no change occurs in the structure of the self; the experience is self-referential.

33. Robert Bellah et al., *Habits of the Heart* (Berkeley: University of California Press, 1985); Robert Bellah et al., *The Good Society* (New York: Knopf, 1991).

34. We acknowledge that if Americans took liberal metaphysics seriously, love and community would be transmogrified, as they are in Hobbes (see infra chap. 4), ceasing to have value in themselves. For the individualist, bonding and cohesion are instruments. Acceptance by the gang is a utility; that is the end of it. *The Wizard of Oz* (movie version) presses this point unconsciously and with uncanny precision, telling the Tin Man that what matters in life is "not how much you love but how much you are loved by others." So far as we know this spectacular moral gaffe has gone unremarked. Perhaps Bellah is right.

35. Iris Murdoch shares our view of the modern mind: "People know about the difference between good and evil, it takes quite a lot of theorising to persuade them to say or imagine that they do not" (*Metaphysics as a Guide to Morals* [New York: Penguin, 1992], 497).

36. Augustine, *Confessions* (New York: Sheed and Ward, 1943), 32.

37. Pepys's diary suggests that the issue is permanent:

He [Carteret] . . . says that he himself hath once taken the liberty to tell the King the necessity of having at least a show of religion in the Government, and sobriety; and that it was that that did set up and keep up Oliver though he was the greatest rogue in the world, and that it is so fixed in the nature of the common Englishman that it will not out of him. (E. Shepard, ed., *Everybody's Pepys* [New York: Harcourt, Brace, 1926], 456)

38. See Jeffrey Stout, *Ethics after Babel: The Languages of Morals and Their Discontents* (Cambridge: James Clark, 1988), 194–200.

39. John Coons, "Intellectual Liberty and the Schools," 4 *Journal of Law, Ethics, and Public Policy* 495–533 (1985).

40. At least nothing reported by Bellah et al. could support such a conclusion. *Habits of the Heart* is based upon long interviews of a handful of individuals. It appears that none of those interviewed was asked in very clear terms whether either natural or religious rules have authority over the individual. Nevertheless, on his own initiative, "Brian" says: "Why is integrity important and lying bad? I don't know. It just is. It's just so basic. I don't want to be bothered with challenging that. It's part of me" (Stout, *Ethics*, 7). Brian might be taken as an example of a threatening individualism, and, of course, he and the other respondents are orthodox Sinatrans about doing it "my way." On the whole, however, Brian recognizes a lateral morality not invented by society. What he lacks is a language. He is a typical case of cultural blindness intensified by miseducation. What Bellah has in fact identified is a crisis of moral communication. Viewed in the round, Brian and the others interviewed are fairly traditional in their real beliefs. They are, however, reduced to stammering incoherence by the secular taboos of their culture, assisted perhaps by the form of the interrogation. Jeffrey Stout has seen what this is about:

> The language of individualism seems to be less his first language of self-understanding than his language of last resort—a set of slogans he reaches for (with obvious reluctance) when somebody won't take storytelling or unprincipled talk of habit and happiness as sufficient for purposes of justification. (Id. at 196)

Stout denies that Brian must be read as an individualist:

> Brian can . . . just as easily be read as offering his own experience as evidence for the claim that one course is objectively better than the other and therefore should be preferred to it. (Id. at 197)

The failure, according to Stout, is the interviewers' abuse of the "Socratic method."

In our reading and observation, Bellah et al. appear nettled that their subjects have lost faith in the political solutions of the New Deal. Their books may have transformed this disapproval into an indictment of the moral theory supposedly favored by the American middle class. No doubt we bourgeoisie deserve a thrashing, but—we think—less for our want of belief in moral responsibility than for our failure to honor it. But readers must judge for themselves. The other book is Bellah et al., *The Good Society*, supra. Both get scored off by Andrew Greeley in "Habits of the Head," *Society* 74 (May–June 1992).

41. Samuel Scheffler, "Responsibility, Reactive Attitudes, and Liberalism in Philosophy and Politics," *Philosophy and Public Affairs* 21 (1992): 303. As for liberalism's incapacity to produce a theory of responsibility, Scheffler is disputed by Arthur Ripstein, "Equality, Luck, and Responsibility," *Philosophy and Public Affairs* 23 (winter 1994): 3. A shrewd reconnaissance of the state and prospect of "Victorian virtues" is G. Himmelfarb, "A De-Moralized Society: The British/American Experience," *The Public Interest* 111 (fall 1994): 57.

42. J. Budziszewski provides their portrait:

> If some theoretician opines, "Morals are a branch of taste; there *are* no objective goods with which we could be brought into right relationship," I readily admit that the point cannot be proven either way. One must take it on faith. But I will add this: I have never known a theoretician who could not suffer indignation— a *moral* passion. Break into his house and see what happens. For an even faster reaction, contradict him! Scratch a subjectivist and you find a moralist every time. The principle, I think, is plain. Many people are *confused* about the distinction between good and evil, but only those *forget* it who have ceased, altogether, to be human. Human beings are so obsessed with it that they will try to derive moral imperatives even from the proposition that there is no moral knowledge. It is one of our most popular parlor games. (J. Budziszewski, *True Tolerance: Liberalism and the Necessity of Judgment* [New Brunswick, N.J.: Transaction, 1992], 6)

And, as John Sisk said of Rosa Luxemburg's murderer, "we can be fairly certain . . . that her killer, like most political assassins, took virtue very seriously" ("Saving the World," *First Things* [May 1993]: 12).

CHAPTER 3
MAKING THE HOST PROPERTY UNIFORM

1. Milton, *Paradise Lost*, book 5, verses 788–93; *The Portable Milton*, 365.

2. Of course convention could have given equality a more elastic definition. Regarding the meaning of signs and symbols, convention is sovereign and might have adopted any imaginable notion; human equality could even have signified a maximum range of deviation in respect of some trait (as John Rawls might have it; see supra at 32–33). We find nothing in common usage, however, that departs from the elemental notion of an absolute individuated sameness. Equality as sameness in degree is part of the grammar of the West. To displace this simple concept with some flabby notion of flux and approximation would be baffling. To speak of the host property as anything but fixed in its possession and identical in its degree would make equality gibberish.

3. The criterion of uniformity means that equality could have no commerce with recent revivals of what should be called *futilism* but which goes under the catchy title "moral luck." This notion is summed up in what is to us a very peculiar assertion by Thomas Nagel: "There is a *morally* significant difference between rescuing someone from a burning building and dropping him from a twelfth-story window while trying to rescue him" ("Moral Luck," in Statman, *Moral Luck*, 58 [emphasis added]). The context—the entire essay—confirms that, for Nagel, you are a better *person* if you succeed in producing some material good; indeed, *blame* properly attaches if you don't. "Actual results influence culpability" (id. at 62). In a companion essay also called "Moral Luck" (id. at 62), Bernard Williams appears to agree. His parting salute on luck includes this lament from a philosopher who cannot be consoled even by his own integrity: "I still cannot see what comfort it is supposed to give to me, or what instruction it offers to other people, if I am shunned, hated, unloved and de-

spised, not least by myself, but am told that these reactions are at any rate not *moral*" ("Postscript," id. at 254). (For a compressed statement by Williams of his objection to "morality" [as opposed to "ethics" or well-being] as a concept, see Bernard Williams, *Morality: An Introduction to Ethics* [San Francisco: Harper and Row, 1972], 79–88.) This sort of argumentation gives us the impression that both have lost their ethical bearings. To a *moralist* who believes that "one is morally at the mercy of fate" (Nagel, "Moral Luck," id. at 65–66), we can only say—good luck.

The recent work of Philip Selznick may leave him also committed to the view that moral fulfillment is essentially objective and depends upon luck: "Without appropriate opportunities and supports, the quest for moral well-being may be confused, frustrated, and aborted; the *telos* may be experienced as dim and incoherent rather than clear and compelling. Therefore the injunction to follow nature must be sustained by a worked-out theory of what the natural end-state is and why it is worthy of our striving" (*The Moral Commonwealth*, 151; see also id. at 227–28). For a balanced and penetrating general treatment of the subject, see A. Duff, "Must a Good Man Be Invulnerable?" *Ethics* 86 (1976): 294.

4. As we shall see in chapters 5 and 8, however, for much of the Western tradition there has been an equivalent ambiguity that is not *merely* linguistic. For Aristotle and his Latinist heirs, the good man can only be one who does good acts. The conflation of human goodness and correct behavior has for many scholars proved nearly irresistible, but see, for example, Bruno Schüller, S.J., "Types of Grounding for Ethical Norms" in *Readings in Moral Theology*, no. 1, ed. C. Curran and R. McCormick (New York: Paulist Press, 1979), 184–98.

5. In this century, in the English-speaking world, the insight that a man can choose the "right act" and yet deserve condemnation as a "bad man" goes under the title "Moore's Paradox." See G. E. Moore, *Ethics* (London: Oxford University Press, 1949). Moore's distinction between the right and the good received refinement from R. M. Hare in *The Language of Morals* (Oxford: Oxford University Press, 1982), 185.

6. Diligence is a moral concept strangely neglected in the literature, perhaps on the theory that correct behaviors are easy to spot. (Of course it is the moralists, not the epistemologists, that one is apt to find describing correct behaviors as "self-evident" and evil ones as "*mala in se*"). An exception is Ryu and Silving's somewhat confusing discussion of the distinction (apparently original to Max Weber) between an ethic merely of "good intention" and one of "responsibility." The latter requires

> consciousness of the duty to *ascertain* the true obligation, the struggle for the *right* decision. Purity of attitude, acting in accordance with the consciousness of duty is but one side of the ethical value of an act; the other, *primary*, side is responsibility for the *substantively* correct decision *within the framework of individual ethical capacity of realization*. Concern with the correct decision is the element that endows the subjectively moral act with full earnestness and existential weight. It imposes upon the person responsibility not only for the purity of his attitude but also for the ethical correctness of his act. (Paul K. Ryu and Helen Silving, "*Error Juris*: A Comparative Study," 24 *University of Chicago Law Review* 421, 453 [1957]; quoting and translating Welzel, *Aktuelle Strafrechtsprobleme im Rahmen der finalen Handlungslehre, Juristische Studiengesellschaft Karlsruhe* 15, 16 [1953])

Another exception to the neglect of diligence as a moral category is Richard Milo's discussion of moral negligence (*Immorality* [Princeton, N.J.: Princeton University Press, 1984], 82–114, esp. 83–90). Milo identifies moral negligence (the failure to be morally diligent) as a distinct form of moral failure. This is consistent with the premises of human equality as we interpret them; both intentional wrongdoing and negligent inadvertence corrupt. See also Aquinas, *Summa theologiae*, Ia–IIae, qq. 54, 64, 79. A perceptive account of moral "trying" is John E. Hare, *The Moral Gap: Kantian Ethics, Human Limits, and God's Assistance* (Oxford: Clarendon, 1996), 112.

7. An exception is the actor who does the objective good by accident; he is not subjectively perfected.

8. Criminal law makes an important exception for conviction of a serious crime, which requires a demonstration that the accused had a "guilty mind."

9. "To be sure, the law—for very good reason—deals only with realizations; the merely would-be lawbreaker lies beyond its condemnation. But morality and law simply differ in this as in other regards. To take the Williams and Nagel law on 'moral luck' is in fact to take an overly legalistic view of morality" (Nicholas Rescher, "Moral Luck," in Statman, *Moral Luck*, 166 n. 18). If by "realizations" Rescher meant the achievement of the objective result intended, he would be in error. The law punishes mere attempts and failed conspiracies. It would be accurate to say that the law deals only with intentions that are evidenced by certain kinds of overt acts. For a lawyer's standpoint on the general question of chance in law, see K. Kessler, "The Role of Luck in the Criminal Law," 142 *Pennsylvania Law Review* 2183 (1994).

10. "They make the exercise of freedom more difficult or less difficult, but they cannot destroy it. . . . In practice it is impossible to do so" (Pope John Paul II, *Centesimus annus* 35–36 ([1989]). Note that this does not clearly support the premises of equality; it allows the possibility that the crucial subjective act of self-commitment is made *easier* for some than for others.

11. Contemporary support for the proposition includes Rescher, "Moral Luck" in Statman, *Moral Luck*, 156–57; and Judith Thompson, "Morality and Bad Luck," id. at 195, 204.

12. Indeed, even the Old Testament has scarcely begun before intention becomes an issue. See infra chap. 8.

13. Though several of the essayists in *Moral Luck* would "blame" actors for altruistic efforts that failed. See supra at 67 n. 3.

14. For the Greeks, even poverty was a moral failure. "The poor man could not, in this ethics, be a good man" (Crane Brinton, *A History of Western Morals* [New York: Harcourt, Brace, 1959], 79). See discussion infra chap. 5 at 127–29. For the Christian, "there is only one sadness; it is not to be a saint" (Leon Bloy, quoted in Jacques Maritain, *The Peasant of the Garonne* [New York: Holt, Reinhart and Winston, 1968], 246).

15. *The Meditations of Marcus Aurelius*, trans. G. Long, *Harvard Classics*, vol. 2 (New York: Collier, 1937), 285.

16. Bernard Lonergan, "The Subject," in Lonergan, *A Second Collection* (Philadelphia: Westminster, 1974), 83.

17. We take John Wilson to have meant something of the sort, and thereby to have taken an important preliminary step toward a theory of equality (see supra at 29–31).

18. Aquinas, *Summa theologiae*, Ia–IIae, q. 18, a. 29; F. C. Copleston, *Aquinas* (New York: Penguin, 1955), 206–7.

19. Such analysis frequently invokes pseudo-Dionysius's dictum that the good of an *act* comes from the whole cause, evil from any defect (see infra chaps. 5 and 8 at 125–29 and 326 n. 37, respectively). This, of course, conflates the good of the act and the state of the actor.

20. *Pensées* (New York: Random House, 1941), § 347. Of course Pascal here remains ambiguous. He could have meant that thinking *well*, not striving to do so, was the principle. The ambiguity continues in another and extended translation of the relevant passages: "All our dignity then consists in thought. We must look to that in order to rise aloft; not to space or time which we can never fill. Strive we then to think aright: that is the first principle of moral life. It is not from space that I get my dignity, but from the control of my thought" (Pascal, *Pensées* [London: Routledge and Kegan Paul, 1950], § 161).

21. The moral theory we describe in this chapter as required by conventional equality largely coincides with what the philosopher Jean Hampton has described as the "insubordination" or "defiance" theory of immorality. (Because Hampton's focus is upon what *corrupts*, she never unqualifiedly embraces the proposition that subordination to an honestly mistaken moral injunction *perfects*.) Arguing against claims that unchosen ignorance or the operation of an internal "Manichean" force (e.g., original sin) justifies judging a person immoral, Hampton concludes:

> [What] "makes [a person] culpable is her [defiant] choice to do an action which she knows to be wrong, i.e., prohibited by a moral injunction, and where she knows this injunction claims to be the ruling principle of her choices. The word "claims" here is important. She doesn't know that this injunction must be authoritative over her; she knows only that it claims to be authoritative. . . . It is this claim that she resists, repudiates, fights off, as she chooses to do otherwise than it directs. The injunction is therefore not something that she can be indifferent towards, because she understands that she is supposed to be governed by it. . . . But by the very act of flouting the moral injunction, she understands that she is supposed to be inside its scope and rejects its power over her. (Jean Hampton, "The Nature of Immorality," *Social Philosophy & Policy* 7, no. 1 (1989): 22, 39–40)

Hampton claims both *Genesis* and Immanuel Kant as allies:

> The Genesis author explains the source of human immorality as, to use Milton's words in *Paradise Lost*, a "foul revolt." . . . [According to Kant,] the immoral person is one who *sides with* his own inclinations over morality; insofar as he reverses the proper order of the incentives, he rebels against the authority of the moral law, and it is in virtue of that rebellion that he is condemned. (Id. at 39, 41 n. 40)

See also Jean Hampton, "*Mens Rea*," *Social Philosophy and Policy* 7, no. 2 (1990). Hampton utterly overlooks the myriad medieval claims (as by Isidore of Seville, Hugh of St. Victor, and Gregory the Great) that Eve sinned *ex ignorantia*.

22. "It is always suspicious when we appeal to our good heart and good intentions in order to get out of doing the deeds of love" (Karl Rahner, *Biblical Homilies* [New

York: Herder and Herder, 1966], 109). And see J. Casey, *Pagan Virtues* (Oxford: Oxford University Press, 1990), 211. Conversely, consider the strange case of the grandmother who stops making cookies for her grandchildren precisely because she has come to realize that her intention is merely to gain their affection (no one we know).

23. At the end of chapter 5 we will see a radically different—though still "realist"—conception of objectivity that might support our conception of human equality.

24. G. Galilei, *Concerning the Two Chief World Systems* (Berkeley: University of California Press, 1953), from Galileo's *Dedication to the Grand Duke of Tuscany.*

25. Thus he says: "If the acts that are in accordance with the virtues have themselves a certain character it does not follow that they are done justly or temperately. The agent also must be in a certain condition when he does them; in the first place he must have knowledge" (Aristotle, *Nicomachean Ethics* II.3, 1105a 28–32). (All our quotations of Aristotle are from R. McKeon, *The Basic Works of Aristotle* [New York: Random House, 1941].) See generally Richard Sorabji, "Aristotle on the Role of Intellect in Virtue" in A. O. Rorty, ed., *Essays on Aristotle's Ethics* (Berkeley: University of California, 1980), 201. Sorabji concludes his study thus: "Aristotle ascribes a major role to the intellect [in virtue] and . . . he does not contradict this ascription" (id. at 218).

26. Plato, *Protagoras*, § 352 *ad finem*; *Meno*, § 77e.

27. A. E. Taylor, *Platonism and Its Influence* (New York: Longmans, Green, 1924), 61.

28. See, for example, Lawrence Kohlberg, *The Philosophy of Moral Development* (San Francisco: Harper and Row, 1981), 30. As Robert Nozick would have it: "A 'perfect' philosophical argument would leave no choice" (*Philosophical Explanations* [Cambridge: Harvard University Press, 1981], 4). For a general criticism of Kohlberg's work, see Paul Vitz, "Critiques of Kohlberg's Model of Moral Development: A Summary," *Revista Española de Pedagogia*, año 52, num. 197 (Enero-abril, 1994): 5.

29. The origins and content of gnosticism—indeed, its identity—are murky and disputed. The modern classic on the subject is Hans Jonas, *The Gnostic Religion* (Boston: Beacon, 1958). The view nearest our own may be that of Eric Voegelin as summarized in his *The New Science of Politics* (Chicago: University of Chicago Press, 1952). Later we will consider the possibility (allegation) that some quarters of contemporary Christianity have been gnosticized (infra chap. 7 at 182–85).

30. Jonas, *The Imperative of Responsibility*, 22.

31. The issue arises at a rather early point in the history of the universe. There is a difficulty about the angelic defection: "[Satan's fall] raises the question whether a rational moral agent could intend to turn away from his ultimate end knowing he would be punished for doing so" (G. Shedler, "Retributive Punishment and the Fall of Satan," 30 *American Journal of Jurisprudence* 137, 138 [1985]). St. Anselm is reported as holding that "ignorance was necessary" (id. at 141). Our own refinement of this would be that knowledge, too, is necessary—but just what this means is not so easy to say. Perhaps this accounts for Augustine's apparent oscillation between (1) a relative insufficiency of knowledge in the bad angels, and (2) their free rejection of sufficient knowledge (*City of God* [Garden City, N.Y.: Doubleday, 1958], 220–22, 257).

32. Kohlberg, *The Philosophy of Moral Development*, 30.

33. "Omniscience excludes the making of decisions" (Alasdair MacIntyre, *After Virtue*, 2d ed. [Notre Dame: University of Notre Dame Press, 1984], 96). The extensive modern debate over the question of how a person might act contrary to his or her own judgment of the good is represented in F. Jackson, "Weakness of Will," *Mind* 93 (1984): 1. For a careful assessment of the problem as it first got worked through by Aristotle under the name *akrasia* (moral weakness), see W.F.R. Hardie, *Aristotle's Ethical Theory*, 2d ed. (Oxford: Clarendon, 1968), 258–93.

34. Murdoch, *Metaphysics as a Guide to Morals*, 505.

35. *Nicomachean Ethics* VII.2, 1145b30.

36. Newman thought their very sophistication a hurdle to clear moral judgment. Of "Philosophers, experimentalists, lawyers" he says: "Even when in their hearts they have no doubt about a conclusion, still often, from the habit of their minds, they are reluctant to own it, and dwell upon the deficiencies of the evidence, or the possibility of error, because they speak by rule and by book, though they judge and determine by common-sense" (John Henry Newman, *A Grammar of Assent* [Garden City, N.Y.: Doubleday, 1955], 227).

37. This does not deny that higher intellectual capacity may turn up a greater number of morally plausible options. "The chief difficulty of moral conflicts is not the choice between obvious good and evil, but the absence of any single, morally binding solution laid down once for all and the necessity for making each time an individual creative act" (Berdyaev, *The Destiny of Man*, 76).

38. And Dryden could have been right in supposing that "great wits are sure to madness near allied" (*Absalom and Achitophel*).

39. Our experience suggests the possibility that educated persons—and especially those whose circumstances allow reflection—tend to a greater degree to apply reason to morality. In the process, the most sincere seeker can become all too vividly aware of his own rich capacity for casuistry and of the temptations it poses; one's very agility raises doubts of the instrument, doubts that would not afflict the simpler (or busier) person. In the amplitude of his own knowledge, he discovers that the path is never coercively clear. Like the rich man, he is burdened by his own possessions. His intellect cannot nail the good decisively, and, with more prosaic skills atrophied, intellect is the only tool left him.

40. Immanuel Kant, *Foundations of the Metaphysics of Morals*, trans. Beck (Indianapolis: Bobbs-Merrill, 1959), 21. This did not prevent Kant from appealing to the gnostic impulse, at least in his own culture. "Kantian idealism [became] the conventional nineteenth-century German belief that their philosophic national depth was all that Germans needed in the way of conventional virtue" (Brinton, *A History of Western Morals* [New York: Harcourt, Brace, 1959], 419). Nietzsche caught the subtlety in Kant's little bow to the masses: "*Kant's joke*. Kant wanted to prove in a way that would dumbfound the common man that the common man was right: that was the secret joke of his soul. He wrote against the scholars in favor of the popular prejudice, but for scholars and not popularly" (*The Gay Science* [1882], in W. Kaufmann, ed., *The Portable Nietzche* [New York: Penguin, 1976], 193). From a certain point of view we see ourselves to be retelling Kant's joke.

41. See Paul Tillich, *A Complete History of Christian Thought* (New York: Harper and Row, 1968), 108 *et seq.* The point, however, does not hold for poets, novelists, and theologians, many of whom see obscurity as a benign phenomenon. See infra chap. 6 at 155–61.

42. Aquinas agreed, though he concluded that this was also the truest liberty. As Gilson puts the Thomist conclusion: "If the human intellect could offer to us, as a known object, the Sovereign Good Himself, our will would cleave to it at once and seize it with an immovable grip which would also be the most perfect liberty" (Etienne Gilson, *History of Christian Philosophy in the Middle Ages* [New York: Random House, 1955], 379). Recognition of fallibility did not stop Aquinas (or Gilson) from holding bewildered moral actors to cognitive standards they could not possibly meet. See infra chap. 8 at 195–98.

43. Pascal has it that "he must not see nothing at all . . . he must see and not see; and that is exactly the state in which he naturally is" (*Pensees* [New York: Random House, 1941], § 555). It may be that in a certain sense we are all gnostics. The authors, for example, are gnostics who "know" that *every* person has in the same degree the knowledge that can save. The "elect" is everybody.

44. Dietrich Bonhoeffer even insisted that "not to know where you are going is the true knowledge" (*The Cost of Discipleship* [New York: Macmillan, 1959], 103). We would stop with this: To grasp that you are going at all is knowledge sufficient to a full moral life.

45. Nozick, *Philosophical Explanations*, 4–8, 197. Or, as Iris Murdoch remarks, "Axioms may not 'win' but must remain in consideration" (*Metaphysics as a Guide to Morals*, 483).

46. Walker Percy observes that fallibility (paradoxically) has a positive role even in the realm of knowing. Winding up a chapter on "Metaphor as Mistake," he tells us:

> This "wrongness" of metaphor is seen to be not a vagary of poets but a special case of that mysterious "error" which is the very condition of our knowing anything at all. This "error," the act of symbolization, is itself the instrument of knowing and is an error only if we do not appreciate its intentional character. If we do not take note of it, or if we try to exorcise it as a primitive residue, we shall find ourselves on the horns of the same dilemma which has plagued philosophers since the eighteenth century. The semanticists, on the one horn . . . do not and cannot say how we know. The behaviorists, on the other, imply that we do not know at all. . . . But we do know, not as the angels know and not as dogs know but as men, who must know one thing through the mirror of another. (Percy, *The Message in the Bottle*, 81–82)

47. There is a substantial literature on the question of whether self-deception is possible or a kind of self-contradiction. An interesting view with a very useful bibliography appended is T. S. Champlin, "Self-deception: A Reflexive Dilemma," *Philosophy* 52 (1977): 281.

48. This wisdom did not arrive with Freud:

> Now some one may say that all men desire the apparent good, but have no control over the appearance, but the end appears to each man in a form answering to his character. We reply that if each man is somehow responsible for his state of mind, he will also be himself somehow responsible for the appearance [and] . . . for his own evildoing. (Aristotle, *Nicomachean Ethics* III.5, 1114a32–1114b4)

49. An observer as sensitive as David Daube is able to credit them (David Daube, "Judas," 82 *California Law Review* 95 [1994]). For a powerful analysis of the limits

of our capacity to pass *moral* judgment even on the Nazi doctors who committed the greatest of atrocities "in all good conscience," see Edward Zukowski, "The Good Conscience of Nazi Doctors," in *Annual of the Society of Christian Ethics* 53 (1994). For practical purposes, of course, the world operates under a *presumption* that the person who is consistently wrong in the objective order has not committed himself to the good; since good intention is unprovable, the presumption is effectively conclusive. And we could agree specifically with Philip Selznick that *moral* "integrity presumes at least a core of morally justifiable commitments" (Selznick, *The Moral Commonwealth*, 322).

50. Dorothy Sayers, *Unnatural Death* (New York: Harper and Row, 1955), 214. Gobbo's own words in *Merchant of Venice*:

> My conscience says "Lancelot, budge not." "Budge," says the fiend. "Budge not," says my conscience. "Conscience," say I, "you counsel well"; "fiend," say I, "you counsel well!"

George Eliot fingers a different specimen in *Middlemarch* (Boston: Houghton Mifflin, 1956), 453:

> The spiritual kind of rescue was a genuine need with him. There may be coarse hypocrites, who consciously affect beliefs and emotions for the sake of gulling the world, but Bulstrode was not one of them. He was simply a man whose desires had been stronger than his theoretic beliefs, and who had gradually explained the gratification of his desires into satisfactory agreement with those beliefs. If this be hypocrisy, it is a process which shows itself occasionally in us all.

For a stage version of the process of *collective* self-delusion terminating in (we think) the wrong choice, see F. Dürrenmatt, *The Visit* (New York: Random House, 1958).

51. Represented in the film, *In the Name of the Father* (1993).

52. Voegelin is prepared to assume the good intention even of the gnostic totalitarians. Given their assumptions, "types of action . . . morally insane . . . will be considered moral in the dream world because they intended an entirely different effect" (Voegelin, *The New Science of Politics*, 169).

53. Even lawyers worry about such matters. R. Loder says, however, that we worry too little ("Moral Skepticism and Lawyers," *Utah Law Review* 47 [1990]).

54. If this capacity remained subject to increase and decrease throughout life according to moral choices made, individual adults could also possess it in its original degree but only contingently as they fall to that specific original quantum that presumably would consist of the minimal grasp of responsibility to seek the lateral good.

55. Though this view would require the assumption that the capacity is immune to mere circumstance, while it alters in its strength according to free choices of the moral actor.

56. See esp. *Paradiso*, canto 3. Dante's array of capacities for beatific perception does not answer *our* question about equality; with the unique exception of Jesus' mother, we do not take Dante to hold that the disparate celestial states of individuals were in any respect a function of inborn differences in their capacity for self-perfection. The circles of *Paradiso* may correspond in some part to levels of individual virtue *achieved*, but there is no suggestion that these degrees of excellence correspond

to the relative puissance of some earthly capacity—natural or developed. Indeed, were it so, it would seem an odd piece of moral theology. At just which temporal moment of our earthly career would our (variable) capacity for virtue determine our heavenly post? There is no principled answer, and in fact it is not a question in which Dante shows any interest. True, those whom he celebrates as having a more ample grasp of the divine reality seem, by and large, to be persons who on earth had exceptional intellectual or related gifts. But if God has power first to endow mankind with such gifts and then to restore them after the dissolution of the body, post mortem, he could presumably bestow upon the warm-hearted dunce the cognitive capacity needed in paradise to grasp whatever Aquinas grasps. What is more threatening to human equality in Dante is the strong suggestion that disparate apprehension of the good is entirely a function of the dispensation of *grace*:

> Not, then, by merit, do these spirits go
> To dwell in varying degrees of bliss;
> Grace-given is the sight which grades them so.
>> (canto 32: verses 73–74, trans. Reynolds
>> [Baltimore: Penguin, 1962], 336)

This would accord with Aquinas, see infra, 167–68. Earlier, however, Dante speaks of righteousness in respect of the angels: "Their sum of merit is the measure of their sight—merit which grace and righteousness beget" (canto 28: verses 111–13, id. at 304).

Reynolds comments on these passages regarding angels as if they applied equally to humans: "The power to see God is greater or less in proportion to the greater or less merit of the soul; and merit itself is grace—given and fostered by the will" (id. at 307–8). If human destiny is affected by a "righteousness" (Dante) that is "fostered by the will" (Reynolds), there seems for both Dante and Reynolds some doubt about the smothering dominance of grace.

57. This *could* be Augustine's meaning as he (like Dante) explains that everyone in heaven gets all the happiness he is capable of and feels no desire for more: "The less rewarded will be linked in perfect peace with the more highly favored. . . . The less endowed will have the high endowment of longing for nothing loftier than their lower gifts" (Augustine, *The City of God*, 541).

58. We accept much of the psychological theory that (beginning with Aristotle) has emphasized the impact of habit. There is a semi-empirical wisdom about psychological formation that applies reasonably well to both the enhancement and erosion of our cognitive moral powers. Those who habitually perform the objective good no doubt come to see its terms more clearly (and vice versa). See infra chap. 5 at 142–43. By definition, however, these behavioral theories could not apply to the unmeasurable capacity of the self to commit to the real good as its ideal.

Meanwhile, we should be clear that we reject altogether those psycho-metaphysical theories that would simply eliminate a continuing self, reducing the individual to the determined sum of his or her experiences. B. F. Skinner is the usual citation for this peculiar form of intellectual self-immolation. See Skinner, *Beyond Freedom and Dignity* (New York: Knopf, 1971). An ontological half-way house is represented in M. Dan-Cohen, "Responsibility and the Boundaries of the Self," 105 *Harvard Law Review* 959 (1992); and "Between Selves and Collectivities: Toward a Jurisprudence of Identity," 61 *University of Chicago Law Review* 1213 (1994). See generally Charles Taylor, *Sources of the Self* (New Haven: Yale University Press, 1989).

59. This same question could be asked separately about cases of well-intended but mistaken choices; here we ask it only of the harder case for equality—that of bad intention. Evil intent presumably is likelier to corrupt the capacity for moral self-perfection than is honest error; refutation of that greater danger simultaneously disposes of the lesser.

60. Nor are we required to disagree with the assessment of Nemesius as paraphrased by Gilson: "Our acquired habits, either good or bad, hang on our acts, and since our acts hang on our own free choice, we carry the responsibility of a life that is truly our own work" (Gilson, *History of Christian Philosophy in the Middle Ages*, 63).

61. Responding to the objection that Aristotle's emphasis on the importance of habit for correct behaviors negates the possibility of uniform human freedom, Joseph Owens explains: "A man may make the wrong choice, as regards either end or means. But that is not the final word. As long as he has choice he remains open to a reversal. . . . [T]he power of choice remains open for the individual. It is not done away with by a bad decision" ("The Grounds of Ethical Universality in Aristotle," in John R. Catan, ed., *Aristotle: The Collected Papers of Joseph Owens* [Albany: SUNY Press, 1981], 148, 162).

62. Francis Thompson, "The Hound of Heaven," in R. Aldington, ed., *The Viking Book of Poetry of the English Speaking World*, vol. 2 (New York: Viking, 1958), 1082.

63. We stress *outcomes* in order to distinguish the kind of choice that pursues a specific objective goal from the disinterested intellectual choice merely to *think about* a subject (say astronomy) or to self-reflect, daydream, or let our imagination run.

64. O.E.D. ascribes this to "Higden (Rolls) V.53."

65. Other candidates not chosen include one Greek root: *peirein* (to attempt); and two Latin: *diligere* (to love), which would allow "diligentism," and so on, and *conari* (to strive), of which Spinoza made cognate use (as "*conatus*," etc.). The English verb *subordinate* could also ramify into the necessary forms, but the word carries distracting baggage. When the elder author exits, the German verb *brennen* (to burn) will offer a plausible set of vaguely eponymic terms: to brenn, brennist, brennism, and so on; all offer a euphony unattainable in variations on the tuneless senior name (J.E.C.).

INTRODUCTION TO PART II

1. Though the correctness of our interpretation of the convention is thus assumed, parts 3 and 4 inevitably will constitute its indirect and informal criticism. If Cicero, Schweizer, and the pope all proclaim equality but define it differently (and intelligibly), we lose credibility. If every responsible authority declares against us, we must wonder whether we heard the butcher correctly.

2. J. Q. Wilson, *The Moral Sense* (New York: Free Press, 1993), xiii.

3. Wills, *Inventing America* (1979), supra.

4. As noted already in the text, the "reality" of this order is problematic for several reasons, including its apparent dependence upon the approval of the participants in any particular social order. See generally Francis Hutcheson, *Illustrations on the*

Moral Sense, ed. B. Peach (Cambridge: Harvard University Press, 1971). Peach's introduction elaborates the ambiguities at great length. Here we simply assume (what we believe) that Hutcheson himself considered obligation to exist independent of our apprehending it.

5. Francis Hutcheson, "An Inquiry into the Original of Our Ideas of Beauty and Virtue," in J. Schneewind, ed., *Moral Philosophy from Montaigne to Kant* (Cambridge: Cambridge University Press, 1990), 505, 517–18.

6. The remaining case for Hutcheson would be that of correct behavior attempted for the wrong reason; a bad motive would also rob the act of benefit for the actor. See Hutcheson, *Illustrations on the Moral Sense*, 160.

7. At one point he seems to make reason itself a potential barrier—and never any help at all—to discernment of the good: "'Tis our reason which presents a false notion . . . to the *moral faculty*. The fault or error is in the opinion or understanding and not in the *moral sense*: what it approves is truly good" (*A System of Moral Philosophy* [London: Foulis, 1755], 91). It thus would seem that to reason at all is to risk mistake. The passage next quoted in the text probably forbids this interpretation.

8. Hutcheson, "The Original of Our Ideas of Beauty and Virtue," 518.

9. Id. at 520.

10. This also seems James Q. Wilson's initial understanding of Hutcheson. The moral sense perceives an "ought" that constitutes "an obligation binding on all people similarly situated" (Wilson, *The Moral Sense*, xii). Duty thus is specifically and objectively determined by circumstances not chosen by the actor. See also id. at 162, 221, 226–27.

11. Hutcheson, *Illustrations on the Moral Sense*, 172.

12. Id. at 173.

13. *Pace* Wills, who believes that Hutcheson rested "political freedom and equality entirely on the basis of *equal* moral faculty in all men" (Wills, *Inventing America*, 228). In support he quotes the following passage from Hutcheson's *Short Introduction to Moral Philosophy* (1747): "In this respect all men are originally equal, that these natural rights equally belong to all, at least as soon as they come to the mature use of reason; and they are equally confirmed to all by the law of nature. . . . Nature makes none masters, none slaves." Insofar as we understand this sentence, it appears to deal with *rights*. That all men enjoy equal rights would say nothing of what it would mean for them to *be* equal. Even unequal men could be thought to deserve the same protections for their freedom.

14. Thomas Reid, *Essays on the Active Powers of the Human Mind* (1788), reprinted in Schneewind, *Moral Philosophy*, 615.

15. Hutcheson and Reid were the intellectual successors of the Earl of Shaftesbury through his *Inquiry Concerning Virtue or Merit* (1711), reprinted in Schneewind, *Moral Philosophy*, 488. The following passages suggest the genealogy of our problem:

> A mistake therefore, in fact . . . can be no cause of vice. But a mistake of right . . . must of necessity be the cause of vicious action in every intelligent or rational being.
>
>   But as there are many occasions where the matter of right may even to the most discerning part of mankind appear difficult, and of doubtful decision, 'tis not a slight mistake of this kind which can destroy the character of a virtuous

or worthy man. But when, either through superstition or ill custom, there come to be very gross mistakes in the assignment or application of the affection; when the mistakes are either in their nature so gross, or so complicated and frequent, that a creature cannot well live in a natural state, nor with due affections, compatible with human society and civil life; then is the character of virtue forfeited. (Id. at 492)

For an assessment of "the leveling and blunting process which Shaftesbury's thoughts suffer at the hands of Hutcheson," see Ernst Cassirer, *The Philosophy of the Enlightenment*, trans. Koelln and Pettegrove (Princeton, N.J.: Princeton University Press, 1951), 321. Adam Smith's *The Theory of Moral Sentiments* (Indianapolis: Liberty Classics, 1993) is a work generally associated with this school and the one best known to contemporary moralists. It does not address our questions.

16. Wilson, *The Moral Sense*, supra.

17. Id. at 23, 40, 44, 70, 123, 126, 132, 148, 158, 169, 186. Wilson even relies specifically on Darwin's words in *Descent of Man*: "Any animal whatever, endowed with well-marked social instincts, would inevitably acquire a moral sense or conscience, as soon as its intellectual powers become as well-developed, or nearly as well-developed, as in man" (id. at 130–31).

18. Ibid.

19. Wills, *Inventing America*, 218–28. Whether or not Jefferson came so far in his thinking, he was anything but the mere egalitarian fabricated by Herrnstein and Murray: "For both Jefferson and Madison, *political* equality was both right and workable. They would have been amazed by the notion that humans are equal in any other sense" (Herrnstein and Murray, *The Bell Curve*, 531).

20. The primary text is Jefferson's brief and delphic observation regarding the American slaves that "in the endowments of . . . the heart [Nature] will be found to have done them justice" (*Notes on the State of Virginia*, in *Thomas Jefferson, Writings* [New York: The Library of America, 1984], 269).

21. *Inventing America*, 225.

22. Id. at 223–28.

23. Julian P. Boyd et al., eds., *The Papers of Thomas Jefferson* (Princeton, N.J.: Princeton University Press, 1958), vol. 12, 15.

24. Ibid.

CHAPTER 4
COULD THE ENLIGHTENMENT BELIEVE?
INDIVIDUALISM, KANT, AND EQUALITY

1. Hobbes's words in their entirety:

Men by nature equal. Nature hath made men so equal, in the faculties of the body, and mind; as that though there be found one man sometimes manifestly stronger in body, or of quicker mind than another; yet when all is reckoned together, the difference between man, and man, is not so considerable, as that one man can thereupon claim to himself any benefit, to which another may not pretend, as well as he. For as to the strength of body, the weakest has strength enough to kill the strongest, either by secret machination, or by confederacy with others, that are in the same danger with himself.

And as to the faculties of the mind, setting aside the arts grounded upon words, and especially that skill of proceeding upon general, and infallible rules, called science; which very few have, and but in few things; as being not a native faculty, born with us; nor attained, as prudence, while we look after somewhat else, I find yet a greater equality amongst men, than that of strength. For prudence, is but experience; which equal time, equally bestows on all men, in those things they equally apply themselves unto. That which may perhaps make such equality incredible, is but a vain conceit of one's own wisdom, which almost all men think they have in a greater degree, than the vulgar; that is, than all men but themselves, and a few others, whom by fame, or for concurring with themselves, they approve. For such is the nature of men, that howsoever they may acknowledge many others to be more witty, or more eloquent, or more learned; yet they will hardly believe there be many so wise as themselves; for they see their own wit at hand, and other men's at a distance. But this proveth rather that men are in that point equal, than unequal. For there is not ordinarily a greater sign of the equal distribution of any thing, than that every man is contented with his share. (*Leviathan*, supra, 98)

2. Ibid.

3. Id. at 119–20.

4. See our discussions of "range properties" in the work of John Rawls, supra, 32–33, 41; infra, 200. Constantly ahead of his time, Hobbes may have anticipated what Tocqueville would observe in the democracies: "It is not simply that in democracies confidence in the superior knowledge of certain individuals has been weakened. . . . [T]he general idea that any man whosoever can attain an intellectual superiority beyond the reach of the rest is soon cast in doubt"(*Democracy in America* [Garden City, N.Y.: Doubleday, 1969], 641).

5. Hobbes, *Leviathan*, 103.

6. Id. at 113–14.

7. Philip Selznick has remarked the essential agreement between Hobbes and Freud in their "view of a primordial, narrowly self-interested ego"(*The Moral Commonwealth*, 211–12).

8. Reason itself has been demoted by Hobbes. Traditional morality had made reason the discoverer of the good; Hobbes makes it servant to the will, a handmaiden whose only task is to discover to the will the probable practical consequences of potential choices. It confides that if you hit Perkins, he will likely hit you back. Ask whether you are entitled to, or even should, hit Perkins, and reason has nothing to say (except about what it would be *prudent* to do). For on the question of "should" there is nothing to reason about. Reason reports for duty to a self that is under the absolute command of the will as it proceeds to choose among the passions and preferences clamoring to be realized. Hobbes and his successors spoke in moral terms, but, in fact, he had turned morality in upon itself. Michael Sandel's *Liberalism and the Limits of Justice* (Cambridge: Cambridge University Press, 1982) is a splendid general exposition of this tendency among individualist philosophers, including

Rawls and Dworkin, to disparage (implicitly) the function of reason. And see Charles Fried, "Liberalism, Community, and the Objectivity of Values," 96 *Harvard Law Review* 960 (1983), a review of Sandel.

9. In any case, that is what *moral* freedom is. Proudhon gave a succinct rendering of the contrary view; liberty is "not the daughter but the *mother* of order" (quoted in Selznick, *The Moral Commonwealth*, 372 n. 21).

10. "*Good*, and *evil*, are names that signify our appetites and aversions; which in different tempers, customs, and doctrines of men, are different" (Hobbes, *Leviathan*, 123). As Hume was soon to conclude, reason *ought* to be slave to the passions. See infra at 115. Now, human equality could accept this latter notion, if it be understood in a certain sense. It would be wholly consistent with the convention for reason to be servant of will and passion, so long as there is a real good that merits rational search, and so long as this good is made the object of our will and passions. In that event, reason is the instrument of the search for that good. This is not Hobbes's meaning.

11. Again, we invoke the wisdom of Iris Murdoch as an expression of the common sense of the race: "There is no unattached will as a prime source of value . . . Good is not an empty receptacle into which the arbitrary will places objects of its choice. . . . [The artist renders] the beauty of the world as an image of obedience. . . . Non-philosophical people do not think that they invent the good" (*Metaphysics as a Guide to Morals*, 507–8).

12. Lacking any preinstitutional morality, any Hobbesian candidate for equality would also flunk even the mushier tests of "importance" and "goodness."

13. Angels, who seem to be enjoying a cultural revival, were a major interest of Thomas Aquinas, earning him the title "The Angelic Doctor." In his *Summa theologiae*, dozens of major articles are devoted to such inquiries as "Whether Angels Assume Bodies" and "Whether an Angel Is in a Place?" See generally *Summa theologiae*, Ia, qq. 50–64.

14. Id. at q. 50, a. 4.

15. It is precisely in this difference that John Dewey locates the primary importance of intellect: "Knowledge, instead of revealing a world in which preference is an illusion and does not count or make a difference, puts in our possession the instrumentality by means of which preference may be an intelligent or intentional factor in constructing a future by wary and prepared action" (*The Quest for Certainty* [New York: Putnam, 1960], 250).

Presumably Hobbes would here remind us of his assertions about the "equality of ability." See supra at 101–2. We find it hard to take him seriously on this point, however, unless he is to be understood as asserting the usual liberal point (we accept it) that all rational persons have the *minimum* capacity necessary to political participation, hence for legal *rights*. But that claim would not be relevant to a descriptive equality; or, more precisely, by suggesting that this capacity varies in degree above the political minimum, it actually would deny the possibility of a descriptive human equality.

16. "Where no covenant hath preceded, there hath no right been transferred, and every man has right to every thing; and consequently, no action can be unjust. But when a covenant is made, then to break it is *unjust*: and the definition of injustice,

is no other than *the not performance of covenant.* And whatsoever is not injust, is *just*" (Hobbes, *Leviathan*, 113).

17. "If there were no responsibility 'by nature' there could be none 'by contract' " (Jonas, *The Imperative of Responsibility*, 95). The point was made earlier and famously by Hans Kelsen.

18. John Locke, *The Second Treatise of Government* (New York: Hafner, 1947), 122–23. Both treatises on government frequently acknowledge man's subjection to obligations imposed by God and nature. See Selznick, *The Moral Commonwealth*, 507. And see generally E. Gardner, "John Locke: Justice and The Social Compact," 9 *Journal of Law and Religion* 347 (1992).

19. Locke, *The Second Treatise of Government*, 189–90.

20. For example, id. at 147, where Locke speaks in the egalitarian mode of every man's "equal right . . . to his natural freedom." This clearly is not a descriptive equality but an equality of political rights. And see id. at 168–69.

21. For all his theoretical skepticism, Hume eventually emerged in general harmony with Hutcheson and the "school of Moral Sense." See supra at 94–97. Indeed, his vague moral doctrine can be understood as a form of natural law which his empiricism would seem to have made impossible:

> *Reason* and *sentiment* concur in almost all moral determinations and conclusions. The final sentence, it is probable, which pronounces characters and actions amiable or odious, praise-worthy or blameable; that which stamps on them the mark of honour or infamy, approbation or censure; that which renders morality an active principle and constitutes virtue our happiness, and vice our misery: it is probable, I say, that this final sentence depends on some internal sense or feeling, which nature has made universal in the whole species. For what else can have an influence of this nature? (David Hume, *An Enquiry Concerning the Principles of Morals*, in C. W. Hendel, ed., *Hume Selections*, sec. 1 [New York: Scribner's, 1927], 198)

22. See David Hume, *An Enquiry Concerning Human Understanding*, in E. A. Burt, ed., *The English Philosophers from Bacon to Mill* (New York: Random House, 1939), 635 *et seq.*; Hume, *An Enquiry Concerning the Principles of Morals*, 194, 198, 219, 230.

23. J. J. Rousseau, *The Social Contract*, ed. C. Frankel (New York: Hafner, 1947), 19.

24. Id. at 18–19. See also id. at 6, 14.

25. We concede that Rousseau flirts with—or even embraces—inconsistency: "What is good, and conformable to order, is so from the nature of things, and independently of human conventions" (id. at 33).

26. J. J. Rousseau, *A Discourse upon the Origin and Foundation of the Inequality among Mankind, Harvard Classics*, vol. 34 (New York: Collier, 1938), 161, 190.

27. Roger J. Sullivan, *Immanuel Kant's Moral Theory* (Cambridge: Cambridge University Press, 1989), 184.

28. Immanuel Kant, *Groundwork of the Metaphysic of Morals*, trans. and ed. H. J. Paton (San Francisco: Harper and Row, 1964), 117/457, Paton, 125.

29. "To say that a moral agent acts freely does not mean that such an agent acts lawlessly. In a lawless (i.e., completely ruleless) world, anything could follow from

anything, and that would make the notions of causality in general and of free, moral agency in particular totally meaningless. . . . To say that a moral agent is one who acts freely must therefore mean that such an agent can exercise causal power on the basis of a law or laws given by his reason alone" (Sullivan, *Immanuel Kant's Moral Theory*, 47–48). See Immanuel Kant, *The Metaphysics of Morals*, trans. and ed. M. Gregor (Cambridge: Cambridge University Press, 1996), 6:213–14, Gregor, 13. See generally Henry Allison, *Kant's Theory of Freedom* (Cambridge: Cambridge University Press, 1990).

30. "As 'a higher faculty of desire,' moral reason must be both a *cognitive* and a *conative* power, *entirely by itself* able to determine how we should act and also able to motivate us to act on those judgments without relying on any prior desires. . . . This is *the* central thesis of Kant's moral theory. . . . In fact, this constitutes what may be called Kant's Copernican revolution in moral philosophy. No one before Kant had thought to suggest that human reason could be so powerful. . . . [A]ll other philosophers had based the motivation or conative power of practical reason on desires. . . " (Sullivan, *Immanuel Kant's Moral Theory*, 45). See Kant, *Groundwork*, 36/412, Paton, 80.

31. "Everything in nature works in accordance with laws. Only a rational being has the power to act in *accordance with his idea* of laws—that is, in accordance with principles—and only so has he a *will*. . . . the will is nothing but practical reason" (Kant, *Groundwork*, 36/412, Paton, 80).

32. "A law has to carry with it absolute necessity if it is to be valid morally—valid, that is, as a ground of obligation; . . . the ground of obligation must be looked for, not in the nature of man nor in the circumstances of the world in which he is placed, but solely *a priori* in the concepts of pure reason" (Kant, *Groundwork*, pref. vi, Paton, 57.

33. "Kant's idea of 'autonomy,' like that of 'freedom,' is far more precise and restricted than the present-day notion. For Kant, the term 'autonomy' denotes our ability and responsibility to know what *morality* [as distinguished from *happiness*] requires of us and our determination not to act immorally. Rather than being a norm for promoting and satisfying our desires, then, the law of autonomy functions fundamentally as 'the supreme limiting condition of all subjective ends.' It is precisely the fact that morally right maxims qualify as universal laws that shows they are not and cannot be essentially self-seeking. Therefore, the autonomous person is one who, by enacting objective principles of conduct, is not only self-legislative but also universally legislative" (Sullivan, *Immanuel Kant's Moral Theory*, 47 [internal citation omitted]).

34. Immanuel Kant, *Critique of Practical Reason*, trans. L. W. Beck, 3d ed. (New York: Macmillan, 1993), 93–94, Beck, 98.

35. "Of that [noumenal] world [man] knows no more than this—that in it reason alone, and indeed pure reason independent of sensibility, is the source of law; and also that . . . he is there his proper self only as intelligence (while as a human being he is merely an appearance of himself)" (Kant, *Groundwork*, 118/457, Paton, 125).

36. Sullivan, *Kant's Moral Theory*, 47.

37. Kant, *Metaphysics of Morals*, 6:226, Gregor, 18.

38. It binds a rational agent as an *imperative* because it commands him, amid his temptations to be egotistical, to choose according to pure reason; it is an imperative

that is *categorical* because it binds the category of rational beings as such, that is, unconditionally or "categorically," not merely hypothetically or conditionally.

39. Kant, *Groundwork*, 40/415, Paton, 82; 43/416, Paton, 83–84.

40. Kant, *Critique of Practical Reason*, 80–82, Beck, 84–85. For Kant's complementary account of how the will becomes evil, see Immanuel Kant, *Religion within the Limits of Reason Alone*, trans. T. Greene and H. Hudson (San Francisco: Harper, 1960), 15–39.

41. Kant, *Critique of Practical Reason*, 82, Beck, 86.

42. Jeffrie Murphy once read Kant this way: "On Kant's view, unlike the Christian view, worthiness of respect as a person would seem to be a matter of *degree*—not something owed equally to all members of the human species. People differ in their degree of rationality" ("Afterword: Constitutionalism, Moral Scepticism, and Religious Belief," in A. Rosenbaum, ed., *Constitutionalism: The Philosophical Dimension* [New York: Greenwood, 1988], 239, 245). See also Jeffrie G. Murphy, *Kant: The Philosophy of Right* (Macon: Mercer University Press, 1994), 63–64. But on our reading of Kant, it is simply man's being under a law that he can fulfill, not upon his free choice to honor it, that gives man his dignity. Our reading has the support of Murphy's more recent work: "Following in the path of Christianity's moral egalitarianism, Kant maintains . . . that *all* human beings are to be regarded as possessing that sacred value he calls dignity. All human beings are to be treated with equal concern and respect simply because they are human beings" ("Human Decency and the Limitations of Kantianism," *Rechtstheorie* [Berlin: Duncker and Humblot, 1993] 215, 220–21). Although we concur in Murphy's more recent reading of Kant on this issue, whether Christianity proffers a "moral egalitarianism" is not so clear, as we show in chapters 7 and 8.

43. Kant, *Critique of Practical Reason*, 127 n., Beck, 134. See Sullivan, *Kant's Moral Theory*, 140. Does this make the "adoption" of the maxim an event always discernible to the adopting self? One's own state of perfection would thus be ever perspicuous to self-reflection and immune to self-delusion. Why this would be so, and why it would be important to Kant, is very puzzling.

44. Kant, *Metaphysics of Morals*, 6:446, Gregor, 196.

45. See Kant, *Metaphysics of Morals*, 6:221, Gregor, 14; Sullivan, *Kant's Moral Theory*, 63–75, 184–92. See also Jeffrie G. Murphy, "Kant's Concept of a Right Action," *The Monist* 51, no. 4 (October 1967): 574–98.

It may be, as Kant's critics insist, that the categorical imperative suffers from "vacuity and indeterminateness" (Richard McKeon, "The Development and Significance of the Concept of Responsibility," in Z. McKeon, ed., *"Freedom and History" and Other Essays* [Chicago: University of Chicago Press, 1990], 62, 76–77). But whether the categorical imperative actually *works*, we need not decide; our only question here is whether Kant affirms an order of lateral correct behaviors, and the answer is certainly yes.

46. "If our ability to act morally rightly were . . . dependent on empirical conditions, . . . that would be the death of morality. . . . What moral reason commands *must always* be within our power to do. . . . What is always possible for us to do is to shape our *intentions* in a morally acceptable manner. . . . Morally significant actions, then, for Kant, are *not primarily* performances in the world. . . . Kant did believe that external, visible performances can have moral significance as a sign of our

moral sincerity. . . . We always need to strive with all our power to carry out our moral decisions in our conduct, for such effort indicates the genuineness of our intentions" (Sullivan, *Kant's Moral Theory*, 66–67 [citations and footnotes omitted]).

47. Kant, *Groundwork*, 3/394, Beck, 10.

48. "What the moral law commands, virtue, is always possible to attain. If obedience to that law depended on empirical possibilities, that would destroy its categorical, that is, its moral, character" (Sullivan, introduction to Kant, *Metaphysics of Morals*, xviii).

49. Kant, *Metaphysics of Morals*, 6:434–35, Gregor, 186. Sullivan summarizes this Kantian theme:

> It is because of being under the moral law that each and every person has an intrinsic, inalienable, unconditional, objective worth or dignity . . . as a person. . . . We have an absolute and irreplaceable worth, for our value is not dependent on our usefulness or desirability. . . . Every person attains moral reason and thereby the ability to achieve the highest achievable good, a good will. To be "a man of principle," that is, an autonomous agent, is possible to a person with "the most ordinary human reason" and is of greater worth than having the greatest talent. (Sullivan, *Kant's Moral Theory*, 197)

See also Thomas E. Hill Jr., *Dignity and Practical Reason in Kant's Moral Theory* (Ithaca: Cornell University Press, 1992), 166–67.

Though he is extremely technical, Kant is not always consistent. Occasionally he takes positions that would sever the nerve of his own enterprise, as, for example, when he asserts that man needs a "moral education" in order to become moral (Immanuel Kant, *Education*, trans. A. Churton [Ann Arbor: University of Michigan Press, 1960], 6). How he would reconcile this to the idea that morality is an obligation all are capable of fulfilling, we cannot say.

50. See Kant, *Groundwork*, 66–67/429, Paton, 96.

> Kant's is an ethics of the people, of moral egalitarianism. Nowhere is this more clearly evident than in his second formula [of the categorical imperative]. . . . Respect is an attitude due equally to *every* person, *simply* because each is a person, a rational being capable of moral self-determination. . . . Every person possess moral reason and thereby the ability to achieve the highest achievable good, a good will." (Sullivan, *Kant's Moral Theory*, 197)

51. Williams, "Moral Luck," 36. On Kant's preference for a more comprehensible (semi-)Pelagian God, see infra at n. 60.

52. In one sense it clearly is not. Kant's is an equality among all *rational* beings qua rational, not merely among all rational humans. But we do not consider this problem separately because it is simply another, weaker version of the next objection we consider, viz., that the noumenal self is too emaciated and other-worldly to be recognizable as a person's true self.

53. Williams, "Morality and the Emotions," 228.

54. Ibid.

55. Ibid. Williams's judgment is that Kant's noumenal self amounts to no more than "extravagant metaphysical luggage" (*Ethics and the Limits of Philosophy* [Cambridge: Harvard University Press, 1985], 64–65), a metaphysical deus ex machina in

the service of a transcendental psychology that is "where not unintelligible, certainly false" ("Morality and the Emotions," 207, 228).

56. Ibid. Cf. Allison, *Kant's Theory of Freedom*, 191–98.

57. Sullivan, *Kant's Moral Theory*, xiii. Leszek Kolakowski makes this point powerfully in "Why Do We Need Kant?" (in Kolakowski, *Modernity on Endless Trial* [Chicago: University of Chicago Press, 1990], 44–54).

58. One prominent historian puts it thus, only slightly out of context: "We are all Kantians now" (A. H. Adkins, *Merit and Responsibility* [Oxford: Oxford University Press, 1960], 2).

59. Williams, "The Idea of Equality," in *Problems of the Self*, 235. Part 3 will suggest that Williams's understanding of the "mainstream" of Christianity is parochial.

60. Kant is not a counterexample. We are treating Kant as a philosopher, which is what Kant would have preferred. But, as Kant's critics are quick to add, Kant was more of a theologian than he himself knew. The philosophical premises of Kantianism that render it congenial to human equality ring with the theological themes that in chapter 7 we argue are necessary to any Christian reconciliation with human equality. The so-called philosopher of Protestantism is, in reality, the theologian of semi-Pelagianism. "Christian ethics . . .," in Kant's judgment, "destroyed man's confidence of being wholly adequate to [salvation], at least in this life; but it reestablished it by enabling us to hope that, if we act as well as lies in our power, what is not in our power will come to our aid from another source" (*Critique of Practical Reason*, 127 n., Paton, 134). Embedded here in the core of Enlightenment ethics is the idea of a divine human synergy that is the germ of the Christian hope for human equality. Our reading of Kant harmonizes with Murphy's suggestion that a religious conception of equal human dignity may be at the core, rather than at the margins, of Kant's account. See Murphy, "Human Decency," 220–21. See also Immanuel Kant, *Lectures on Ethics* (New York: Harper Row, 1963), 66. For a detailed and sensitive analysis of the role Kant assigns God in the moral life, see Hare, *The Moral Gap*, 7–98.

CHAPTER 5
NATURE, NATURAL LAW, AND EQUALITY

1. *The African Queen*, based on the 1935 novel by C. S. Forester.

2. Oscar Wilde, *The Picture of Dorian Gray* (Harmondsworth: Penguin, 1985), 102.

3. See Joseph Biden Jr., "Law and Natural Law: Questions for Judge Thomas," *The Washington Post*, September 8, 1991, p. C1; and Philip Soper, "Some Natural Confusions about Natural Law," 90 *Michigan Law Review* 2393, 2403–9 (1992).

4. Rousseau observed: "Knowing nature so little, and agreeing so poorly upon the meaning of the word *law*, it would be very difficult to agree upon a good definition of natural law" (*The First and Second Discourses*, preface to "Discourse on the Origins and Foundations of Inequality," 95). Hobbes took much the same view (*Philosophical Rudiments Concerning Government*, in *English Works*, ed. W. Molesworth [London: Bohn, 1841], vol. 2, 14).

5. Kai Nielsen, *Ethics Without God*, rev. ed. (Buffalo: Prometheus, 1990), 38.

6. " 'Nature'—the image of a reality possessed of an origin, a solidity, and a stability independent of human intervention; a sign for what does not depend on human desire or design; and because of these special characteristics, endowed with an authority that is normative for human conduct" (John T. Noonan Jr., "The Metaphors of Morals," in W. O'Brien, ed., *Riding Time Like a River: The Catholic Moral Tradition since Vatican II* [Washington, D.C.: Georgetown University Press, 1993], 35, 36).

7. Philip Selznick, "Sociology and Natural Law," 6 *Natural Law Forum* 84, 91 (1961).

8. Until Machiavelli dispensed the prince, it would not yield even to the extreme plight of the Italian states and the city of Florence. Machiavelli was a watershed in natural law theory. "It is this rock [of the natural law]," writes Isaiah Berlin, "upon which western beliefs and lives had been founded, that Machiavelli seems, in effect, to have split open" ("The Originality of Machiavelli," in Isaiah Berlin, *Against the Current*, ed. H. Harold [Oxford: Oxford University Press, 1981], 68; see also 36). Unlike Hobbes and his radical individualist successors, Machiavelli did not deny the existence of the natural law; his signal accomplishment was to suppose that there could be exigencies so critical that some people (*viz.*, the new prince) could, indeed must, disregard the natural law. While Machiavelli continued to recognize the reality of a nature that one is to act *against* in emergency, he also proposed the novel suggestion that moral *self*-perfection might come—for a limited few, in limited circumstances—from doing in this manner what is contrary to that nature. See Sebastian de Grazia, *Machiavelli in Hell* (Princeton, N.J.: Princeton University Press, 1989); cf. John Geerken, "Elements of Natural Law Theory in Machiavelli," in H. Johnson, ed., *The Medieval Tradition of Natural Law* (Kalamazoo: Medieval Institute, 1987), 37. The Hobbesian belief that nature is morally mute was the quick and easy expansion of Machiavelli's exception.

9. Obviously "the laws of nature" taken as empirical science are not our topic. Our interest is not in the prediction of phenomena but in natural law as a norm and guide to human moral self-perfection. See A. P. d'Entrèves, *Natural Law: An Introduction to Legal Philosophy* (London: Hutchinson, 1951), 7, 10–11. We are also uninterested in those common American renditions of natural law that view it as an uncontroversial statement of the minima of social justice. See Lon Fuller, *The Morality of Law* (New Haven: Yale University Press, 1969); Russell Hittinger, "Natural Law and Virtue," in Robert George, ed., *Natural Law Theory* (Oxford: Clarendon, 1992), 42. Note, finally, that despite their labels, the literary inventions by the Enlightenment of "states of nature" also do not qualify for discussion in this chapter. This fictional device was (and remains) a favorite of moralists, such as Rousseau and Locke, looking to escape theocratic sources without dishing morality itself. The comparisons we must make are not among contingent conditions of the world that the self inhabits but, rather, among concepts of the selves that do the inhabiting.

10. Our neglect of Aquinas is not an oversight. He would command a place in any fair consideration of the history of natural law theorizing, but we found that the issue of equality comes into bolder relief in the comparison of other natural law theories. (Each of these four theories claims Aquinas as support, and each may be correct.) Natural law is, in any event, only one of the aspects under which Aquinas describes man's morality; we consider the theological perspectives infra, chapter 8.

Our own judgment favors the understanding of Aquinas's doctrine of natural law proposed by Stephen L. Brock, "The Legal Character of Natural Law According to

St. Thomas Aquinas" (unpublished dissertation, University of Toronto, 1988); *accord* James P. Reilly Jr., "Saint Thomas on Law" (*The Etienne Gilson Lecture, 1988*) (Toronto: Pontifical Institute of Medieval Studies, 1990). On this reading, knowledge of the natural law is "knowledge, albeit imperfect, of the very order that the eternal law has instituted or imposed upon God's creatures, even if it is not yet a comprehension of this order in its properly divine or eternal being, nor even an awareness of the fact of its eternal institution by a divine legislator" (id. at 119). So far, a uniform capacity to satisfy the natural law is plausible. But what Brock must conclude later is threatening.

> Even if the original understanding of the principles of natural law is immediate and requires no advertence to God whatsoever, the theoretical judgment on the truth of these principles is rather closely connected with their status as laws of God. And their status as laws of God is much more easily grasped with the help of revelation than through any process of human reasoning. (Id. at 251 [citation omitted])

The plain problem for equality is the gnostic advantage of those who encounter revelation over those who do not.

11. As we proceed to disparage Common Sense natural law, we should be careful to spare that broader version of common sense on which we have rested our own position. Our project has supposed that obtensionalism is not our own invention but is, rather, that version of morality and of the moral self that—for consistency with the convention—must be believed by those who claim that humans are descriptively equal. We think that most people do believe it.

12. "As Aristotle is uniquely the philosopher of common sense, so his moral philosophy is uniquely the ethics of common sense" (Mortimer Adler, *The Time of Our Lives: The Ethics of Common Sense* [New York: Holt, Rinehart and Winston, 1970], 236). See Henry Veatch, *Rational Man: A Modern Interpretation of Aristotelian Ethics* (Bloomington: Indiana University Press, 1964), 69–71; and Vernon Bourke, "Two Approaches to Natural Law," 1 *Natural Law Forum* 92 (1956).

13. We have in mind the following sort of statement:

> There is a universal moral law, as distinct from a moral code, which consists of certain statements of fact about the nature of man; and by behaving in conformity with which, man enjoys his true freedom. This is what the Christian Church calls "the natural law." . . . The universal moral *law* (or natural law of humanity) is discoverable, like any other law of nature, by experience. It cannot be promulgated, it can only be ascertained, because it is a question not of opinion but of fact. . . . At the back of the Christian moral code we find a number of pronouncements about the moral *law*, which are not regulations at all, but which purport to be statements of fact about man and the universe. . . . These statements do not rest on human consent; they are either true or false. If they are true, man runs counter to them at his own peril. (Dorothy Sayers, *The Mind of the Maker* [San Francisco: Harper and Row, 1979], 9–11)

For other examples see C. S. Lewis, *Mere Christianity* (New York: Macmillan, 1952), 18; A. P. d'Entrèves, "The Case For Natural Law Re-examined," 1 *Natural Law Forum* 44–45 (1956); and Joseph Fuchs, *Natural Law: A Theological Investigation* (Dublin: Gill, 1965), 8.

14. For a classic statement of this essentialist aspect of morality, see Josef Pieper, *Living the Truth* (San Francisco: Ignatius Press, 1989), 109–77. "Action is really determined by the objective reality itself" (id. at 144).

15. For a typical exposition of this neo-Aristotelian, but-not-quite-natural-law position, see Jude Dougherty, "What Judge Thomas Did Not Say," *The Modern Schoolman* 69 (1992): 395, 400.

16. Ibid. See also the discussion of Veatch's position in Robert George, "Natural Law and Human Nature" in George, *Natural Law Theory*, 31, 33.

17. See Aristotle, *Physics*, II.3, 194b32–195a2. See also W.K.C. Guthrie, *A History of Greek Philosophy*, vol 6, *Aristotle: An Encounter* (Cambridge: Cambridge University Press, 1981), 117–18; Jacques Maritain, *Moral Philosophy* (London: Bles, 1964), 58: "In Aristotle's dynamic conception all essence is the assignment of an end, a telos—which beings endowed with reason pursue freely, not by necessity. Become in your action what you are in your essence—here is the primordial rule of ethics"; Walter Farrell, *The Natural Moral Law According to St. Thomas and Suarez* (dissertation, University of Fribourg, Switzerland) (Ditchling: St. Dominic's Press, 1930), 132; Leo Strauss, *Natural Right and History* (Chicago: University of Chicago Press, 1953), 7–8; and Veatch, *Human Rights*, 68–86.

18. Veatch, *Human Rights*, 56.

19. Vernon Bourke, "Is Thomas Aquinas a Natural Law Ethicist?" *The Monist* 58 (1974): 52, 65. Cf. Jacques Maritain, "Natural Law and Moral Law," in R. Anshen, ed., *The Moral Principles of Action: Man's Ethical Imperative* (New York: Harper and Brothers, 1952), 62, 62–63. Joseph Owens correctly has Aristotle in accord, the necessary relations being ones of "seemliness" or "congruence" ("The Grounds of Ethical Universality in Aristotle," 162).

20. Vernon Bourke, *History of Ethics* (New York: Doubleday, 1968), 90. The word "complexus" has a long history in the Latin language and many denotations, but Bourke's meaning here seems to be the core one of a "union" or "coming together."

21. "Natural law is not a written law. Men know it with greater or less difficulty, and in different degrees, running the risk of error here as elsewhere. . . . That every sort of error and deviation is possible in the determination of these things [of the natural law] merely proves that our sight is weak, our nature coarse, and that innumerable accidents can corrupt our judgment" (Jacques Maritain, "Natural Law in Aquinas," in C. Curran and R. McCormick, eds., *Readings in Moral Theology*, no. 7 (New York: Paulist Press, 1991), 114, 118.

22. This quotation from MacIntyre continues: "Modern ethics asks, What ought I do if I am to do right? and it asks this question in such a way that doing right is made something quite independent of faring well" (Alasdair MacIntyre, *A Short History of Ethics* [New York: Macmillan, 1966], 84). See also Martha Nussbaum, *The Fragility of Goodness* (Cambridge: Cambridge University Press, 1986), 5; Williams, *Ethics and the Limits of Philosophy*, supra; and Werner Jaeger, *Paideia: The Ideals of Greek Culture* (Oxford: Blackwell, 1961), vol. 3, 25–26; vol. 1, 303–4.

23. See generally Georg Wieland, "Happiness: The Perfection of Man," in N. Kretzman et al., eds., *The Cambridge History of Later Medieval Philosophy* (Cambridge: Cambridge University Press, 1982), 673. See infra chap. 8 at 198. The Greek word literally means to have a good god watching over.

24. Maritain, *Moral Philosophy*, 34.

25. Id. at 48. See Aristotle, *Nicomachean Ethics*, I.7, 1098a17–19 ("One swallow does not make a summer . . . and . . . a short time . . . does not make a man blessed and happy"); I.8, 1099a31–1099b8; I.10, 1101a14–20; X.6–9, 1176a30–1181b25; VII.13, 1153b16–21; *Magna Moralia*, II.8, 1206b30–35. See also Nussbaum, *The Fragility of Goodness*, 318–72; cf. 373–77.

26. Indeed, Aristotle can be read as correcting the abstract excesses of Plato.

27. Maritain, *Moral Philosophy*, 47–48 (emphasis added).

28. Id. at 33.

29. But even this is not so clear:

Many changes occur in life, and all manner of chances, and the most prosperous may fall into great misfortunes in old age, as is told of Priam in the Trojan Cycle; and one who has experienced such chances and has ended wretchedly no one calls happy. (*Nicomachean Ethics* I.9, 1100a1)

30. Even Dodds can be read to share this perception:

Oedipus is great . . . in virtue of his . . . strength to pursue the truth at whatever personal cost, and strength to accept it and endure it when found. "This horror is mine," he cries, "and none but I is strong enough to bear it." Oedipus is great because he accepts the responsibility for *all* his acts, including those which are objectively most horrible, though subjectively innocent. (E. R. Dodds, "On Misunderstanding the *Oedipus Rex*," in *Greece and Rome* 13 [1966]: 37, 48)

Cf. Stanley Hauerwas, *Truthfulness and Tragedy* (Notre Dame: Notre Dame University Press, 1977), 64–70.

No doubt there are many possible meanings for "tragedy," and the specifically Greek idea of it had the signal virtue of assuring that the Greeks would write the most perfect specimens of one great form of literature. We also agree (*pace* Plato) with the conclusion of Aristotle and Nussbaum that human life is genuinely diminished by disease, loneliness, and lucklessness. Nussbaum is correct: "I am an agent, but also a plant" (Nussbaum, *The Fragility of Goodness*, 5). What the authors— and equality—could not accept is that the highest human worth—moral worth—is snatched away in the withering of the plant. Nussbaum insists:

How many who live together really *live* together, "sharing in speech and reason"? . . . It is, in fact, an extraordinary demand to make on the world; those who make it are likely to be unhappy. But since the goal of the Aristotelian is not so much happiness in the sense of contentment as it is fullness of life and richness of value, it is no solution to omit a value for happiness's sake, to reduce your demands on the world in order to get more pleasing answers from the world. The Aristotelian will simply take on the world and see what can be done with it. (Id. at 369)

This is part and parcel of Nussbaum's diatribe against Kant (see supra chap. 4 at 121). But this refuses, deliberately, even to distinguish between moral and nonmoral goods. Nussbaum thereby creates a false dilemma. Equality omits no value, and it encourages "fullness of life"; it insists, however, that the highest kind of personal worth, even in those who have the least control of their environment, is invulnerable to chance.

31. Hannah Arendt, *On Revolution* (Harmondsworth: Penguin, 1977), 190. For another statement of this "trouble" with natural law, see Yves Simon, *The Tradition of Natural Law* (New York: Fordham, 1965), 110–45, esp. 136–45. See also Kai Nielsen, "The Myth of Natural Law," in S. Hook, ed., *Law and Philosophy* (New York: New York University Press, 1964), 122, 129 ("If there is no God . . . [then] the classical natural law theory is absurd"); and G.E.M. Anscombe, "Modern Moral Philosophy," in *The Collected Philosophical Papers of G.E.M. Anscombe*, Vol. 3: *Ethics, Religion and Politics* (Minneapolis: University of Minnesota Press, 1981), 26, 30–31.

32. See, for example, I. Gury, S.I., *Compendium Theologiae Moralis*, 15th ed. (1907), vol. 1, 122–23, § 122 n. 1:

> Objectum vero legis naturalis *formale* non quidem in convenientia cum natura rationali, non in perfectione eidem naturae debita, quae ideo quaerenda sit, neque in necessitate quadam aut convenientia cum felici statu naturae humanae sive in individuis, sive in societate debet reponi; *sed in ratione praecepti a Deo hominibus impositi*; adeo ut dictamen rationis haberi debeat tanquam promulgatio divinae ordinationis, seu signum divinae voluntatis aut praecipientis aut vetantis. Unde illud s. Anselmi: *Quicumque legi naturali obviat, Dei voluntatem non servat.* Quocirca concinne ac proprie definiri lex naturalis posset: *Iudicium intellectus de voluntate Dei supremi naturae gubernatoris, mala vetantis ac bona praecipientis.*

> The formal object of the natural law should be placed not in a harmony with rational nature, nor in the perfection owed that nature (which therefore should be sought), nor even in some exigence of or harmony with a flourishing state of human nature, whether in individuals or in society; but rather in the rationale of a precept imposed on man by God, so that the command of reason should be as a promulgation of a divine decree or as a sign of the divine will both commanding and prohibiting. Thus St. Anselm says, "Whoever opposes the natural law does not obey the will of God." Wherefore natural law can nicely and properly be defined as the judgment of the intellect regarding the will of God, the supreme governor of nature, prohibiting evil and commanding good. (Brennan's translation)

33. See, for example, Bourke, *History of Ethics*, 124: "It would be difficult to overstate the scope of Suarez's influence in ethics."

34. Suarez had been a law student before becoming a Jesuit (id. at 123).

35. All references to the text of Suarez are to the *Tractatus de Legibus, ac Deo Legislatore* (1612) by book, chapter, and section. The translations are from *Selections from Three Works of Francisco Suarez, S.J.*, vol. 2 (Oxford: Clarendon, 1944), although in a few places we have adapted the translation based on the Latin text of the *Tractatus de Legibus* in Francisco Suarez, *Opera Omnia*, vols. 5, 6, ed. C. Berton (Paris: Vives, 1856).

36. The "as it were" is necessary because, as we shall see, although Suarez maintains, on the one hand, that it is the real relation of man's rational nature to other natures that founds these conformities, his predominating opinion is that they are contained not in the world but in a set of deductive propositions. The two positions appear to us incompatible.

37. Cf. John Finnis, *Natural Law and Natural Rights* (Oxford: Oxford University Press, 1988), 45–46, 59, 61.

38. "As a result of this diminished reality in the universality of human nature, Suarez is forced to adopt a teaching on ethical obligation that stresses the basing of this oughtness on God's will" (Bourke, *History of Ethics*, 122).

39. See also 2.13.9; 2.16.3; 2.8.3.

40. "In the end the function of reason remains purely informative, not legislative" (Louis Dupré, *Passage to Modernity: An Essay in the Hermeneutics of Nature and Culture* [New Haven: Yale University Press, 1993], 137).

41. See Suarez, *Tractatus de Legibus*, 2.6.11–13; 2.5.9; 2.5.5; 2.6.5–6. See also id. at 2.6.13.

42. See Farrell, *The Natural Moral Law*, 148–54. See also Bourke, *History of Ethics*, 123: "Natural law has an obligatory force from the will of God."; Suarez, *Tractatus de Legibus* 2.6.17; and Brock, *The Legal Character of Natural Law According to St. Thomas Aquinas*, 45 n.48.

43. Suarez reasons that from the time God freely willed to create humans with the capacity to know and do good and evil, God was obliged to command that humans so act, for it would be "in the highest degree foreign to the divine wisdom and goodness" to fail to command humans to do what is good and to avoid what is evil. "The morality caused by the Natural Moral Law is indeed distinct from the 'natural honesty and malice' of acts, according to Suarez, yet de facto these two moralities are inseparable and God cannot refrain from commanding and prohibiting the acts which form the subject matter of the Natural Moral Law" (Farrell, *The Natural Moral Law*, 122).

44. See 2.6.8, 12–13.

45. Id. at introduction to book 2. See 2.9.6.

46. Cf. 2.15.15.

47. Suarez hedges with the Latin word "*parum*," which we translate as "particularly."

48. See id. at 2.7.4; 2.4.4; 2.7.10; 2.8.4. These two formulations, one having to do with natural perfection, the other with "rectitude," reflect the duality in Suarez's conception of the natural law: natural finality and command. Cf. preface to *De Legibus*.

49. Immanuel Kant, *Fundamental Principles of the Metaphysics of Morals*, in Kant, *"Critique of Practical Reason" and Other Works on the Theory of Ethics*, 6th ed., trans. T. Abbot (London: Longmans, Green, 1909), 43.

50. Pope Leo XIII's encyclical *Aeterni patris* (1879) identified the crisis and prescribed a renewal of Thomistic thought.

51. Cf. Stout, "Truth, Natural Law, and Ethical Theory," in George, *Natural Law Theory*, 95:

> Many theorists decided that something less cosmological, something having to do with *human* nature or practical reason or collective intersubjectivity, would have to be substituted for the traditional correspondence relation if the notion of moral truth was to be retained. Some of the resulting programmes, which I am calling anti-realist, called themselves natural law theories, but they were hardly of the traditional kind.

See also George, "Natural Law and Human Nature," in id. at 31.

52. Finnis's and Grisez's criticism of the traditional natural law theories clarifies their own theory in these respects.

> The scholastic natural law theory must be rejected. It moves by a logically illicit step—from human nature as a given reality, to what ought and what ought not to be chosen. Its proponents attempt to reinforce this move, from what is to what ought to be, by appealing to God's command. But for two reasons this fails to help matters. First, unless there is a logically prior moral norm indicating that God's commands are to be obeyed, any command of God considered by itself would merely be another fact which tells us nothing about how we ought to respond. Second, even leaving this problem aside, the difficulty remains that human persons are unlike other natural entities; it is not human nature as a given, but possible human fulfillment which must provide the intelligible norms for free choices. (Germain Grisez, *The Way of the Lord Jesus*, vol. 1, *Christian Moral Principles* [Chicago: Franciscan Herald, 1983], 105 [citations and italics omitted])

See also Finnis, *Natural Law and Natural Rights*, 42–46, 342–43, 348–50; Germain Grisez, "The First Principle of Practical Reason: A Commentary on the *Summa theologiae* Question 94, Article 2," 10 *Natural Law Forum* 168 (1965). Cf. Russell Hittinger, *A Critique of the New Natural Law Theory* (Notre Dame: Notre Dame University Press, 1987), 14–20.

53. George, "Natural Law and Human Nature," in George, *Natural Law Theory*, 34.

54. Id. Contra Common Sense and Classic, it is on this account that Integration claims that "practical knowledge cannot have its truth by conformity to what is known. Rather, a practical proposition is true by anticipating the realization of that which is possible through acting in conformity with that proposition, and by directing one's action toward that realization" (Germain Grisez, Joseph Boyle, and John Finnis, "Practical Principles, Moral Truth, and Ultimate Ends," 32 *American Journal of Jurisprudence* 99, 114, 116 [1987]).

55. See Finnis, *Natural Law and Natural Rights*, 59–99, esp. 85–90; Grisez, Boyle, and Finnis, "Practical Principles, Moral Truth, and Ultimate Ends," 106–8.

56. George, "Natural Law and Human Nature," 31.

57. "Self-evident principles are *per se nota*—known just by knowing the meaning of their terms. This does not mean that they are mere linguistic clarifications, nor that they are intuitions—insights unrelated to data" (Grisez, Boyle, and Finnis, "Practical Principles, Moral Truth, and Ultimate Ends," 106).

58. Letter of Joseph Boyle to Brennan, July 6, 1992.

59. See Finnis, *Natural Law and Natural Rights*, 92–95. "The distinguishing characteristic of Finnis' system is the independence of one value from another so that each is self-asserting because of its intrinsic worth" (Terence Kennedy, "The Originality of John Finnis' Conception of the Natural Law," in C. Curran and R. McCormick, eds., *Readings in Moral Theology*, no. 7 [Mahwah, N.J.: Paulist Press, 1991], 124, 132).

60. Grisez, *Christian Moral Principles*, 105.

61. Abstracted from the seven basic goods in which it is given, this principle is known as the *first principle of practical reason*.

62. Grisez, Boyle, and Finnis, "Practical Principles, Moral Truth, and Ultimate Ends," 121.

63. John Finnis, "Natural Law and Legal Reasoning," 38 *Cleveland State Law Review* 1, 3 (1990).

64. Cf. Grisez, Boyle, and Finnis, "Practical Principles, Moral Truth, and Ultimate Ends," 127–28.

65. Ibid., 132. See also John Finnis, *Fundamentals of Ethics* (Washington, D.C.: Georgetown University Press, 1987), 72.

66. "While the basic goods, considered as principles of practical knowledge, are not ordered among themselves, it does not follow that these principles are an unordered crowd. Prior to anyone's choice, unfettered practical reason, together with the conditions which human nature inevitably sets for moral life, establish certain natural priorities among a good person's basic interests. It follows that these priorities set necessary conditions for any morally good life plan" (Grisez, Boyle, and Finnis, "Practical Principles, Moral Truth, and Ultimate Ends," 138–39). Cf. George, "Natural Law and Human Nature," 35–36; and cf. Ralph McInerny, *Ethica Thomistica* (Washington D.C.: Catholic University of America Press, 1982), 48–56.

67. See Hittinger, *A Critique of the New Natural Law Theory*, 93–154.

68. R. A. Connor, review of Russell Hittinger's *A Critique of the New Natural Law Theory*, 33 *American Journal of Jurisprudence* 250, 254, 255–56 (1988).

69. These doubts are increased by the generous comment of a collaborator of Finnis and Grisez. In a letter to Brennan (July 6, 1992), Joseph Boyle observes: "I am not sure what you . . . mean by 'does his best but still gets it wrong.' " We can appreciate the puzzlement. In a sincere attempt to engage the equality issue as we posed it, he considers a number of permutations of the "does his best but gets it wrong" theme. He *excuses* the person who does an intrinsically evil act, because he had to act without sufficient reflection; but he will not concede that in making this choice this mistaken person is morally *perfected.*

Its incompatibility with human equality is just the beginning of the trouble created by the natural lawyer's taking refuge in excuse. Christian moral *theology*, as we shall see (infra chap. 8), has God excusing persons that act wrongly out of certain kinds of ignorance. In that context, the category of the excused makes some sense, because there is, as a part of the system, a person, namely God, to do the excusing. In its own right, however, natural law lacks any such person. Acts are either in accord with nature (or integral human fulfillment) or they are not. If people who perform acts of the latter sort are found to be "excused," it will have been through the beneficent agency of *someone*—not, we submit, by nature. What it would mean for nature to excuse the good faith wrongdoer (or anyone, for that matter), we cannot understand.

70. Robert P. George, *Making Men Moral: Civil Liberties and Public Morality* (Oxford: Clarendon, 1993), 39.

71. Ibid. See also id. at 102.

72. In this respect, Integration amounts to a distinction from Aristotle without an important difference and with all the dangers:

For [Aristotle], it is always important to ask whether two human beings are equally capable of virtuous activity, before we determine whether the good of one should be given greater weight than the good of the other. If they are equals, then it may be appropriate for them to compromise and share the good; and if they are unequals, then one should serve the other, promoting his own interests primarily because this helps another achieve a superior way of life. (Richard Kraut, *Aristotle on the Human Good* [Princeton, N.J.: Princeton University Press, 1989], 109)

See also supra chap. 1 at 35.

73. There are at least five useful, general introductions to Lonergan's work. See Joseph Flanagan, *Quest for Self-Knowledge* (Toronto: University of Toronto, 1997); Frederick Crowe, *Lonergan* (Collegeville: The Liturgical Press, 1992); Hugo Meynell, *An Introduction to the Philosophy of Bernard Lonergan*, 2d ed. (Toronto: University of Toronto Press, 1991); Patrick Byrne, "The Fabric of Lonergan's Thought," in Fred Lawrence, ed., *Lonergan Workshop*, vol. 6 (Atlanta: Scholars Press, 1986), 1–84; and David Tracy, *The Achievement of Bernard Lonergan* (New York: Herder, 1970) (completed before Lonergan had finished what he regarded as his magnum opus). A superb introduction to Lonergan's ethics is Frederick Crowe, "An Exploration of Lonergan's New Notion of Value," in Michael Vertin, ed., *Appropriating the Lonergan Idea* (Washington, D.C.: Catholic University of America Press, 1989), 51. To appreciate the person of Lonergan interacting with his ideas, see Richard Liddy, *Transforming Light: Intellectual Conversion in the Early Lonergan* (Collegeville: Liturgical Press, 1993). A succint exposition of Lonergan's basic stance is presented in Patrick Brennan, "Discovering the Archimedean Element in (Judicial) Judgment," *Law and Philosophy* 17 (1998): 177–92.

74. See Thomas Nagel, *The View From Nowhere* (Oxford: Oxford University Press, 1986); "The Limits of Objectivity," in S. McMurrin, ed., *The Tanner Lectures on Human Values*, vol. 1 (Salt Lake City: University of Utah Press, 1980), 75–140.

75. Bernard Lonergan, *Understanding and Being: The Halifax Lectures on Insight*, 2d ed., vol. 5, *The Collected Works of Bernard Lonergan* (Toronto: University of Toronto Press, 1990), 175–76; Lonergan, *Insight*, 377, 634.

76. Richard Rorty, *Philosophy and the Mirror of Nature*, (Princeton, N.J.: Princeton University Press, 1979), 340; see also Rorty, "Solidarity or Objectivity?" in Rorty, ed., *Objectivity, Relativism, and Truth: Philosophical Papers*, vol. 1 (Cambridge: Cambridge University Press, 1991), 21–34.

77. Bernard Lonergan, *Method in Theology* (Minneapolis: Seabury, 1972), 19–20.

78. Ibid.

79. See Bernard Lonergan, "Cognitional Structure," in *Collection*, 2d ed., vol. 4, *The Collected Works of Bernard Lonergan* (Toronto: University of Toronto Press, 1988), 205, 208–11.

80. Bernard J. F. Lonergan, "The Subject," in *A Second Collection*, 69.

81. On these three operations, see Lonergan, *Method*, 9; Lonergan, *Insight*, 271–78. On probabilistic judgments, see infra at 224. To anticipate a little, it is their availability that makes equality possible: "The variety of possible answers makes full allowance for the misfortunes and shortcomings of the person answering, and by the same stroke it closes the door on possible excuses for mistakes. A judgment is the responsibility of the one that judges. It is a personal commitment" (id. at 272).

82. Lonergan, "The Subject," 79.

83. Lonergan, *Method*, 121. See also Lonergan, *Insight*, 599.

84. Lonergan, *Method*, 19; *Insight*, 276–77.

85. Lonergan, *Method*, 17.

86. Id. at 16. "The unity of consciousness is itself given; the pattern of operations is part of the experience of the operations; and inquiry and discovery are needed, not to effect the synthesis of a manifold that, as given, is unrelated, but to analyze a functional and functioning unity" (id. at 17). In *Insight* Lonergan characterizes this eros as one of the mind, whereas in *Method* it emerges more clearly as one that involves understanding but passes *beyond* to responsibility. See Crowe, "An Exploration of Lonergan's New Notion of Value," 54. For Lonergan's own characterization of the difference in the treatment he gives this level in *Insight* and *Method*, respectively, see "*Insight* Revisited," in *A Second Collection*, 263, 272.

87. Lonergan, *Method*, 13.

88. Lonergan, *Insight*, 332.

89. Lonergan, *Method*, 20.

90. Id. at 20.

91. Id. at 18.

92. Lonergan describes this as "sublation," but it must not be understood in the Hegelian sense of rejecting what is surpassed. See id. at 241. See also Lonergan, "Cognitional Structure," 220; and "The Subject," 80.

93. Bernard Lonergan, "Mission and the Spirit," in *A Third Collection: Papers by Bernard J. F. Lonergan, S.J.*, ed. F. Crowe (London: Chapman, 1985), 23, 29. See Lonergan, *Insight*, 604.

94. "Objective knowing is not yet authentic human living; but without objective knowing there is no authentic living; for one knows objectively just insofar as one is neither unperceptive, nor stupid, nor silly; and one does not live authentically inasmuch as one is either unperceptive or stupid or silly" (Lonergan, "Cognitional Structure," 220).

95. Lonergan, *Method*, 292.

96. Lonergan, "Cognitional Structure," 213.

97. Lonergan, *Understanding and Being*, 172.

98. Lionel Trilling, *Sincerity and Authenticity* (Cambridge: Harvard University Press, 1971).

99. See Lonergan, *Insight*, 115–28, 259–62, 272, 299–304, 510, 549–52.

100. First there must be "conversion." "Moral conversion changes the criterion of one's decisions and choices from satisfactions to values. . . . Such conversion . . . falls far short of moral perfection" (Lonergan, *Method*, 240). And with that the work has just begun. "One has *yet to uncover and root out* . . . bias. One has to *keep developing* one's knowledge. . . . One has to *keep scrutinizing* one's intentional responses. . . . One has to *listen to criticism* and to protest. One has to *remain ready to learn* from others. For moral knowledge is the proper possession only of morally good men and, until one has merited that title, one has still to *advance* and to *learn*" (ibid.; footnote omitted, emphasis added). See id. at 52, 268. "It is . . . only by reaching the sustained self-transcendence of the virtuous man that one becomes a good judge, not on this or that human act, but on the whole range of human goodness" (Lonergan, *Method*, 35). See Crowe, "Lonergan's New Notion of Value," 61–62.

101. Tad Dunne, *Lonergan and Spirituality* (Chicago: Loyola University Press, 1985), 62.

102. Lonergan, *Insight*, 689.

103. Dunne, *Lonergan and Spirituality*, 62.

104. "Concretely it remains difficult to tell whether or not we are being authentic" (id. at 61).

105. Id. at 66.

106. Lonergan, "The Subject," 83. Here we can put in context the words we first encountered in chapter 3: "By his own acts the human subject makes himself what he is to be, and he does so freely and responsibly; indeed, he does so precisely because his acts are the free and responsible expressions of himself" (id. at 79). See Lonergan, *Method*, 38; Lonergan, *Understanding and Being*, 234; and Crowe, *Lonergan*, 131.

107. Lonergan, *Insight*, 278.

108. See id. at 689.

109. See ibid.

110. Bernard J. F. Lonergan, "The Transition from a Classicist World-View to Historical Mindedness," in *A Second Collection*, 1, 2; Lonergan, *Insight*, 618; David Granfield, *The Inner Experience of Law: A Jurisprudence of Subjectivity* (Washington, D.C.: Catholic University of America Press, 1988), 177–216, passim; Michael Novak, "Bernard Lonergan: A New Approach to Natural Law" in *Proceedings of the American Catholic Philosophical Association* 41 (1967): 246: "Natural law is not constituted by an 'objective code'; it is constituted by a set of dynamically related operations on the part of each individual person" (id. at 248–49 [citation omitted]).

111. We do more to show Lonergan's harmony with human equality in John Coons and Patrick Brennan, "Created Equal: Lonergan Explains Jefferson," ed. Fred Lawrence, *Lonergan Workshop* (Boston College, 1995), vol. 12, 45–76.

112. Cf. Lonergan, "Natural Right and Historical Mindedness," in *A Third Collection*, ed. F. Crowe (Mahwah: Paulist Press, 1985), 172: "Now Aristotle defined a nature as an immanent principle of movement and of rest. In man such a principle is the human spirit as raising and answering questions. As raising questions, it is an immanent principle of movement. As answering questions and doing so satisfactorily, it is an immanent principle of rest."

113. See Aquinas, *Summa theologiae*, Ia–IIae, prologue to "Treatise on Habits" and prologue to "Treatise on Law." See also *Summa theologiae*, Ia–IIae, q. 58, a. 2.

114. Kenneth L. Woodward, "What Is Virtue?" *Newsweek*, June 13, 1994, 38, 39.

115. Preeminent among these are Alasdair MacIntyre's *After Virtue*, supra, in which MacIntyre argues for something like Aristotle's account of the virtues but shorn of Aristotle's "metaphysical biology" (148), and Stanley Hauerwas's *Character and the Christian Life: A Study in Theological Ethics* (San Antonio: Trinity University Press, 1985), in which Hauerwas makes virtue and character, in the tradition of Aristotle and Aquinas, a concern for Protestant ethics.

116. This is an instance of the general Aristotelian preference for act over potency. See also Nussbaum, *The Fragility of Goodness*, 322–27, esp. 324.

117. Woodward, "What Is Virtue?" (emphasis in original). Aquinas, for example, limits virtue to those states of character that are in accord with right reason and thus incline their possessor to specific real goods. See James Keenan, *Goodness and*

Rightness in Thomas Aquinas's Summa Theologiae (Washington, D.C.: Georgetown University Press, 1992), 92–116. "The moral virtues concern attainment, not striving. . . . In the ambit of Thomas's discussion on the moral virtues, his goodness always means our rightness" (id. at 105).

PART III
COULD THE CHRISTIANS BELIEVE IN HUMAN EQUALITY?

1. Brennan's translation. *The New Jerusalem Bible* renders the text thus: "The Word was the real light that gives light to everyone; he was coming into the world." Both the Greek and Latin texts allow other translations, and *The New Jerusalem Bible* provides these English alternatives: "The true light, that which enlightens every man, was coming into the world," or "He (the Word) was the real light that enlightens every man who comes into the world." For a collection of interpretations, remarkable for their capacity to make "every" mean "some," see Thomas Aquinas, *Super Evangelium S. Ioannis Lectura*, ed. P. Cal, O.P. (Turin: Marietti, 1952), Lectura 5, §§ 124–36.

CHAPTER 6
THE FRAMEWORK FOR A CHRISTIAN OBTENSIONALISM

1. Something like this moved Hasidics in their reaction to the elitism of the learned. See Joseph Telushkin, *Jewish Literacy* (New York: William Morrow, 1991), 214–18; and Stephen Wylen, *Settings of Silver: An Introduction to Judaism* (Mahwah, N.J.: Paulist Press, 1991), 250–57; bibliography, 378. "Instead of remaining the province of a few esoteric specialists, the mystical concern to hasten the time of redemption became a responsibility of ordinary people as well" (Roy Rosenberg, *The Concise Guide to Judaism: History, Practice, Faith* [New York: Mentor, 1991], 156).

2. As the whole of this book affirms, viewing the moral impulse as an *invitation* to a possible perfection is not exclusive to theistic systems: "All of our ways of looking at men carry with them, explicitly or implicitly, requests to take up an attitude toward life, to complete oneself by acquiring a distinctive set of sentiments and motivations" (John Chapman, "Toward a General Theory of Human Nature and Dynamics," in J. R. Pennock and J. Chapman, eds., *Nomos XVII: Human Nature in Politics* [New York: New York University Press, 1977], 292, 312).

3. That the Christian's call to salvation is a call to "perfection" is amply demonstrated in Robert Flew, *The Idea of Perfection in Christian Theology* (London: Oxford University Press, 1934), as is the multiplicity of ways in which Christians have conceived of perfection. Flew has twenty-two chapters, each presenting a distinctive answer to the question, what is Christian perfection. "Like some phrase of music which summarizes and concludes a symphony, so the aspiration after perfection gives unity and harmony to the whole [Christian] discourse" (id. at 5).

4. In a third version (e.g., *Luke* 14:23), attendance is by compulsion rather than invitation. Were this the rule, conventional human equality would be an impossibility. However, as the detailed discussions of chapters 7 and 8 reveal, few theologians today have God totally eliminating the requirement of some free human response.

5. This "deal" between God and man is not intended as an analogy to contract with its central metaphor of offer and acceptance between equal parties; lawyers will recognize the further technical difficulty about "consideration." The relation has aspects of "promissory estoppel," but the best jurisprudential analogy seems to be "gift on condition."

6. "Oration on the Dignity of Man," in V. Gollancz, ed., *A Year of Grace* (London: Gollancz, 1950), 276–77.

7. One signal advantage for equality is the commitment of scripture to a single original pair and their *common* corruption in the Fall, one that is transmissible in a fixed form. Neither Cain's spectacular defection (nor any succeeding sin) introduces any change of essence among the ramifying bloodlines.

8. Gene Outka's magisterial statement of the elements and implications of Kierkegaard's vision of equality could serve as the outline of a separate book. See supra chap. 1 at 36–37.

9. Andrew Greeley has a way of putting this sort of question to Catholics that might be extended to all Christians: "I don't like the way the bottom line is worded. I would much prefer to say not, 'What do we *have* to believe?' or 'What must we believe?' but 'What *may* we believe?' Even better, 'What are we lucky enough to believe?' Best of all 'What are we *privileged* to believe?' " (*The Bottom Line Catechism* [Chicago: Thomas More, 1982], 7).

10. M. Harrington, *The Long Distance Runner* (New York: Henry Holt, 1988), 240–41.

11. Roberto Unger, *Knowledge and Politics* (New York: Free Press, 1975), 295. Still a third style of response to God's reserve is that of Bertrand Russell:

A woman . . . [wanted to know] what would he say, if when the moment came, it turned out that he had been wrong all this time and now found himself standing outside the Pearly Gates? Russell's eyes lit up, she told me, and he responded with eagerness. "Why, I should say," he cried, in his high, thin voice, "I should say, 'God, you gave us insufficient evidence!' " (R. Angell, "First Tuesday," *The New Yorker*, November 9, 1992, 148)

12. For example, Arthur Leff, "Unspeakable Ethics, Unnatural Law," 6 *Duke Law Review* 1229 (1979).

13. In *Rosencrantz and Guildenstern* Tom Stoppard sees that no departure of this sort could ever wholly succeed in its object:

Guil: A man breaking his journey between one place and another at a third place of no name, character, population or significance, sees a unicorn cross his path and disappear. That in itself is startling, but there are precedents for mystical encounters of various kinds, or to be less extreme, a choice of persuasions to put it down to fancy; until—"My God," says a second man, "I must be dreaming, I thought I saw a unicorn." At which point, a dimension is added that makes the experience as alarming as it will ever be. A third witness, you understand, adds no further dimension but only spreads it thinner, and a fourth thinner still, and the more witnesses there are the thinner it gets and the more reasonable it becomes until it is as thin as reality, the name we give to the common experience. . . . "Look, look!" recites the crowd. "A horse with an arrow in its forehead! It must have been mistaken for a deer." (*Rosencrantz and Guilden-stern Are Dead* [New York: Grove, 1967], 21)

14. When Dante wrote "I came to myself within a dark wood where the straight way was lost," he could—up to that point—have been reporting the daily experience of all of us. And seldom in the dark wood of real life do the rest of us encounter a Virgil—much less a Beatrice—either of whom might be recommended to Roberto Unger as his second choice.

15. "God prefers rather to incline the will than the intellect. Perfect clearness would be of use to the intellect, and would harm the will" (Pascal, *Pensees* § 580).

16. Gilson, *The History of Christian Philosophy in the Middle Ages*, 138–39.

17. Eric Voegelin would go a good deal further: "Uncertainty is the very essence of Christianity," and failure to grasp this is the fatal first step on the easy road to gnosticism (*The New Science of Politics*, 122). And the tragedy of twentieth-century politics in Europe was that "gnostic speculation overcame the uncertainty of faith" (id. at 129).

18. Iris Murdoch nicely compresses the picture of what she calls Kant's "agnosticism," which we would describe as the saving obscurity of his vision:

Kant says that if we were certain of God's existence and were able to see him, we would have no free will and would be merely puppets. He thus establishes agnosticism as a condition of morality . . . [L]ater . . . he explains his agnostic position in more passionate and informal and less metaphysical terms. . . . [H]e repeats that the subjective ground is inscrutable and that if we had certain knowledge of God we would lose our freedom. (Murdoch, *Metaphysics as a Guide to Morals*, 446)

19. We are not proposing Tertullian's "*credo quia absurdum*" as part of the model. Most theologians understand faith as consistent with, and many consider it the outcome of, reason. "In coming to faith, believers normally employ a 'logic of discovery' in which the mind, pondering the clues, is guided by a hope-filled anticipation of God's self-revelation. . . . Reason operates not only in the approach to faith but also in the act of faith and in the subsequent reflection in which one's understanding of the mysteries of faith is deepened" (Avery Dulles, *The Assurance of Things Hoped For* [Oxford: Oxford University Press, 1994], 221).

20. *A New Catechism: Catholic Faith for Adults* (authorized edition of the Dutch Catechism) (New York: Seabury, 1969), 294.

21. Id. at 126.

22. Id. at 293–94. However we put this, it is a distinction between two states of the will:

The difference between the two states of mind is moral, not intellectual. Faith says, Yes, I will, *though* I am not sure. Doubt says, No, I will not, *because* I am not sure, but they agree in not being sure. Both faith and doubt would be swallowed up in actual knowledge and direct experience. (James Stephen, *Liberty, Equality, Fraternity* [London: Smith, Elder, 1873], 323)

23. *A New Catechism*, 297. Only slightly out of context, John Henry Newman adds this: "Doubt itself is a positive state, and implies a definite habit of mind, and

thereby necessarily involves a system of principles and doctrines all its own" (*A Grammar of Assent*, 294).

24. *A New Catechism*, 293.

25. Isaac Singer, *The Collected Stories* (New York: Farrar, Straus & Giroux, 1953), 35.

26. "Is it simply a kind of godlessness . . . that cries for the forbidden fruit that Kierkegaard called 'direct information' . . .?" (Karl Barth, *The Word of God and the Word of Man* [New York: Harper and Row, 1957], 175).

27. Graham Greene, *Monsignor Quixote* (New York: Washington Square Press, 1982), 68. Though man never can confirm the providential role of obscurity, he can speak of it with confidence: "The world of creation cannot as yet see Reality, not because it chooses to be blind, but because in God's purpose it has been so limited" (J. Ferguson, *Pelagius* [Cambridge: Heffer, 1956], 180; referring to *Romans*, 8:20). Josef Ratzinger calls this the "law of disguise." God uses every "sign" that "by concealing him more, shows more truly his intrinsic nature" (Ratzinger, *Introduction to Christianity*, 191–93). Origen (ca. 185–254) had it that "the knowledge manifested to those worthy of it in the present time comes through a mirror and in an enigma . . . It is foolish not to suppose that it is the same way with the other virtues" (*Origen*, trans. R. Greer [New York: Paulist Press, 1979], 120). Aeschylus conveyed his ambivalence about this divine strategy in a sarcasm:

> *Prometheus:* I caused mortals to cease foreseeing doom.
> *Chorus:* What cure did you provide against this sickness?
> *Prometheus:* I placed them in blind hopes.
> *Chorus:* That was a great gift you gave to men.
>
> (*Prometheus Bound*)

28. The senior author knows this classic quatrain but is unable to discover its embodiment in the library.

29. This thought suggests a related difficulty in the traditional picture of a hell that is no fun at all. That there is a Christian alternative to that picture—one presenting the self with plausible trade-offs—may be less radical than it sounds. The thought has the support of C. S. Lewis in *The Great Divorce*, supra, and even Dante makes room for the satisfaction that consists precisely in being the person we choose to be. See M. Smith, "Punishment in the *Divine Comedy*" (manuscript on file with the authors). Dorothy Sayers agrees:

> The accusation of cruelty, so often urged against the *Purgatorio* as well as against the *Inferno*, is therefore without meaning or relevance. Whether in Hell or in Purgatory, you get what you want--if that is what you really do want. If you insist on having your own way, you will get it: Hell is the enjoyment of your own way for ever. (Sayers's introduction to Dante, *The Divine Comedy*, vol. 2, *Purgatory* [Baltimore: Penguin, 1955], 16)

On every aspect of the hellish experience, we recommend D. Walker, *The Decline of Hell*, supra. We only regret Walker's title which suggests that giving the damned their heart's desire is a slacking off of Christian rigor. Imagine a Darwinist being condemned to give an endless lecture on natural selection to an audience of adoring freshmen, or a dedicated consumer joined forever to George Orwell's "race of enlightened sunbathers" (*The Road to Wigan Pier* [New York: Harcourt, Brace, 1961], 169).

30. As it is known from its use in the Greek of the New Testament.

31. See Anders Nygren, *Agape and Eros*, trans. P. Watson (New York: Harper and Row, 1953), 200–32.

32. See, for example, Gene Outka, *Agape: An Ethical Analysis* (New Haven: Yale University Press, 1972), 11.

33. Id. at 15, 12–13, 155–61, passim.

34. Some agape writers see a threat to descriptive equality in the frustration of their favorite egalitarian social schemes. This, of course, is nonsense. Whether the levelers or the plutocrats have their way in society, "essential" human equality (if it exists) has been protected by locating it safely in our nature. It may be slighted by politicians, but it is hardly erased or even altered.

35. Still another imaginable objection is that our view makes the relation of human equality rest upon the *capacity* of humans for moral self-perfection without emphasizing that this capacity is emergent in the fulfillment of an antecedent *need*. Our focus on human power risks being mistaken as merely another species of narcissism. Even though persons are under obligation to others, if the hope of "self-perfection" is the only reason to honor that obligation, the image of the isolated human monad is not wholly exorcised. It takes the emphasis upon need to make our claim "religiously interesting" (Jay Johnson, "Knowledge, History, and the Turn to Experience: An Investigation of Sources in the American Intellectual Tradition for Making Human Equality Theologically Interesting"; this review of an early draft of this book is on file with the authors). Abandoned by individualism and neglected by natural law, it would be the final calamity for human equality to wind up boring the theologians.

We chose not to concentrate upon human *need*, because it did not seem promising as either the meaning or the reality of human equality. Gene Outka is in accord. Rejecting "need" as the basis of human equality, Outka concludes that "personal agency [is] decidedly more representative of how equality is understood" ("Equality and Individuality," 199). Nevertheless, we take the point, and it is peculiarly germane in respect to religion. We cannot properly celebrate the initiation of lateral moral obligation and power in the individual person without recognizing the prefatory human need for which that power is the cure. To be plain, each of us comes to life empty, fit only for futility until simultaneously one is commissioned and encumbered by the experience of moral connection. To know the Other is the generative occasion of all my specifically interhuman possibility. It admits both of us to the two hopes worth having. These hopes are symmetrical. On the one hand, the encounter draws us outward toward engagement and responsibility—toward love in all its inscrutable and insistent forms. On the other hand, this connectedness with the Other becomes a possibility only insofar as we are simultaneously rescued from our native emptiness. To be capable of love, we must first have become *somebody*. And this we cannot manage for ourselves, for our need is total. A good deal more is going on than ego satisfaction. If anything in this work suggests otherwise, we have been irresponsible.

CHAPTER 7
REPAVING THE ROAD TO HELL:
THE PELAGIAN ISSUES

1. In Latin generally rendered as "*Facienti quod in se est Deus non denegat gratiam.*" Luther's version is even stronger, as appears in the work cited in succeeding note.

2. This is our rough paraphrase of Martin Luther's words. *D. Martin Luthers Werke* (Weimar, 1883–), 56.503, quoted in Heiko Oberman, "*Facientibus quod in se est Deus non denegat gratiam*: Robert Holcot O.P. and the Beginnings of Luther's Theology," in Heiko Oberman, *The Dawn of the Reformation* (Grand Rapids, Mich.: Eerdmans, 1992), 84, 98 n. 83.

3. See J. Mahoney, *The Making of Moral Theology* (Oxford: Clarendon, 1987), 38.

4. Id. at 40 (quoting John Henry Newman).

5. John K. Ryan, trans., *The Confessions of St. Augustine* (New York: Image, 1960), 198.

6. See John M. Rist, *Augustine: Ancient Thought Baptized* (Cambridge: Cambridge University Press, 1994), 183.

7. Augustine, *The City of God*, XIX.26 (quoted in Mahoney, *Moral Theology*, 88). Louis Dupré discerns in Augustine the beginnings of the "fateful separation" of grace from nature:

> Augustine [lays] the groundwork for the later separation between the order of nature and that of redemption. In part this was due to the more moral and medicinal view of grace that, from the beginning, had dominated the Latin tradition. But in Augustine's case an additional historical controversy played a part. Against the one-sided stress placed on the need of good works by the emerging Pelagians, Augustine reemphasized that the fall had wounded and incapacitated nature and hence that nature first had to be cured by the remedy of grace. Eventually this remedy will be viewed as a quasi-independent entity, rather than as the deification of human nature it had been for Greek Christians. (Dupré, *Passage to Modernity*, 169–70)

8. Ferguson, *Pelagius*, 39–45. The sad tale of this interesting man and his irrepressible idea is well told by Ferguson.

9. Mahoney, *Moral Theology*, 48–49.

10. Before Augustine, Origen had said as much as anyone: See "On Prayer," in Greer, *Origen*, 157. In his introduction to the volume quoted, Hans Urs von Balthasar identifies Origen as committed to the sort of practical moral freedom that Augustine soon would doom: "It should be emphasized that the soul does not lose its freedom in the fall, even though the conditions in which it then finds itself make it more difficult for freedom to be exercised. Origen's emphasis is retained by his successors and ultimately becomes what can be called the Pelagian theme, namely, that a human being can still take the first steps toward God" (id. at 13).

11. Mahoney, *Moral Theology*, 47 (internal quotation omitted).

12. Augustine got Pelagius's views rejected by the African bishops in 415 and by the pope in 417 and 418. From about 412 until his death in 430, Augustine poured out a steady stream of anti-Pelagian works. The major and some of the minor ones

are collected in *The Nicene and Post-Nicene Fathers*, 1st ser., vol. 5, *Augustine: Writings Against the Pelagians* (Grand Rapids: Eerdmans, 1991). Moreover, in the *Retractationes*, which he composed near the end of his life, Augustine modified the relevant portions of *De libero arbitrio*.

13. Etienne Gilson, *History of Christian Philosophy in the Middle Ages*, 595 n. 37. Ferguson notes that even this "original" infusion of grace was an afterthought for Pelagius and an adjustment in response to criticism (*Pelagius*, 70). See also id. at 106 *et seq*. Ferguson puts the final positions of Pelagius as follows: "Man enjoys free will and . . . God does not will the damnation of any man. Two propositions follow. . . . [M]en damn themselves by severing themselves from the love of God, and . . . the only sense in which God can be said to predestinate men is by his foreknowledge" (id. at 141). The bulk of the early Pelagian texts are collected and translated in B. R. Rees, *The Letters of Pelagius and His Followers* (St Edmundsbury: Boydell, 1991).

14. For a brief history of this doctrine, see Mahoney, *Moral Theology*, 194–202. Cyprian's remark was in the context of the Church's attitude toward schismatics and heretics.

15. Rist, *Augustine*, 260, 133–34.

16. Id. at 273.

17. Alister McGrath, *Iustitia Dei: A History of the Christian Doctrine of Justification* (Cambridge: Cambridge University Press, 1986), vol. 1, 28 n. 33. For a discussion of the ambiguities as to exactly what Augustine held on predestination, see Rist, *Augustine*, 268–70. Even where Augustine has God predestinating only to salvation and merely "permitting" the damnation of the rest, equality is excluded; for God has coerced some into salvation and denied salvation to the rest.

18. Prosper of Aquitaine, (quoted in Jaroslav Pelikan, *The Christian Tradition: A History of the Development of Doctrine*, 5 vols. (Chicago: University of Chicago Press, 1971–1989), vol. 1, 320). Fatalism of this sort they recognized as pagan.

19. Pelikan, *The Christian Tradition*, vol. 1, 320, 322.

Augustine's understanding of the workings of grace "dismayed" the monks of his day (Mahoney, *Moral Theology*, 51; see also Rist, *Augustine*, 288–89). Monks, it turns out, have been perennial defenders of man's capacity to choose God and denouncers of the "lazy argument" that God does everything for man through grace. Monks (including the female version, nuns) voluntarily undertake the "evangelical counsels" of poverty, chastity, and obedience—disciplines that scripture commends but does not command. In undertaking them and resolving to persevere in them to the end, the monk undertakes a spiritual athleticism—striving to do all he can to please God. "Monasticism is," in short, "the boldest organized attempt to attain to Christian perfection in all the long history of the Church" (Flew, *The Idea of Perfection in Christian Theology*, 158). As such, it is a powerful affirmation of what equality asks of Christianity, namely, that man be able freely to respond to God's invitation to fellowship. The flip side, however, poses a predictable threat. If what one does matters, and monasticism furthers one's chances, what of those who are not free to join, ignorant of the possibility, or simply have no vocation? Are they at a disadvantage? At certain moments in the history of the Church, the answer was in the affirmative; monks were moral elites. Today, by contrast, most agree that the monk's obligation and opportunity are the same as every Christian's: to seek God's will and to submit to it as he finds it.

20. For confirmation of the deep relevance of the Pelagian issues to any credible Christian commitment to equality, see Outka, "Equality and Individuality," 198 n. 7, 180–81.

21. The canons of Orange II are collected in Denzinger and Schönmetzer, *Enchiridion*, 36th ed. (Rome: Herder, 1965) (hereafter, DS), §§ 371–97. The sixth canon of Orange II (DS § 376) leaves no example of the worthlessness of human effort unmentioned.

22. Pelikan, *The Christian Tradition*, vol. 1, 329 (emphasis added) (quoting Augustine, *On the Predestination of the Saints*).

23. Mahoney, *The Making of Moral Theology*, 50.

24. "There is no doubt that Augustine came to think—indeed probably always thought—that the majority of mankind, after death, will come to a bad end" (Rist, *Augustine*, 267). Augustine "plainly and simply *knows* about the outcome of divine judgment. And all those bowing to his authority, from Gregory the Great through the early and High Middle Ages—Anselm, Bonaventure, and Thomas not excepted—to the Reformers and Jansenists will become *knowers* in the same sense, taking this knowledge as a fully secure basis upon which to construct their further speculations about God's twofold predetermination *post* or *ante praevisa merita*" (Hans Urs von Balthasar, *Dare We Hope "That All Men Be Saved"?* [San Francisco: Ignatius, 1988], 65).

25. See Rist, *Augustine*, 270–72. Referring to the Augustinians' treatment of 1 *Timothy* 2:4 and like scriptural language, Kolakowski observes that "it turned out, as in many other cases, that what seems unambiguous in the canonical text may, by skilful exegesis, be made ambiguous and then unambiguous again but in a sense opposite to what it seemed to mean at first glance" (*God Owes Us Nothing*, 25).

26. See Aquinas, *Summa theologiae*, Ia, qq. 23–24.

27. "As predestination includes the will to confer grace and glory, so also reprobation includes the will to permit a person to fall into sin, and to impose the punishment of damnation" (Aquinas, *Summa theologiae*, Ia, q. 23, a. 3, c.).

28. Ibid., Ia, q. 23, a. 4, *ad* 1.

29. Ibid., Ia, q. 19, a. 6, *ad* 1. Thomas here mentions and does not endorse Augustine's view that God wills all the elect to be saved. See also id. at Ia, q. 23, a. 4, *ad* 4.

30. Aquinas, *De subst. sep.*, 14; see Bernard Lonergan, *Grace and Freedom: Operative Grace in the Thought of St. Thomas Aquinas*, ed. J. Patout Burns (London: Darton, Longman, and Todd, 1971), 84.

31. Lonergan, *Grace and Freedom*, 116.

32. Ibid.

33. Id. at 115.

Reprobation differs in its causality from predestination. This latter is the cause both of what is expected in the future life by the predestined—namely, glory—and of what is received in this life—namely, grace. Reprobation, however, is not the cause of what is in the present—namely, sin; but it is the cause of abandonment by God. It is the cause, however, of what is assigned in the future—

namely, eternal punishment. But guilt proceeds from the free-will of the person who is reprobated and deserted by grace. (Aquinas, *Summa theologiae*, Ia, q. 23, a. 3, *ad* 2)

34. The position is defended by able scholars. Brian Davies, for example: "One may, of course, say that if my actions are ultimately caused by God then I do not act freely at all. Aquinas, however, would reply that my actions are free if nothing in the world is acting on me so as to make me perform them, not if God is not acting in me" (Brian Davies, *The Thought of Thomas Aquinas* [Oxford: Oxford University Press, 1992], 177). Cf. R. Garrigou-Lagrange, *Grace* (London: Herder, 1952), 421–22.

We confess bewilderment at the idea of a unidirectional freedom. If a man is free to sin, by definition he is free not to sin; but if this free negative act of restraint is not his own free act of acceptance, what is it? Is there a third category of acts by which man's free avoidance of sin leaves him somewhere between damnation and salvation?

Earlier in life (1254–57) Thomas had said that if man freely makes the initial and necessary first step toward salvation, God comes out to meet him and completes the process with transforming grace. Just a few years later (1258–64), however, Thomas rejected his original position as Pelagian (*Summa contra Gentiles*, 2.149.8.), and in his unfinished last work, writes, "if we speak of grace as it signifies a help from God to move us to good, no preparation is required on man's part, that, as it were, anticipates the Divine help, but rather, every preparation in man must be by the help of God moving the soul to good"(Aquinas, *Summa theologiae*, Ia–IIae, q. 112, a. 2, c.). Aquinas's final position is that if a man is saved, it is thanks to God alone.

35. The complete history of this maxim has not been written. We piece some of it together infra, this chapter. The standard accounts, which are complementary but still far from exhaustive, are Jean Riviere, "*Quelques antecedents patristique de la formule: 'Facienti quod in se est,' "* in 7 *Revue des Sciences Religieuses* 93 (1927), and Artur Landgraf, *Dogmengeschichte der Frühscholastik* (Regensburg: Pustet, 1952), vol. 1, 249–63. See also McGrath, *Iustitia Dei*, vol. 1, 83–91, passim; and Heiko Oberman, *The Harvest of Medieval Theology* (Durham: Labyrinth, 1983), 129–45, passim.

As Landgraf notes and Riviere emphasizes, Origen had found the principle of the "*facienti*" embodied in *Matthew* 25:29: "*Omni enim habenti dabitur et abundabit.*"

36. Aquinas, *Summa theologiae*, Ia–IIae, q. 109, a. 6, *ad* 2 (Brennan's translation).

37. Ibid., Ia, q. 23, a. 5, c. (emphasis added). For a confirmation of our reading of Aquinas, see Kolakowski, *God Owes Us Nothing*, 39–42.

38. In chapter 8 we reach the conclusion, troubling to a Christian equality, that Aquinas's general approach to the morality of acts and intentions continues, at least at the ceremonial level, to be endorsed by the Church that sometimes forgets Thomas's starting point in election and predestination.

39. A condition is "sufficient" if its satisfaction effects salvation; it is "necessary" if its satisfaction is required but leaves another such condition to be fulfilled.

40. What we have in mind is what the tradition denominated variously as the *concursus generalis, influxus generalis, influentia generalis*. See Oberman, *The Harvest of Medieval Theology*, 47–48, 142–45, passim; Lonergan, *Grace and Freedom*, 24 nn. 13, 14; and Ferguson, *Pelagius*, 70, 172–75.

41. Kolakowski casts the "semi-Pelagian" position in language cognate with our own: "We do not need divine grace to do good but 'sufficient grace' is given to all, and it needs only our free will to make it efficient. Since this efficient grace is a constant condition of our life, we may say that moral perfection and salvation depend on our effort and will" (Kolakowski, *God Owes Us Nothing*, 13).

42. This is not to say that Biel was without antecedents. Duns Scotus (ca. 1265–1308) and William of Ockham (ca. 1300–1349) each espoused a theology of justification conceding more effect to man's initiative than Aquinas had allowed. There is even evidence that what later would be termed the "Gabrielistic theology of justification" was the most popular in the universities in the early fourteenth century (Oberman, "Duns Scotus, Nominalism and the Council of Trent," in Oberman, *The Dawn of the Reformation*, 220.)

43. *D. Martin Luthers Werke* (Weimar, 1883–), 56.503, quoted in Oberman, ""Facientibus," 92. As Josef Ratzinger would have it, God exercises his "creative freedom which creates further freedoms" (*Introduction to Christianity* [New York: Herder, 1971], 110).

44. Oberman, *The Harvest of Medieval Theology*, 177 (emphasis omitted). Cf. McGrath, *Iustitia Dei*, vol. 2, 89.

45. The medieval theologians had an extensive vocabulary to express these ideas. The central notion is that of the pact God has created, by fiat, with man. It alone establishes the terms of human justification and salvation. God did not have to reward man's best efforts (*potentia absoluta*); he could have insisted upon strict justice (*meritum de condigno*). In fact, however, God has willed (*de potentia ordinata*) to accept man's best efforts as meritorious (*meritum de congruo*); God did not have to abide by the *facienti*, but he has chosen to. The *facienti* is God's "contract" with man. See McGrath, *Iustitia Dei*, vol. 1, 109–28, 83–91; Oberman, "Facientibus," 98; Oberman, "Duns Scotus," 204–33; Oberman, *The Harvest of Medieval Theology*, 166–78; and Francis Oakley, *The Western Church in the Later Middle Ages* (Ithaca: Cornell University Press, 1979), 142–48.

46. Alister McGrath, *Reformation Thought*, 2d. ed. (Oxford: Blackwell, 1993), 77.

47. McGrath, *Iustitia Dei*, vol. 2, 4; see also id. at vol. 2, 18–19; and vol. 2, 4–10; McGrath, *Reformation Thought*, 91–93; see also Oberman, "Facientibus," 99–100, 101.

48. McGrath, *Reformation Thought*, 94.

49. Ibid.; Pelikan, *The Christian Tradition*, vol. 4, 146.

50. McGrath, *Iustitia Dei*, vol.2, 8.

51. Quoted in McGrath, *Reformation Thought*, 93–94.

52. See Oberman, "Facientibus," 98 n. 82; McGrath, *Reformation Thought*, 95–96. See also Pelikan, *The Christian Tradition*, vol. 4, 139.

53. Pelikan, *The Christian Tradition*, vol. 4, 139. Luther never understood that Aquinas was his ally. See supra at 167–68.

54. Quoted in Pelikan, *The Christian Tradition*, vol. 4, 140–41.

55. Id. at 138, 140, 142.

56. Louis Bouyer, *The Spirit and Forms of Protestantism*, trans. A. V. Littledale (Westminster: Newman, 1961), 46.

57. Quoted in Pelikan, *The Christian Tradition*, vol. 4, 141.

58. McGrath, *Iustitia Dei*, vol. 2, 18, 10–32.

59. See McGrath *Reformation*, 100–101; McGrath, *Iustitia Dei*, vol. 2, 16–17.

60. Quoted in Pelikan, *The Christian Tradition*, vol. 4, 149–50.

61. Luther preferred to keep silent on this question because of the doctrine's tendency to induce either despair or presumption (Pelikan, *The Christian Tradition*, vol. 4, 218–19).

62. Id. at 217–32; McGrath, *Iustitia Dei*, vol. 2, 37.

63. Pelikan, *The Christian Tradition*, vol. 4, 222, (quoting Calvin, *Institutes*, 3.23.1: "Reprobation to damnation by the eternal will of God was an ineluctable corollary of election to salvation by the same eternal will of God; it was not based on God's foreknowledge of human conduct any more than salvation was"). "With unrelenting vigor, Calvin pressed his rejection of the notion of divine permission all the way to the point of attributing to God's active predestinating will even the fall of Adam into sin and the consequent verdict of eternal death on 'so many peoples, together with their infant offspring' " (Pelikan, *The Christian Tradition*, vol. 4, 224 [internal citation omitted]).

64. Pelikan, *The Christian Tradition*, vol. 4, 221 (quoting Augustine).

65. Lakoff, *Equality*, 42.

66. John Calvin, *Institutes of the Christian Religion*, 3.21, trans. H. Beveridge (Grand Rapids: Eerdmans, 1957), vol. 2, 206.

67. Pelikan, *The Christian Tradition*, vol. 4, 227.

68. McGrath, *Iustitia Dei*, vol. 2, 86.

69. Emphasis added. Some of the translations of the documents of Trent are Brennan's; others are from H. J. Schroeder, O.P., ed., *Canons and Decrees of the Council of Trent* (London: Herder, 1941).

70. Oberman, "Duns Scotus," 212. "The rule that God does not deny his grace to those who do their very best is a rule of grace" (id. at 213). "It is usually said that the Council of Trent in its definition of the truly Catholic doctrine of justification opted for the *via media*, steering away from both the Scylla of Lutheranism and the Charybdis of Nominalistic Pelagianism. If our interpretation is *e mente auctorum*, a true presentation of the mind of the Fathers of Trent, the nominalistic doctrine of justification has substantially contributed to the final formulation of the decree, and the Scotistic interest in the *meritum de congruo* has been fully validated, taken into account and safeguarded" (Oberman, "Duns Scotus," 218).

71. Internal citations omitted.

72. *John* 3:5 (quoted in DS at § 1524).

73. Though they maintained that faith in Christ alone was necessary to salvation, Calvin and Luther did not tarry over the fate of those who never had an opportunity to hear Christ preached; they easily concluded that such pagans had been predestinated to reprobation. The great voyages of discovery in the sixteenth century, however, raised the stakes, and the earlier hope that angelic missionaries would reach the otherwise unevangelized was now supplemented by increasingly sophisticated speculation as to how such folk could be saved. None of these interesting schemes was raised to the level of doctrine, however. The version perhaps most promising to equality is that propounded by one Juan de Lugo, who held that those who do what is in their power to find the way to salvation will be justified, so long as they make an act of faith in whatever revelation is available to them. See Dulles, *The Assurance of Things Hoped For*, 58–60.

74. Father Hardon is typical of many modern Catholic theologians when he claims for the doctrine of the baptism of desire an origin in the "earliest times" (John A. Hardon, *A Catholic Catechism* [New York: Doubleday, 1981], 234). It remains the case that the principal early expositor of the Church's sacramental theology, St. Augustine, had no "substantive thesis" regarding the baptism of desire (Rist, *Augustine*, 286).

75. Trent teaches that the adult whom God chooses does not begin his justification with baptism; he must be prepared for it. And for Trent the preparation is work that God seems to perform only on those who have received the gospel; part of the adult's preparation for baptism is coming to believe as true the "things divinely revealed and promised" (DS § 1526). It is not enough, moreover, merely to believe in divine mercy or simply to believe oneself justified (DS §§ 1562, 1564). One must believe in the redemption that is in Jesus Christ (see DS §§ 1562, 1564).

So long, of course, as salvation presupposes a preparation involving belief in the revelation of Jesus Christ, the doctrine of baptism of desire is good news only to those who receive the Christian revelation and wish to embrace it. That this alone is baptism of desire may be too restrictive a reading of Trent. It is, however, a reading that would have sufficed to contradict the reformers' specific denial of the Church's role in mediating salvation.

76. *The Catechism of the Catholic Church* (Mahwah, N.J.: Paulist Press, 1994), § 1257.

77. *Catechism* § 1260 (emphasis in original).

78. Whether the Eucharist and other sacraments are a *relative advantage* to Christians is a different but also relevant question. To that possibility it is a plausible response that the positive effect of the sacraments received in liturgical form is accompanied by an added and balancing responsibility, foreclosing the perception of any net Christian moral advantage. See infra at 333 n. 110. Conversely, if baptism may be had by unconscious desire, why would not such a general disposition of the will produce the benign effects of the other relevant sacraments?

79. By 1567 Pope Pius V had already condemned seventy-nine propositions of one Baius who maintained that man was naturally created in such a way that God owed and had to provide man whatever gracious help is necessary for his salvation (McGrath, *Iustitia Dei*, vol. 2, 90–93; DS §§ 1906, 1911, 1913). Baius's view is anti-Pelagian in the sense that man is totally reliant upon God for his salvation but apparently congenial to equality insofar as men are *naturally* entitled to the grace that restores man to a state of merit in the eyes of God. (But was man free to refuse it?)

80. McGrath, *Iustitia Dei*, vol. 2, 93–94; Dale van Kley, *The Jansenists and the Expulsion of the Jesuits from France, 1757–1765* (New Haven: Yale University Press, 1975), 7–8.

81. McGrath, *Iustitia Dei*, vol. 2, 95; Pelikan, *The Christian Tradition*, vol. 1, 319.

82. In preparing to write, Jansen had read the whole of Augustine's writings ten times and the anti-Pelagian writings thirty times (Charles Beard, *Port Royal* [London: Longman, Green, Longman, and Roberts, 1861], vol. 1, 242).

83. McGrath, *Iustitia Dei*, vol. 2, 96. See also van Kley, *The Jansenists*, 9.

84. Quoted in Dulles, *The Assurance of Things Hoped For*, 60.

85. The reason for what seems to be magisterial diffidence, while perhaps not satisfying, is plain enough, as it had been since Augustine:

It is not easy to conceive of a territory of belief intervening between the Semi-Pelagianism, which holds the free and valid co-operation of the human will with the Divine Spirit, and the theory of Predestination commonly called Calvinist, which unconditionally refers all salvation to the efficacy of grace. (Beard, *Port Royal*, vol. 1, 259)

86. Ibid.

87. See Mahoney, *The Making of Moral Theology*, 94. If there is an identifiable doctrine of semi-Pelagianism, the villain has *never* been officially condemned by that name. The semi-Pelagianism of John Cassian appears still to be within the bounds of Roman Catholic orthodoxy. See Ferguson, *Augustine*, 184. See also Kolakowski, *God Owes Us Nothing*, 56.

88. Pope John Paul II, Apostolic Constitution, *Fidei depositum*, sec. 3.

89. Kolakowski, *God Owes Us Nothing*, 230 n. 66.

90. See also *Catechism* at § 1991: "Justification is at the same time the acceptance of God's righteousness through faith in Jesus Christ" (emphasis omitted).

91. Cf. id. at § 2022.

92. *Catechism* at § 2025 (Brennan's translation). The linguistic device by which this division of labor is clarified has changed from the one Oberman found in the documents of Trent to the following, of which the quoted English is a translation: "*Meritum imprimis pertinet ad Dei gratiam, secundo loco ad hominis cooperationem*" (*Catechismus Catholicae Ecclesiae* [Vatican City: Libreria Editrice Vaticana, 1997]).

93. Catholics have been rewriting Augustine for centuries—by silent omission: "In Catholic historical works the hardness—or cruelty—of Augustine's doctrine of predestination is often mitigated by omission; this applies even to Gilson's classic" on Augustine (Kolakowski, *God Owes Us Nothing*, 208 n. 61).

94. See also § 836.

95. Quoting Vatican II, *Ad gentes*.

96. The groundwork for the emancipation was laid at the Second Vatican Council (1962–65), of which we shall have much more to say in chapter 8. Before that ecumenical council, the most influential Catholic theological treatises felt free to hew to a line verging, in relevant respects, on Augustine. For an example of the highly exclusivistic theology that was possible for Catholics before Vatican II, see Ludovicus Lercher, S.I., *Institutiones Theologiae Dogmaticae*, 4th ed. (Barcelona: Herder, 1945), vol. iv/1, §§ 182–420, esp. §§ 305, 357–85. Here, as in Aquinas, the *facienti* is incorporated but gutted, and great effort is expended explaining that God's salvific will is "unequal" and thus a "mystery of the divine predilection."

97. "In spite of all the condemnations of Pelagian and semi-Pelagian teaching, and in spite of the great popularity of Augustine's writings among today's active Catholics, the cornerstone of his theology of predestination seems to have been nearly lost. The Roman Church largely adopted, following the Jesuit philosophy, a doctrine which seemed more in keeping with the modern rationalist notion of justice, and this implies, ultimately, the long tradition notwithstanding, that salvation is not offered or denied gratuitously" (Kolakowski, *God Owes Us Nothing*, 109). Indeed, "it was the teaching of Augustine that the pope declared heretical" in the Jansenist controversy (id. at 14).

98. "It was plain to the Puritans that the visible church in England stood too far from the invisible; it indiscriminately embraced the flagrantly wicked along with the good or sincerely repentant" (Edmund S. Morgan, *Visible Saints: The History of a Puritan Idea* [New York: New York University Press, 1963], 10).

99. Id. at 26.

100. Id. at 41.

101. Id. at 47.

102. Id. at 67–68.

103. Id. at 68–69.

104. Id. at 73; see also 89–90, 93–112. "New England was an effort to reduce the gap between God and man."

105. Norman Pettit, *The Heart Prepared: Grace and Conversion in Puritan Spiritual Life*, 2d. ed. (Middletown, Conn.: Wesleyan University Press, 1989), 18.

106. Perry Miller, *The New England Mind: From Colony to Province* (Cambridge: Harvard University Press, 1953), 56.

107. Pettit, *The Heart Prepared*, 7.

108. Miller, *From Colony to Province*, 55. Miller adds: "A phenomenon of Calvinism everywhere in the century was a tendency to analyze the process of regeneration into a series of moments, but that strain which invented the federal theology was impelled, by the nature of the metaphor, to set off an initial period where he who is about to believe begins to learn what to expect" (ibid.).

109. Id. at 53.

110. "In the seventeenth century Arminianism stood as a ghastly warning to all Calvinists. . . . The Arminians yielded too far to the pressure for . . . smuggling too much human freedom into the ethics of predestination" (Perry Miller, *Errand into the Wilderness* [Cambridge: Harvard University Press, 1956], 56–57). See Francis Christie, "The Beginnings of Arminianism in New England," in W. Rockwell, ed., *Papers of the American Society of Church History*, 2d ser. (New York: Knickerbocker, 1912), vol. 3, 153.

111. Opposing the Calvinist *decretum absolutum* on the ground that it denied some people salvation through no fault of their own, Arminius taught that Christ's atonement was intended for all men, that men need God's grace to be saved, and that to be saved men must freely concur in God's plan. As for the meaning of the *facienti*, Arminius argued that it would be altogether wrong if it meant that God's original grace is not at work in the beginning of man's conversion. But, insisted Arminius: "If [the *facienti*] be understood in the following sense, 'To him who does what he can by the primary grace already conferred upon him,' then there is no absurdity in this sentence, 'God will bestow further grace upon him who profitably uses that which is primary' " (Article 17 of "The Apology or Defence of James Arminius, D.D., Against Thirty-One Theological Articles," in *The Works of James Arminius*, trans. J. Nichols [reprint of the London edition] [Grand Rapids: Baker, 1986], vol. 2, 19–20). John Milton's God was Arminian:

> To prayer, repentance, and obedience due,
> Though but endeavored with sincere intent,
> Mine ear shall not be slow, mine eye not shut.
> And I will place within them as a guide

My umpire Conscience, whom if they will hear,
Light after light well used they shall attain,
And to the end persisting, safe arrive.

>   (Milton, *Paradise Lost*, book 3, verses 191–97,
>   *The Portable Milton*, 294)

112. Pelikan, *The Christian Tradition*, vol. 4, 225. See generally McGrath, *Iustitia Dei*, vol. 2, 115–21.

113. Miller, *From Colony to Province*, 64.

114. Ibid.

115. Ibid.

116. Ibid.

117. Ibid.

118. Ibid. (emphasis added).

119. Pettit's study of preparationism, *The Heart Prepared*, supra, is a sustained criticism of Miller's argument that preparationism became a virtual synergism.

120. Perry Miller, " 'Preparation for Salvation' in Seventeenth Century New England," in *The Journal of the History of Ideas* 4 (1943): 253, 286. See also Perry Miller, *The New England Mind: The Seventeenth Century* (New York: Macmillan, 1939), 396.

121. Miller, *The Seventeenth Century*, 395.

122. Ralph Perry, *Puritanism and Democracy* (New York: Vanguard, 1944), 296. See also Miller, *The Seventeenth Century*, 397.

123. Max Weber, *The Protestant Ethic and the Spirit of Capitalism*, trans. T. Parsons (New York: Scribner's, 1930), 121. We find in Weber no apprehension that beyond confirming his election, the Puritan also was preparing for—even inducing—his justification just a little. Cf. id. at 115 n. 64.

124. Id. at 117. Weber is not alone in this judgment. See Philip Lee, *Against the Protestant Gnostics* (Oxford: Oxford University Press, 1987), 126. Everyone who "at every moment stands before the inexorable alternative, chosen or damned" (id. at 115), has an interest in a rational handling of the side of the divide on which he falls. James Maclear argues forcefully that early American millennialist hopes encouraged the foundation of a *nation* (not just a church) dedicated to moral exertion ("The Republic and the Millennium," in Elwin A. Smith, ed., *The Religion of the Republic* [Philadelphia: Fortress, 1971], 183–216).

125. See supra chap. 3.

126. Lee, *Against the Protestant Gnostics*, 21.

127. Id. at 26 (quoting Hans Jonas).

128. Lee, *Against the Protestant Gnostics*, 33–40.

129. Harold Bloom, *The American Religion* (New York: Simon and Schuster, 1992), 32–33, 49, 102–3, 206–7.

130. Cf. Lee, *Against the Protestant Gnostics*, 13–44, esp. 35–38.

131. Bloom confirms Lee in respect of Southern baptists. "So far as I can tell, the Southern Jesus, which is to say the American Jesus, is not so much an agent of redemption as he is an imparter of knowledge. . . . Jesus is not so much an event in history for the American Religionist as he is a knower of the secrets of God who in return can be known by the individual. Hidden in this process is a sense that depravity is only a lack of saving knowledge. Salvation, through knowing the knowing

Jesus, is a reversal wholly experiential in nature, an internalization of a self already internalized" (*The American Religion*, 65).

132. Lee's historical analysis treats both Puritanism and the "enthusiastic" religion of the Great Awakening as pure and cohesive causes of gnostic decay. If Perry Miller's version of Puritan religion is anywhere near the mark, however, it is doubtful that every mutation of Protestantism has been in the direction of gnosticism.

133. Id. at 28.

134. Id. at 49.

135. Karl Barth, *Church Dogmatics* (Edinburgh: Clark, 1957), vol. 2, part 2, 72. (Because all our citations to Barth's *Church Dogmatics* are to vol. 2, part 2, subsequent citations will indicate only page numbers.)

136. Id. at 77.

137. Id. at 74.

138. Ibid.

139. Ibid.

140. Id. at 75.

141. Ibid.

142. C. Berkouwer, *The Triumph of Grace in the Theology of Karl Barth* (Grand Rapids, Mich.: Eerdmans, 1956), 91. Here Barth is in rough harmony with Pelagius: "The harshness of Augustine's outlook . . . is due to the fact that in his philosophy grace has its origin in the arbitrary will of God, and not in His love. Pelagius has a far juster awareness that our love springs from the love that is the nature of God, and that we love Him because He first loved us" (Ferguson, *Pelagius*, 177).

143. Barth, *Church Dogmatics*, 115 (emphasis added).

144. Id. at 122. "Calvin's *decretum absolutum* has been replaced by a decree that is Jesus Christ" (Berkouwer, *The Triumph of Grace*, 262).

145. Barth, *Church Dogmatics*, 116–17. Election is God's free grace, and that grace alone is election's source (id. at 112). See Berkouwer, *The Triumph of Grace*, 262.

146. Id. at 106.

147. "Predestination is never a mankind-condemning No of God. It does indeed involve rejection, but it is the rejection of *Christ*. Mankind, we, deserved this reprobation . . . [but] our rejection is borne in [Christ's] and thereby it is borne away" (ibid.).

148. Id. at 172, 173, 174.

149. Id. at 118 (emphasis added).

150. Our own conclusion is that Barth rejects, while Trent cautiously allows, a theology of grace and freedom compatible with human equality. This runs afoul of Hans Küng's judgment that Barth's and Trent's teachings are essentially *the same*. See Hans Küng, *Justification: The Doctrine of Karl Barth and a Catholic Reflection*, trans. T. Collins et al. (New York: Nelson, 1964). Nor can our reply to Küng simply be that he misunderstands Barth, for Barth wrote to Küng that "you have me say what I actually do say and . . . I mean it in the way you have me say it" (id. at xix). Our only possible reply is twofold. First, Küng seems to have overlooked Trent's apparent toleration of the *facienti* and its acknowledgment that man's free efforts may have *some* merit that God has agreed to reward (see supra at 174–76); cf. id. at 266–67. Second, Küng underestimates the symbolic importance of the real differences in emphases that he admits. The Barthian/Calvinist *stress* upon man's passivity is out

of harmony with equality in a way Trent's *stress* upon man's obligation and capacity to cooperate with God is not.

151. Berkouwer, *The Triumph of Grace*, 266 (citations omitted).

152. James Livingston, *Modern Christian Thought* (New York: Macmillan, 1971), 339.

153. Barth, *Church Dogmatics*, 76.

154. Almost certainly Barth would have been happy with the trade-off.

155. Berkouwer, *The Triumph of Grace*, 265 (citations omitted).

156. See id. at 262–65, 89–92; McGrath, *Iustitia Dei*, vol. 2, 182–83; and Berkouwer, *The Triumph of Grace*, 114.

157. "No serious *kerugmatic* significance can be ascribed to what Barth calls the 'fatal danger' of unbelief. In the same moment in which it would become kerugmatically meaningful, unbelief *as a human decision* would again become a competitor of *God's* decision. All of Barth's objections against human co-operation and synergism, against every construction of balance between grace and freedom, would again return" (Berkouwer, *The Triumph of Grace*, 267).

158. "If synergism had a legitimate place in the doctrine of the Church we could place the human decision next to the divine decision. The divine decision, however, has been taken precisely *over against* the human and godless decision and can *therefore* not be undone by any human decision" (Berkouwer, *The Triumph of Grace*, 113).

159. McGrath, *Iustitia Dei*, vol. 2, 181.

160. Barth, *Church Dogmatics*, 417. See Berkouwer, *Triumph of Grace*, 114, 263.

Logically, [Barth's doctrine of election] would entail the doctrine of [universal salvation]. However, believing in a higher divine logic . . ., Barth maintains in view of the freedom of the divine grace and on scriptural grounds that the question of whether or not ultimately all men will be saved must remain an open one. (Herbert Hartwell, *The Theology of Karl Barth* [London: Duckworth, 1964], 110–11)

161. See Berkouwer, *The Triumph of Grace*, 114–16.

162. McGrath, *Iustitia Dei*, vol. 2, 182.

163. Id. at 184.

164. Cf. Lee, *Against the Protestant Gnostics*, 226–27.

165. Helmut Thielicke, *Theological Ethics*, vol. 1, *Foundations*, ed. W. Lazareth (Grand Rapids, Mich.: Eerdmans, 1984) (a translation and abridgement of *Theologische Ethik* [Tübingen: Mohr, 1958], 86). We should at least mention here that in Thielicke's ethics we find a metaphysics (or, more to the point, the anti-metaphysics) that we rejected in chapter 2 as incompatible with equality. Our interpretation of human equality is that it is the unique relation that results from people's sharing the sameness of *capacity* for moral self-perfection. In giving this interpretation to the convention we declined the suggestion (pressed by our friend and tutor Richard Schenk, O.P.—no Protestant he), that, if there is a descriptive human equality, it is one based not on sameness of capacity but of *vocation*. We declined to identify the "host property" as a vocation because to do so has the effect of transferring the ground of equality from man himself to the person who gives the vocation, namely, God. To be sure, equality does not insist that man manufacture and own his capacity for self-perfection; the concept is perfectly at home with the belief that God created

and sustains the capacity. But what equality will not allow is that the host property be located outside man in, for example, a vocation. But it is exactly in terms of a vocation, rather than a capacity, that Thielicke insists on understanding man. Man is not a being whom God has endowed with the capacity to be self-perfecting; man has no dignity grounded properly in himself. Man "is" only because God remembers man and summons him into union. "The divine address constitutes the person" (id. at 164). See id. at 147–70. Thielicke rejects the view that man "exists" ontically, because it is, he insists, a Greek and unbiblical idea that has the effect of separating man from God. Equality cannot accept such an anti-metaphysics, for unless there exist humans with their own qualities and capacities, there can be no equality among them—or so, at least, we interpret the convention to require.

166. Id. at 499. "Ethics does not solve problems; it intensifies them" (id. at 621).

167. See id. at 623.

168. Id. at 500.

169. Id. at 602. "The dilemma, the ambiguity . . . is due to the mists of this aeon, in which a clear beam of light becomes a diffused cloud of light. The sun itself is not darkened. It is simply concealed by the clouds in the atmosphere of this aeon" (id. at 611).

170. Id. at 386. Our own conflicting view appears supra 72, 128–29, and 297 n. 30.

171. Id. at 597.

172. Id. at 577.

173. Ibid.

174. Id. at 570.

175. See id. at 84–85.

176. The more representative view seems that of Mark Noll, "The Lutheran Difference," *First Things* 20 (1992): 31, 39. Noll sees the *sola fide* as swamped by American activism: "Augustinianism . . . was doomed. In America it was simply too much to believe that *sinfulness*—the ineluctable curvature of the self in upon itself—was a greater problem than *sins*, the freely chosen actions of the will."

177. Tillich, *A History of Christian Thought*, 124. B. R. Rees collects and reports confirming evidence for the Anglo-Saxon world (*Pelagius: A Reluctant Heretic* [St Edmundsbury: Boydell, 1988]).

178. "It was the heretics Luther and Calvin, not the orthodox Catholics, who were the real heirs of Augustine" (Ferguson, *Pelagius*, 184).

CHAPTER 8
THE REPAVING PROJECT, PART II:
AN EQUAL-OPPORTUNITY CREATOR

1. Søren Kierkegaard, *Fear and Trembling* (Garden City, N.Y.: Doubleday, 1953), 31: "Abraham . . . left his earthly understanding behind and took faith with him."

2. Bruce Vawter, *A Path Through Genesis* (New York: Sheed and Ward, 1956), 169:

The sacrifice of a human being, so repugnant to us and with such difficulty associated with a divine command, would not have appeared too strange to Abraham. There is no evidence that human sacrifice was ever practiced by the

Hebrews, but it was common among the Canaanites with whom Abraham lived, and how was he to know that God, the ruler of life, would not require this thing of him?

3. G. von Rad, *Genesis*, trans. J. Marks (Philadelphia: Westminster, 1961), 234.

4. Helmut Thielicke's reading of the incident is illuminating. Abraham was faced with what seemed an insoluble contradiction. Were he to sacrifice Isaac, he would no longer be taking seriously God's promise about his descendants; he would cease to be a believer. But should he refuse to offer up Isaac because of his belief in the promise of descendants, he would disobey God's command. The situation "was too hopeless to be a subject of reflection or conversation." Faced with the apparent choice between disbelief and disobedience, Abraham improvises. And this, says Thielicke, "is precisely the quintessence of faith, namely, to trust God that behind what seems to be a hopeless situation there is hidden God's own way. . . . [Abraham] does not believe in a tragic cleavage in the ultimate power of being. He believes in the unity of God, even though he does not see it. Indeed, it is because he does not see that he really believes" (Thielicke, *Theological Ethics*, 665–66).

5. Kierkegaard, *Fear and Trembling*, 71.

6. Note, by the way, that the tempter is a gnostic who invites his victims to self-perfect by acquiring special knowledge.

7. Herbert Morris might be a sympathetic lawyer for Eve: "The serpent's guile with Eve was no straightforward case of fraud. It is not as if he outright lied to her, promising her something he knew she would not get. He simply left out a few pertinent details of what she would get in addition to what he told her she would. He was a subtle salesman" (Herbert Morris, "Lost Innocence," *On Guilt and Innocence: Essays in Legal Philosophy and Moral Psychology* [Berkeley: University of California Press, 1976], 139, 161).

8. *New Oxford*. According to Zwingli, however, Paul was "thrown to the ground and rebuked" ("Of the Clarity and Certainty of the Word," in *The Library of Christian Classics*, vol. 24, *Zwingli and Bullinger*, ed. G. Bromiley [Philadelphia: Westminster, 1953], 82).

9. Much depends on the punctuation. The best Latin version inserts none at all, allowing Saul's ignorance to be read as a cause (*quia*) of grace: "*sed misericordiam consecutus sum quia ignorans feci in incredulitate superabundavit autem gratia Domini nostri cum fide et dilectione quae est in Christo Iesu.*" *Biblia Sacra: Iuxta Vulgatem Versionem*, 3d rev. ed. (1983). A popular English version connects ignorance only to excuse and not to overflowing grace: "Mercy, however, was shown me, because while I lacked faith I acted in ignorance; but the grace of our Lord filled me" (*The New Jerusalem Bible* [1985]). The original Greek, as it appears in *Novum Testamentum Graece*, 26th ed. (Stuttgart: Nestle-Aland, 1985), is punctuated in this same manner.

10. See the following two works by David Daube: "For They Know Not What They Do: *Luke 23.34*," *Studia Patristica* 4, no. 2 (Berlin: Akadamie, 1961), 58–70; and *Sin, Ignorance, and Forgiveness in the Bible* (Berkeley: University of California Press, 1985). Another interestingly ambiguous case is that of the lying midwives in *Exodus* 1:15–21. One reading is that the midwives were rewarded for the good intention with which they performed the evil act of lying. For analysis of Aquinas's efforts to disarm the passage, see Keenan, *Goodness and Rightness*, 168–75.

11. Was Eckhardt a heretic when he made the following claim:

A man has little reason to be afraid of anything if he knows his will to be good. . . . If you have good will, you shall lack for nothing. (B. Blakney, trans., *Meister Eckhardt* [New York: Harper and Row, 1941], 12–13)

Or did he save himself only by this addition?

You may now be asking when the will is perfect. It is perfect . . . when it is transformed and adapted to the will of God. (Id. at 13)

Or is he back in trouble when he concludes that,

God does not look at what you do but only at your love and at the devotion and will behind your deeds. (Id. at 22)

12. Here we can insert an observation about mysticism that parallels the one we made about monasticism early in chapter 7. In nearly all Christian theology, and particularly in moral theology focused upon man's vocation to love God, the possibility of mystical experience in this life, as a kind of foretaste of the hereafter, is emphasized. Often the asceticism of the monastic life has been undertaken in the hope of "inducing" mystical experience. If mysticism should turn out to be a moral advantage available only to those special persons capable of it, equality again would be threatened.

While mystics apparently have been blessed by God in a specific and excelling way, it would not follow that they are superior in their capacity for moral perfection. Theologians tend to hold that mystical experience is not a *moral* advantage. Further, as long as this life lasts, the mystic's obligations to her brothers and sisters continue. And, although in mystical union one may gain knowledge of God that is inaccessible to others, still and always her obligation is to do the best she can to know and to do the good. Aquinas is perhaps typical when, after receiving mystical visions near the end of his life, he considered it his duty to try to share what he had seen; his lateral duties were confirmed, not obviated, by his mystical experience (Edward Synan, "Saint Thomas Aquinas: His Good Life and Hard Times," in Leonard Kennedy, ed., *Thomistic Papers III* [Houston: Center for Thomistic Studies, 1987], 35, 47). Whatever special relationship he offers people in this life, God, it seems, never cancels man's lateral duties. See generally R. Garrigou-Lagrange, *Christian Perfection and Contemplation According to St. Thomas Aquinas and St. John of the Cross* (St. Louis: Herder, 1951).

13. See generally Rist, *Augustine*, 148–202. And see Mahoney, *The Making of Moral Theology*, 76–77. See also supra 312 n. 24.

14. We are grateful to Giles Constable, of the Institute for Advanced Study at Princeton, New Jersey, for the revelation that the medievals worried lest this imperative, known as the "*dilige*," be understood as moral license. This led, in turn, to their deflation of Augustine's apparent emphasis on the subjective element of morality.

15. Augustine was confident that "we always know exactly what God's commands are" (Mahoney, *The Making of Moral Theology*, 57).

16. Id. at 49 n. 41. Cf. id. at 52. Augustine's reassurance "is primarily a statement about God, and not about man's moral abilities" (id. at 56). Hare confirms this reading of Augustine (Hare, *The Moral Gap*, 26–27, 113–14).

17. Thus Augustine himself was more believable than Trent when it quoted his "God does not require the impossible" ((DS § 1536). Where man is not determined by grace, the aphorism functions as a *sub silentio* refusal to "excuse" the actor for wrong actions taken in good faith.

18. D. E. Luscombe, ed., *Peter Abelard's Ethics* (Oxford: Clarendon, 1971), 45. Further, "we say that an intention is good, that is, right in itself, but that an action does not bear anything good in itself but proceeds from a good intention" (id. at 53).

19. Id. at 55. See also id. at 12–13.

20. Id. at xxxii.

21. Armand Maurer, *Medieval Philosophy*, rev. ed. (Toronto: Pontifical Institute of Medieval Studies, 1982), 70.

22. Luscombe, *Ethics*, xxxv.

23. Jesus himself put Abelard (and equality) at a disadvantage when he noted that forgiveness was indeed appropriate.

24. See Maurer, *Medieval Philosophy*, 69–70:

In his *Christian Theology* [Abelard] teaches that God granted a revelation to the great pagan philosophers who lived holy lives and came very close to Christian truth. Through them, pagans were enlightened concerning God's will, and hence moral goodness and salvation were within their reach.

But compare with this Abelard's *Ethics*, where he notes specifically that if intention were allowed to be salvific without reference to whether or not its object pleases God, "even the unbelievers" would be able to perform acts accompanied by good intentions (Luscombe, *Ethics*, 54–55). The crimes unbelievers pursue through ignorance or innocent unbelief are no sin; but salvation requires belief (id. at 62–63).

25. Abelard thus fell short of his ambition "to extend to the whole field of the morality of our acts the subjective principle of intention which St. Augustine had applied only to the good morality of virtuous actions" (Mahoney, *The Making of Moral Theology*, 178 [internal quotes omitted]).

26. Peculiarly, however, Abelard took the position that ecclesiastical courts *must* infer a bad intention from a bad act—lest the courts in assessing criminal guilt presume to know men's hearts (Harold Berman, *Law and Revolution* [Cambridge: Harvard University Press, 1983], 189). The ecclesiastical authorities rejected Abelard's strategy, but Abelard, perhaps unintentionally, had encouraged the belief that the naked act determines the actor's goodness or corruption.

27. The relevant propositions rejected at the Council of Sens (1140–41) are collected at DS §§ 725, 729, 733, 739.

28. See Josef Fuchs, "Morality: Person and Acts," in Josef Fuchs, *Christian Morality: The Word Becomes Flesh*, trans. B. McNeil (Washington, D.C.: Georgetown University Press, 1987), 105, 107. It was St. Bernard, long Abelard's nemesis, who secured the latter's condemnation.

29. Etienne Gilson, *The Philosophy of St. Bonaventure* (Paterson, N.J.: St. Anthony Guild, 1965), 378–79.

30. Examples of this extraordinary but neglected genre are collected in *Medieval Handbooks of Penance*, trans. J. McNeill and H. Gamer (New York: Octagon, 1965).

31. Mahoney, *The Making of Moral Theology*, 31. See generally id. at 1–36; Berman, *Law and Revolution*, 164–98.

32. Prologue to the *Prima Secundae* of the *Summa theologiae*. We do not understand how Aquinas's account of freedom here can be reconciled with his deterministic conclusions earlier reported regarding the manner of our salvation. See supra at 167–68.

33. *Summa theologiae*, Ia–IIae, q. 6, a. 8, c.

34. See also id. at Ia–IIae, q. 76, arts. 3–4. "If, however, the ignorance be such as to be entirely involuntary, either through being invincible, or through being of matters one is not bound to know, then such like ignorance excuses from sin altogether" (id. at Ia–IIae, q. 76, a. 3, c.

35. Id. at Ia–IIae, q. 19, a. 5, *ad* 2.

36. Id. at Ia–IIae, q. 19, a. 6, c.

37. John Mahoney's comment is understated:

It may be significant that Aquinas, while granting that action which proceeds from invincible ignorance is not sinful, appears to shrink from describing it as actually good. In [*Summa theologiae*] Ia 2ae, q. 19, a. 6, for instance, the introductory question to be discussed is "Utrum voluntas concordans rationi erranti, sit bona," but Aquinas begins by rephrasing the question as "utrum conscientia erronea excuset." The three preliminary objections which preface the article all conclude "Ergo voluntas concordans rationi (etiam) erranti, est bona," and Aquinas's approach is invariably to take up a different position from such preliminaries, even if only nuanced. The first consideration draws from him the response based on Pseudo-Dionysius that for an act to be good it must be so in every respect, although it can be bad as a whole from only one defect . . . And yet, according to Aquinas, no particular human act can be morally indifferent. (Mahoney, *The Making of Moral Theology*, 193–94 n. 60)

38. "But if a man's reason errs in mistaking another for his wife, and he wish to give her her right when she ask for it, his will is excused from being evil: because this error arises from ignorance of a circumstance, which ignorance excuses, and causes the act to be involuntary" (*Summa theologiae*, Ia–IIae, q. 19, a. 6, c.).

39. Ibid.

40. See generally Stanley Bertke, *The Possibility of Invincible Ignorance of the Natural Law* (Washington, D.C.: Catholic University of America Press, 1941).

41. It was and remains the general Christian view that the acquisition of reason by the individual is a process and not a discrete event. Access to the Eucharist at age seven was an adoption of that age as a convenient threshold of responsibility. Later it was to become the earliest moment of potential liability for crime, but this responsibility was always subject to the prosecutor's burden of showing the capacity for "*mens rea.*" See J. Coons, R. Mnookin, and S. Sugarman, "Puzzling Over Children's Rights," *Brigham Young Utah Law Review* 307, 327–28 (1991). It is mystifying that Catholic theologians tended toward an on-off view of culpable knowledge in specific cases while Canon Law and Christian society interpreted the possibility of humans' committing serious objective wrongs in a state of practical confusion as an enduring problematic.

42. Aquinas's handling of the question in his treatise "On Evil" ("*De Malo*"), another of his mature works, is no different:

But because a person is said to be negligent only when he omits what he is obliged to do, it does not seem to pertain to negligence that he fails to apply his mind to know anything whatsoever but only if he fails to apply his mind to know those things he ought to know, either simply and at any time—hence ignorance of the law is rightly regarded as negligence—or in a particular case as he who shoots an arrow in some place where men are accustomed to pass is considered guilty of negligence if he makes no effort to know whether anyone is passing at that time. And such ignorance which occurs by reason of negligence is considered voluntary. (Aquinas, *De Malo*, trans. J. Oesterle (Notre Dame: University of Notre Dame Press, 1995), q. 3, a. 8., p. 133.

43. Davies, *The Thought of St. Thomas Aquinas*, 231; see id. at n. 13. Of course for Aquinas, unlike Aristotle, man's fullest and final happiness is the beatitude of the vision of God; but whether man chooses (and achieves) what is good in this life affects whether he reaches his final good in the next. See id. at 230.

44. The distinction between the "right" and the "good" is familiar to consumers of ethical theory presented in the English language. See supra chap. 3 at 67–69, 276 nn. 4 and 5. That the distinction only recently has been made in Catholic moral theology results in part from peculiarities of the Latin language that was used by Aquinas and by Catholic theologians until the other day. See Mahoney, *The Making of Moral Theology*, 322–23.

45. There is no evidence that Thomas measures human *striving* in any of his writings on the moral act and the acquired [natural] moral virtues. Instead, he restricts himself to the object and proximate end, wherein reason presents the former and measures both. (Keenan, *Goodness and Rightness*, 119)

We admire Keenan's own reformulation of the nature of Christian moral obligation; it shows the influence of his mentor, Josef Fuchs, S.J., whose ethics we discuss infra:

Goodness as antecedent to rightness depends on effort, not attainment. . . . We sin often, not in our mistakes, errors or wrongdoing, but by not bothering, not trying, not striving. Sin is not the failure to attain but the failure to attempt. (James Keenan, "The Problem with Thomas Aquinas's Concept of Sin," *The Heythrop Journal* 35 [1994]: 401)

Not every student of moral theology shares our esteem for Keenan's balanced efforts to find in Thomas an ethics that credits human striving. John Cuddeback, for example, castigates Keenan for cutting morality loose from right reason. Correct reason, Cuddeback asserts, "is always required for moral goodness" (*The Thomist* 58 (1994): 342, 347). Cuddeback does not tarry over those whom reason and faith do not teach the specific answers.

46. There is, however, a curious partial exception in Aquinas that is worth brief notice. James Keenan catches it in his perceptive study of Thomas's moral theory. At least for the specific case of believing Christians, Thomas's understanding of "charity" is a kind of parallel to what moderns mean by moral goodness and what we have called "obtension." Charity, for Thomas, is an infused theological virtue. By it, the soul is already, in this life, united to God in a way that is continuous with—if far short of—the union the soul will have in final beatitude. What characterizes the

charitable soul in this life is its striving for ever fuller union with God (*Goodness and Rightness*, 127). Charity, as Thomas understands it, directs and moves Christians to seek union with God and to do rightly ordered acts. But the measure of charity is not whether we do rightly ordered acts but whether we are striving to do so. The way we lose charity is not by errors of reason but by failing to strive.

This is the promising beginning of a Thomistic accommodation with obtensional-ism, but one that could not succeed even when confined to believers. First, within Thomas's own thought there is an incoherence; his understanding of charity is for-gotten (or at least inoperative) when he comes to consider the nature of sin. For Thomas, sin occurs specifically where the will of the Christian believer accepts an object that is unreasonable. "But the question of why the will is inordinate does not arise" (id. at 153). Thomas proposes a long list of acts that are generically sinful, and he concludes that the Christian who voluntarily does them is bad. True, for the act to be mortally sinful, there must be deliberate consent to the generically sinful act; but Thomas often infers that there has been such consent simply from the agent's having done the act. But this procedure overlooks entirely whether and how much the agent has striven to do what is correct. "In the long run," concludes Keenan, "Thomas's moral description is still derived from objects. . . . Thomas does not ask the antecedent question of whether the agent is striving out of love to find the right" (id. at 157; see generally id. at 148–75).

But even had Thomas's understanding of charity shaped his analysis of sin, the result would have been equality only among Christians. Unlike the virtues we con-sidered at the end of chapter 5, charity is, as Augustine and then the Church taught, a gift "from above" that distinguishes Christians and sets them apart. "Thomas pro-vides . . . no description of moral motivation for the non-Christian" (id. at 143; see also id. at 54). It would take seven hundred more years for the insight (by Karl Rahner) that man's "natural" striving for the good might be the charity of the "anony-mous Christian."

47. Somehow the fact of equality would reinforce liberal goals. Noting that the virtue of which men are capable is determined by grace, Porter concludes: "Thus, whatever inequalities in virtue exist among the justified cannot be tied to particular classes of persons and therefore cannot be used as a basis for justifying or reinforcing social inequalities" (Jean Porter, "The Subversion of Virtue: Acquired and Infused Virtues in the *Summa theologiae*," in *The Annual of the Society of Christian Ethics* [1992]). Does anyone hold anything like the position Porter rejects?

48. See Harry V. Jaffa, *Thomism and Aristotelianism: A Study of the Commentary by Thomas Aquinas on the Nicomachean Ethics* (Chicago: University of Chicago Press, 1952).

49. Porter, "The Subversion of Virtue," 26.

50. Id. at 25.

51. Id. at 28.

52. Id. at 23, 28.

53. *Summa theologiae*, Ia, q. 23, a. 5, *ad* 3. Porter sees that Aquinas's theory of predestination has relevance to descriptive equality. Incomprehensibly, however, she judges it to be a "rationale for equality" that Aquinas does not adopt (*The Recovery of Virtue: The Relevance of Aquinas for Christian Ethics* [Louisville: Westminster/John Knox, 1990], 139).

54. Porter, "The Subversion of Virtue," 33–37, esp. 37.

55. Carlyle, *A History of Political Theory*, vol. 1, 8 (cited in Porter, *The Recovery of Virtue*, 137 n. 14). See supra chap. 1 at 34–36.

56. Porter, *The Recovery of Virtue*, 140.

57. Ibid.

58. Porter, "The Subversion of Virtue," 28.

59. Porter, *The Recovery of Virtue*, 70 (citations omitted).

60. Porter, "The Subversion of Virtue," 37.

61. Cf. id. at 37.

62. Id. at 23.

63. Albert Jonsen and Stephen Toulmin, *The Abuse of Casuistry: A History of Moral Reasoning* (Berkeley: University of California Press, 1988), 175.

The influential Catholic moral theologian Bernard Häring is an exception to this pattern of neglect. He notes approvingly that Liguori "advocat[ed] respect for conscience. . . . [and] insisted on the universal vocation to holiness" ("Learning More about God's Plan in a Worldwide Community," 11 *Journal of Law and Religion* 177, 179 (1994–95). See also Bernard Häring, *Free and Faithful in Christ* (New York: Crossroad, 1982), vol. 1, 240–41.

64. We have simplified the discussion of Liguori by ignoring cases of *excuse* for mistake of fact. Cf. supra at 195–98.

65. Alphonsus Liguori, *Theologia Moralis*, 1.1.6, in *Liguori Opere* (Turin: Marietti, 1846), vol. 5, 2.

66. No American lawyer can hear the word "proximate" without a mild autonomic response. It has been the vehicle of thousands of decisions declaring that a particular event in a series of events leading to an injury was (or was not) close enough to that injury in the chain of causation to justify liability for the one initiating that event. Liguori's usage seems cognate. In judging *who is good* he considers only what is immediate or "proximate" to the acting self. We were not surprised to learn that Liguori had a successful career as a practicing lawyer.

67. Bernard Häring, "Saint Alphonsus de Liguori—Advocate of the Defence of Conscience," *Readings in Redemptorist Spirituality*, English ed., vol. 4, 60, 67.

68. Liguori, *Theologia Moralis*, 1.1.7, vol. 5, 2 (quoting Aquinas, *Quodlibetal Question 3*, a. 27).

69. Häring, "Saint Alphonsus de Liguori," 62.

70. For a critical analysis of the "breakdown" of Aquinas's reasoning that prevented his reaching Liguori's position, see Eric D'Arcy, *Conscience and Its Right to Freedom* (New York: Sheed and Ward, 1961), 49–189.

71. See James Keenan, S.J., "Can a Wrong Action Be Good? The Development of Theological Opinion on Erroneous Conscience," *Eglise et Théologie* 24 (1993): 205. We hedge with the word "potential" because this capacity could, in theory, be enjoyed in different degrees. We likewise decline to make much of Pope Alexander VIII's condemnation (in 1690) of the Jansenist proposition that there would be personal sin if one were to act against the natural law while invincibly ignorant of that law. (DS § 2302). This was virtually a costless concession (not to mention a dig at the Jansenists) because the regnant view was that ignorance of the natural law *was* vincible.

72. John Henry Newman, "A Letter Addressed to His Grace the Duke of Norfolk," in *Conscience, Consensus, and the Development of Doctrine*, ed. James Gaffney (London: Doubleday, 1992), 434, 457.

73. Newman, *Grammar of Assent*, 277–78.

74. Id. at 183.

75. Id. at 230. This sentence could be Lonergan's. It was with his study of Newman that Lonergan said his philosophic development began. See Crowe, *Lonergan*, 39.

76. Newman, *Grammar of Assent*, 15.

77. Id. at 16.

78. See, for example, "Discourse X: Faith and Private Judgment," in John Henry Newman, *Discourses to Mixed Congregations* (New York: Longmans, Green, 1929), 192–213. This is in sharp distinction from his perception of the barbarian: "You know, it is one opinion entertained among divines and holy men, that the number of Catholics that are to be saved will on the whole be small. Multitudes of those who never knew the Gospel will rise up in the judgment against the children of the Church, and will be shown to have done more with scantier opportunities" (id., "Discourse VIII: Nature and Grace," 160). Rabbi Robinson gives the Jewish perspective on the chances for the gentiles. "It was much easier, according to the thinking of the rabbis, to be righteous as a non-Jew than as a Jew, and the reward at the end of days was the same for both" (*The Concise Guide to Judaism*, 98).

79. See id., "Discourse XI: Faith and Doubt," 214–37, esp. 215: "The Church does not allow her children to entertain any doubt of her teaching; and that, first of all, simply for this reason, because they are Catholics only while they have faith, and faith is incompatible with doubt."

80. John T. Noonan, "Development in Moral Doctrine," *Theological Studies* 54 (1993): 662.

81. See Mahoney, *The Making of Moral Theology*, 119, 325, 294–99; and James M. Gustafson, *Protestant and Roman Catholic Ethics: Prospects for Rapprochement* (Chicago: University of Chicago Press, 1978), 58.

82. Bernard Lonergan considered his work vindicated in the adjustments made: "The meaning of Vatican II was the acknowledgement of history" (in J. M. O'Hara, ed., *Curiosity at the Center of One's Life* [Montreal: Thomas More Institute, 1987], 426). Not wanting to call development "change," Vatican II put this different, slightly ambiguous spin on it: "Insight grows both into the words and the realities that have been handed on" (*Dei verbum*, sec. 8). See also *Gaudium et spes*, sec. 5.

The theological reasons for the magisterial change were abetted by a variety of secular influences. One was the twentieth-century experience of a daily social life shared by Christians and pagans in the modern city. Where governments had failed peacefully to unite the two, the industrial revolution to a degree succeeded; many men and women experienced the possibility of friendship across lines of fundamental division. And after wars the likes of which man had never seen, there was the discovery that even atheism can take an unselfish form: "Pity may become a source of rebellion against God. Man may renounce the Creator out of pity and compassion for the creature. Atheism may have a very lofty source" (Berdyaev, *The Destiny of Man*, 120). Finally, psychology had added its evidence regarding the vulnerability of the grasp of the good by individual humans. See L. Rulla et al., "Anthropology of the Christian Vocation," in Latourelle, *Vatican II: Assessment and Perspectives*, vol. 2, 402.

83. For example, the emperor Trajan appears in Purgatory (canto 10: verses 73–96); Abraham and other Old Testament figures are identified "among the blest" in Inferno (canto 4). Dante was on solid theological ground. In the second century St. Justin, for example, already had exceeded Dante in the inclusiveness of the Christian opportunity. In his *Dialogue with Trypho*, Justin concluded that, even before Christ, "those who lived according to the Word, whether pagans or Jews, were therefore, properly speaking, Christians" (Etienne Gilson, *The Spirit of Medieval Philosophy* (New York: Scribner's, 1940), 27). Justin conceived this possibility because, refusing sharply to distinguish between the natural and the supernatural, he considered the Word of God a seed of truth knowable by all men and life in conformity with it pleasing to God (Mahoney, *The Making of Moral Theology*, 101–2).

84. DS § 3870. Whether this subsequent clarification was meant to have a restrictive effect is hard to say: "*Requiritur enim, ut votum, quo quis ad Ecclesiam ordinetur perfecta caritate informetur; nec votum implicitum effectum habere potest, nisi homo fidem habeat supernaturalem*" (DS § 3872). The result all depends upon to whom the required supernatural faith is available; if only to official Church members, again inequality ensues.

It should be noted that this decree cites DS § 3869 as support for the doctrine of baptism of desire taught by the Council of Trent. But whether Trent actually provides that support is dubious, for the reasons set out in chapter 7, supra, at 175–76. Trent generally was not hopeful about the prospects of nonbelievers. See DS § 1544.

85. Murray's position and its development are summarized and well analyzed in the editorial and introductory materials by J. Leon Hooper, S.J., ed., in John Courtney Murray, *Religious Liberty: Catholic Struggles with Pluralism* (Louisville: Westminster/John Knox, 1993).

86. *Dignitatis humanae*, secs. 2, 3, 11.

87. Häring, "Saint Alphonsus de Liguori," 61.

88. *Gaudium et spes*, sec. 16 (emphasis added).

89. *Lumen gentium* ("Dogmatic Constitution on the Church"), sec. 16. It is noteworthy that for this proposition *Lumen gentium* cites only the Holy Office's 1949 letter to Archbishop Cushing regarding Father Feeney—hardly a venerable precedent.

90. *Dignitatis humanae*, like most legislative creations, is an unwieldy collection of ideas, debated and bartered. Murray's influence is nonetheless unmistakable in the primary justification selected for the historical shift to religious liberty. It is an insight born of humility and realism: everyone is a pilgrim seeker after truth, ever obligated to search and often to revise his understanding. When the truth unfolds, it must do so historically and incrementally. Its discovery is never more than a contingent possibility. Whether one is lucky enough to make the discovery does not decide one's moral destiny. That depends, rather, upon whether one looks for the truth.

91. *Ad Gentes* ("Decree on the Church's Missionary Activity"), sec. 7.

92. *Lumen gentium*, sec. 16. See also *Gaudium et spes*, sec. 10.

93. *Gaudium et spes*, sec. 29. Henri de Lubac, like Maritain (supra chap. 1 at 36), eschews both "capacities" and "calling" in favor of an undefined "essential equality": "In spite of great differences of understanding and of function, all members of the

human race enjoy the same essential equality before God" (Henri de Lubac, *Catholicism* [London: Universe, 1962], 118). Whether "the same essential" allows for degrees is left unaddressed.

94. Vatican II's emphasis upon the importance of the *search* for truth, so dependent upon Murray, reminds us of Bernard Lonergan and his emphasis upon personal commitment to the search rather than to its realized externals. As it happened, Murray was deeply influenced by the work of his fellow Jesuit (Murray, *Religious Liberty*, 34 n. 16). See also J. Leon Hooper. S.J., *The Ethics of Discourse: The Social Philosophy of John Courtney Murray* (Washington, D.C.: Georgetown University Press, 1986), 121–25).

95. John Courtney Murray, *We Hold These Truths: Catholic Reflections on the American Proposition* (Kansas City: Sheed and Ward, 1988), vii–viii.

96. Id. at viii–ix.

97. Paul Knitter, *No Other Name? A Critical Survey of Christian Attitudes Toward the World Religions* (Maryknoll, N.Y.: Orbis, 1985), 125–30.

98. Rahner himself is said to have been agog at how few controversies arose during the council with regard to the new optimism concerning salvation.

99. Karl Rahner, "Anonymous Christians," in Karl Rahner, *Theological Investigations*, vol. 6 (New York: Seabury, 1974), 390, 391.

100. Ibid.

101. Ibid.

102. Karl Rahner, "Concerning the Relationship Between Nature and Grace," in Karl Rahner, *Theological Investigations*, vol. 1 (Baltimore: Helicon, 1961), 297, 312; see also "Nature and Grace," in Rahner, *Theological Investigations*, vol. 4 (Baltimore: Helicon, 1966), 165 *et seq.*

103. Mahoney, *The Making of Moral Theology*, 98.

104. Dulles, *The Assurance of Things Hoped For*, 151–52.

> Grace is in the world *qua* world; it is in humans *qua* human. . . . What distinguishes Rahner's theological ethics from the received tradition of "natural law," which is knowable and acted upon by all persons, is, theologically speaking, Christian; it is graced. . . . Persons . . . who are acting in conformity with their true natures are acting in grace. . . . Those who properly love their neighbors are at the same time loving God; whether they are atheists, Hindus, Catholics, or Protestants is not a decisive factor. (Gustafson, *Protestant and Roman Catholic Ethics*, 117–18)

105. Karl Rahner, "Anonymous and Explicit Faith," in Karl Rahner, *Theological Investigations*, vol. 16 (New York: Seabury, 1979) 52, 57–58.

106. Hans Küng considers this surreptitious colonization offensive:

> The formula, "no salvation outside the Church," is then as true as ever, because all in fact are in the Church from the very beginning: not as formal but as "anonymous Christians." . . . Does this solve the problem? . . . It would be impossible to find anywhere in the world a sincere Jew, Muslim or atheist who would not regard the assertion that he is an "anonymous Christian" as presumptuous. . . . [W]hat would Christians say if they were graciously recognized by Buddhists as "anonymous Buddhists"? (Hans Küng, *On Being a Christian*, 98)

107. Karl Rahner, "Faith Between Rationality and Emotion," in Rahner, *Theological Investigations*, vol. 16, 61, 67.

108. Karl Rahner, "Some Thoughts on 'A Good Intention,' " in Karl Rahner, *Theological Investigations*, vol. 3 (Baltimore: Helicon, 1967), 105, 122. "Life is [to be] given a chance to educate us" (id. at 127).

109. Karl Rahner, "The Dignity and Freedom of Man," in Karl Rahner, *Theological Investigations*, vol. 2 (Baltimore: Helicon, 1963), 235, 253 (emphasis added).

110. Rahner, "Some Thoughts on 'A Good Intention,' " 128. See also "Reflections on the Problem of the Gradual Ascent to Christian Perfection," in Karl Rahner, *Theological Investigations*, vol. 3, 21. Thus if Rahner satisfies the criteria of conventional human equality, he may do so at the expense of the traditional theology of the sacraments. For him, saving grace reaches man, first of all, through and in nature rather than coming "from above" as the effect of the sacraments alone. This leaves the function of the sacraments obscure. For Rahner, people are already incorporated into Christ (hence the Church) exactly by Christ's becoming a man; God has triumphed already—and completely—in the incarnation.

Just how one's official membership in the institutional Church and the reception of baptism and the other sacraments "add" anything to this already established regime of grace is hard to see. Rahner emphasizes that the sacraments guarantee the grace they promise, but to us this seems just as true of the grace God promises man at the core of his being. Hard pressed to distinguish the grace mediated through the sacraments from that already mediated to all through the incarnation, Rahner designates the sacraments as thematizations or reminders of God's existing commonwealth of grace. The sacraments are historically mediated and community-celebrated instances of the grace God already offers to everybody (Karl Rahner, *The Church and the Sacraments* [New York: Herder and Herder, 1963]). The sacraments may be a help, but they are not necessary. That they are even a help would, of course, raise a question for equality. See supra chap. 7 at n. 78. Rahner's harmony with human equality may depend upon whether this "help" is of a sort that, *mutatis mutandis*, makes salvation more accessible to believers than to unbelievers. On this question Rahner is simply unclear.

111. "Rahner has often defended [his] solution as compatible with the teaching of Vatican II—teaching that he may have had a hand in formulating. But it is not necessary to interpret the statements of Vatican II as supporting the Rahnerian doctrine of 'anonymous Christianity.' That doctrine is, moreover, somewhat difficult to harmonize with the teaching of earlier councils and with the New Testament view of faith. In the New Testament and in traditional Christian theology, faith generally means explicit acceptance of the gospel" (Dulles, *The Assurance of Things Hoped For*, 153). Dulles nonetheless concludes that faith is a possibility open to all people (id. at 280).

112. Other, "unofficial" catechisms issued after Vatican II held that what scripture holds necessary for salvation is attainable without regard to a person's intellectual capacities:

Since God draws faith from the deepest core of man's being, its degree and vitality are not tied to intellectual endowments. . . . If the way of faith was that of pure reasoning the cleverest and most cultured people would find God most easily. The less learned and the less gifted would be less enlightened than they as regards the final end of life. But the knowledge through which God is found stems rather from man's inner orientation than from his talents. (*A New Catechism: Catholic Faith for Adults*, 125–26)

113. *Veritatis splendor* § 78 (emphasis added) (quoting the *Catechism of the Catholic Church*; the *Catechism* was first published in 1992, but it took until 1994 for the English version to appear).

114. Id. at § 78.

115. Id. at §§ 62–63 (citations omitted; emphasis in original).

116. We do not read the encyclical's condemnation of the moral theology of the "fundamental option" as extending to obtensionalism. In the former there supposedly is "an intention [of charity] with no corresponding positive effort to fulfill the different obligations of the moral life" (§ 67), whereas the latter—as we define it— measures moral goodness by whether there is a diligent intention of the real good.

117. Alasdair MacIntyre, for one, has read the encyclical as requiring right answers: "What we all have to learn is how to make right choices" ("How Can We Learn What *Veritatis Splendor* Has to Teach?" in *The Thomist* 58 (1994): 171, 183) because "the human good can be achieved only through a form of life in which the positive and negative precepts of the natural law are the norms governing our relationships" (id. at 173). MacIntyre thus continues his refusal (which we noted supra chap. 5 n. 22) to distinguish moral and nonmoral goods. Indeed, this appears to drive him to repudiate even the obligation to follow the involuntarily erroneous conscience: "Conscience has no authority in and by itself, but only insofar as its subjective deliverances conform (*sic*) to . . . objective [moral] standards" (id. at 187). Can MacIntyre mean what he has written? We would have thought—and *Veritatis splendor* teaches (§ 62)—that conscience derives its authority from its good faith *claim* to speak the truth to the human actor, not from conformity to the truth.

118. For example, can it be that it is Christian baptism that actually *creates* "fundamental equality with regard to dignity"? That seems the position of canon 208 of the *Code of Canon Law* (1983), which limits the precious equality it postulates to the "Christian faithful." We suspect confusion.

119. See "Vatican II: Salvation, Personal Morality, Right Behavior," in Josef Fuchs, *Personal Responsibility and Christian Morality*, trans. W. Cleves et al. (Washington, D.C.: Georgetown University Press, 1983), 19, 25; and "The Phenomenon of Conscience: Subject-Orientation and Object-Orientation," in Fuchs, *Christian Morality*, 118, 125.

120. "Innovative Morality," in Josef Fuchs, *Moral Demands and Personal Obligations*, trans. B. McNeil (Washington, D.C.: Georgetown University Press, 1993), 109, 116–17. Fuchs's understanding of objectivity is close to Lonergan's. See "Natural Law or Naturalistic Fallacy," in Fuchs, *Moral Demands and Personal Obligations*, 30, 40–41. See also "The Absolute in Moral Theology," in Fuchs, *Moral Demands and Personal Obligations*, 15, 25–26.

121. Fuchs, "Morality: Person and Acts," 109. See also "Early Christianity in Search of a Christian Morality: 1 Cor. 7," in Fuchs, *Christian Morality*, 83–101.

122. Fuchs, "Vatican II," 26.

123. Fuchs, "Morality: Person and Acts," 108.

124. Id. at 117.

125. Id. at 114. "In reality, the conscience is not sheer subjectivity, but a reflection on objectively available facts and discoverable evaluations that strives responsibly to reach the conclusion of ethical discourse in order to make a responsible decision" ("Conscience and Conscientious Fidelity," in *Moral Demands and Personal Obligations*, 153).

126. Fuchs, "Morality: Personal Acts," 108–9.

127. As to this we offer Fuchs's own response to *Veritatis splendor*:

> The encyclical attacks the idea that the moral quality of individual acts may be determined only by the intention, the basic orientation and the fundamental option of the person concerned (67). I must ask: who says anything remotely like this? Every particular act involves some reference to good or evil, and no one wishes to deny it; the problem is how this relates to the ethical status of the person as a whole, which is on another level. (Josef Fuchs, "Good Acts and Good Persons," in *The Tablet* [November 6, 1993]: 1444–45)

128. Tillich, *A History of Christian Thought*, 267. For a subtle analysis by a Protestant of the dearth of Protestant opinion on the salvific efficacy of good intentions, see Gustafson, *Protestant and Roman Catholic Ethics*, 1–29. "If salvation . . . comes through God's imputation of righteousness to persons, then the moral life no longer has the same *religious* seriousness" (id. at 10).

129. We must, however, note the overwhelming relevance of the emergent dispute among Protestant pastors over whether nonbelievers can be saved (Gustav Niebuhr, "Christian Split: Can Nonbelievers Be Saved?" *New York Times*, August 22, 1996, at A1.)

130. Lakoff, "Christianity and Equality," 123. Lakoff also has "Christianity . . . contending that degrees of rationality made no difference. What mattered was that every man had a soul and that in the eyes of God all souls were equally worthy" (id. at 118). Regrettably, this promising generality is never explained and would face serious opposition from predestinarians, Thomists, and others.

131. At least there is no historical dogmatic preference for the sophisticated or clever. Gilson recaptures the early resolution of the question: Who is the best Christian?

> Against the Gnostic thesis which reserved for a spiritual aristocracy the privilege of the knowledge that saves, Clement maintains that, since all are baptized, all Christians are equally able to achieve salvation. In the sight of God even the most learned among the Christians are but children, while, inversely, the most humble among the Christians are just as much the children of God as the most learned ones. So, when he speaks of a Christian *Gnosis*, Clement does not have in mind a selected group of super-Christians whose religion would be superior in perfection to that of the common flock of the faithful. On the contrary, he means to say that all the Christians are the true Gnostics. No doubt, some Christians know more and better than the other ones, but they are not more Christian than those who know less, or who know it less well. (Gilson, *History of Christian Philosophy in the Middle Ages*, 30)

And see E. Hamel, "The Foundation of Human Rights in Biblical Theology," in Latourelle, *Vatican II*, 460, 475–76.

132. *The New Catholic Encyclopedia*, vol. 6, 658.

133. See supra chap. 7 at 186–87.

134. Rahner, *Foundations of Christian Faith*, 97–106.

INTRODUCTION TO PART IV

1. Bernard Williams, "The Idea of Equality," 157–58.

CHAPTER 9
HARMONIES OF THE MORAL SPHERES

1. "Man is thus a member of two worlds. . . . He is responsible for *willing* to promote the moral law, within the sensible world, but he must be resigned about the *actual* results" (J. Collins, *A History of Modern European Philosophy* [Milwaukee: Bruce, 1954], 567 [interpreting Fichte's *Vocation of Man*]).

2. Well-intended moral catastrophes of the collective sort are assembled in M. Magnet, *The Dream and the Nightmare* (New York: Morrow, 1993). Such failures tell us nothing of the moral effects upon the actors, but they emphasize the fragility of our grasp of the good of others, hence of our own duty toward them. This is all the more true when the action to be undertaken is positive *policy* exceeding the minima prescribed by the Decalogue.

3. The Christians have worried considerably over this issue. "If God's purpose is not related to the betterment of the social order, why should Christians have a concern which God does not share?" (L. Gilkey, *Reaping the Whirlwind* [New York: Seabury, 1976], 215). We suppose one answer would be that God has given us the betterment of the social order as a project in whose service we simultaneously undertake the personal perfection (salvation) that he wills each of us freely to achieve or reject. Fixing the world may prove to be the vocation of Sisyphus, but this is irrelevant. "The gods" of Albert Camus may have "thought . . . that there is no more dreadful punishment," but they were wrong. Even if, in the end, the labor of Sisyphus proves "futile," they were wrong, for he is saved (*The Myth of Sisyphus and Other Essays* [New York: Vintage, 1955], 88).

4. See discussion supra at 80–82, 155–61.

5. We concede that distinguished moralists have sometimes incorrectly assumed that belief in moral perfection by intention *entails* rejection of an external standard. See, for example, J. C. Murray, *We Hold These Truths*, supra, 276 *et seq.*

6. Isaac Watts thought society could exist very well, as Rome did, by honestly worshipping even false gods—so long as there were, indeed, a real God and a true religion (J. Maclear, "Isaac Watts and the Idea of Public Religion," *Journal of the History of Ideas* [1992]: 25, 34). The parallel gets closer to our case when Watts insists upon the additional reality of a universal lateral obligation apart from revelation (id. at 31, 42).

7. Robert Pirsig says we must start with ourselves before we can expect to make any contribution to the common good (Robert Pirsig, *Zen and the Art of Motorcycle*

Maintenance [New York: Bantam, 1974], 267). We could agree if it were understood that we can start perfecting ourselves *only* by seeking the common good.

8. The importance of this distinction has been reinforced for us by reading chapter 9 ("Responsibility") of Robert Spaemann's manuscript "*Glück und Wohlsollen*" (translated by Alberg and Schenk and shared—with Spaemann's permission—by Richard Schenk). R. Spaemann, *Basic Moral Concepts*, trans. T. Armstrong (London: Routledge, 1989), has also been a useful guide.

9. We are reminded that Kant distinguished duties *regarding* animals or God from duties *toward* either, reserving the latter to human persons (Kant, *Doctrine of Virtue*, 442).

10. Some of the more Nietzschean versions of Darwinism (including that of Darwin himself) may be exceptions. And, both before and after Darwin, a few Europeans were tempted to convert racial genocide and/or slavery into moral crusades. (We are unable to determine whether General George Custer had the advantage of reading Herbert Spencer's *Social Statics*.) On the whole, however, that portion of the slaughter and human bondage effected in the New World by Europeans was perceived even by its perpetrators as a necessary evil. Sherman's assertion that "the only good Indian is a dead Indian" never acquired a rationale. And we should not forget the ongoing influence of counterculture figures such as Las Casas. See H. R. Parish, ed., *The Only Way*, trans. F. P. Sullivan (New York: Paulist Press, 1992); and *In Defense of the Indians*, ed. and trans. S. Poole (De Kalb: Northern Illinois University Press, 1974).

11. See *Restatement (Second) of Contracts*, 302, 304, 315 (1981). To be sure, the law is interested only in the intentions of the promisor and promisee, and it is they (and the law) who create the relation to the Other.

12. J. C. Murray has it about right: "The traditional ethic, which asserts the doctrine of reason in public affairs, does not expect that man's historical success in installing reason in its rightful rule will be much more than marginal. But the margin makes the difference" (*We Hold These Truths*, 289).

13. It is sometimes suggested that "pure agents" (those supposed to be unaffected by bad moral luck) make bad citizens. See, for example, M. Walker, "The Virtues of Impure Agency," in Statman, *Moral Luck*, 235–50. "Pure agents will have far less to account for, and will bear, in total, far less responsibility" (id. at 245). Similar criticisms appear in other essays in the same volume. See, for example, J. Andre, id. at 129. Note that these concerns do not attach to obtension. Walker may take Kant as a target, reading him to suppose that "pure agents are free, on their own, to determine what and how much they may be brought to account for" (id. at 245). Even were he right about Kant, this would be irrelevant for any theory in which the actor is responsible to seek a sovereign and independent good. Andre, too, is beside the point when she asserts that "the 'morally accident-prone' can learn to be better; but they are unlikely to change if all our moral assessment is concentrated on intention and none on actual result" (id. at 129). The first duty of obtension is to concentrate on the actual result; that concentration is the *precondition* of a good intention.

14. According to a separate criticism, the supposed lenity of obtension actually cheapens the achievement of personal goodness. But in what would this debasement consist? The objection could not be that moral self-perfection is simply made easier; for, by definition, nothing would be lost if perfection itself were more accessible. The question is whether perfection itself retains its nature or shrinks exactly as it becomes

available. The principle could be that things have worth in proportion to what we suffer to attain them. Not only is lunch not free; the more expensive it is, the better it tastes for the one who must pay. Where that idea originated, we cannot say. It would be a heresy to Christians, for it devalues unmerited grace.

15. Gilson, supra chap. 8 at 195.

16. Rousseau thought Christians lacked the capacity for good citizenship because their eye was on eternity: "True Christians . . . hardly endeavor to avoid slavery; this short life is of too little consequence in their eyes" (Rousseau, *The Social Contract*, 122). If we have read the Christian's moral incentives correctly, the opposite is true; if salvation rests upon diligent pursuit of the objective good, the Christian is playing exactly the same game as Rousseau but for much higher stakes. Maritain agrees: "Human weakness is always trying to go to sleep. . . . But Christianity is the very opposite of such a sleep. Authentic Christianity has a horror of the pessimism of inertia" (Jacques Maritain, *True Humanism* [New York: Scribner's, 1938], 48).

17. Mahoney gives a useful taxonomy:

> To sum up the different systematic replies elaborated in the sixteenth to the eighteenth centuries to answer the question of what to do when in doubt, the tutiorist would advocate obedience to the law or any other course which was the safer to follow, the probabiliorist would urge doing what seemed the more likely to be right, the aequiprobabilist would judge that either of equally balanced alternatives could be followed, and the simple probabilist would reply that any action was morally justified for which a good case could be made.
>
> Below this elaborate moral shorthand, of course, a fundamentally important moral debate was in fact being conducted on the nature of moral responsibility, the competing claims of truth and security, and the ever-present tension between freedom and responsibility and between freedom and authority. (Mahoney, *The Making of Moral Theology*, 137)

Pascal denounced casuistry of this sort in a manner that would leave him at odds with us. "The earnestness of the saints in seeking the truth was useless, if the probable is trustworthy" (*Pensees* [Random House, 1941], § 916). Pascal misses the possibilities that it is earnestness alone that counts and that some saints may not be so obvious.

18. It was all this industry, of course, that drove Luther to repudiate the *facienti*. It was also typical of the Reformers, such as Luther, to reject the "evangelical counsels," the traditional Catholic designation for what we refer to as supererogation.

19. See, for example, Frederick Schauer, *Playing by the Rules* (Oxford: Clarendon, 1991), 229–33.

20. The reference here is to Lon L. Fuller's distinction between the "morality of duty" and the "morality of aspiration" (*The Morality of Law* [New Haven: Yale University Press, 1964]). See also Joel Feinberg, "Supererogation and Rules," *Ethics* 71 (1961): 276–88.

21. Its modern naturalistic version preserves this spirit of questing "supererogation"—the never-quite-finished commitment—as the central motif of environmental ethics. It includes the ceaseless duty to know what we can and to recognize the range of our ignorance as a primary datum (Jonas, *The Imperative of Responsibility*, 7–8). The Christian existentialist would add that "personality must come out of itself,

must transcend itself—this is the task set to it by God" (Berdyaev, *The Destiny of Man*, 57).

22. It is, however, "not the will to be peculiar and unlike anybody else; it means the desire to derive one's consciousness from its primary source" (id. at 163).

23. Obtension also entails the obligation of mutual education which now has two aspects. First, we must share whatever wisdom we can muster about specific good behaviors; second, we must teach one another the vocation to transcend the minimum. In that regard, note that belief in the obtensional view assists the moralist who seeks to define the minimum of good conduct and thereby to contribute to the common good. No longer need the sensitive casuist be concerned that less gifted persons will be unable to grasp the terms of his objective message. Once the perfection of the luckless is no longer at stake, the moralist is strengthened against undue lenity in his assessment of what counts as good behavior.

24. Carole Pateman, *The Sexual Contract* (Stanford: Stanford University Press, 1988), 78.

25. *Declaration of the Rights of Man and of the Citizen*, adopted by the National Assembly on August 26, 1789, and reaffirmed by the Constitution of 1958. In 1790 Edmund Burke's *Reflections* had set the intellectual agenda, focusing upon liberty and equality (*Reflections on the Revolution in France*, Harvard Classics, vol. 24 [New York: Collier, 1937], 143). Burke himself held for a "true moral equality" which, however, he did not specify (id. at 176).

26. In the motion adopted by the Cordeliers in June 1793: *Unite, indivisibilité de la Republique, Liberté, Egalité Fraternité ou la mort.* "Aulard . . . gives the first official use of the phrase in the motion passed by the Club" (*Journal de Paris*, no. 182; *Oxford Dictionary of Quotations*, 2d ed. [London: Oxford University Press, 1953], 12).

27. F. Engels, "History of the Communist League," in L. Feuer, ed., *Marx and Engels: Basic Writings on Politics and Philosophy* (Garden City, N.Y.: Doubleday, 1959), 459–70.

28. Id. at 469. Cf. F. Toennies, *Karl Marx: His Life and Teachings*, trans. C. Loomis and I. Paulus (East Lansing: Michigan State University Press, 1974), 31.

29. Rechristened "brotherhood," fraternity has played ambiguous, historic roles. On the one hand it has been inclusive and on the other exclusive—a case of us against them. Under that same banner of brotherhood it continues its career today as a vague sentiment about proper relations among races and nations. Overall, fraternity still does not seem to have acquired any theoretical base of its own distinct from equality. There is modest analytical effort to this end in the one major compendium in English purporting to be the history of the concept, W. C. McWilliams's *The Idea of Fraternity in America* (Berkeley: University of California Press, 1973). The book is a useful but somewhat unfocused collection of essays on psycho-social historical notions about the nature of community. It is a model of coherence, however, in comparison with T. V. Smith and E. C. Lindeman, "The Fraternity Motif," in their *The Democratic Way of Life*, chap. 2 (New York: New American Library, 1951). Recently, there has been a spate of friendly attention to fraternity among liberal and socialist commentators who enlist it on the side of "community" and "solidarity" but continue to conflate it with egalitarian ideals of sameness in treatment. Several of these works are considered briefly in Pateman, *The Sexual Contract*, 78–82.

30. James Fitzjames Stephen, *Liberty, Equality, Fraternity* (New York: Holt and Williams, 1873). Stephen saw the distinctive element in fraternity to be a vague, abstract, and ineffectual love of humanity—a secular religion lacking any theory that could make strangers worthy of love (id. at 256 *et seq.*). If the nature of fraternity and its relation to a real equality were to be left in this vague state, we would agree with Stephen's conclusion.

31. E. Wilson, *To the Finland Station* (Garden City, N.Y.: Doubleday, 1940), 308.

32. Though fraternity could be interpreted to embrace all manner of human good, it has a special claim to the domain John Finnis labels the good of "friendship" (see Finnis, supra chap. 5 at 133). And John Rawls at least briefly associates his own concept of distributive justice—"the difference principle"—with fraternity (*A Theory of Justice*, 105–6).

33. Even Hobbes conceived of it so—as a kind of personal power or capacity. We have done the same throughout this essay. The only difference between Hobbes and us is over the question of whether liberty is sovereign and defines the good. Obtension limits moral autonomy to the choice for or against an obligation that is independent of consent; but for the moment we can stand with Hobbes, leaving only the determinists to reject freedom as a fact.

34. Grand designs and final social solutions seldom offer a compelling reason for wanting to *be* a just *person*. The good life is not the triumph of the right theory but the embrace of personal responsibility. And, in any case, "without good men you cannot have a good society" (C. S. Lewis, *Mere Christianity*, 72).

35. Alasdair MacIntyre seems to have attached his moral hopes to the fraternal ideal: According to MacIntyre the West needs another, doubtless very different, St. Benedict. For a millenium and a half Benedicts's *Rule* has shaped the fraternal life of monasteries (for monasteries and nunneries) (MacIntyre, *After Virtue*, 245). That Ronald Dworkin and Anthony Kronman have also set their sights on fraternity only confirms our judgment that the concept wants moral fortification. Richard Rorty's embrace of fraternity is likewise only half-encouraging:

> Here, in the late 21st century (*sic*), as talk of fraternity and unselfishness has replaced talk of rights, American political discourse has come to be dominated by quotations from Scripture and literature, rather than from political theorists or social scientists. Fraternity, like friendship, was not a concept that either philosophers or lawyers knew how to handle. They could formulate principles of justice, equality and liberty, and invoke these principles when weighing hard moral or legal issues. But how to formulate a "principle of fraternity"? Fraternity is an inclination of the heart, one that produces a sense of shame at having much when others have little. It is not the sort of thing that anybody can have a theory about or that people can be argued into having. (Richard Rorty, "Fraternity Reigns," *New York Times Magazine*, September 29, 1996, 155, 157)

36. For example, Pateman, *The Sexual Contract*, supra.

37. The current effort to make something of "communitarianism" may yet bear fraternal fruit. The *Responsive Communitarian Platform*, announced in 1991 and adorned with varied and appropriate signatures, could be interpreted to accept a descriptive human equality. It declares that "we should . . . recognize our basic equality . . . as moral agents," and remarks upon "the equal moral dignity of all individu-

als" (*The Responsive Community*, 12, 17). Unfortunately the *Platform* evidences no awareness that these propositions remain ambiguous and fragile until they are grounded in a particular theory of personhood—one that many of the signatories could find unacceptable for its recognition of a preinstitutional order of obligation.

38. The preamble to the constitution of the Wobblies imagined "a society in which it is easier for people to be good" (Dorothy Day, *The Long Loneliness* [San Francisco: Harper and Row, 1972], 170). If there is a word better than fraternity to encourage this state of affairs, let it be heard.

39. Curiously, the word "responsibility" becomes a serious political term roughly around the time of the French Revolution. It appears to have been proferred in response to concerns for the common good of the sort canvassed in the text. See Richard McKeon, "The Development and the Significance of the Concept of Responsibility," 62–87.

CHAPTER 10
HARVESTS OF EQUALITY

1. Indeed, apart from the power attributed to God, variability may be definitional of *any* power (human or otherwise) including the capacity for moral self-perfection.

2. Charles Taylor sees the problem clearly enough:

> The politics of equal dignity is based on the idea that all humans are equally worthy of respect. It is underpinned by a notion of what in human beings commands respect, however we may try to shy away from this "metaphysical" background . . . [W]hat commanded respect in us was our status as rational agents, capable of directing our lives through principles. Something like this has been the basis for our intuitions of equal dignity . . . a *universal human potential*, a capacity that all humans share. This potential, rather than anything a person may have made of it, is what ensures that each person deserves respect. ("The Politics of Recognition," in A. Gutman, ed., *Multiculturalism* [Princeton, N.J.: Princeton University Press, 1994], 41)

Taylor avoids serious encounters with the metaphysics that poses the real problem.

3. "Let us make man in our image, after our likeness" (*Genesis* 1:26).

4. The Jewish sage, Philo, comments on the *Genesis* idea in *De Opificio Mundi*, stressing that the mind is the core of the image. The second-century Christian, Origen, does the same. See Origen in *On First Principles*, book 4, in Greer, *Origen*, 14–16; and *Prologue to the Commentary on the Song of Songs*, id. at 220. The obvious Latin example is Augustine in *De Genesi ad litteram*. See also J. E. Sullivan, *The Image of God: The Doctrine of St. Augustine and Its Influence* (Dubuque, Iowa: Priory, 1963). A medieval representative is Peter Lombard, *Commentary on the Sentences*, 2.16.17. References are collected in the excellent essay of Charles Trinkhaus, "The Renaissance Idea of the Dignity of Man," *Dictionary of the History of Ideas* (New York: Scribner's, 1973), vol. 4, 136.

5. Few of the early sources use the specific term "dignity," but by the Middle Ages it is clear that the discussions of the "*imago Dei*" and of "dignity" concern the same subject matter.

6. Cicero specifically applies the term "dignity" to the uniquely human element: "Man's mind [as distinguished from that of animals] is developed by study and reflection. . . . From this we may learn that sensual pleasure is wholly unworthy of the dignity of the human race" (*De Officiis* [Cambridge: Harvard University Press, 1979], vol. 1, 30).

7. Thus Article I(1) of the *German Basic Law*: "The dignity of man shall be inviolable. To respect and protect it shall be the duty of all state authority."

8. O. Schachter, "Human Dignity as a Normative Concept," 77 *American Journal of International Law* 848 (1983). *The International Covenant on Civil and Political Rights* contains several clear references to dignity as a descriptive. See 20 *Georgia Journal of International and Comparative Law*, appendix C, 441 (Preamble) and 445 (article 10).

9. Likewise, the question of whether a person *has* dignity sometimes is confused with the question of whether a person acts in a dignified manner. But dignity is not lost by a breach of Victorian etiquette; it is made of sterner stuff. Thus it would be a facile mistake to suppose that a person's weeping at his own execution would dissolve his dignity and therewith any reason to spare him.

10. B. F. Skinner, *Beyond Freedom and Dignity*, supra.

11. This point is not strictly necessary in the case of religious believers. Their dignity could, no doubt, be provided for independently in the ascendant order by a private relation to God (as with Adam before the arrival of Eve). However, no one has given such an exclusively vertical interpretation to the concept, and, for the Christian, the imperative of charity would be enough to locate human dignity emphatically in the lateral dimension. We *have* dignity, in part, because we *are* moral interactors.

12. Incurably nonrational humans—even human remains—are entitled to respectful treatment, but the sources of this entitlement lie outside the domain of the dignity entailed in human equality. See supra at 53–54.

13. Conversely, if all are "equal in dignity" this would seem to entail the authors' version of equality, especially when dignity is associated with "reason and conscience," as it often is. See, for example, United Nations' *Universal Declaration of Human Rights*, (December 10, 1948). Failure to perceive the danger to dignity is widespread even among those who cherish the concept and associate it with equality. Mortimer Adler conflates dignity with a fragile equality he would ground in the capacity for rational morality or "the power of free choice" (*Six Great Ideas*, 164). Though variable reason is a constituent element, Adler treats dignity as if it were incapable of degree: "The dignity we attribute to being a person rather than a thing is not subject to differences in degree. The equality of all human beings is the equality of their dignity as persons" (id. at 165). He then warns of the relativization that unconsciously he has just invited: "Were all human beings not equal in their common humanity, did they not all equally have the dignity of persons, they would not all be entitled to equalities of condition" (ibid.). A dignity so vulnerable even to its friends needs to be reconceptualized.

14. On precisely this distinction Garry Wills contrasts modern society with that of Revolutionary America: "Our culture takes reason and intellect to be the highest of man's faculties" (Wills, *Inventing America*, 224). We think this attitude to be largely a phenomenon of the media and the academy.

15. See supra at 72–76.

16. See supra at 73–76.

17. "The intellectual can advance in proper time to the position of a court theologian. . . . And, if you are bright, you will follow him" (Voegelin, *The New Science of Politics*, 175). Voegelin portrays Hobbes as opposed to the attitude of the Puritans and other gnostic enthusiasts. Nevertheless, Hobbes himself, though seemingly indifferent to individual moral self-perfection, lays the groundwork for the moral rule of the intellectual in both the objective and internal orders.

18. Once again we decline to take seriously Hobbes's tactical premise that humans are equal in strength and intellect. See supra at 101–2.

19. "Why Do We Need Kant?" in Kolakowski, *Modernity on Endless Trial*, 44, 54.

Kant indeed believed in the essential equality of human beings with respect to their dignity as free beings endowed with reason. In this point, he certainly continued the seventeenth-century doctrine of natural law—he was an heir of Puffendorf [*sic*] and Grotius—even if he based his doctrine on different anthropological presuppositions. (Id. at 49)

20. Nietzsche is less at home in Nuremberg than in the halls of ivy:

Be robbers and conquerors, as long as you cannot be rulers and owners, you lovers of knowledge! Soon the age will be past when you could be satisfied to live like shy deer hidden in the woods. At long last the pursuit of knowledge will reach out for its due: it will want to *rule* and *own*, and you with it. (*The Gay Science*, 979–98; emphasis in original)

21. The authors' evidence for this is primarily the firsthand reports of the West German academics who, in so many instances, became their (gnostic?) replacements. See also K. Meyer, "Berlin's Lost Generation," *New York Times*, January 3, 1995; I. Markovitz, "Children of a Lesser God: GDR Lawyers in Post-Socialist Germany," 94 *Michigan Law Review* 2270 (1996).

22. Voegelin, *The New Science of Politics*, 181 (quoting Hobbes, *The Elements of Law, Natural and Political*, ed. F. Toennies [1928], part 1, chap. ix, sec. 21).

23. This is portrayed imaginatively in the sensationally successful 1994 movie *Forrest Gump*. The various bullies who would dominate and brutalize the dim-witted Gump are themselves mostly marginal nincompoops of the gnostic sort. We might note in passing that the public's emotional embrace of this film provides some confirmation of our interpretation of the convention. It is not conclusive of the question, however, because in the film Gump (by luck or otherwise) *correctly* assesses every moral issue. He is, as it were, a moral idiot savant. We would appreciate a sequel in which the obtending and self-perfecting Gump makes all the objectively *wrong* choices, thereby presenting his neighbors a rather more interesting moral question. That would be a harder movie to make.

24. See supra chap. 7 at 182.

25. T. Carlyle, *On Heroes, Hero-Worship, and the Heroic in History* (London: Chapman and Hall, 1841); *Past and Present* (New York: W. H. Colyer, 1843); *Oliver Cromwell's Letters and Speeches: With Elucidations* (London: Chapman and Hall, 1845); *The History of Friedrich II of Prussia, Called Frederick the Great* (London: Chapman and Hall, 1865).

26. The story is well, if critically, told by J. Hunter in *Culture Wars: The Struggle to Define America* (New York: Basic Books, 1991); and in *Before the Shooting Begins* (New York: Free Press, 1994).

27. For the Shakespeare imbroglio, see P. Cantor, "Shakespeare—'For All Time?' " *The Public Interest* (winter 1993): 34.

28. The hero is not himself a person but a name:

> The marbles of what he was stand
> Like a white abstraction only, a feeling
> In a feeling mass, blank emotion,
> An anti-pathos, until we call it
> Xenophon, its implement and actor.
> (Wallace Stevens, "Examination of the Hero in a Time of War,"
> *The Collected Poems* [New York: Vintage, 1990], 276–77)

And see "Paisant Chronicles," id. at 334–35.

29. Harold Bloom, *The Western Canon: The Books and School of the Ages* (New York: Harcourt, Brace, 1994).

30. We do not suppose that heroic literature celebrates *mere* role playing by plastic and adaptive wimps of the sort identified in the studies by Erving Goffman. All roles offer at least the twofold choice to play or to revolt. Cast in the occasional role that is potentially heroic, one chooses between the great and the pedestrian response. Roles are a subspecies of the invitation to self-perfection through commitment to the good. Cf. MacIntyre, *After Virtue*, 119.

31. If he was great, it may be for his very ordinariness. Harold Bloom makes him sound like a good fourth for bridge (*The Western Canon*, 55–56, 61–62).

32. C. S. Lewis, "The World's Last Night," in *The World's Last Night and Other Essays* (San Diego: Harcourt, Brace, Jovanovich, 1973), 105.

33. This does not deny that from time to time our experience delivers signals of an apparent real goodness or a real corruption at the heart of another person. Nor can humans conduct their practical affairs without the rule of thumb that the behavior of others is evidence of intention. The only message is this: Make no ultimate judgment of the person nor any judgment of her at all beyond that required for the business at hand. See supra at 70–72.

34. Samuel Pufendorf may mean something of the sort: "No one can live a social life with a person by whom he is not rated as at least a fellow man" (*De jure naturae et gentium*, vol. 8, chap. 2, 330). Philip Selznick quotes Rousseau to similar effect: "One cannot live in peace with people one regards as damned" (*The Moral Commonwealth*, 425). Our proposition is, of course, more specific in requiring the perception of *equals*.

35. Just what the practical aim of the communitarian movement really is cannot be specified in any consistent way, at least if all those traveling under that banner are to be given equal weight. See "Freedom and Community," unsigned editorial in *The Economist*, December 24, 1994, 33 (commenting upon A. Etzioni, *The Spirit of Community* [New York: Crown, 1993]). Nevertheless, it is not hard to identify the general metaphysical position the communitarian will have to take on the nature of equality, if he is to avoid fomenting further social fracture along lines of intellectual power and insight. In this subsection we make the assumption that this is his hope,

ascribing that position to him even though we recognize that some signatories of the *Platform* reject the view of human moral life that is necessary to descriptive equality.

36. The following sort of observation is very common: "[All of us] . . . are influenced by notions that . . . nonwhites are more like animated things than full-fledged human beings." Note, "It's Not Easy Bein' Green: The Psychology of Racism, Environmental Discrimination, and the Argument for Modernizing Equal Protection Analysis," 46 *Vanderbilt Law Review* 937 (1993). Unfortunately, such insights tell us little of what a full-fledged human being would be.

37. As to whether Jefferson himself actually held this view see supra at 97–99.

38. Here it would be hard to improve on the insight of the old anarchist Michael Bakunin who despised Marx's division of function between intellectuals and workers. The outcome would, he said, be

the reign of scientific intelligence, the most aristocratic, despotic, arrogant, and contemptuous of all regimes. There will be a new class, a new hierarchy of real and pretended scientists and scholars, and the world will be divided into a minority ruling in the name of knowledge and an immense ignorant majority. And then, woe betide the mass of ignorant ones! (J. Karabel, "Revolutionary Contradictions: Antonio Gramsci and the Problem of Intellectuals," *Politics and Society* 6 [1976]: 123, 124)

39. The group need not, of course, be racially defined. See, for example, W. E. Channing, "On the Elevation of the Laboring Classes," in *Essays English and American, Harvard Classics*, vol. 28 (New York: Collier, 1938), 311, esp. 323.

40. This provides the occasion to note G. K. Chesterton's contrary interpretation of the nineteenth-century American public reaction to Dickens's concern about collecting his fees:

Nothing is more likely than that the Americans thought it very shocking in Dickens, the divine author, to talk about being done out of money. Nothing would be more American than to expect a genius to be too high-toned for trade. . . . For it is quite unjust to say that the Americans worship the dollar. They really do worship intellect—another of the passing superstitions of our time. (*Charles Dickens: The Last of the Great Men* [New York: The Readers Club, 1942], 102–3)

That was nineteenth-century America, and—writing in 1906, even before the Great Wars—Chesterton himself foresaw the passing of this democratic gnosticism. There is something left of it, but the modern overexposure of the intellectual in the media has taken its toll on brain worship among ordinary people. And the humiliating end of the ideological dictatorships has left us, if anything, too morally condescending to the embattled intellectuals. In 1997 one could prudently fear a gnosticism of the ignorant. As Voegelin foresaw, "the reaction against gnosticism will be as world wide as its expansion" (*The New Science of Politics*, 165).

41. The notion of a gnostic equality is a contradiction, as is any other equality grounded on a measurable and variable trait (e.g., the ability to dunk a basketball). The celebration of equality within the academy is the canard of a guild secure in its possession of a peculiar excellence that it would like to make the universal measure

of human worth. When academics apply for affirmative action places in athletic events, we will reconsider.

42. As Harold Bloom observes of the Southern Baptist Convention, gnosticism easily tends to anti-intellectualism (*The American Religion*, 43–44).

43. "It is but a step from the idea that a person's worth is bound up with achievement to the conclusion that some people are *inherently* more [capable of becoming?] worthy than others. The 'opportunity society' invites the return of moral inequality—and does so with an easy conscience" (Selznick, *The Moral Commonwealth*, 494). The classic moral complaint about efficiency in role assignments is M. Young, *The Rise of the Meritocracy* (London: Thames and Hudson, 1958). See also D. Bell, *The Coming of Post-Industrial Society* (New York: Basic Books, 1973).

44. A nearly uniform blindness on this point explains the hysteria over the appearance of *The Bell Curve*, supra. Whether Herrnstein and Murray proved their own case is not for us to say (nor do we think it important). What *was* proved is that their detractors perceive brains as a moral category; gnostics to the core, these ingenuous critics exorcise their own contempt for the ignorant by projecting it. *The Bell Curve* at least recognizes that intelligence is "just a noun, not an accolade" (id. at 22) and emphasizes "how little an IQ score tells about whether [to] . . . admire or cherish" a person (id. at 21). Sadly, the book never denies that IQ affects one's *capacity* for moral self-perfection; nor does it suggest much about whom we should cherish and thus may leave a gnostic impression.

45. We, of course, would see such persons as threatened by a kind of moral "false consciousness."

46. George Orwell, "Charles Dickens," in *A Collection of Essays by George Orwell* (Garden City, N.Y.: Doubleday Anchor, 1954), 55, 71.

47. The graphics in *The Bell Curve*, supra, are a relentless repetition of this metaphor.

48. In truth, even this poor chap's literary creator seems to take a gnostic view of his possibilities (E. Markham, "The Man with the Hoe").

49. L. Bloy, *The Woman Who Was Poor*, trans. I. J. Collins (New York: Sheed and Ward, 1947).

50. C. Lasch, "Progress: The Last Superstition," *Tikkun* 4, no. 3 (1989).

51. There were, to be sure, dissenters: "I think that the progress has been mixed, partly good and partly bad. I suspect that in many ways it has been a progress from strength to weakness" (Stephen, *Liberty, Equality, Fraternity*, 220).

52. Alasdair MacIntyre concludes that our culture has overall degenerated from a higher intellectual and cultural order into an antirational emotivism (*After Virtue*, 21 et seq.).

53. "Precisely such hopes . . . for a morally 'better' man . . . are the core of the ideal" (Jonas, *The Imperative of Responsibility*, 159).

54. As Paul Cantor puts it of Shakespeare's modern deconstructors, they are "obsessed with asserting their superiority as people of the twentieth century over Shakespeare, the Elizabethan" (Cantor, "Shakespeare—'For All Time?' " 44). Crane Brinton reminds us that this claim is typical of the twentieth-century gnostic: "An ordinary Englishman in 1901 had, in this system, to be a morally superior being to an ordinary Athenian in 416 B.C." (Brinton, *A History of Western Morals*, 421).

55. A naive lawyer would suppose their survival to have proved them "fitter"!

56. As is the contempt of the modern gnostic for women who decline the rationalist turn and for clergy who are not smart but merely Christian.

57. Jonas, *The Imperative of Responsibility*, 16–17. Jonas later adds this tribute to our "primitive" ancestors: "Being human, though different each time, was not therefore more provisional and 'unfinished' at any time than it is today" (id. at 110).

58. "The doctrine of progress is bound to be a religious faith, since there can be no positive science of progress" (Berdyaev, *The Meaning of History* [London: Bles, 1949], 187). And Tocqueville reminds us that another source of romantic perfectionism is the egalitarian element in democratic politics: "Equality puts many ideas into the human mind . . . and it changes almost all the ideas that were there before. I take the concept of human perfectibility as an example" (A. de Tocqueville, *Democracy in America*, 452). Reinhold Niebuhr would add that "there is a millennial hope in every vital religion" (*Moral Man and Immoral Society* [New York: Scribner's, 1932], 60). We hope not.

59. Again, Jonas in his classic work, *The Gnostic Religion*, supra, and Voegelin, *The New Science of Politics*, supra.

60. See Gilson, *History of Christian Philosophy in the Middle Ages*, 59. And see generally C. Dawson, *Progress and Religion* (New York: Sheed and Ward, 1938); and C. Lasch, *The True and Only Heaven* (New York: Norton, 1991). The latter contains an invaluable bibliographical essay.

61. C. Lasch, "Progress: The Last Superstition," supra.

62. T. de Chardin, *The Phenomenon of Man*, trans. B. Wall (New York: Harper and Brothers, 1959), 276.

63. Id. at 288 (emphasis omitted).

64. Id. at 244. He adds the specifically gnostic point: "The great human machine is designed to work and *must* work—by producing a superabundance of mind" (id. at 257; emphasis in original).

65. Julian Huxley, introduction to Chardin, *The Phenomenon of Man*, 12.

66. Id. at 19.

67. Id. at 20.

68. Rahner, *Foundations of Christian Faith*, 190.

69. The Lutheran theologian Helmut Thielicke notes that "there is no biblical foundation whatever for the concept of historical progress. By nature, i.e., in its innermost structure, history is implicated in the fall. This is why it cannot sever itself from its own roots and approximate more and more to the kingdom of God" (*Theological Ethics*, 439).

70. "One need not be a conservative to believe that our grandparents knew, in things that matter, as much or more than we" (Richard Neuhaus, *The Naked Public Square* [Grand Rapids, Mich.: Eerdmans, 1984], 226).

71. By contrast, "the Gnostic fallacy destroys the oldest wisdom of mankind concerning the rhythm of growth and decay which is the fate of all things under the sun" (Voegelin, *The New Science of Politics*, 166).

72. With Berdyaev we conclude that progress in the moral sense is an inhuman concept: "Every generation is in contact with the Absolute and Divine and . . . it is precisely in this that the Divine truth and justice consist. What could be more unjust than a monopoly of the divine life and mysteries reserved for a generation at the apex of progress" (Berdyaev, *The Meaning of History*, 193).

73. Chardin, *The Phenomenon of Man*, 230–31.

74. Our conversation with Chardin replays a century-old Chekhov dialogue:

"If the limits of progress lie in infinity, as you say, it follows that its aims are indeterminate," I replied. "Which means living without definitely knowing what you are living for!"

"That may be! But this 'not knowing' is not so dull as your 'knowing.' I am climbing a ladder known as progress, civilization, culture, I go on and on, not knowing definitely where I am going, but, truly, it's worth living just for the sake of this marvelous ladder; you, meanwhile, know what you are living for: so that some should not enslave others, so that the artist and the man who grinds his colors for him should dine equally well. But that's the bourgeois, the gray, kitchen side of life, and to live for that alone—that really would be disgusting, now wouldn't it?" (A. Chekhov, "My Life (The Story of a Provincial)," in *Ward Six and Other Stories* [New York: New American Library, 1965], 246–47)

75. If it is important to accommodate eschatology, this picture would suffice. It vindicates the judgment of the early Christians whose "predictions" were, in essence, an emerging but incomplete consciousness of the new reality, namely, that a fully redeemed world would be one in which humanity had received the invitation, and each could choose, one by one, to accept or reject. The Christians had the inchoate conviction that this had now become the case.

76. Bloom, *The Western Canon*, 110.

77. Pangloss is a caricature of Leibniz and his doctrine of preestablished and universal harmony in which all things are for the best under the reign of a beneficent though distinctly mechanistic God (G. Leibniz, *The Monadology*, trans. R. Latta [Oxford: Oxford University Press, 1968]).

78. Augustine, *City of God*, 365, 367. In his gentler moments, he made grace gather all into a seeming human equality: "*You created man male and female*, but all one in your spiritual grace, where there is neither male nor female according to sex, just as *there is neither Jew nor Greek nor bond nor free*" (Augustine, *The Confessions*, trans. F. J. Sheed [New York: Sheed and Ward, 1950], 341).

79. Thus we encounter cosmic moralisms of the following sort: "Unity and right human relations—individual, communal, national and international—can be brought about by the united action of the men and women of goodwill in every country" (from *International Unity*, a pamphlet of World Goodwill). If such a global condition were attained, we would wonder (with Walker Percy) that someone (well-intentioned) had slipped something into the water system. See Walker Percy, *The Thanatos Syndrome* (New York: Farrar Straus and Giroux, 1987).

80. And under any cultural or political regime. But this is not because obtension is an abstract universalist morality; quite the opposite. It is at home with *both* the universalist and the tribal perspective; each is needed in a morality that would focus upon fraternity. Cf. Selznick, *The Moral Commonwealth*, 197.

INDEX

NEW FORUM BOOKS

New Forum Books makes available to general readers outstanding original interdisciplinary scholarship with a special focus on the juncture of culture, law, and politics. New Forum Books is guided by the conviction that law and politics not only reflect culture but help to shape it. Authors include leading political scientists, sociologists, legal scholars, philosophers, theologians, historians, and economists writing for non-specialist readers and scholars across a range of fields. Looking at questions such as political equality, the concept of rights, the problem of virtue in liberal politics, crime and punishment, population, poverty, economic development, and the international legal and political order, New Forum Books seeks to explain—not explain away—the difficult issues we face today.

Paul Edward Gottfried, *After Liberalism:
Mass Democracy in the Managerial State*

Peter Berkowitz, *Virtue and the Making of
Modern Liberalism*

John E. Coons and Patrick M. Brennan, *By Nature Equal:
The Anatomy of a Western Insight*